W9-BEH-333

The Berlin–Baghdad Express

SEAN MCMEEKIN

The Berlin–Baghdad Express

*The Ottoman Empire and Germany's
Bid for World Power*

The Belknap Press of
Harvard University Press
Cambridge, Massachusetts

Copyright © 2010 by Sean McMeekin
All rights reserved
Printed in the United States of America

First published in the United Kingdom by Penguin Books Ltd. 2010

First Harvard University Press paperback edition, 2012

Library of Congress Cataloging-in-Publication Data

McMeekin, Sean, 1974–
The Berlin-Baghdad express : the Ottoman Empire
and Germany's bid for world power / Sean McMeekin.
p.   cm.
First published in the United Kingdom in 2010 by Penguin Books Ltd.
Includes bibliographical references and index.
ISBN 978-0-674-05739-5 (cloth : alk. paper)
ISBN 978-0-674-06432-4 (pbk.)
1. World War, 1914–1918—Turkey.   2. World War, 1914–1918—
Islamic countries.   3. Jihad.   4. Germany—Foreign relations—1888–1918.
5. Geopolitics—Germany—History.   6. Germany—Foreign relations—Turkey.
7. Turkey—Foreign relations—Germany.   I. Title.
D520.T8M36   2010
940.3'1—dc22   2010019199

For Nesrin

Some day, when the full history is written – sober history with ample documents – the poor romancer will give up business and fall to reading Miss Austen in a hermitage.

John Buchan, *Greenmantle* (1916)

Contents

CONTENTS

List of Maps

List of Abbreviations

AVPRI   Arkhiv vneshnei politiki Rossiiskoi Imperii (Archive of the Foreign Policy of the Russian Empire), Moscow, Russia

BOA   Başbakanlık Osmanlı Arşivleri (Ottoman Government Archive), Sultanahmet, Istanbul, Turkey

DBB   Deutsches Bundesarchiv Berlin, Lichterfelde, Berlin, Germany

EJP   Ernst Jäckh Papers, Yale University, New Haven, Connecticut

GPA   Geheimes Preussisches Staatsarchiv, Berlin, Germany

HHSA   Haus-, Hof-und Staatsarchiv, Vienna, Austria

KW   Kriegsarchiv Wien, Vienna, Austria

MvO   Max von Oppenheim Stiftung, Sal. Oppenheim jr. & Cie KGaA, Cologne, Germany

NA   National Archives of the United States (NA), US Embassy, Ankara, Turkey

PAAA   Politisches Archiv des Auswärtigen Amtes, Berlin, Germany

PRO   National Archives of the United Kingdom (formerly Public Record Office), Kew Gardens, London, United Kingdom*

---

* Although it has been several years now since the Public Record Office was renamed the National Archives of the United Kingdom, I do not know of a single researcher who refers to it by the new name. For the sake of tradition and to preserve common currency, I continue to reference it in this book as the PRO.

QO	Quai d'Orsay Archives, Paris, France
RGVIA	Rossiiskii Gosudarstvennyi Voenno-Istoricheskii Arkhiv (Russian Government Military-Historical Archive), Moscow, Russia

A Note on Names and Translations

With apologies to my Turkish friends, I have generally gone with 'Constantinople', as it was still called in the pre-First World War and wartime era, even by Ottoman government officials, unless I am talking about the city today, in which case it is indeed 'Istanbul'. Living in Ankara myself, I could not, however, countenance using the classical 'Angora', much as I like the sound of it. With most other cities I have used the contemporary form with modern usage in parentheses, thus 'Adrianople (Edirne)' or 'Üsküp (Skopje)'. Today's St Petersburg was likewise 'St Petersburg' until 31 August 1914, after which date Peter's Germanic sounding city was Slavicized as 'Petrograd' (in the current narrative, we do not have to contend with its years as 'Leningrad').

With regard to Turkish spellings, I have generally rendered the 'c' as 'dj' (as in *Djavid* and *Djemal*) and used the dotless 'ı' where appropriate (it sounds a bit like 'uh') to differentiate from the Turkish 'i', which sounds like 'ee'. Likewise, I have tried to render properly 'ş' (sh) and 'ç' (ch) to add Turkish flavour to the text, even if these letters are really post-1928 concoctions of Atatürk's language reforms. It is impossible to be consistent in all these things; may common sense prevail.

All translations from the French, German, Russian and Turkish, unless otherwise noted, are my own.

Prologue: The View from Haydarpasha

On a small promontory jutting out from the Asian shoreline of Istanbul, where the Bosphorus meets the Sea of Marmara, sits the stunning neo-classical façade of Haydarpasha station. So perfectly does the edifice fit the small peninsular setting that, from a distance, Haydarpasha appears almost to float on the water. This is no accident. A masterpiece of German architecture of the late Wilhelmine era, Haydarpasha in fact rests not on the shore itself but on over a thousand wooden piles, each driven into the earth by steam-hammer, which support a state-of-the-art steel-carcass bearing system. Although damaged over the years by fires, explosions and sabotage, the original structure still stands as a monument to German engineering in its golden age.

The dramatic setting brilliantly captures the allure of the city which lies astride two continents. Haydarpasha, Istanbul's railroad gateway to Asiatic Turkey and the East, is physically oriented towards the West, commanding one of the finest views of Istanbul's European shoreline. The minarets of the Blue Mosque beckon across the upper reaches of the Sea of Marmara, along with the golden cupola and faded red brick of the Hagia Sofia, and the outlines of Topkapı Palace and the Sublime Porte, just above the old fortress walls of Byzantium. Scanning to the right, one takes in the entrance to the Golden Horn, and further north, on a very clear day, it is just possible to catch a glimpse of the suspension bridges spanning the Bosphorus.

Like many of the world's great buildings, Haydarpasha seems to come from a vanished era, its very grandeur a reproach to the bland mediocrity of the present age. Built almost exactly one hundred years ago, Haydarpasha conjures up the astonishing confidence of Europe's *fin de siècle* era, the crusading imperial spirit of an age which knew neither irony nor apology. There is nothing subtle about the station, or the intent behind it. Haydarpasha was designed to be a flagship station of the beloved Berlin to Baghdad railway of Kaiser Wilhelm II. Here the German Emperor's *Weltpolitik* first took concrete form, seeking to unite East and West, Asia and Europe, and put imperial Germany firmly on the path to world power.

It was an intoxicating vision, one of the all-time great gambits of history; and yet it is all but forgotten today. The Kaiser's dream of empire has mostly fallen down the memory hole, a victim both of the amnesia accorded history's great losers and of its having been overlaid by the nihilistic horrors of Nazism. Even without the comparison of the ideas of his hideous successors, the Kaiser's vision remains oddly appealing. Wilhelm's oriental fixation had something of the feeling of a love affair, as he courted the affections of the various peoples of the Ottoman Empire. To be sure, Wilhelm wanted Germans to lead the way in 'civilizing' the Middle East, reinvigorating its moribund economy and integrating it with Europe's. In this sense, Germany's Wilhelmine *Drang nach Osten* was akin to the Russian push into Siberia and Central Asia or America's path to the Pacific under Manifest Destiny – and a good deal more sensible in economic terms than the mad European Scramble for Africa. The Kaiser's vision was the most romantic, and arguably the most sympathetic, of all of these imperial projects. The subjects he wished to bring into the modern age were not primitive tribesmen, but the once-great peoples of the Near East, whose ancestors had given the world writing, Abrahamic religion, democracy, philosophy and science. Let the Americans have the plains, the Russians Siberia, the French and Belgians and British various malaria-ridden lands in Africa. Germany would build her own economic empire in the very cradle of Western civilization.

Wilhelm's motivation was not exclusively economic, of course. Rummaging around in a London apartment vacated by a German family after the outbreak of war in 1914, the new English tenant 'came across a German geographical globe with a system of projected and completed railways clearly marked from Berlin to Madras via Constantinople, southern Persia, Baluchistan, and Bombay'.[1] Here was the map of an empire to crown all empires, with Wilhelm strutting across the world stage as a true modern Alexander, taking in Anatolia, Mesopotamia and Persia and toppling the British Raj. German steel rails would conquer this vast expanse, fording deserts, mountains and swamps to introduce European technology to Asia, while bringing the silks, spices, minerals and raw materials of the Orient to the markets of the West. Whereas Hitler was willing to concede the British their global, sea-based empire in exchange for recognition of his own domination of the Eurasian landmass, Wilhelm wanted the British Empire too, including its crown jewels of Egypt and India.

It may have seemed like a pipe dream, but Wilhelm had a trump card up his sleeve: Islam. Long before the formal crowning of the Triple Entente in 1907, the Kaiser had begun sizing up the enemy coalition coalescing against him. Russia, France and particularly Great Britain all shared one colossal Achilles heel: they each now ruled over millions of unruly Muslim subjects, whose resentment at being dictated to by infidels might easily be inflamed in a European war. Strange as it might seem today in our post-colonial age, the greatest Muslim power on earth a hundred years ago was not Afghanistan, Persia or even Ottoman Turkey (then the only independent Islamic countries of note) but the British Empire, which counted over 100 million Muslim subjects, scattered across the Indian subcontinent, the Gulf States, Egypt and Anglo-Egyptian Sudan. Even Tsarist Russia's count of 19 million Islamic subjects was greater than the entire Ottoman population, infidel and Muslim alike, and France was not far behind. Imperial latecomer Germany, by contrast, could reasonably claim innocence in the Islamic world, having only a smattering of Islamic subjects in her own tiny African empire.

That the world's Muslims had less ground for resenting Germany than her enemies in the Triple Entente did not, of course, necessarily mean they saw themselves as German allies. Not for nothing, however, had the ancient Chinese notion that 'the enemy of my enemy is my friend' become a favoured proverb in the Arab world. The Kaiser would not have to make Muslims love him if he was to weaken the Entente powers, merely ensure that the furies of their pent-up *ressentiment* were directed at their proper target – and far away from the Germans. So long as the powers remained at peace, Wilhelm would have to be reasonably careful about spreading sedition in the colonial territories of the Entente. If a war of the Great Powers ever came, however, the gloves would come off.

In the meantime, Wilhelm could busy himself with one of history's great diplomatic charm offensives. Sultan Abdul Hamid II, whose paranoia about foreign designs on his Ottoman realm was legendary, was a promising target for seduction. Menaced by the Russians in the Balkans, the French in North Africa, and the British in Egypt and Arabia, the 'Sick Man of Europe' was desperate for a strong European ally who could stand up to the Entente bullies. The Kaiser, who dreamed of extending German influence into the Islamic world of the Near East, was in need of a sponsor who could give him credibility with Muslims – and Sultan Abdul Hamid was by title also Caliph, or supreme religious authority, of Sunni Islam. It was a match made in heaven.

Although there were fits and starts along the way, the romance between Kaiser and Sultan was in full flower by the first decade of the twentieth century. Spurred on by a sense of shared threat of Entente encirclement, a team of German engineers and Turkish workmen broke ground at Haydarpasha in May 1906. The signing of the long-feared Anglo-Russian Convention in August 1907 only heightened the sense of urgency, and the great neo-classical masterpiece on the Asian shore was completed ahead of schedule in summer 1908, shortly after the signing of the third and final Baghdad railway convention between Kaiser and Sultan. As German railway experts began the first surveying work on the Taurus mountains near the Cilician Gates once traversed by Alexander's army, it seemed there was nothing that could stop the expansion of German influence in the Near East, as Teutonic engineers began prospecting for oil and mineral resources in Anatolia, Syria, Mesopotamia and Arabia, even as salesmen plied German machines, manufactures and medicines. Once the Orient Express was up and running from Berlin to Baghdad and the Persian Gulf, it would be game, set and match in the German bid for world power.

I
The Vision

We must not forget that everything taking place in a Mohammedan country sends waves across the entire world of Islam.

Baron Max Oppenheim

I

The Kaiser, the Baron and
the Dragoman

Pour chasser les démons, il faudrait un prophète.[1]

King Louis Philippe to François Guizot

As the *Hohenzollern* passed through the Dardanelles en route for Constantinople in the first week of November in 1889, an astonishing spectacle greeted its distinguished passengers, all crammed onto the outer decks. 'From Settl-Bahar and Kum-Kaleh to Abydos,' wrote an English journalist observing from the shore, 'all the forts hoisted the German flag, the military bands played the German anthem, and as the Imperial yacht passed between the castles where the straits are narrowest the forts on either side thundered forth their welcome in a salute of 101 guns.' After docking at the Golden Horn, the German royal party was received with elaborate ceremony by Sultan Abdul Hamid II at the imperial palace of Yıldız: official visits to the even grander Dolmabahçe and Beylerbey palaces would follow. A particular highlight was a tour of the Bosphorus aboard elegant Ottoman court caiques, each one 'rowed by ten pairs of oars'. So warm was the Sultan's reception, so beguiling the oriental sights on display, that the German delegation extended its official visit to four full days filled with pomp and panoply.[2]

It was a heady experience for young Kaiser Wilhelm II. Having ascended to the German throne the previous year, his thirtieth, the Kaiser was anxious to make a name for himself and emerge from the shadow of Germany's long-serving Chancellor, Prince Otto von Bismarck. The state visit to Constantinople accomplished both tricks at once, not least because Bismarck had made clear his stout opposition to the trip, for fear of offending Russia to no good purpose. Ever since the unification of Germany under Prussian leadership in 1871, Bismarck had been content to consolidate the boundaries of the new German empire, trying to avoid unnecessary foreign adventures at all costs. Bismarck's famous remark about the Balkans not being 'worth the bones of a single Pomeranian grenadier' is in fact a misquote: what he actually said was that 'the whole Orient' – meaning the entire Ottoman Empire – should not be a concern of Germany's foreign policy.[3] Although Bismarck did support the spread of German influence in Turkey, personally approving the dispatch of a German military mission led by Generalmajor Otto Kaehler on Abdul Hamid's request in 1883, he did so as quietly as possible, for fear of ruining Germany's fragile relations with Russia, which viewed the Straits at Constantinople with greedy eyes.[*4] In 1887, Bismarck had tried to counter Russian suspicions with his 'Reinsurance Treaty', in which Russia and Germany pledged to remain neutral in wars with third countries (including Ottoman Turkey).[†] And now here was the Kaiser making an unprecedented state visit to the Sultan, confirming the Russians' worst fears about German intentions in the Near East.

What was a diplomatic nightmare for Bismarck, however, was for the young Kaiser very good fun. Wilhelm was fêted everywhere he went in Constantinople, even by the English colony, which took him in as one of their own (he was, after all, the grandson of Queen Victoria). Aside from the salutes and cannonades, there was enough political intrigue in four days to fill a book. Addressing his German counterpart, in accordance with Islamic tradition, through a pair of interpreters (despite knowing French perfectly well), Sultan Abdul Hamid took the impressionable young Kaiser into his confidence, complaining of palace plots, unflattering embassy gossip and, more pointedly, the designs of other European sovereigns on his domains. Because Germany had not, as of yet, displayed similar territorial ambitions, Wilhelm remembered the Sultan telling him, with an air of conspiracy, that

---

* After Kaehler's death in 1885 the mission was headed by Lieutenant Colonel Freiherr von der Goltz, with whose name the pre-war initiative is usually associated.

† A secret clause spelled out that Germany would remain neutral in the event of Russian naval intervention in the Bosphorus or the Straits.

'my visit would make these powers very nervous'. This was music to the ears of an ambitious young Emperor keen to make his mark on the world.[5]

In the young Kaiser's ostentatious state visit to Constantinople in 1889, we can see those qualities which would soon both fascinate and repel the world. On the one hand, it is easy to see why the visit was so well received. Wilhelm's childlike curiosity and capacity for wonder, his ability to be fascinated by new sights and sensations, from the Ottoman caiques and palaces to the 'gracious, delightful, rhythmic dances of the Circassians' in the Sultan's *harem*: all this went over very well with Constantinople's residents. An ancient caravan people known for their hospitality to travellers, Turks have always responded well to visitors' attentions and compliments. Kaiser Wilhelm did not disappoint them, thanking the Sultan effusively for his 'splendid hospitality' and declaring himself 'much moved by the feelings of cordiality and sympathy shown towards their Majesties both by the Sovereign of Turkey and his subjects'. The Kaiser then gave the Sultan's Grand Vizier a diamond-set Prussian Order of the Eagle.[6]

The flip side to the flattery on display during the Kaiser's state visit was Wilhelm's vanity and insecurity, his need to be the centre of attention, which has been remarked on by nearly all of his biographers. Born in the breech position after an agonizing ten-hour delivery which his mother barely survived, the future Kaiser suffered nerve damage that crippled his left arm, which by adulthood was six inches shorter than the right and essentially useless. As a result of his deformity, Wilhelm could not even cut his own meat without help, let alone handle weapons like the soldier he always wanted to be. The young Kaiser had thus grown up with a very large chip on his shoulder, a sense that he had always to prove himself and win acclaim. Kaiser Wilhelm, it was said, had to be 'the stag at every hunt, the bride at every wedding, and the corpse at every funeral'. This was not a man likely to resist the lure of oriental gifts and blandishments.[7]

The trip to Constantinople also highlighted Wilhelm's reckless sense of statecraft, born of his restless, unbalanced character. Able to muster up sudden enthusiasms on a moment's notice, Wilhelm yet lacked the ability to focus on essentials, or note contradictions. It is of more than passing historical interest, for example, that the Kaiser befriended not only the soon-to-be-notorious 'Bloody Sultan' on this inaugural visit to the Ottoman capital, but also Theodor Herzl, the Viennese journalist usually considered the father of Zionism. Converted by Herzl, with astonishing swiftness, to the Zionist cause, the Kaiser promptly lobbied Sultan Abdul Hamid on Herzl's behalf. It does not seem to have occurred to young Wilhelm that the Sultan's Muslim subjects may not have viewed the prospect of further Jewish settlement in Palestine favourably, or that the Sultan-Caliph of Sunni Islam might have resented this officious intervention in Ottoman religious affairs. Nor does the Kaiser seem to have given much thought to how, exactly, this meddling served the German national interest. For Bismarck's cool and careful indifference to the Orient, the Kaiser had now substituted the emotional improvisations of amateur hour. The Eastern Question would never be the same again.[8]

The Kaiser, to be sure, did not follow up directly on his overtures to either the Sultan or the Zionists: his attention, characteristically, wandered elsewhere soon after returning home from Constantinople. Still, Wilhelm's 1889 trip was a harbinger of things to come. The ageing Bismarck was pushed out of office in March 1890, ostensibly because his reactionary predilections were out of step with the more progressive Reichstag elected that year: but the Kaiser was equally keen on breaking the Iron Chancellor's hold on foreign policy. Within weeks of Bismarck's fall, the Reinsurance Treaty with Russia was allowed to lapse, despite open Russian overtures in Berlin in favour of renewal. A natural alliance between the two reactionary powers had been replaced, perhaps quite needlessly, by an antagonism which would dominate two world wars. Not only did the lapse open the door for France's courting of a defensive alliance with Russia (concluded in 1894), it also put the Tsar's diplomats on notice that the Germans would no longer acquiesce in Russian designs on the Straits. Had the Kaiser made an effort to renew Bismarck's Reinsurance Treaty, it is possible the Russian government would have ignored the Kaiser's flirtations with the Ottoman Sultan, and refrained from rushing headlong into French arms for fear of an out-of-control Germany. Instead, Wilhelm's state visit to Constantinople, followed by the expiration of the Reinsurance Treaty, confirmed the Russians' worst fears about German intentions at the Porte, with momentous consequences for the European strategic balance.

Considering the serious diplomatic price Germany may have paid for the Kaiser's dalliance with the Sultan in 1889, it is peculiar that nine years passed before Wilhelm bothered to visit his friend Abdul Hamid again. The Kaiser's oriental fixation, it would seem, was only one of his passing fancies, which had evaporated as quickly as it came over him. It is true that, following the Sultan's repression of an Armenian uprising in August 1896, Wilhelm famously sent a signed photograph of himself to Abdul Hamid to mark the latter's birthday, just as everyone else in Europe was condemning the Kaiser's friend as the 'Bloody Sultan' and 'Abdul the Damned'. It is less well known, however, that the Kaiser also conspired at this very time with the British Prime Minister Lord Salisbury to reach an agreement on the partition of the Ottoman Empire in the case of its collapse, with the aim of tempting Russia to abandon her alliance with France. Luckily for Wilhelm's relations with Abdul Hamid, Lord Salisbury quickly dropped the idea, and the news of the Kaiser's approach to Salisbury was not leaked to the press.[9]

Still, Wilhelm never forgot the charms of Constantinople. When at last he returned to the Bosphorus in October 1898, there was little left to restrain the Kaiser from a full-blown diplomatic offensive. Old Bismarck had died earlier that summer, banishing any lingering qualms the Kaiser might have felt over pursuing his more assertive foreign policy. None of the great man's successors in the Chancellery or Foreign Office – Caprivi, Holstein, Marschall, Hohenlohe or Bülow – had yet figured out how to rein in the Kaiser's exuberance. Alarm had recently been growing in Britain about the Kaiser's burgeoning *Weltpolitik* – from his notorious encouragement of the rebellious anti-British Boers in South Africa with the 'Krüger telegram' in 1896, to the German naval expansion programme begun in 1897 – but if anything, the disdain Wilhelm's English cousins increasingly felt for him only goaded him on further in his efforts to upstage them. And so Wilhelm resolved not only on a state visit to the Ottoman capital, but to make a grand tour of the Orient, taking in Rhodes, Malta, Jerusalem, Lebanon and Damascus.

As if to underscore the historic nature of the Kaiser's geopolitical voyage, it was launched on the 100-year anniversary of Napoleon's invasion of Egypt, which had inaugurated the first great age of European

Orientalism. Napoleon's invasion had been a disaster for the Ottoman Empire, showing up the military inferiority of the Muslim world against European armies: although the French forces were ultimately repulsed, it was due only to British intervention. The Kaiser's visit, by contrast, was friendly and by invitation; but in its way it was just as portentous as Napoleon's invasion. A throng of Western reporters followed the Kaiser almost everywhere he went, recording the impressions he made and speculating wildly on his motives. It seemed impossible Wilhelm was really just making the rounds and seeing the sights. Was the Kaiser seeking to shore up the Sultan's rule and frustrate Russian, British and French designs on his domains? Or was Wilhelm himself staking a claim to the Ottoman inheritance?

The Kaiser's exuberant behaviour did little to quell these speculations. In Constantinople, Wilhelm presented to the Ottoman people 'a huge and ornate fountain', which still stands in the Hippodrome (known today as the Alman Çeşmesi, or German Fountain). To the Sultan, he wished to have sent a Prussian rifle of the latest design, on which the Ottoman coat of arms was specially mounted. To the Kaiser's chagrin, however, Abdul Hamid declined, at first, to receive his gift, apparently because a rumour had reached his ears that Armenian terrorists were conspiring to kill him with a bomb smuggled into his palace. At last Wilhelm himself brought the Sultan his gift weapon in person, in a trunk carefully protected by a 'wrought iron fire screen', which Abdul Hamid inspected 'with an unmistakable air of elevated mistrust'. To appease his suspicions, the Kaiser bowed before the Sultan with great ceremony and slowly opened the 'ominous casket' with his own hands. Finally reassured that no bombs were inside, Abdul Hamid fondly examined the Kaiser's gun. For the rest of the evening, amity and good cheer prevailed.[10]

The curious incident in Constantinople was hardly an encouraging omen for the Kaiser's trip. If the paranoid Abdul Hamid did not trust Wilhelm in his own home, he could hardly have been reassured when the Kaiser rode triumphantly into Jerusalem on 29 October 1898 through a specially cut breach in the city walls, in a Prussian field marshal's uniform and 'mounted on a black charger', as if he were conquering the Sultan's city, rather than visiting it as his guest.[11] The ostensible purpose of the visit to Jerusalem was to help dedicate the new Church of the Redeemer, constructed by German Protestants. But Wilhelm also made a point of pleasing German Catholics, by taking into his protection the *Dormitio beatae virginis*, or presumed site of the Assumption of the Virgin Mary. So overwhelmed was Wilhelm when he visited the site that he immediately 'placed himself, his army, and his Empire in the service of the Mother of Christ'.[12] The Kaiser then telegraphed Pope Leo XIII, to make official his protection of Catholics in the Holy Land. Not that Wilhelm was playing favourites: to please northern German Protestants he next offered his sovereign protection to a German evangelical *Weihnachtskirche* in Bethlehem. Piling intrigue upon intrigue, Wilhelm received Theodor Herzl again on 2 November in Jerusalem. Herzl wanted the Kaiser to charter a company to promote German Jewish colonization of Ottoman Palestine, and of course to win the Sultan's backing for the project. The first international Zionist Congress, slated to convene later that month in Basel, would benefit enormously from an endorsement from Kaiser Wilhelm, because of his presumed influence on the Sultan. As always, the Kaiser was swayed quite easily by Herzl's arguments, assuring him solemnly that 'Your movement ... is based on a sound, healthy idea. There is room here for everyone. My personal observations convince me that the land is arable. Only provide water and trees.' In the end, Wilhelm was warned by the Ottoman Foreign Minister Ahmed Tevfik (who was accompanying the tour) that Abdul Hamid was not friendly to Zionism, and quietly dropped the idea.[13] But the Kaiser's public embrace of Zionism, in the holiest city of Christianity, then under Muslim rule, was dizzying enough whether sincere or not. How could he ever top this?

As it turned out, quite easily. Following a brief stopover in Beirut, the Kaiser made another ceremonial entrance, this time into Damascus. Wilhelm was intoxicated by the first truly Arab town he had ever visited, 'with its characteristic concealed courtyards and their splashing fountains, its fascinating bazaars, and the whole charm of the Saracenic architecture and the Arabs' mode of life'. Wherever Wilhelm went, recalled his State Secretary Bernhard von Bülow, 'the populace welcomed him with a peculiar cry of greeting, a long drawn-out, repeated guttural bellow of "Lululu, Lululu, Lululu", and the monotonous noise intoxicated him as though it had been hashish'.[14]

Entranced, Wilhelm laid a wreath on the tomb of the great Muslim warrior Saladin and 'hung a lamp of solid silver before ordering that a mausoleum of the finest marble be built around it at his expense'. Moved by the Kaiser's honouring of a great hero of Islam, the city's leading cleric, Sheikh Abdullah Effendi, organized a banquet in Wilhelm's honour on 8 November 1898. Here, in one of the most notorious in a career marked by many notorious speeches, the Kaiser paid gushing tribute to the medieval hero of Islam as 'one of the most chivalrous rulers of all times, the great Sultan Saladin ... a knight without fear or fault'. Making the obvious leap from Saladin to the current Sultan, Wilhelm next saluted the great Abdul Hamid. 'May the Sultan,' Wilhelm declaimed with dramatic flourish, 'and his 300 million Muslim subjects scattered across the earth, who venerate him as their Caliph, be assured that the German Kaiser will be their friend for all time.'[15]

Had Kaiser Wilhelm gone around the bend? It was one thing to offer protection to Christians in the Holy Land – although even this sort of manoeuvre could have serious consequences, as Napoleon III had discovered when his courting of Levantine Christians in 1852 had lit the spark which led to the Crimean War.* But here was a powerful Christian sovereign declaring a proprietary interest in nearly all the subjects of the Ottoman Middle East – no less than three Christian denominations, the Jews of Palestine and all of the Muslims to boot. This was not all. By offering his protection, via the Sultan, to '300 million Muslims' around the world, Wilhelm was meddling in the affairs of other powers with Muslim subjects – not least French North Africa, Russian Central Asia and the British Empire, which alone contained some 100 million Muslims spread out over British India, Egypt and the Gulf States. Then, too, there was Persia and southern Mesopotamia, where Shia Muslims had never accepted the Ottoman Sultan as their Caliph. No wonder the Kaiser's State Secretary for Foreign Affairs, Bernhard von Bülow, tried desperately to edit the text of Wilhelm's speech before it was released to the press, for fear

---

* Of course, this may have been what the French Emperor had wanted to do – to provoke Russia into overreacting. In this, Napoleon III was much like the erratic Kaiser Wilhelm II. Both men were far better at conjuring up crises than at profiting from them.

of 'arousing suspicion in ... Paris, London and St Petersburg'. But it was too late: the German Ambassador in Constantinople, Baron Marschall, had already given the text to the Wolff news agency, 'on a direct order from His Majesty'.[16]

What was the Kaiser thinking? Interestingly, there does exist a record of the Kaiser's thoughts during this historic tour of the Orient – in the letters he dispatched, improbably, to his 'dear friend Nicky' in St Petersburg. Judging from this correspondence, Wilhelm's strategic goal was to convince both Sultan and Tsar that their true enemy was Great Britain, thus threatening Germany's great rival for global supremacy with a pincer movement. The trump card, Wilhelm believed, was the Muslim world, whose fury had most recently been unleashed against British intervention on behalf of the Christians in Crete in 1897. 'What an effect this act of pillage has had on the Mahometan world,' Wilhelm wrote the Russian Tsar from Constantinople on 20 October 1898: 'What a terrible blow to the prestige of the Christian *en général* in the eyes of the Mussulman and renewal of hatred you can hardly imagine!' Taking 'Nicky' into his confidence, as if the two were already allies in battle with perfidious Albion, the Kaiser told the Tsar to 'Remember what you and I agreed upon at Peterhof never to forget that the Mahometans were a tremendous card in our game in case you or I were suddenly confronted by a war with the certain meddlesome Power!' British India, that is, could be brought low by an Islamic jihad, launched by either Sultan or Tsar, who was himself the 'master of millions of Mahometans'.[17] The idea that Russia was just as vulnerable to Muslim unrest as Britain does not seem to have occurred to Wilhelm – not yet, anyway.

Tossing discretion aside, Kaiser Wilhelm now revealed to the Tsar the underlying motivation for his Muslim charm offensive: he had fallen in love with Islam. Wilhelm decried the ostentation of the Christian churches of the Holy Land, which contrasted unfavourably with the simple adornments of the mosques. 'Fetish adoration,' the Kaiser wrote to Nicholas II from Jerusalem, 'has created a supreme contempt for the Christians with the Moslems', and Wilhelm was inclined to agree with them. All but proclaiming his conversion, the Kaiser now confessed to the Tsar that 'My personal feeling in leaving the holy city was that I felt profoundly ashamed before the Moslems and that if I had come there without any Religion at all I certainly would have turned Mahommetan!'[18]

Thus was born *Hajji Wilhelm*, the mythical Muslim Emperor of Germany, who would cut such a grandiose, yet confusing figure on the world stage in the decades to come. Following the visit to Damascus, rumours of the Kaiser's conversion to Islam spread widely throughout the bazaars of the Middle East, helped along by the discovery of 'passages in the Koran' which 'showed that the Kaiser had been ordained by God to free Muslims from infidel rule'.[19] It helped that Germany, unlike Britain and France, was still relatively little known in Ottoman lands: her image was a tabula rasa onto which German propagandists could write whatever they wished. The Kaiser had now given them the script. Germany, led by Hajji Wilhelm, would be the Western protector of Islam, saving this noble faith from the depredations of European imperialism. Like the Kaiser's conversion, it was a half-truth at best: Germany had her own Muslim colonies, principally in West Africa, which put the lie to the claim that her hands were clean.*[20] But contradictions have never bothered visionaries.

Where before the budding pan-German activists of the Kaiserreich had little geographical focus for their imperial striving, aside from unedifying disputes with the British over poor scraps of African territory which few Germans really wanted to settle anyway, the Kaiser's grand tour of 1898 gave the movement the inspiration it needed. Wilhelm himself may not have been clear on the goals of the Ottoman offensive – he changed his mind too often. But pan-German theorists easily remedied this deficiency. Inspired by their Kaiser's powerful vision, a new generation of intellectuals and adventurers would sketch in the contours of Germany's *Drang nach Osten*.

Foremost among these visionaries was Max von Oppenheim, the wayward son of the Oppenheim banking dynasty whose family fortune allowed him to moonlight alternately as explorer, writer, diplomat, archaeologist and prospector. Oppenheim, born in 1860, was nearly an exact contemporary of his hero, Kaiser Wilhelm: the two first met

---

* As of 1900, Germany had some 2.6 million Muslim subjects, most of them in German East Africa.

while serving in similar aristocratic Guards regiments in 1879. The men were introduced by Oppenheim's friend in his 15th Ulan regiment, Albano von Jacobi, following a regimental parade in Strasbourg Wilhelm had come to observe. It is doubtful that young Max made much of an impression on the Hohenzollern prince, but Oppenheim never forgot the encounter, from which he dated 'my respect for our future Kaiser'.[21]

Oppenheim does not say what it was, exactly, that he respected about the then twenty-year-old Wilhelm, but it was not likely to be his soldierly bearing. The future Kaiser's interest in the Prussian army was famously confined to a fascination with its stupendous variety of medals and uniforms; Oppenheim seems to have enjoyed mainly the entrée his smart Ulan Guards get-up gave him to the Strasbourg salons and the Derby races at Baden-Baden. Neither man was cut out for the discipline of military life. The quality Oppenheim responded to in his future Emperor was, rather, Wilhelm's restless curiosity and wander-lust. In this the two men were kindred spirits. But whereas it took Wilhelm a decade's worth of sovereign state visits finally to focus his passion on the Ottoman world (and even then, fleetingly), Oppen-heim knew from an early age that his fate lay in the Orient.

As a small boy Max had been given an illustrated edition of *The Thousand and One Nights* for Christmas.* The picaresque tales and exotic images awakened a powerful longing for the East, which Oppen-heim would never outgrow. Simply to placate his father, who wanted him to take over the family banking business, Oppenheim did study law in Berlin after leaving the Guards, attaining the rank of *Referen-dar* (junior barrister) and entering the civil service; but he was not cut out for professional life. In the winter of 1883–4, at the impressionable age of twenty-three, Oppenheim embarked on his first oriental voyage, taking in Athens, Smyrna and Constantinople, where he claims to have danced with half the Greek girls in the city. He never forgot this intro-duction to the charms of Eastern women: in fact he began collecting

---

* The Oppenheims, including Max's father Albert, were Jewish; but his mother Paula was Catholic. For professional reasons, Albert Oppenheim converted to Christianity after his marriage. Because of the principle of matrilineal descent in Judaism, Max was thus a gentile twice over – but, as we shall see below, he was never quite able to shake the Jewish connection.

oriental women's costumes, assembling over the years nearly 150 complete ensembles.[22]

In 1886, Oppenheim set off on another *Bildungsreise*, this time taking in the Maghreb. It was a more ambitious trip than the first: he could no longer rely on German-speaking Greek girls to ease him gently into the local culture. In the Moroccan capital of Fez, Oppenheim picked up enough Arabic to jabber a bit with the locals. He also picked up his first concubine, an Arab-Berber beauty he purchased in one of the local slave markets. It is curious to note that Oppenheim – counting on local slavers' inability to distinguish between foreign tongues – passed himself off as a Turk, having been told by his interpreter of the 'frightful penalties for Muslim girls who fornicated with infidels'. Islamic sexual morality in Morocco seemed both forbidding and strangely titillating: with impersonal Western-style prostitution unknown, men instead purchased temporary female sex-slaves (*Sklavinnen*), savoured their sensual delights as if monogamously, and then 'freed' them, as Oppenheim did after enjoying his concubine for about a month.*

As his foray into the slave market implies, Oppenheim was not lacking in daring. Despite still knowing only the barest smattering of spoken Arabic, the young adventurer made a point of entering every single mosque in Fez, knowing full well that 'as the first European to do so', he was 'evidently risking his life'.† Oppenheim also risked his own skin – and those of his companions – when he confronted bandits attempting to rob his caravan in the Rif mountains between Wezzan and Fez. A fine shot – young Max had honed his markmanship by shooting daily whenever he visited his uncle Heinrich at the latter's rural estate in Wiesbaden – Oppenheim fired off five bullets, piercing with each one the water-bottles carried by the robbers, then fired in the air, before quickly reloading his six-shooter. 'After a brief discussion,'

---

* Oppenheim's half-Berber concubine was later betrothed to the nephew of Oppenheim's guide/interpreter, Omar Barrade.

† Adding strangeness to these already improbable adventures, Oppenheim claims to have been accompanied on his mosque tour by the very nephew who was betrothed to his concubine. It is not known whether the two men discussed their shared object of desire while praying together.

he recalls, 'the robbers quickly fled and had soon disappeared from sight'. He may not have spoken Arabic fluently yet, but Oppenheim had already mastered the real lingua franca of the Orient: superior force.[23]

It was not until he finally resigned from the civil service in 1892, however, that Oppenheim could truly devote himself to the Orient. This time the young explorer spared no expense in preparing his voyage, assembling a small team of archaeologists and hiring a full-time Arab instructor soon after his caravan arrived in Egypt. Determined not only to taste the delights of the Orient, but to become a true connoisseur of its culture, religion and customs, Oppenheim leased a small house in an old Arab neighbourhood in Cairo on Crocodile Alley, in which none of the servants spoke anything but Arabic. Financially independent, and to all purposes unemployed, Oppenheim was ready to 'go native'. Using Cairo as his home base – which it would remain, with brief interruptions, until 1909 – he now began the scholarly exploration of the Middle East which would be his life's work.

After docking at Beirut, the Oppenheim caravan carried on to Damascus, where they purchased camels and supplies for the long journey across the desert to Mesopotamia. The ostensible purpose of the exploring party was to scour for archaeological ruins, such as those of the ancient city of Palmyra, which they found near the modern settlement of Deir ez Zor. An abiding distraction, however, was the threat of Bedouin raids. The Turkish authorities provided an armed escort of twenty soldiers to accompany Oppenheim's party as they ventured south into Bedouin territory. But Oppenheim was more curious than afraid of the nomads. Here was a sort of living anthropology: groups of hardy survivors who still lived as they had for centuries, roaming freely across thinly populated desert areas and living off the booty from raids, tribute and protection money. What were their customs and beliefs? Were they proper Muslims, or did they retain pre-Muslim tribal superstitions? And what was their relation to the Ottoman authorities, and the holy cities of Arabia?

Oppenheim was particularly taken with the Bedouins of the Shammar tribe, based in central Arabia but whose wanderings brought them frequently into desert areas of present-day Iraq, the Sinai and Syria. The Shammar were led by the Rashid clan, one of the three main contenders – along with Ibn Saud's Wahhabis in the Nejd and the Hashemites of Mecca – for primacy in the Arabian peninsula. Faris Pasha, the Sheikh of the Shammar, invited Oppenheim to stay in the Bedouin camp for several nights as an honoured guest. He was obviously enthralled with the ways of the Shammar, snapping a series of romantic black-and-white photographs and describing their customs with great empathy and care. He was quite taken with the tribe's old-fashioned virtues, such as fierce courage in battle and hospitality to strangers. The Shammar's characteristic vices he found equally striking: 'his caprice, his covetousness and taste for robbery, and his violent temper'. Perhaps it was as well that Oppenheim stayed only for a few days.[24]

His reports on the Shammar, sent in to the German government and later expanded into a political travelogue, *From the Mediterranean to the Persian Gulf*, began to establish his reputation as a regional expert: T. E. Lawrence later cited Oppenheim's work as 'the best book on the area I know'.[25] It was not yet clear, however, just what, exactly, the young explorer was an expert *on*. Although Oppenheim would usually find an archaeological pretext for his trips into Bedouin country, it was not until 1899 that he made his first real find, the Neolithic settlement at Tell Halaf, in north-eastern Syria close to the Turkish border (and he would not begin excavating this site until 1911).

Nourished by his servants and teachers in the Arab quarter of Cairo, Oppenheim's spoken Arabic was coming along well, although his accent was noticeable. This allowed him to speak with Bedouins like the Shammar in their own language, and to pass when needed as a Muslim (he usually dressed in Arab garb on his travels). But there is little evidence that he did any serious reading of Arab literature or Islamic history. In this, the golden era of European, and particularly German, Orientalism – the age of titans like Ignaz Goldziher, Snouck Hurgronje, Theodor Nöldeke and Carl Heinrich Becker – the contributions of Max von Oppenheim seem to have made scarcely a ripple.*

If his scholarship did not win him acceptance into the ranks of academic Orientalism, however, Oppenheim's Arabist travelogues

---

* Oppenheim is not mentioned, for example, in Robert Irwin's examination of German Orientalism in *For Lust of Knowing. The Orientalists and their Enemies* (2006).

were more successful on a political level, as a kind of audition for the German Foreign Office (*Auswärtiges Amt*). Having rejected the discipline of army life and the boredom of the civil service, he still wished to serve his country and his entrée into native Arab circles in the Near East was his main selling point with the Foreign Service, which did not generally admit non-nobles, and was particularly unwelcoming to Jews.*[26]

To get around the obstacle of his Jewish background, Oppenheim willingly renounced his ancestral Jewish faith and claimed to have fully embraced his mother Paula's Catholicism. (Considering that he frequently told Arabs he was a Muslim, this may not have seemed like a great stretch to him.) His claim was backed up by Paul Graf von Hatzfeldt, one of Bismarck's protégés and a former State Secretary, who was then German Ambassador to London. Sponsorship by the illustrious Hatzfeldt, who spoke highly of Oppenheim's potential as a regional analyst, at last secured the ambitious young traveller a paid post in the Cairo Consulate in 1896. Curiously, however, he seems never to have been given a proper diplomatic title or rank. Whether this was because of his Jewish origins, or to offer the Foreign Office plausible deniability in case the young adventurer got into trouble, is unclear. But it rankled with Oppenheim. Try though he might to pass as a Christian or a Muslim, he repeatedly ran up against the iron law of the Orient (and, evidently, the German Foreign Office): once a Jew, always a Jew.

Oppenheim was far too ambitious, however, to be discouraged by the reluctance of the Foreign Office grandees to admit him into the highest social circles. Besides, he had always preferred the native quarter of Cairo to the European, the dust and din of the Arab souk to the artificial polished order of the diplomats' quarter, the call of the muezzin to the dinner bell at Embassy banquets. His ambition was far too

---

* Although there was no formal ban on Jews serving in the *Auswärtiges Amt*, the anti-Semitism was not subtle. Friedrich von Holstein, senior counsellor since the 1870s, specifically ruled out Oppenheim as a candidate for the Foreign Service in 1891, on two 'disqualifying grounds': that he was a 'full-blooded Jew' (i.e. both of his parents were Jewish: which was incorrect) and that he was 'from a banking family'.

grand for him to concern himself with petty consular politics and his dream was to reach the ear of the Emperor himself. By the time of Wilhelm's grand Near Eastern tour of 1898, Oppenheim was well placed, as the Germans' main Arab political analyst in Cairo, to capitalize on the Kaiser's oriental diplomacy. Knowing Wilhelm's taste for flattery, Oppenheim felt no need to be subtle as he began salting his consular reports with obsequious references to the great figure Wilhelm had cut in the Arab world. He wrote in one dispatch, describing his own 1899 journey in Asiatic Turkey:

> In Damascus as on my further travels I was struck by the powerful impression the visit of His Majesty the Kaiser had made on the Mohammedans of Syria, and it was not difficult to observe what a particularly fine reputation the German name is endowed with, now more than ever ... German businessmen in Beirut, Damascus and Aleppo have assured me, that the blessing of His Majesty's visit has expanded their business opportunities in tangible measure. The wreath, which His Majesty laid at the tomb of Saladin in Damascus, has been enshrined as a relic in a glass case ... A memorial tablet commemorating the Kaiser's visit was placed in a special protective display case in the glorious temple to Jupiter in Ba'albek.[27]

With buttery praise like this, it is not surprising that Oppenheim came to the Kaiser's attention as a man he could count on to spread the good word about Germany in the Near East. Although the extent of his influence on the Kaiser's foreign policy ideas remains unclear, there was undoubtedly an important meeting of these similar minds in Potsdam in summer 1900, just two years after Wilhelm's visit to Damascus, arranged by the Cairo Consul-General, Paul Graf von Metternich. Having read (or at least skimmed) several of Oppenheim's reports on Arab politics, the Kaiser invited his contemporary to dine. Following dinner, Oppenheim showed Wilhelm several hundred photographs he had taken on his 1899 journey through eastern Turkey, Syria and Mesopotamia. The Kaiser was predictably enthralled, and bombarded Oppenheim with questions about Islam, the desert bedouins and their customs. As a reward for his copious counsel on a region close to Wilhelm's own heart, the Kaiser promoted Oppenheim to the rank of Chief Legal Counsel (*Legationsrat*).[28]

Thus began an annual tradition, as Oppenheim returned to Berlin each summer to escape the brutal heat of Cairo and entertained the Kaiser with tales of oriental life. Wilhelm was not always an inveterate talker, as many suspected from his sometimes incontinent speechifying: in fact he quite enjoyed listening while he ate.[29] This was particularly true with Oppenheim, who was so loquacious that he often neglected his food, to the Kaiser's amusement. On one occasion Oppenheim's favourite dish in the world, lobster with melted butter, was served up, but removed by the waiters before the poor man had the chance to taste it. The Kaiser laughed boisterously at his talkative friend's misfortune, but made no move to recall the waiter to bring the lobster back. This was just the kind of teasing Wilhelm had always revelled in.[30]

Convinced that he was now the Kaiser's own personal envoy to the Islamic world, Oppenheim's work in Cairo took on an almost hypomanic quality. Between 1896 and 1909, he filed no less than 467 reports on Arab politics for the German Foreign Office, many of them running to a hundred pages or more. The subjects ranged from pan-Islam (a theme of particular interest to Kaiser Wilhelm) to Christian minorities; from plans for restoring irrigation networks in the Valley of Babylon to possible routes for the Baghdad railway; from Egyptian dynastic politics to the depredations of the British occupation authorities; from the British navy and its influence on the Muslim hajj to the Sherifate of Mecca and the tribal politics of the Hejaz; from the nature of the Caliphate and the Sunni–Shia divide to messianic Islamic cults and the followers of the Mahdi in Sudan. If Oppenheim's approach to these subjects was not especially fresh, he still brought to all of them a wide-ranging curiosity and single-minded passion – that passion being the need for Germany to defend the Ottoman Empire against the British bogeyman, or what he liked to call the 'English-Mohammedan-African-Asian Colonial Empire'.*

Oppenheim's reports have a relentless and repetitive quality, and yet we should not dismiss their importance on grounds of lack of originality. Like all hack-work, his dispatches from Cairo reveal the

---

* These reports are all preserved in the German Foreign Office archives in Berlin (PAAA). Some are also available in the US. They will be referred to individually below.

animating obsessions of his time and place, in this case the increasingly chauvinistic and anti-British thinking of pan-Germans encouraged by the Kaiser's *Weltpolitik*, and how their pan-Germanism opportunistically merged together with anti-imperialist pan-Islam.* Reporting on a wave of Lebanese Christian migration to America in spring 1903, for example, he deplored the economic impact of this brain drain on Beirut, before launching into a tirade against the local French, English, Russian and American missionary schools. It was these institutions of Western Christian imperialism, Oppenheim thundered, which 'implanted in the native Christians of Syria and Lebanon instinctive anti-Turkish sentiments and a desire for secession from the Ottoman Empire'. Because this population of would-be rebels knew that Germans were 'friends of the Sultan and opponents of the separation of any part of the Ottoman Empire', Syria's Christians would always remain 'hostile to us' (i.e. to Germans). And so he galloped home to his conclusion: Syrian Christians should be ignored in Germany's regional plans. They were 'the most unscrupulous and unreliable elements … among the many races of the Orient'.[31]

In this way the great ethnic mosaic of the Near East was ground down in the pan-German mind to the crude categories of pro-German and anti-German, of groups who would be useful to the expansion of German influence or should be summarily brushed aside. The dividing factor was not necessarily confessional, but whether a given population supported the Kaiser's friend Sultan Abdul Hamid or not: thus Zionist Jews were OK (for now), but Maronites, Coptic and Armenian Christians were anathema, as like as not British stooges.[†] Muslims could fall into either category. For the most part, Sunni Muslims were reliable, but possible rivals to Sultan Abdul Hamid's spiritual authority as Caliph, like the self-proclaimed Mahdi and his followers in Sudan, needed to

---

* In its original form, the idea of pan-Germanism referred merely to the unification of the German-speaking peoples of Europe in a single state. By the 1890s, however, the idea had taken on distinctly imperialist overtones. The Pan-German League (*Alldeutscher Verband*), founded in 1894, was openly expansionist, promoting German colonization in Africa and the Near East.

† For example, Oppenheim thought most Armenians in Cairo were in the pay of Lord Cromer, the Consul-General.

be carefully monitored.[32] Oppenheim was also suspicious of both the Sherif of Mecca and his rival Ibn Saud's tribe of Wahhabi Muslims, believing both (correctly, as it turned out) to be in the pay of British agents. Ibn Rashid, by contrast, and his Shammar Bedouins, were loyal to the Sultan, and thus implicitly pro-German.[33]

Egyptian nationalists, too, were useful, because their opposition to the British occupation implied an endorsement of the Sultan's sovereign claim over Cairo. And so Oppenheim befriended them all, from the sulking Khedive Abbas Hilmi, to Mustafa Kamil, founder of the Egyptian National Party and editor of *al Liwa*, to Sheikh Ali Yusuf, editor of *Al-Mu'ayyad*, to the faculty firebreathers at al-Azhar University. Not surprisingly, these men told him what he wanted to hear: they were all great admirers of the Kaiser. Oppenheim even organized a banquet in Mustafa Kamil's honour in Berlin in 1905, after which occasion Kamil was given a regular column in the *Berliner Tageblatt* ('Letter From an Egyptian Patriot') in which he berated the British on behalf of Germany.[34] The Wilhelmstrasse may have denied that it viewed Britain with hostility, but the German press knew otherwise. Any enemy of Germany's enemy was a friend.

Like the Kaiser on his grand tours, Oppenheim was in his element in the back streets of Cairo, living the life he had dreamed of having since boyhood. He resided in the old Arab quarter of Bab el Louk, in an early nineteenth-century pasha's palace fitted out with all the delights of the Orient. There was a proper dining room (*Selamlık*) in which Oppenheim greeted European visitors, but the beating heart of the place was the inner *harem*, where he kept his concubines. Every autumn, after his return from Berlin, Oppenheim's head servant Soliman would procure him a new slave girl (he called them his *Zeitfrauen*, or temporary concubines), who would become mistress of the harem until the following year, and who was herself served by two female attendants. He lived a double life, entertaining consular colleagues or visiting German politicians (like future Chancellor Bethmann Hollweg) in his outer *Selamlık*, while carefully concealing the women's *harem* within. Only on one occasion did the veil come loose. Intrigued by a married woman named Zenab, whose bewitching figure had attracted him on the street through her *burqa*, Oppenheim arranged a secret rendezvous which quickly blossomed into a steamy affair: he even kicked his current *Zeitfrau* out of the house so that Zenab would not be jealous. But Zenab's husband found them out, and drowned her in the Nile.[35]

Considering the swaggering figure Oppenheim was cutting around Cairo, and the vitriolic anti-English tone of his consular reports, it is not surprising that he came to the attention of the British authorities there. His house, located near al-Azhar University and the headquarters of the radical paper *al Liwa*, was notorious as a meeting place for would-be revolutionaries. Lord Cromer, the controversial Consul-General who had more or less ruled Egypt since the 1880s, had long suspected Oppenheim as a renegade German agent sent by the Kaiser to stir up Egyptian nationalists and Islamic agitators. When the so-called Kaba or Aqaba border crisis broke in 1906,* these suspicions boiled over into full-scale paranoia. 'Baron Max von Oppenheim',† British and French papers began reporting from Cairo, was in constant communication with Moukhtar Pasha, the Ottoman High Commissioner in Egypt representing the Sultan; he was hosting rabble-rousers in his home; he was distributing blood-curdling pamphlets urging on pan-Islamic jihadi massacres of European colonists; and he was intriguing with anti-French Algerian and anti-Italian Tripolitan rebels too.[36] All this was more or less true, as was implicitly confirmed by the non-denial denial issued by the German Consulate. The mysterious Baron, German Consul-General Graf Metternich told Sir Charles Hardinge, 'had no official position in Cairo', although Metternich admitted, in a seeming contradiction, that Oppenheim did receive a salary and enjoyed diplomatic privileges.[37]

Oppenheim himself, meanwhile, responded to the British accusation that he was inciting Arab subjects to a dangerous level of anti-British

---

* In part because Egypt was still nominally part of the Ottoman Empire under international law, the 'Egyptian-Ottoman' border remained very loosely defined. In 1905, Heinrich August Meissner 'Pasha' proposed to the Porte the extension of the Hejaz railway to Aqaba on the Gulf coast, which would turn the southern Sinai desert into important strategic real estate. Both the Ottoman government and the British sent troops to the area, and the crisis very nearly blew up into a war.

† The origin of Oppenheim's title of Baron ('Freiherr' in German) remains unclear, aside from the fact that he put it on his own calling card. It took some time, but eventually the moniker stuck. After his name burst into the headlines in 1906, he was generally referred to both inside and outside Germany as 'Baron Oppenheim'.

hatred by sending the German Foreign Office even more vitriolic anti-British screeds. Their press campaign against him over Aqaba, Oppenheim tried to explain to the Wilhelmstrasse, showed that the British had 'thrown off the mask and have now begun openly to turn on the Sultan'. The Aqaba border question was turning into 'a struggle for prestige in the eyes of the entire Mohammedan world, being played out in the Sinai between England and Turkey'. Far from being something for Germans to worry about, this presented Berlin with a golden opportunity. In any war between Great Britain and the Ottoman Empire, Oppenheim predicted, 'the embers of rebellion would burst into flames in all of [Britain's] Muslim colonies, and in so frightful a way that England would have to use all her troops and a great portion of her navy to put them out'.[38] The green turban had been quiescent for centuries, but 'in the future', he prophesied, 'Islam will play a much larger role ... the striking power and demographic strength of Islamic lands will one day have a great significance for European states'. 'We must not forget,' he wrote to the Wilhelmstrasse, 'that everything taking place in a Mohammedan country sends waves across the entire world of Islam.' Germany, Oppenheim believed, could ride the crest of this wave of anti-British pan-Islamism to world power.[39]

Like all would-be prophets, Oppenheim was ahead of his time. Although they appreciated his informative reporting on Egyptian and broader Arab politics, Oppenheim's superiors in the Foreign Office were not yet ready to risk a war with Great Britain over Ottoman border disputes. His position in Cairo did improve temporarily after Lord Cromer finally stepped down from his post in 1907, but it was only a matter of time before another scandal broke. In the event, it was a relatively minor incident, Oppenheim's reputed takeover in autumn 1909 of a radical newspaper, *Masr el Fatat*, which did the trick. Once again, the English and French newspapers were lit up with wild speculation about the Kaiser's spy, this 'occult agent of Germany'.[40] Oppenheim was publicly denounced by the new British-appointed Egyptian Minister-President Boutros Ghali,* a Coptic Christian who does not seem to have appreciated the Baron's promotion of pan-Islam (this

---

* Grandfather of Boutros Boutros-Ghali, Secretary-General of the United Nations from 1992 to 1997.

was Oppenheim's own interpretation). Another Christian, a Cairo businessman of Levantine origin, wrote to the President of the German Reichstag that Oppenheim was ruining Germany's reputation with his intrigues, warning that 'the presence of this man in Egypt is a perpetual danger, a grave menace to peace'.[41] This was too much even for Oppenheim's sponsors in the Wilhelmstrasse, who finally washed their hands of him. He was given a year's paid vacation, then formally sacked from the Foreign Office in November 1910. However, Kaiser Wilhelm, to cushion the blow to one of his favourites, gave Oppenheim the title of a Minister Resident at large.[42]

Oppenheim was not the only German Orientalist to run afoul of the British in pre-war Cairo. Just as the Baron's bravado had often put his caravan companions – and his Cairo lovers – into harm's way, Oppenheim had gradually roped a promising young German scholar into his dangerous adventures in pan-Islam. This was Curt Prüfer (born 1881), who began work at the German Consulate in Cairo in 1907. Like that of his mentor (and that of their mutual hero, Kaiser Wilhelm), Prüfer's restlessness seems to have arisen in large part from his strained relations with his family. His father Carl, a schoolteacher of liberal democratic views, tried to dissuade his son from government service, warning that the creeping authoritarianism of Wilhelmine Germany would corrupt him. But Curt would have none of this. Burning with the ambition of the lower middle class, he studied both law and Oriental languages at the University of Berlin, in the hope of preparing for the prestigious (and socially exclusive) Foreign Office. A far more serious student than Oppenheim, Prüfer completed a doctoral dissertation in Egyptology at the University of Erlangen in 1906. By this time, Prüfer had already mastered French, English, Italian and Arabic, and 'could understand Turkish, Russian, Spanish, and Portuguese'. It was clear, said an admiring Orientalist colleague, that Prüfer 'possessed phenomenal linguistic talent'. He made a perfect choice for dragoman, a kind of all-purpose translator, interpreter and cultural consultant, of Germany's Consulate in Cairo in 1907, and was rapidly promoted to Oriental Secretary.[43]

Had Prüfer's career followed its natural course, he would have established himself as one of the leading Western scholars in Cairo. By diplomatic convention, enshrined in a treaty between Germany and

(British-occupied) Egypt in 1904, a German national was always to be appointed as director of the Khedivial Library in Cairo, one of the most prestigious positions for Orientalists in the entire world. When Professor Bernhard Moritz prepared to step down from the coveted post in September 1911, the new German Consul-General, Hermann Graf von Hatzfeldt, put Prüfer's name forward for the position of library director, to no one's surprise. Prüfer was a rising star, indisputably the top young German Orientalist in town.

Yet Curt Prüfer had not strictly followed the career path of a scholar. Baron Oppenheim, twenty years his senior and grand man about town, had introduced the young dragoman to his fiery nationalist friends, particularly Sheikh Abdul Aziz Shawish, successor to the now-deceased Mustafa Kamil at *al Liwa*. Sheikh Shawish, a Tunisian pan-Islamist who ran guns to Libya during the Turco-Italian war which broke out in September 1911, was seen by the British as 'an incredibly venomous opponent', owing to 'his unreasoning fanaticism, his overwhelming egoism, and his malignant perversion and disregard of truth'.*[44] Oppenheim had also dragooned Prüfer along on his voyages into Bedouin country, both men dressing as Arabs as they searched for 'ancient ruins' (or gathered intelligence, as the British suspected). All this was sufficient for the British to rule Prüfer out as a candidate for the Khedivial Library directorship, on the grounds that his 'activities are those of a confidential political agent, rather than those of a student of Arabic'.[45]

Lord Kitchener, the conqueror of Khartoum who had recently been seconded to the British Consulate in Cairo, had good reason to be concerned about Prüfer's political activities. Earlier in 1911, Boutros Ghali, the Coptic Christian Minister-President whose objection to Oppenheim's pan-Islamist intrigues had provoked the latter's removal from Cairo, was assassinated by a young Muslim fanatic. Christian-Islamic tensions in Cairo were thus already running high when the Turco-Italian war erupted in September, just as the diplomatic crisis over the Khedivial Library appointment was breaking. It hardly

---

* This was the description of John Romich Alexander, in *The Truth About Egypt* (1911). Curiously, this excerpt on Shawish from Alexander's book was later used by the Germans as a *recommendation* for putting Shawish on the imperial payroll.

helped Prüfer's case that he was observed recruiting Egyptian Muslim volunteers to cross into Libya to fight the Christian Italians, jihad-style.[46] Because the Khedivial Library housed ancient Islamic manuscripts and was used primarily by Muslims, Kitchener was worried that it could easily 'become a natural centre of ... Pan-Islamic doctrine', particularly if a German agent like Prüfer was in charge.[47] To beat the Germans at their own game, Kitchener proposed in October that, because of its importance for Islam, the Khedivial Library should henceforth have only a Muslim as director.[48] To win German acquiescence to the rejection of Prüfer's appointment, Kitchener would allow the Germans to have the post of assistant library director, and the directorship of the Cairo Museum. As a sop to his bruised ego, Curt Prüfer would be given a scholarly award.[49]

Still, the Germans stood by their man. Consul-General Hatzfeldt was adamant that Prüfer was the most qualified for the position. His animated correspondence with Kitchener on the subject reveals a great deal about the burgeoning rift in Cairo caused by the German embrace of pan-Islam, and by Baron Oppenheim's activities in particular. As a final trump card, Kitchener threw Oppenheim's name at Hatzfeldt as proof positive of Prüfer's unsuitability for the library directorship, claiming that as the Baron's 'personal secretary', Prüfer had sullied himself with spy work. In another classic non-denial denial, Hatzfeldt replied that Prüfer's 'relations with Baron Oppenheim have always been purely social ones and these too were very slight'. Somewhat painfully, Hatzfeldt offered to enlist Oppenheim himself (now cataloguing his Tell Halaf ruins) to clear Prüfer's name – by issuing a sworn affidavit denying that he had any influence over him.[50] Poor Oppenheim had now been disowned entirely by the Foreign Office he had striven so mightily to join. And yet the Baron must have felt even worse for his young protégé Curt Prüfer, who, unlike him, did not have a private fortune to fall back on.

Deprived of his dream job and still only thirty years old, Prüfer would never forget the snub, or the men who had snubbed him. Nor would Oppenheim easily forgive that 'certain meddlesome power' whose representatives had forced him to leave his beloved Cairo in disgrace. Like their hero Wilhelm II, sneered at his whole life by his arrogant British cousins for his social awkwardness,

Oppenheim and Prüfer had a score to settle with Albion. And so it was that three privileged, well-travelled cosmopolitans, raised amidst the splendour of European civilization at the height of its glory, each serving a young empire entering its golden age of prosperity, achievement and influence, came to burn with seething resentment against the established power whose continued pre-eminence mocked German pretentions to world leadership. Pursued by demons only they understood, the Kaiser, the Baron, the Dragoman, and those who served them, would make the world pay for its failure to recognize their greatness.

2

Berlin to Baghdad

To extend the railway from Haydarpasha to Baghdad ... to build this line with only German materials and for the purpose of bringing goods and people to [Asia] via the most direct path from the heart of Germany ... will bring closer the day when [Bismarck's] remark about the entire Orient not being worth the bones of a Pomeranian Grenadier will seem like a curious historical memory.

Baron Marschall von Bieberstein, German Ambassador
to Constantinople, 1899[1]

Heading east from Istanbul by train today, alert travellers may be struck by architectural anomalies which seem out of place in contemporary Anatolia. If the stately *fin de siècle* German imperial style of the railway stations at Haydarpasha and at Adana, the gateway to the eastern Mediterranean, seems at least congruous with the importance of these cities, the same cannot be said for identical-looking stations at tiny villages along the way. From modest-sized stops at Karaman and Ereğli to virtual ghost towns like Durak (population: 148), the same yellow Swabian stucco stationhouses with white trim and red-tiled roofs greet those few passengers alighting en route. So light is the traffic on the line that only one passenger train per day sets off in both directions. Because there is only a single track, the east- and west-bound trains must wait in a station to pass each other. Now, as in its earliest days, the cross-Anatolian 'express' serves mostly through-traffic, crawling along at a snail's pace through a dry, windswept plateau almost entirely devoid of human habitation.

It has been a long, hard fall for the Baghdad railway and the Germans who planned, financed and built it. Most people now associate the line not with Germany at all, but with British authors and heroes. James Bond stows the Soviet code machine away aboard the Orient Express as he escapes from Istanbul in *From Russia With Love*. Graham Greene sets one of his classic thrillers blending political intrigue, crime and romance aboard the *Stamboul Train*. Hercule Poirot solves one of Agatha Christie's most famous murder mysteries aboard the legendary line, picking up clues in Syria which help him solve the crime somewhere in Bulgaria. *Murder on the Orient Express* has even been turned into a tourist attraction by the owners of the Pera Palace Hotel in Beyoğlu, the old European quarter of Istanbul.

There is something curious about these stories and their hold on the popular imagination. While not immune to the charms of the East, neither James Bond nor any of the characters in *Stamboul Train* or Agatha Christie's bestseller is remotely an Orientalist. Their concerns are exclusively Western, related to socialism and class warfare, European anti-Semitism, the Cold War, or domestic affairs back home. The minarets and muezzins of Islam do not factor at all.

It takes a leap of imagination, then, to voyage back in time to the bitter *fin de siècle* struggles over the Baghdad railway, when the Orient was still full of mystery, a romantic dream world to the West, still partly unmapped, the last and potentially greatest frontier of European exploration. Baghdad itself was a name of mythic grandeur, conjuring up images of *The Thousand and One Nights*, Baron Oppenheim's boyhood bedtime reading. Mesopotamia, the legendary Land of Two Rivers, had been slumbering in economic stagnation for centuries, ever since the Europeans' circumnavigation of Africa in the 1400s had put paid to the landward trade routes. Even before the collapse of the oriental carry trade, the Mongol invasion of the thirteenth century had ruined the old Persian and Mesopotamian irrigation networks, such that the ancient breadbasket of the world now lay barren. And yet, if the floods of the Tigris and Euphrates were again harnessed and controlled, wrote one English irrigation engineer:

> the delta of the two rivers would attain a fertility of which history has no record; and we should see men coming from the West, as well as from the East, making the Plain of Shamar a rival of the land of Egypt. The flaming swords of inundation and drought would have been taken out of the hands of the offended Seraphim, and the Garden of Eden would have again been planted.[2]

Baghdad, to be sure, was not much to look at in the late nineteenth century. A city of only some 150,000 people, which served mostly as a way-station for nomads and caravan traffic, it was a sleepy backwater of the Ottoman Empire, by general consensus the Sick Man of Europe. It would take a heroic effort to bring Mesopotamia's economy back to life, let alone connect it by steel railhead with Constantinople, 2,000 miles distant across swampy marshland, deserts and two forbidding mountain ranges. But this was just the kind of half-mad imperial enterprise *fin de siècle* Europeans excelled in. With Africa's terrors now tamed by the anti-malarial quinine which had allowed the continent to be carved up by European colonists, and Asia and the Americas connected by steam-powered sea vessels to the hubs of global commerce, only Asiatic Turkey remained a key zone outside the expanding web of world trade. Baghdad may not have itself been much of a prize, but just 500 miles beyond it to the south-east lay the port of Basra on the Persian Gulf, whence flowed sea-borne traffic to India and the Far East. A railway linking Europe with the Persian Gulf could offer a faster trade route to the Orient, outpacing not only the long sea voyage around Cape of Good Hope but even the shorter Suez Canal route (by three days, if the calculations of railway planners held true).

It was an entrancing vision for the European powers, beginning with the British, already the predominant trading power in the Persian Gulf. As the traditional protector of Turkey against Napoleonic and then Russian encroachment, Great Britain seemed, at first glance, a natural candidate to develop the infrastructure of the Ottoman Empire. It was not only the breadbasket of Babylon which beckoned to the British classical imagination: there was also Asia Minor, ancient cockpit of Alexander's army, now poor and sparsely populated, a pale remnant of its former glories under Persia, Hellas, Byzantium and the Ottoman Empire's own salad days under Süleyman the Magnificent. 'Verily Anatolia,' wrote D. G. Hogarth, the Oxford mentor of Lawrence of Arabia, 'is one of the gardens of the temperate earth, and perhaps some day European colonists may return from the lands of fever and fly ... to take up this portion of their more legitimate heritage.'[3]

Just as we might expect from her position as historic protector of the Porte, Britain had first made the running in Ottoman rail construction, building the lines from Smyrna (Izmir) on the Aegean Sea inland to Kasaba in the 1860s, and from Mersin to Adana along the Mediterranean. Together with the British buyout of the French shares in the Suez Canal Company in 1875, these coastal railways in Asiatic Turkey seemed to herald British dominance of Near Eastern trade traffic. The special relationship between London and Constantinople, however, took serious knocks in the years that followed. Sultan Abdul Hamid's deposition of the newly formed Turkish parliament and constitution in 1878, during the emergency posed by war with the Russians, whose army had reached as far as San Stefano (Yeşilköy, site of today's Atatürk airport), inaugurated an era of palace paranoia at the Porte. Abdul Hamid was particularly suspicious of rail construction near Turkey's coastlines, fearing they would be vulnerable to naval blackmail or bombardment in wartime.[4] Although the British Tory premier Benjamin Disraeli had, with Bismarck, negotiated a settlement at Berlin in 1878 which forced back the Russians and returned much conquered territory to the Ottomans, Abdul Hamid was not reassured by the return of the notoriously anti-Turkish Liberal William Gladstone to office in 1880. The British annexation of Cyprus in 1878, and the invasion of Ottoman Egypt ordered by the Gladstone government in 1882, marked the beginning of the end of London's special relationship with the Porte, which would never truly recover.

Among the other European powers, France seemed most likely to replace the British as the self-interested European sponsor of the Ottoman Empire. It was Napoleon III, after all, whose courting of Syria's Christians had sparked the Crimean War, in which Britain and France had stood together with the Ottomans against the Russian invaders. Sure enough, it was the French who moved in when the British began disengaging from Turkey, taking over the Smyrna–Kasaba and Mersin–Adana railways in the 1880s, and assuming a dominant position in the Ottoman Public Debt Administration in Constantinople, just as the British took over Egyptian government finances in Cairo. And it was the French, of course, who had first come up with the idea of a romantic rail route to Turkey: the original 'Orient Express' train ran from the Gare de l'Est in Paris to Sirkeci station on Constantinople's European shoreline in 1889.* But the Franco-Russian defence treaty, concluded in 1894, damaged France's position at the Porte no less dramatically than had the British occupation of Egypt a decade earlier. If there was a single unshakeable law underlining the Eastern Question, it was that one could not be friends with both Turkey and her historic northern enemy at the same time.

As for France's new ally, Russia viewed the prospect of Ottoman railway development with unrestrained hostility. Russian diplomats did take a keen interest in rail development in north-eastern Turkey along the Black Sea coast, and in the Armenian areas of eastern Anatolia: but this was only in order to make sure that no lines would ever be built in either region.† Likewise, Russia sought to block plans for a Baghdad railway at every opportunity, making clear to the Porte that any rail construction even remotely near the Russian border would be regarded as a *casus belli*, as it would speed up Turkish troop deployments to the Caucasus. When negotiations over the concession for a Baghdad line heated up in 1899, the Russian press issued dire warnings about possible 'military consequences'. Behind the dangerous Baghdad railway plan, believed Russian War Minister Kuropatkin (incorrectly), lay the British government.[5]

---

* By way of Munich, Vienna, Budapest and Belgrade. The original 'Express d'Orient', chartered in 1883, had run from Paris to Vienna. The Agatha Christie/James Bond version of the line was actually the 'Simplon Orient Express', a more southerly line via Sofia, Zaghreb, Trieste, Venice and Milan, established following the opening of the Simplon tunnel through the Swiss-Italian Alps in 1919.

† By the terms of the Russian-Ottoman Black Sea Agreement of 1900, the Russian Tsar reserved the right to veto any railway development projects in northern or eastern Anatolian areas abutting the Caucasus.

When we consider the suspicions beginning to swirl around both of Turkey's Crimean War allies at the Porte, it is not surprising that Abdul Hamid began lobbying for imperial Germany to replace them as his protector against the Russian threat. There were promising grounds for an Ottoman-German alliance. The lack of a long German imperial tradition was reassuring to the morbidly suspicious Sultan, as was Germany's geographic remoteness from his domains. The Ottoman Empire shared volatile borders with Austria-Hungary, Russia and now British Egypt, and there was a substantial population of French settlers stirring up Christian minorities in Syria. Germany's footprint in Asiatic Turkey, by contrast, was negligible, confined mostly to the military mission headed by General von der Goltz 'Pasha', which many credited for improved Ottoman performance in the 1897 war with Greece, when the Turks won a series of impressive victories in Thessaly.*

Meanwhile, the astonishing German industrialization spurt which began in the 1880s stimulated enormous demand for imported metals and minerals, not to mention foodstuffs to feed the growing German population. And Asiatic Turkey, European prospectors were beginning to report, was rich in almost everything modern industry requires, from lead, zinc, copper and chrome to lignite and liquid petroleum, this last discovered near Mosul as early as 1871, in what seemed to be inexhaustible quantities. If German steel rail could tame the Anatolian steppe and break through the Taurus mountains, the abundant resources of the Near East could begin feeding the voracious German economy, even while the Sultan's ability to deploy troops to trouble areas was enhanced. Strategically speaking, it was a perfect marriage.

German interests in Ottoman rail were already in full swing when the Kaiser began his courtship of Abdul Hamid. It was a German engineer, Wilhelm von Pressel, who had designed and helped build the first leg of what would become the Baghdad railway, the sixty-mile line stretching from Istanbul's Asian shore along the Sea of Marmara inland to Izmit, completed in 1872. Pressel, sometimes called the 'Father of the Baghdad Railway', grew fond during his years in

---

* Von der Goltz was given the Ottoman honorific 'Pasha' upon returning to Germany in 1895, following ten years in the Sultan's service.

Anatolia of both Turkey and Turks, believing that the planned railway would reinvigorate the beleaguered Ottoman Empire and allow its peoples to seize control of their own destiny. It is noteworthy that the arch anti-Orientalist Bismarck took personal note of Pressel's advocacy of the Ottoman cause, denouncing him as a 'simple Swabian engineer' who dares to 'tell me what to do'.[6]

If Pressel's vision inspired the creation of the Baghdad railway, however, it was not Pressel who would build it. The proposed line to Basra, covering 2,000 miles of arid and largely inhospitable steppe-land, mountains, deserts and swamps, was such an immensely costly undertaking that serious financial backing was necessary – not least because Ottoman Turkey had declared bankruptcy in 1875, its finances now under strict European oversight.* Pressel himself was too stubborn and idealistic to get on with the German moneymen who began descending on Constantinople in the 1880s and 1890s, in particular Georg von Siemens, director of Deutsche Bank, whose granting of an emergency loan of 30 million Marks to the Sultan in 1888 put Germany in the driver's seat for the Baghdad concession.[7] Whereas Pressel wanted to internationalize the Baghdad project as broadly as possible so as to cushion the Ottoman Empire against imperial encroachment by Germany (or any other European power), Siemens was a staunch imperialist who put German interests first. In this Siemens was seconded by Baron Marschall von Bieberstein, Germany's State Secretary and, from 1897, Ambassador to the Porte. In order to supplant French and British influence in Turkey and the Near East, the Baghdad railway, Marschall declared emphatically in 1899, must be constructed 'with only German materials and for the purpose of bringing goods and people to [Asia] via the most direct path from the heart of Germany'.[†8]

---

* By the terms of the Decree of Mouharrem signed in 1881, the European-dominated Ottoman Public Debt Administration had control of all revenues raised through customs and tax collection in the empire, from monopoly duties on salt, silk and tobacco production to sales taxes on alcohol and stamps. No less than four-fifths of the revenues collected from these duties went to payment of interest on the Ottoman debt.
† The Berlin-to-Baghdad version of the line (which, in the ideal North Sea to Persian Gulf version, would also incorporate Hamburg and Basra at the far ends) joined up with the old Parisian 'Orient Express' at Vienna, by way of Dresden and Prague.

This was much easier said than done. The Deutsche Bank-owned Anatolian Railway Company (Société du Chemin de fer Ottoman d'Anatolie), chartered in 1889 on the heels of Siemens' generous loan to Abdul Hamid the previous year, did complete the extension of the Izmit line to Ankara by 1892 on its own. But even this comparatively modest project, covering only about 250 miles, including a southern detour via Eskişehir (which allowed the railway to bypass the steeper mountain passes of Bolu), had required a million pounds sterling laid down by British bankers to get off the ground (the Germans later bought out the British-owned shares in 1890 in the wake of a credit crunch in the City of London, but this was an emergency measure, not a political move).[9] A rail line to Baghdad and Basra would likely require outlays of hundreds of millions, which would necessitate 'kilometric revenue guarantees' (a kind of promissory note or bond pegged to each section of line constructed) to reassure investors. Because such revenue could only be processed via the French-dominated Ottoman Public Debt Administration, this meant French interests, too, had to be taken into account.

Even setting aside Pressel's moral case against German domination of the Baghdad railway, there were very good reasons for internationalizing the financing. Had the Germans succeeded in raising enough revenue on their own to begin construction – an unlikely prospect – this would only have excited French, British and Russian suspicions. The more 'German' the Baghdad railway appeared, the more cause Paris, London and St Petersburg would have for trying to sabotage it, or for putting up rival bids for the concession. By contrast, if the Anatolian Railway Company sold shares broadly to French and British interests, it would cushion the financial risk faced by Deutsche Bank, and increase the likelihood the Great Powers would approve the Baghdad concession. The essential thing was camouflage: Germany must appear not to be building the railway alone, while somehow still securing the strategic benefit.

Despite the political difficulties, the Germans had a major advantage in the bidding for the Baghdad concession: the Sultan's personal backing. The proliferating 'Capitulations' which allowed Europeans to run the Ottoman Empire's finances, postal services and transport made Abdul Hamid something of a guest in his own house, but he was still the nominal sovereign of his empire, and only the sovereign could sign off on the Baghdad concession. After all, selling the right to build this 2,000-mile railway, and to raise the huge customs, ticket and mining concession revenues needed to pay off its sure-to-be-colossal construction debts, was akin to mortgaging the financial future of Ottoman Turkey. So long as the suspicious Sultan lived, he would never mortgage his empire to the British, who had already taken Egypt, one of the crown jewels of his empire. Nor did he trust the French, who were already occupying the (theoretically) Ottoman provinces in the Maghreb and making imperial inroads in Syria, not to mention intriguing openly with Russia, Turkey's mortal enemy. If any Europeans would build the new strategic artery of Asiatic Turkey, it would be the Germans – or no one.

The Kaiser's visit to Constantinople in 1898 raised the stakes in the game, but did not really alter the fundamentals. The Germans wanted to build an Ottoman railway stretching all the way to the Persian Gulf with German steel and skilled labour, but not to take on all the financial risk. The Sultan wanted the Germans to build the Baghdad–Basra line, but only to his own specifications: as far as possible from Turkey's vulnerable Mediterranean coastline, and passing through the volatile Armenian regions of eastern Anatolia, to speed up troop deployments there, whether to meet an Armenian rebellion or a Russian invasion. The British wanted a railway of some kind but one that would link the Mediterranean coast to the Persian Gulf, to stimulate trade. The French, for their part, would have preferred to expand their own Ottoman railway inland from Smyrna, or to build up a serious network stretching into Lebanon and Syria. The Russians wanted to derail, or at least complicate, all of these building projects, except for the regional French lines.

It was impossible, of course, to reconcile all these interests, but the German negotiators did their best. Despite the Sultan's strong preference for a Baghdad line routed eastward from Ankara through Sivas and Diyarbakır, which would avoid the coastline but might wind suspiciously close to the Caucasus, the Germans jettisoned this plan in favour of a more westerly line departing from the existing Anatolian Company railhead at Eskişehir south-east via Konya (reached in 1896), Karaman, Ereğli and Bulgurlu. Ostensibly undertaken to alleviate

Russian concerns, this re-routing in fact made good economic sense, as the new route covered flatter ground (thus cheaper construction costs) and crossed more populated areas (which meant, potentially at least, more profitable traffic). It did, however, bring the German line into west Anatolian territory eyed hungrily by the French-owned Smyrna–Kasaba rail company still building lines inland from the Aegean. Avoiding one potential landmine, the German planners nearly stepped on another. To win over the acquiescence of the Smyrna–Kasaba company (and to avoid a price war over regional fares), the Germans promised in May 1899 that French bankers would receive at least 40 per cent of the capital stock floated by the Baghdad railway undertaking, and that two Smyrna–Kasaba representatives would sit on its board of directors.[10]

Meanwhile, a British group fronted by an Austrian banker named Ernest Rechnitzer was proposing to build a rail link from the Turkish port of Alexandretta (today's Iskenderun) direct to Basra. This plan had the obvious advantage of being inexpensive, avoiding the Taurus and Amanus mountain ranges between Anatolia and Syria, and thus (in theory) making unnecessary the imposing 'kilometric guarantees' by which the Sultan would be asked to pledge future tax revenues to railway bondholders.[11] By speeding up the transport of goods from the Mediterranean to the Persian Gulf and the Indian Ocean beyond, the Rechnitzer line had fantastic economic potential. Its disadvantage, of course, was that Rechnitzer's backers were British.

The Sultan's position, no less than the Germans', was delicate. Financially, he may have been better off going with Rechnitzer's consortium, which was offering to lay down initial construction costs all by itself. But a railway which failed to link Constantinople with eastern Anatolia and the Arab Near East would defeat the strategic point for the Sultan.* By stimulating the economies of Syria and Mesopotamia, the Rechnitzer railway might even indirectly promote the cause of Arab independence. Abdul Hamid mostly trusted the

---

* And for the Germans, who would lose out on the chance of replacing the British-dominated trade routes to the East or the French-dominated tourist traffic to Constantinople, if a full-on Constantinople-to-Baghdad line were not built.

Germans on Siemens' negotiating team, but if they were to build the Baghdad railway he knew they would probably have to raise British and French capital, and administer repayment via the French-dominated Ottoman Public Debt Administration, both of which conditions raised the prospect of further European encroachment on the Sultan's sovereign authority. Trusting no one entirely, the Sultan wished to reserve final control over the railway's routing and construction for himself.

One can hardly blame Abdul Hamid for his caution. Kaiser Wilhelm's disavowal of acquisitive intentions towards the Ottoman Empire during his friendly visit in 1898 was reassuring up to a point, but then this was the same Wilhelm who would famously react to the Boxer Rebellion in China in 1900 by vowing to crush the 'heathens' with such overwhelming force that 'for a thousand years ... no Chinaman ... will dare to look a German in the face'.[12] It was only after vigorous lobbying by German Ambassador Marschall, and the deposit of 200,000 Turkish lira (pounds) (nearly $1 million at the time, the equivalent of $100 million today) in the Ottoman Treasury, that Abdul Hamid finally made a decision. On 23 December 1899, the Ottoman Minister of Public Works, Zihni Pasha, signed an agreement with Georg Siemens, representing Deutsche Bank and the Anatolian Railway Company, which obliged the German group to build a railway 'within a *maximum* period of eight years' from Konya to Basra via Baghdad.[13]

It appeared to be a golden deal – for the Sultan. The Germans had pledged themselves to plan and build a vital strategic artery for Abdul Hamid, in less than eight years, and to raise all the capital necessary for the undertaking. Meanwhile, in a clause negotiated at the last minute on the Sultan's personal insistence, the Germans had agreed that the Ottoman government, 'on its side reserves the power of using, whenever it may desire to do so, its right of buying up the line from Konya to Baghdad and Basra'.[14] Since the Sultan's regime was still, effectively, bankrupt, the prospect of his buying out the Baghdad railway was unrealistic, to say the least. But by insisting on the right, the Sultan was drawing a line in the sand. If the Germans crossed this line and somehow violated his sovereignty, he would retaliate. To reiterate the point, Abdul Hamid announced a ban on all foreign mining concessions in the Ottoman Empire in February 1900, only several months after giving the Germans the Baghdad concession, which cast into doubt the financial viability of the entire undertaking.[15] This was not reassuring to men proposing to invest hundreds of millions of Marks in the railway. As Siemens himself complained, 'the so-called Baghdad Railway Concession is only a piece of paper for which I paid 200,000 Turkish lira!'[16]

This was not the only price the Germans had paid for the right to build the Baghdad railway. Although the details were (understandably) never released to the public, the Sultan had demanded a serious political quid pro quo for the deal. As early as June 1898, Abdul Hamid, through his Ambassador to Berlin, had demanded that the Germans share intelligence on revolutionary opponents of his regime, and be ready to deport, on request, specifically named 'agitators' from Germany.[17] In the years following the awarding of the Baghdad concession in 1899, the Kaiser's spies duly provided Abdul Hamid with regular reports on the whereabouts and activities of his 'Young Turk' opponents.*

Still, the German negotiators did not leave Constantinople empty-handed, either. Contradicting the Sultan's public repudiation of foreign mining concessions, Abdul Hamid had quietly agreed to give German prospectors working for the railway company generous exploration rights inside his domains, including copper- and coal-mining grants and broad excavation rights within twenty kilometres of the Baghdad line on either side.[18] A secret imperial *Iradé* (decree) dated 15 November 1899 – just five weeks before the Baghdad concession was granted – gave the Berlin Museum further rights to keep artefacts German miners or archaeologists might discover while excavating on Ottoman territory. The results, as anyone who has visited the Museum Island in Berlin knows, were dramatic.[19]

The Baghdad railway, we might say, was born in sin. Not surprisingly, in light of the political shenanigans surrounding the

---

* See below, chapter 3.

concession, progress in building it was not swift in coming. It did not help that the concession was signed in the midst of a worldwide depression at the turn of the twentieth century, which scared off many prospective investors. A German expedition sent to scout possible routes to Baghdad in 1899 reported that at least 500 million francs would be needed for construction, and the full eight years allotted by the Sultan's concession, if not more. The Anatolian plains through which the railway would begin its eastward progress from Konya were woefully underdeveloped, with few towns of note, poor agriculture, and no mining or manufacturing to speak of. 'One could ride for hours,' wrote Consul-General Stemrich, the expedition leader, 'without seeing a single cultivated field.'* Without serious investment from outside, central Anatolia offered little potential for profitable traffic.

The Taurus range, meanwhile, was a logistical nightmare, with impassable mountains as far as the eye could see, interrupted only by a few yawning chasms carved by ancient rivers. The famous Cilician passes used by Alexander's army were far too steep for safe rail transport. The mountains could be crossed at a serviceable rail grade only through extensive blasting and the excavation of thousands of tons of rock. In the end, some three dozen tunnels were needed, many of them several kilometres in length.† A daunting proposition with the latest technology today, the degree of difficulty of blasting away nearly twelve miles worth of tunnels in 1900 boggles the imagination. Little wonder it took German engineers years of planning and preparation before they could begin tunnelling the Taurus section of the Baghdad railway.

The Syrian and Mesopotamian stretches on the other side of the mountains were no picnic either. Here the railway would have to pass through miles of nomad country, plagued by marauding Kurds, Bedouins and opportunistic bandits of all kinds. What was good fun for adventure-seekers like Baron Oppenheim (who himself did prospecting for the Baghdad Railway Company, among his other covert

---

* Sad to say, the same is true today.
† On a recent train trip through the Taurus, the author counted thirty-seven tunnels.

activities) was a horrible challenge for railway builders.[*][20] It was not merely the security problem posed by tribal raids which discouraged the German scouts, but the unsuitability of nomadic populations for work on the railway. Nomads were, almost by definition, unsuited to sedentary labour. Armenians and other settled Christian minorities, who dominated what little agricultural cultivation there was in the region, were more promising as a workforce, but if they were enlisted to work on the railway, who would till the land? Skilled foreign workers could, of course, be imported, but they would need higher wages and costly protection. Then there were the swampy, malarial marshes between Baghdad and Basra, where huge quantities of quinine would be necessary to treat workers against disease. All in all, concluded Stemrich's scouting team after outlining likely costs, there was little chance of the railway turning a profit in the near future.[21]

With so many risks surrounding the undertaking, it is not surprising that the financing for the Baghdad railway took years to arrange. Not until 1903 did construction on the line begin, and even then only on the first, flat section from Konya to the foot of the Taurus mountains. In the updated convention signed on 5 March 1903, the new German-dominated Baghdad Railway Company (BRC) was given what seemed to be advantageous terms, such as unlimited use of Ottoman state forests for lumber and state land for 'right of way', both dispensed free of charge. The BRC also received a tax exemption in perpetuity for railway property and revenue. But these concessions were in the Sultan's interest too, designed to get the railway built as quickly as possible. Station depots, post offices and police outposts along the route would all be built by the Germans. The BRC also promised to clear all construction plans with the Porte; to give hiring preference to Ottoman subjects; to discourage further European migration to the Ottoman Empire; to make an annual charity payment of 500 Turkish lira (about $2,500 then, or $2.5 million today)

---

[*] Several of Oppenheim's visits to his beloved ruins of Tell Halaf, for example, were funded by the Baghdad Railway Company, which was planning to route the railway through nearby Ras el 'Ain in north-eastern Syria. Although the moneymen seem to have taken Oppenheim's gushing reports on future railway revenue potential with a large pinch of salt, they did pick up the tab for his scouting trips.

to Islamic foundations for the poor; and to turn over day-to-day management of the railway to the Ottoman government within five years. More significantly for Abdul Hamid, the BRC agreed to erect telegraph poles at 65-metre intervals along the entire line, to spend 4 million francs on Ottoman military installations along the route and, in case of war, to place at the Sultan's disposal its 'entire rolling stock, or such as might be necessary, for the transportation of officers and men of the army, navy, police and gendarmerie, together with any or all equipment'.[22]

Considering how tailor-made these terms were to the extension of the Sultan's sovereign authority over his realm, it is curious to reflect that the press reaction abroad to the Baghdad concession pointed not to the Sultan's clever coup, but to the impending German takeover of the Ottoman Empire. In St Petersburg, *Novoe Vremya* warned that by the time construction of the railway was finished on schedule in 1911, 'Turkey will be completely subjected to German economic control', with 'German merchandise transported from Hamburg to the Persian Gulf exclusively on German railways'. A special report commissioned by French army intelligence concluded the new Baghdad concession to be the work of Moltke the Younger at the German General Staff, with a view to opening up a German line of communication 'from Hamburg to the Far East by way of Berlin, without passing the Suez Canal, that is independent of English influence'.* Although the British government had not followed the BRC negotiations very closely, as Paul Cambon, French Ambassador in London, complained, by April Downing Street, too, was expressing concern about German domination of the railway.[23]

The British, French and Russians were right to worry about the expansion of German influence entailed in the Baghdad railway concession of 1903, even if the terms seemed to be personally designed for Sultan Abdul Hamid. There must have been a good reason why German banks had put up nearly two-thirds of the 3 million francs in

---

* Much as the Germans themselves would have loved this to be true, the Russian and French complaints omitted a crucial fact. The Balkan 'Orient Express' section of the proposed Berlin-to-Baghdad line had a long section winding through Russophile Serbia, as the Central Powers would be reminded to their chagrin in 1914.

	Berlin–Baghdad railway existing and under construction
	Projected extension
	Borders of 1912
	Ottoman Empire

0   500 km

0   250 miles

1. 'Mitteleuropa': from Hamburg to the Persian Gulf, 1912

start-up capital the BRC required to begin construction.[24] The Germans *were* trying to support the Sultan, perceiving him as their most indispensable ally in an increasingly hostile international environment. If Europe descended into a Great Power war, Austria-Hungary could do little more for her German ally than deflect some of Russia's strength on the eastern front, while Italy, Germany's only other European ally, could not do even that. The Ottoman Empire, by contrast, could threaten Russia's vulnerable Caucasian underbelly, along with Egypt and the Suez Canal, the strategic linchpin of the entire British Empire. It could only do this, however, if the Sultan's largely phantom authority over the distant provinces of his empire was buttressed by a great trunk railway to the Near East. If it was in Abdul Hamid's interest to ensure that the railway would serve Ottoman security needs, then it was in Germany's interest too. As Paul Rohrbach wrote in his classic pan-German primer, *Die Bagdadbahn*, 'Not a pfennig for a weak Turkey, but for a strong Turkey we can give everything!'[25]

In building the Baghdad railway, then, the Germans were betting on the Sultan's political future. A railway connecting Constantinople to the Near East could easily be linked to the Hejaz railway (begun in 1901) and thus the holy cities of Medina and Mecca, helping to resurrect the Sultan's authority as Caliph of Sunni Islam and bring his restive Kurdish and Arab subjects back into the imperial fold.[*26] Abdul Hamid's brand of resurgent Islam also had great potential, from the German perspective, for stirring up seditious sentiments among the Muslim subjects of Britain and France. Pan-Islam, spreading eastwards on the Baghdad railway, could be Germany's ticket to world power.

Were the Sultan's precarious hold on his empire to falter, however, the German hand might turn out to be a busted flush. The more closely German diplomats, spies and railway engineers tied their fortunes to Abdul Hamid's reactionary regime, the greater the risk they would burn their bridges with everyone else in the empire, from political

---

* Unlike the Baghdad railway, the Hejaz line (which ran from Damascus to Medina) was directly financed to the tune of 75 million gold francs by subscription from Muslims around the world, as it would directly aid hajj pilgrims. Still, like the Baghdad line, it was mostly built by Germans, including head engineer Heinrich August Meissner.

reformers and go-ahead army officers to Jews and Christian minorities. The Armenians were particularly hostile to Abdul Hamid following the massacres, both spontaneous and organized, which had followed an Armenian uprising in Constantinople in 1896. Thousands of Armenians lived in south-eastern Anatolian districts through which the Baghdad railway would pass en route to Mesopotamia and their skills as mechanics, blacksmiths, metalworkers and artisans would be desperately needed. Then there were Kurds, Arabs, Greeks and Levantine Christians, none of whom took a kind view of Germany's cultivation of the Sultan.

Nor would the Sultan himself look kindly on his German benefactors if their promises were not fulfilled. As progress on the railway inevitably slowed after the first flatlands were forded, the strategic partnership between Berlin and the Porte was engulfed in acrimony. As Turkish officials complained to Hugo Grothe of the German-Anatolian Society, the Germans had 'given new meaning to the Turkish expression "yavaş yavaş"' ('slowly but surely').[27] By 1905, when construction ground to a halt, the BRC had finished barely 200 kilometres, or less than one tenth of the distance to Basra. Rather than a railway to Baghdad, the Germans had built a line to Bulgurlu, a town so small it is no longer a stop on the Anatolian express. For this 'railway to nowhere' the Ottoman government had borrowed 54 million francs, payable at 4 per cent annual interest over ninety-eight years, in order to meet the BRC's kilometric revenue guarantees. It was hefty bill for an empire in financial receivership – and would burden Turkish taxpayers for decades.

To the Germans financing and building the railway, of course, matters looked considerably different. The BRC, aided by German companies like Philipp Holzmann Construction, had built a smoothly functioning railway across the arid wastes of Anatolia, with German steel and engineering skill, to state-of-the-art specifications (the tracks were Prussian type 7).[28] True, progress had stalled after the line reached Bulgurlu, but this was largely due to the Sultan's insistence that construction proceed in stages, one section at a time from west to east, to ensure that none of his restive subjects south-east of the Taurus and Amanus mountains benefited prematurely from the railway's construction. Without being allowed to build a line across the more commercially viable Mediterranean plains, there was no way the BRC could hope to recoup the colossal outlays needed to begin blasting and tunnelling the Taurus mountains. Revenue from the first 200-kilometre section, meanwhile, had proved disappointing. Before the through line was finished, there was little advantage for passengers or freight traffic in travelling from Konya to Bulgurlu by train, only to be forced back on to the caravan route for the mountains. This left the BRC wholly dependent on the Sultan's kilometric guarantees (11,000 francs per finished kilometre, or 4,500 per kilometre in sections under construction) to pay down railway bonds. Profits, even on a flat section of the railway the Germans had finished under cost and ahead of schedule, had simply not materialized. Were the BRC to begin serious work on the Taurus section of the railway, the prospect of profit would become nothing more than a fevered fantasy.

In a sense, the German team was right back where it started. Having proved themselves unable to finance the railway alone,* the Germans would need to raise substantially the kilometric guarantees the BRC demanded of the beleaguered Ottoman government, which by 1906 was again facing bankruptcy. This would necessitate substantial rises in Ottoman tax and customs duties, which could only be approved by the Great Powers – not only the French, who dominated the Ottoman Public Debt Administration, but Russia and Great Britain too. In the diplomacy surrounding the Baghdad concessions of 1899 and 1903, Germany had been able to count on London's tacit support, or at least indifference. But in 1904 Britain had reached a historic Entente Cordiale with France. Meanwhile, the Liberal landslide of December 1905 would inaugurate an era of outright Russophilia in Downing Street. Whereas Tory statesmen like Benjamin Disraeli and Lord Salisbury had favoured propping up the Ottomans to block any threat of a Russian advance, the new Liberal Prime Minister Herbert Asquith and Foreign Secretary Sir Edward Grey,

---

* Although the French-controlled Banque Impériale Ottomane held a significant chunk of BRC stock, the French government had refused to give official listing on the Paris bourse to the railway bonds floated in 1903, which had seriously hampered efforts to raise capital. The British government, too, had refused to underwrite bond issues in the City of London. So the BRC bonds had mostly been sold to German banks.

owing to both the Liberal tradition of favouring Russia over 'barbarous' Turkey and to the mounting German threat, were keen to bury the hatchet with Britain's Great Game rival. If the Germans wanted to secure international financing for the crucial mountain stages of the Baghdad railway, Berlin, cornered by the budding new tripartite Entente, would have to beg.

Luckily, negotiations over raising the Ottoman customs rates had begun earlier in 1905, before the Liberal takeover in London signalled the coming diplomatic revolution. Sultan Abdul Hamid had then proposed raising the duty on imports entering Ottoman ports from 8 to 11 per cent. After a year of agonizing negotiations, the powers agreed, but not before attaching political conditions, including expensive new reforms and restrictions on the use of customs revenue increases to pay the BRC's kilometric revenue guarantees. The increase, moreover, would not kick in until July 1907, by which time construction on the Baghdad line would have been halted for three years.[29] While helping to keep the Sultan's myriad creditors at bay for a time, the customs deal would do little to kick-start construction on the railway that Abdul Hamid so desperately needed to strengthen his empire. And the financial riders attached made it perfectly clear that the Entente powers had no desire to help him do so.

Interestingly, it was the Russian government, which had never signed off on any of the earlier Baghdad concessions, which petitioned Germany first over a new Baghdad railway convention. Russian Foreign Minister Alexander Isvolsky proposed a straight-up imperial bargain while visiting Berlin in October 1906. Russia would 'allow' construction of the Baghdad railway, he told German State Secretary Baron von Schoen, in exchange for German recognition of Russian interests in Persia, and a promise that Germany would never build rail or telegraph lines there.[30]

It was a curious proposal. As interpreted by Marschall, German Ambassador to the Porte, Russia was merely up to her old dirty tricks. To all appearances, Russian industrialists had no plans of their own to build many railways in Persia, and certainly not in Asiatic Turkey. Isvolsky's demand that Germany desist from developing Persia's minuscule rail network was consistent, Marschall believed, with 'the general tendency of Russia's entire policy towards the Orient, to stymie the Islamic countries in their economic development and in this way to exacerbate their political and military weakness'. Berlin, by contrast, wanted to strengthen the Ottoman Empire's communications, and shore up the Sultan's political and spiritual authority in the process. Thus Germany, Marschall advised Chancellor von Bülow in March 1907, must not agree to Russia's veto on Persian rail development, which would 'completely destroy our entire freedom of action', along with Germany's reputation as friend and patron of the Muslim world.[31] Considering the result of Russia's campaign for recognition of its Persian sphere of influence – the Anglo-Russian Convention signed just four months later, which cynically divided Persia into zones of influence, to guarantee the British position in India and the Russians' in Central Asia – Marschall's warning was prescient.

The solidification of the Triple Entente in 1907 only hardened German resolve to go it alone in financing the Baghdad railway. Now that the hostile Russians seemed to have a veto over both French and British policy, there was little hope of moving major new railway bond issues in Paris and London. Sultan Abdul Hamid also shared Marschall's frustrations with Entente machinations, and the two men began negotiating their own counter-Entente accord. Although the terms of the new BRC concession were not finalized until 2 June 1908, Marschall and Abdul Hamid seem to have reached an oral agreement earlier that winter, in which the Sultan promised that 'he would make sufficient guarantees available for the continuation of the Baghdad railway'.[32] The higher customs duties, to the chagrin of the Entente powers, had shored up the Ottoman government's financial position enough that the Sultan could float his own Baghdad railway bonds, pledging to their future repayment any revenue surpluses turned over to his government by the Public Debt Administration. If these surpluses did not materialize, the Sultan promised to make up the gap with local taxes, like the livestock levy on cattle in provinces through which the railway passed, such as Konya, Adana and Aleppo.[33]

However the kilometric guarantees would be paid, the important thing was that construction could finally resume. In exchange for the Sultan's financial pledges, the BRC had vowed to get to work within three months. Urged on by Marschall and led by a brilliant German railway expert, Ernst Mackensen, the BRC moved even faster than this.

By late June, German engineers had begun surveying the Taurus mountains from both directions, the northern team setting up shop at Ereğli and the southern unit at Adana. There were no more concerns about building multiple sections simultaneously: the Sultan had expressly demanded that the Germans work as quickly as possible.[34]

It was a heady time in Anatolia, with the strategic partnership between Kaiser Wilhelm and Abdul Hamid finally bearing fruit. With both sovereigns threatened by diplomatic encirclement, there was a hint of menace in the air which brought urgency to the relationship. Haydarpasha station, now rising ominously on the Asian shore of the Bosphorus, embodied the new potency of the partnership between Berlin and the Porte. Without the help of the other powers, Germany and the Ottoman Empire would build the railway of the world's dreams, linking together East and West, Europe and the Orient, and rewakening the Islamic world from its long economic sleep. The Germans had bet the farm on the Sultan just as everyone else in the world was writing him off, and Abdul Hamid was eager to reward their loyalty. It was a brilliant move, but a risky one. As with so many of history's great gambits, the prize was just beginning to fall into Germany's grasp when fate snatched it rudely away.

3

Young Turks and Old Caliphs

With the triumph of Liberal Ideas in Turkey the great moral influence which Constantinople possesses over Islam at large is destined to assume an intellectual character. Such an influence would then serve as a powerful agent of reconciliation between East and West.

Prince Sabahaddin, August 1906[1]

Since the [failed counter-revolutionary coup] of 13 April [1909] the [Young Turks] have become more careful. Women's emancipation is being put to the side, and once again Sharia law is spoken of. Nevertheless strict Muslims regard the whole [CUP] regime with deep mistrust, if not with outright hostility.

Baron Marschall, October 1909[2]

The generous early returns Germany had received from its gamble on Abdul Hamid were largely owing to the Sultan's precarious perch on his throne. Palace intrigue was nothing new in a monarchy which depended on the peculiar institution of the *harem* to propagate the royal bloodline: in its earliest days newly crowned Sultans had routinely put their brothers to death to prevent succession struggles. In later, ostensibly more humane times, would-be heirs to the throne (or deposed Sultans) were instead confined to the *kafes*, a kind of gilded cage where many went mad in solitary confinement. Although Abdul Hamid was fortunate enough to escape these fates, his troubled reign was literally born of inner-palace bloodshed in 1876. After replacing the long-serving Abdul Aziz as Sultan earlier that year, Abdul Hamid's older brother Murad V had suffered a nervous breakdown. He had cause: the deposed Abdul Aziz had (reportedly) killed himself,* where-upon an army captain close to the martyred Sultan went on murder-ous rampage inside a Cabinet meeting, killing the War Minister, among others. One can hardly blame Abdul Hamid for his para-noia, considering the fate of his predecessors. It did not help that attempts to depose him by force came close to succeeding in both 1878 and 1896.

For understandable reasons, Abdul Hamid's government devoted a great deal of its energy to assuring the sovereign's physical survival. Refusing to live at Dolmabahçe palace because of its unpleasant asso-ciations with the ghoulishly martyred Abdul Aziz, the new Sultan con-structed a veritable fortress at Yıldız, on a rise overlooking Dolmabahçe and the Bosphorus (although significantly, below the towering new imperial German Embassy atop the higher hill at Taksim, opened in December 1877). On the express instructions of the new Sultan, Yıldız had been surrounded by two encircling walls, the second directly abutting the barracks of the Ottoman Imperial Guard, 7,000 strong. As if preparing for a siege, Abdul Hamid had installed inside the forti-fied Yıldız complex 'a farm, a small artificial lake, stables, workshops, a menagerie, and an aviary'.[3]

If the Sultan sometimes seemed to conflate his own fate with that of his empire, he had good reasons for doing so. It was not simply that there were, indisputably, active plots against his life and throne; there were also plots afoot to dismantle the Ottoman Empire, and to a strik-ing extent these could be dated to 1876, the date of Abdul Hamid's accession. In that fateful year, the empire had faced bankruptcy, insur-rections in Bosnia, Serbia, Montenegro and Bulgaria, and the threat of a Russian invasion piggybacking on the southern Slav revolts – which indeed transpired the following April. In Abdul Hamid's first year in power, the Ottoman Empire, long ailing, seemed to be on its death-bed. That both Sultan and empire survived this crisis together only reinforced Abdul Hamid's belief that his own fate was intertwined with that of the House of Osman.

---

* By slashing his wrists – both of them, which may have been a difficult trick, the second wrist cut by a knife-wielding hand already incapacitated by the first thrust.

More to the political point, because both an Ottoman constitution and parliament had been inaugurated in winter 1876–7, while the powers were meeting in Constantinople to decide the fate of the empire with the Balkans in rebellion and the Russians threatening, Abdul Hamid associated Western-style political reform with imperial humiliation. He was not entirely wrong to do so: previous bouts of Ottoman liberalism had all coincided with moments of Turkish weakness, from the suppression of the reactionary Janissary corps in 1826 (during the final throes of the Greek war of independence), to the launch of the Tanzimat reforms in 1839 (after the Egyptian Muhammad Ali's victory over the Ottoman army at Nezib), to the Imperial Rescript of 1856, which followed the empire's embarrassing delivery from Russian invasion by her British and French Crimean War allies. Abdul Hamid, by contrast, used the occasion of a damaging armistice with Russia in February 1878 to prorogue the new parliament, as if to declare Ottoman independence from European political tutelage.*[4]

The Sultan's suspicions about liberal reform were only reinforced by the larger trends in European diplomacy. Since the promulgation of the Rescript of the Rose Bower in 1839, which kicked off the Tanzimat, Ottoman Westernizers had looked to Paris and London for inspiration. But the loss of French face in the Franco-Prussian War of 1870–71 had taken the bloom off the liberal rose. The discrediting of liberalism in Abdul Hamid's mind was completed by the French occupation of Ottoman Tunisia in 1881 and the British occupation of Egypt by the archetypically Liberal Gladstone government in 1882.[5] German prestige, by contrast, was rising steadily, and the Kaiserreich, particularly after the ascension of Wilhelm II in 1888, was anything but liberal. Metternich's Holy Alliance of the conservative Eastern Emperors may have been killed off by the Crimean War (when Austria had split with Russia), but its spirit lived on in Potsdam.

The various steps in the Kaiser's progressive courtship of Abdul Hamid seemed almost uncannily timed to poke a stick in the eye of Ottoman liberals. It was in 1889, the year Wilhelm sang the Sultan's praises while touring Constantinople, that the first serious 'Young Turk'

---

* During the framing of the constitution in 1876–7, Abdul Hamid had cleverly inserted a clause giving the Sultan the 'sacred right' to dissolve parliament: so his action was, technically, legal.

committee, the Ittihad-ı Osmanî Cemiyeti (Society of Ottoman Unity), was formed at the empire's Military Medical College in Gülhane. In the same year, Ahmed Rıza, the former director of state education in Bursa, arrived in Paris to galvanize Ottoman exiles against the despotism of Abdul Hamid. Rıza's journal *Meşveret*, published in Paris and smuggled into Constantinople via the foreign post offices, would soon christen the name for the opposition movement: Ittihad ve Terakki Cemiyeti, or Committee of Union and Progress (CUP). In September 1896, on the heels of a short-lived Armenian rebellion and the subsequent massacres which turned Abdul Hamid into the 'Bloody Sultan' of legend, the CUP's Constantinople branch, working with the Armenian revolutionary Dashnaktsutiun committee (the 'Dashnaks'), prepared an opportunistic *coup d'état*. Betrayed by government informers who had penetrated the movement, the plot was thoroughly snuffed out, with 350 CUP conspirators in the army and civil service arrested or exiled to distant provinces. Yet again Ottoman weakness had given impetus to liberal reform, and yet again Abdul Hamid had proven too wily an opponent. Right on cue, Kaiser Wilhelm now wrote his famous birthday greeting to the Sultan, congratulating Abdul Hamid on another year of imperial survival just as most Europeans were mourning his repression of Armenians and liberal reformers alike. 'Bloody Sultan' or not, Abdul Hamid was now confident of the Kaiser's support.[6]

In much the same manner, the Baghdad railway concession of 1899, following on the heels of the Kaiser's oriental grand tour the previous year, coincided almost exactly with the recuperation of the Young Turk movement from its apparent eclipse three years previously. Just as the Deutsche Bank negotiators were applying the finishing touches to an ambitious railway deal designed to strengthen the Sultan's authority over his fractious subjects that December, Abdul Hamid's half-brother, Damad Mahmud Pasha, fled to Paris with his sons Sabahaddin and Lütfullah, where they would team up with Ahmed Rıza.* At once, the introduction of three possible imperial pretenders transformed the CUP

---

*Damad Mahmud Celâleddin Pasha, the grandson of Sultan Mahmud II, was not only a prince of the blood in the Ottoman line and half-brother to the Sultan: he was also married to Abdul Hamid's sister. His departure on 14 December 1899 (just nine days before the Baghdad railway concession was given to the German team) was thus a very serious matter for the Ottoman government.

from a beleaguered outfit of angry exiles into a serious factor in international politics. The Ottoman pretender sent a note to the British government almost immediately after arriving in Paris, asking for London's backing of his opposition movement (there was no reply).[7] Mahmud, Sabahaddin and Lütfullah also wrote direct appeals to Wilhelm II, hoping the Kaiser might lean on his friend Abdul Hamid to restore the Constitution of 1876 (the answer, unsurprisingly, was no).[8] The Kaiser had made his bet on the Sultan, and would stick with him. European and Ottoman liberals who dreamed of toppling the 'Bloody Sultan', however, now had their own cards to play.

The 'Damad Mahmud affair' furnished a dry run of the international propaganda wars which would increasingly poison Great Power politics in the new century. On the one side, there was 'respectable opinion', mainly British- and French-inflected, which predictably lined up behind Mahmud and his sons. 'Yes, it is true that I fled from my country,' the Sultan's brother-in-law told a sympathetic reporter from *Le Matin* in January 1900, 'because the whole [Ottoman] empire is a prison. Abdul Hamid keeps us all in prison, from [deposed] Sultan Murad V to the lowliest member of the *ulema* in Istanbul.' Mahmud spoke even more freely to the London *Standard*, informing British sympathizers that the wicked despot of Constantinople had 'annihilated thousands of human beings – Muslims and Christians'. The German press, by contrast, taking its cues from the Kaiser's pro-Hamidian *Orientpolitik*, smeared Mahmud at every opportunity. *Die Post* suggested the Ottoman pretender was fronting for the Rechnitzer group, embittered after losing out on the Baghdad railway concession.*[9] *Neue Preussiche Zeitung* and the *Frankfurter Allgemeine Zeitung* dismissed Mahmud as an out-and-out English spy. Or perhaps, suggested *Der Bund* with a sneer, this wayward son of the Ottoman dynasty was blackmailing the Sultan in order to increase his allowance, from 3 to 5 million Swiss francs.[10] Long before the Anglo-French Entente Cordiale formalized the anti-German alliance in 1904, Europe's press barons (many directly subsidized by their governments) had their parts in the drama down pat.

---

* This may have been true. Damad Mahmud indeed offered to help the British gain concessions in the Ottoman Empire in exchange for their help in overthrowing Abdul Hamid. It is likely this would have included a renewed Rechnitzer bid on the Baghdad railway.

When the diplomats and spies threw their hats in the ring, the international row over the Young Turks grew nastier still. Even before Mahmud and his sons had left Constantinople, the German government had been spreading rumours about assassination plots being hatched in Europe against Abdul Hamid. Geneva, then as today an international playground of rich and well-connected exiles, was second only to Paris as a Young Turk refuge. Damad Mahmud himself had set up shop there, injecting a great deal of his fortune into Young Turk propaganda. Because so much CUP literature smuggled into Constantinople was being printed in Geneva, German insinuations about conspiracies against the Sultan were potentially embarrassing to the Swiss authorities if anything did happen to Abdul Hamid. Quietly, the Swiss Ambassador in Berlin assured German State Secretary Bülow that his government 'would do everything possible to assure that no plot (*Attentat*) against the Sultan or his government could be organized from Geneva'.[11]

With a characteristic mixture of boldness and blundering, the Germans seem to have taken this promise as a blanket invitation to crack down on Young Turk plotters in Switzerland. Not long after Mahmud and his sons fled Constantinople in winter 1899–1900, Phillip von Richthofen, a shadowy associate of Baron Oppenheim, surfaced in Geneva. Curiously, Richthofen signed his correspondence as the 'Consul-General of the Ottoman Empire for Switzerland', despite his rather obvious Germanic name and title (like Oppenheim, Richthofen called himself Freiherr or 'Baron', although the origin of his title is unclear), and despite the fact that there was already another Ottoman Consul in Switzerland. Richthofen was almost certainly working for German intelligence, which furnished him with extremely detailed reports on the movements of Young Turk agitators in Europe. In his guise as 'Ottoman Consul' in Geneva, Richthofen forwarded these reports on to Munir Bey, Abdul Hamid's Ambassador in Paris – until, that is, Richthofen was outed as an imposter by the Swiss police, to the delight of the Young Turks and their supporters in the Western press.[12]

In defence of the Germans, it must be said that many CUP leaders were all but begging to be spied upon. It was not only Mahmud and his sons who wrote openly to the Kaiser about their plans to overthrow Abdul Hamid. So, too, did Young Turk activists like Ahmed Rıza, who had addressed a passionate appeal to Wilhelm in November 1898.

'You have already seen our beautiful country,' Rıza wrote to the Kaiser on the occasion of his visits to Jerusalem and Damascus, but asked him also to reflect on the 'sad condition of the Ottoman Empire ... its ruins and misery'. You must, Rıza enjoined Wilhelm, 'dare to listen to the people; hear their voices, as once Moses and Muhammad heard the voice of God in these parts'.[13] With touching naïveté, Rıza continued sending copies of *Meşveret* to the German Foreign Office, hoping they might be passed on to the Kaiser so as to enlighten him about the true state of affairs under the despotic Sultan. Instead, the Wilhelmstrasse passed along Rıza's missives against Abdul Hamid to – Abdul Hamid.[14]

As the Young Turk movement in Europe gathered steam, German efforts to quash it grew more desperate. Spying for the Sultan took on a self-perpetuating quality: the more intelligence on CUP conspiracies reached Abdul Hamid's ears, the more terrified he became, which led him to demand yet more intelligence. Thus in August 1905, a single revolutionary pamphlet occasioned a full-blown investigation, in which the Wilhelmstrasse enlisted the regular German police. 'The Sultan would be most grateful to the German Imperial Government,' Marschall's deputy wrote from the Embassy summer residence at Therapia, 'if the police authorities in Munich could ... [inform him] from which circles (workers, students, Young Turks, Armenians, Macedonians) the pamphlet ... could have originated', as well as 'which individuals and leaders it has reached'. Goaded on by State Secretary Bülow, the Munich authorities duly complied.[15]

German surveillance of the Ottoman pretenders was even more thorough. Prince Sabahaddin, who had replaced Ahmed Rıza as the public face of the CUP organization in Paris, sought an audience with Pope Pius X in March 1906, ostensibly on behalf of the official Ottoman heir apparent Mehmed Reshad, to discuss relations between the Vatican and the Porte and the prospects for reform, particularly relating to the status of Catholic minorities in the Ottoman Empire. After long and tortuous negotiations over protocol, it was agreed that the Ottoman prince would be personally presented to the Pope by the Vatican Secretary of State on the strict condition that no one learn of the meeting. If news leaked out, it could be embarrassing to the Vatican, which would appear to be interfering in Ottoman religious affairs. Even worse, however, would be the damage done to Sabahaddin's reputation among the Muslim faithful, if it seemed he was intriguing with the prelate of Rome. Even the Young Turks might object to such brazen cynicism. Naturally, the German Ambassador in Rome made sure to pass on everything he knew about Sabahaddin's courting of the Pope to State Secretary Bülow, to be forwarded on to Abdul Hamid.[16] The Sultan, in turn, seems to have leaked the Germans' intelligence on the Vatican meeting to his spies in the Young Turk movement (or encouraged the Germans themselves to do so). Before long, Prince Sabahaddin was accused by rivals in the Paris CUP of 'taking money from the Pope'.*[17]

Like his father Mahmud and his rival Ahmed Rıza, Sabahaddin was an easy mark for the Germans. Despite numerous rebuffs, the Ottoman prince continued to seek an audience with the German Emperor, as he did, yet again, after meeting the Pope. Not surprisingly, the German Embassy in Rome declined his visa request, on direct orders from State Secretary Bülow in Berlin (the grounds were that 'the Porte [i.e. Sultan Abdul Hamid] is pursuing the named individual as a revolutionary dangerous to the State').[18] Whereas many of Sabahaddin's CUP and Armenian co-conspirators took pains to conceal their authorship of anti-Hamidian literature, the Prince-pretender openly addressed his revolutionary screeds to European chancelleries, inviting them to intervene in the Ottoman Empire to promote minority rights.[19] Sabahaddin wore sedition on his sleeve.

Succession controversies, of course, were nothing new in European politics. Still, there was something fundamentally different about the conspiracies against Abdul Hamid. Prince Sabahaddin was not simply staking a claim to a disputed throne, in the manner of European royal houses trying to one-up each other in territorial horse-trading. He was setting himself up as a vehicle for reforming the Ottoman Empire – and with it, the entire Islamic world. As Sabahaddin wrote to British Foreign Secretary Sir Edward Grey from Paris in August 1906,

---

*The initial accusation was made by Ali Haydar Midhat of the Paris branch of the CUP. It is unclear what Midhat's source was, but as the only extant reports of this meeting are in the archives of the German Foreign Office (and these are copious), the likeliest explanation is that either the Germans themselves leaked the story, or else Sultan Abdul Hamid did after learning of it from the Germans. The Vatican, for its part, has always stringently denied that the Sabahaddin meeting took place.

Constantinople was still 'the seat of the Caliphate', with supreme authority over (Sunni) Islam. Thus, 'with the triumph of Liberal Ideas in Turkey', Sabahaddin promised Grey, 'the great moral influence which Constantinople possesses over Islam at large is destined to assume an intellectual character. Such an influence would then serve as a powerful agent of reconciliation between East and West.' Unlike Abdul Hamid, he and his Young Turk allies possessed 'an intellectual outlook which is quite up to date': they were ready 'to adopt the ideas of Western civilization'.[20]

Music to the ears of Western liberals, Prince Sabahaddin's vision of modernizing the Caliphate on Western lines was unlikely to inspire much of a following in the Muslim world. His letter to Grey was published just as the Aqaba conflict was reaching fever pitch, whipping up Islamic passions from Constantinople to Cairo, where Egyptian nationalists took up the Sultan's claim to the Sinai peninsula (as against that of British Egypt). Confronting the spectre of pan-Islam veering dangerously close to the great imperial chokepoint at the Suez Canal, British diplomats were hardly going to back an Ottoman imperial pretender already notorious for his support of Christian minorities – and reputed to be intriguing with the Pope. Indulging Prince Sabahaddin's liberalism was a luxury the British could ill afford.

Paradoxically, the weaker Sultan Abdul Hamid's hold on his tottering empire appeared, the more successful was his promotion of pan-Islam, which is to say, his claim to be Caliph of the global *umma* of believers.[21] Attempts by the powers to pry loose Ottoman territory, no less than periodic threats against the Sultan's life and throne, won Abdul Hamid the sympathies of the entire Islamic world. The appearance of British bullying of the Sultan-Caliph was bound to stir up Muslim rage, whatever the facts on the ground. In the case of the Aqaba border dispute, Lord Cromer was actually supporting Egypt's claim on the Sinai: and yet Egyptian nationalists emphatically took Turkey's position. So, too, did British Indian Muslims, who discovered a newfound interest in the troubles of the Ottoman Sultan-Caliph after making their hajj in late 1906. It mattered little that these pilgrims travelled to Mecca, via British ports, on British-owned vessels, protected by the British navy: Abdul Hamid was their man, and Lord Cromer the villain.[22]

Short of withdrawing from Egypt entirely, there was little London could do to dispel the widespread impression among Muslims that Abdul Hamid was a victim of British imperialism. Embracing the Young Turks would only make things worse, as they were, arguably, the most dangerous enemy of the Sultan-Caliph, and thus implicitly anti-Islamic in the eyes of the global *umma*. What men like Lord Cromer needed was a way of somehow detaching the Caliphate from the Ottoman throne. As a leader-writer for the pro-British *Egyptian Gazette* intoned in May 1906, 'the Sultan, no doubt, likes to pretend that when he is touched all Islam is wounded. We must try and see if we cannot correct this artfully propagated delusion.' Perhaps, the propagandist craftily suggested, Britain's Muslim subjects could be gently reminded that 'it is Mecca, not Constantinople, which is the centre of the Muslim faith. It is towards the Kaabah, not towards the St Sophia, that the Moslem turns his eyes as he prays.'[23] Throughout 1906 and 1907, the *Gazette* ran a whole series of articles by Muslim jurists mocking Sultan Abdul Hamid's claim to be Caliph.[24] Clearly, the British were already thinking along the lines of installing a new, Mecca-based Caliph, nearly a decade before Kitchener famously proposed the idea in the first winter of the Great War.[25]

By long-standing tradition, the title of Caliph, or spiritual successor of the Prophet Muhammad, was bestowed on the most powerful sovereign in the Islamic world, who had the honour of 'protecting' the holy places. Since the conquest of Arabia and Egypt by Sultan Selim 'the Grim' in 1517, the Ottomans had a good claim on the title, enforced (usually) by a standing military garrison at Mecca itself. By the early twentieth century, however, Turkish authority in the entire region of the Hejaz, still largely Bedouin country, was fragile: this is why Abdul Hamid was building a railway there. So long as the Germans could build him the rail lines he needed to restore his authority in the Hejaz, Abdul Hamid's claim to be the protector of the holy places of Islam would be safe. If the Sultan were toppled from his throne, however, then whichever Arabian pretender had the powerful British navy at his back – protecting passage for hajj pilgrims coming in from Africa and Asia – might have a fighting chance to take over the Caliphate.

The likeliest candidate to replace the Sultan as Caliph was Sherif Ali Abdullah Pasha of Mecca (the future King Hussein, famous father of T. E. Lawrence's friend Faisal, would not assume this office until 1908). In theory, the Sherifs of Mecca, born of the 'Banu Hashim' or 'Hashemite' dynasty, could claim direct descent by blood from Muhammad's own tribe, the Koreish, via the Prophet's grandson, al-Hassan ibn Ali. According to most Muslim Jurists, this gave the ruler of Mecca a much better legal claim on the Caliphate than the Ottomans – although it was moot in practice, because the Sherifs had nearly always recognized the Sultan's political authority, which is to say his superior army.[26]

The Sherifiate was a peculiar institution, which had evolved to fill the power vacuum left in Arabia as the seat of Islamic power moved from Mecca to Damascus (until AD 750), Baghdad (until the Mongol sack of 1258), Cairo (until 1517), and then Ottoman Constantinople. The root of the problem was that no Muslim sovereign worth his salt had ever wanted to actually *live* in Mecca, in the brutal desert climate of the Hejaz, surrounded by marauding Bedouin tribesmen. In practice the Sherifiate was a glorified protection racket, which for nearly a thousand years had exploited its monopoly over Mecca to shake down hajj pilgrims foolish enough to arrive in the Hejaz without armed escort. Although the Sherif, in military terms, was never a match for the Egyptian Mamelukes or Ottoman Janissaries – even at their strongest Sherifian forces usually consisted of only 'a few hundred slaves, the same number of mercenaries, and ... a few Bedouin clans' – the Sultans had preferred to leave well enough alone in the Hejaz, so long as the Sherif continued toasting them as 'Caliph' in official Mecca prayers, which confirmed their supremacy over all other Muslim princes.[27]

The Ottoman claim on the Caliphate, therefore, rested precariously on military supremacy in Arabia. Not that the Sherifian hold on Mecca was any stronger: in fact the Wahhabi forces of the Saud clan had dislodged the Hashemites from the holy cities in 1802. Mecca had been reconquered from the Wahhabis in 1813, not by the Sherifs, nor the Ottoman army, but by the forces of the reformist Egyptian Khedive, Muhammad Ali. Throughout the nineteenth century, the Sherifs had openly flouted Ottoman power, until the Porte finally figured out how to bring them to heel: giving Hashemite pretenders (and deposed Sherifs) palaces on the Bosphorus, in the 'gilded cage' manner of the *kafes*.*

The problem with Britain's courting of the Mecca Sherifs, then, was not necessarily that the Ottoman hold on the Caliphate was inviolable, but that they may have been backing the wrong horse in the Hejaz. By the early twentieth century, the Sherifiate was notoriously corrupt, with various Hashemite pretenders making annual reverse pilgrimages of their own to sample the urban delights of Cairo and Constantinople.[28] It was this sort of worldly temptation which had first given the Sherifs leverage over the Caliphate, as Muslim sovereigns preferred cosmopolitan capitals to the Hejaz desert; and it was now weakening the Sherifiate itself.[†] Hashemite corruption played right into the hands of Ibn Saud, whose purist Wahhabi followers were again making waves in central Arabia, winning battle after battle against the Shammar Bedouins of Ibn Rashid, and threatening the Hashemite hold on the Hejaz as well. Whether or not officials in London understood all this, the Cairo residency was game enough to play both sides. As Oppenheim complained to Berlin as early as April 1905, the perfidious British were subsidizing both the Sherif and Ibn Saud, which gave them no less than two possible candidates for a new Caliphate detached from the Ottoman throne.[29]

The Germans, of course, had their own horse in the race, and Abdul Hamid was still the favourite. British attempts to discredit the Sultan's claim on the Caliphate were a sign of fear. As the Baron Oppenheim wrote to Bülow (now Chancellor) from Cairo in May 1908, the 'detachment of the Caliphate from the Turkish Sultanate ... and the weakening of the Ottoman Empire' had turned into the overriding goal of 'British *Orientpolitik*'. The reason was easy to grasp: Britain ruled over roughly 100 million Muslim subjects, nearly all Sunnis, in a strategic arc stretching from Nigeria to Egypt, the Gulf States and the Indian subcontinent.

---

* Sherif Ali Abdullah Pasha, for example, was pensioned off in style in Constantinople after being deposed in 1908.
† Much as today the notorious corruption of the oil-rich Saudi royals inspires many Wahhabi critics to support Saudi pretenders like the ascetic Osama Bin Laden.

In the case of a general European war, these Sunnis would, it was assumed, inevitably 'flock to the banner of the moral leader [of Islam], the Sultan-Caliph', which would all but 'guarantee a general uprising of Mohammedans' in England's colonies. This is why Abdul Hamid was Britain's 'most dangerous enemy', whom Germany should support with all her power – for example, by speeding up construction on the Baghdad railway (as if taking dictation, the Deutsche Bank team signed the deal to begin blasting the Taurus mountains exactly one week after Oppenheim wrote this letter).[30]

There was something absurd about this shadow-boxing between two Christian powers over the Caliphate, an ancient Islamic institution most educated Muslims themselves no longer took very seriously. Until Sultan Abdul Hamid had tried to resuscitate pan-Islam in recent decades, most Turkish sovereigns had rather downplayed the title of Caliph, using it more in dealings with 'infidel' states than with other Muslim sovereigns who might have been offended by the suggestion of superiority inherent in the office. European diplomats tended to regard the Caliph as a sort of Pope – that is, a spiritual, not political, leader. Their Turkish counterparts were happy to entertain this entirely false notion of the Caliphate, believing it to be largely harmless.[31]

Pumped up by the British and German propaganda machines, however, the idea of the Caliphate may not have been harmless any longer. Buoyed by the Aqaba border crisis, the Germans' pro-Hamidian pan-Islamism had frightened the British into subsidizing Wahhabism and the Sherifate of Mecca, which in turn had convinced the Germans that they needed to try still harder to strengthen the Ottoman Sultan-Caliph's hold on his far-flung subjects. It was like a race to the reactionary bottom, to see which 'infidel' power could conjure up the purist strain of fundamentalist Islam.

Lost in the crossfire, of course, were the Sultan's Muslim subjects, who had not been consulted as to whether they wanted to live under the strict Sharia law of a revived Caliphate, whether originating from Constantinople, Mecca or the puritanical Wahhabi heartland of the Nejd. Even more lost were the non-Islamic minorities of the Ottoman Empire, who in some areas (like European Turkey, including Constantinople) were numerically equal to or even outnumbered the Muslims.* Hard as it is to imagine today following the modern demographic explosion in the Middle East, in 1900 the Sultan ruled over fewer than twenty million subjects in the entire Ottoman Empire, stretching from the Balkans to the Arabian desert sands, and of those roughly two-thirds were Muslims.[†32] How strange it was, then, that the two greatest Christian powers in Europe were trying to outdo each other in their public embrace of unreformed, backwards-looking Islam. Stranger still, the Germans and British were fighting to resurrect the ancient Caliphate at a time when Young Turk reformers were themselves trying desperately to modernize the Ottoman Empire, making common cause with many beleaguered Christian minorities (particularly the Armenians) to do so.

Of the two imperial rivals, Berlin was better informed about the burgeoning CUP conspiracy of 1908 than London, mostly because of contacts with the Ottoman military dating back to the 1880s. The extent of German influence on the Turkish army has often been exaggerated, in part owing to the illustrious name of the first Prussian adviser hired by the Sultan in 1835, Moltke the Elder (whose fame dates not to his short-lived experience advising the Ottoman army, which he himself deemed to have been ineffectual, but to his role as mastermind of the Prussian victory over France in 1870–71).** Before the notorious Liman von Sanders-led mission of forty officers was dispatched to Turkey in winter 1913–14, there were never more than a handful

---

* In 1885, the population of Constantinople was officially counted at 873,565, of whom 384,410, or about 44 per cent, were Muslims. The Islamic population of the capital seems to have surpassed 50 per cent sometime around the turn of the century, such that by 1914 there were some 390,000 Christians and Jews out of 910,000 city residents (about 43 per cent). In Ottoman Europe, as late as 1911, the population of Jews, Orthodox and Catholic Christians was about 3.11 million out of 6.3 million total, almost exactly half.

† Ottoman demography is a highly contested subject, and after 1877 the numbers were in constant flux, as each successive Balkan and Caucasian war produced refugees – generally Christians leaving and Muslims arriving. In the most thorough pre-war census, completed in 1893, the empire's population was 17.4 million, of which 12.5 million were Muslims, or 70 per cent. By 1914, the proportion of Muslims, following the Balkan wars, was probably more than three-quarters, nearing 80 per cent.

** Moltke did write a book about his experiences in Turkey, which contains the memorable observation that 'a Turk will concede without hesitation that the Europeans are superior to his nation in science, skill, wealth, daring and strength, without its ever occurring to him that a Frank might therefore put himself on a par with a Muslim'.

of German military advisers in Turkey – usually no more than there were British officers advising the Ottoman navy. Nevertheless, German influence in the army was real, and it was the army which counted.

While exiles were getting most of the press attention – Ahmed Rıza and Prince Sabahadhin staged a grand reconciliation at a Paris CUP Congress in December 1907, with the Armenian Dashnaks also attending – it was the quiet spread of revolutionary 'cells' through the army in Turkey which mattered in the end. As von der Goltz Pasha wrote to Kaiser Wilhelm II on 11 December 1907, 'feelings of Turkish nationalism have grown astonishingly and found supporters … there is no doubt that the military expects various radical improvements in the country'. Presciently, von der Goltz pointed to the Third Army in Macedonia as a potential danger zone for Sultan Abdul Hamid.[33] Still, despite having slightly better intelligence on the army, the Germans were blindsided just like everyone else by anti-Hamidian mutinies in the Second and Third Armies which, compounded by a wave of demonstrations in the capital, at last forced the autocratic Sultan to reinstate the constitution and call for parliamentary elections on 23 July 1908. Considering how poor and muddled most of the historical literature on this so-called 'Young Turk revolution' remains, it should not be surprising that European chancelleries were taken by surprise at the time.[34] The German reading of events was not helped by the fact that Germany's powerful Ambassador, Baron Marschall, was on leave from early June to late August 1908, missing the entire revolution. Taking the reins in his absence was Alfred von Kiderlen-Wächter, an experienced but unimaginative diplomat who wrote to Chancellor Bülow on 10 July 1908, as the army mutiny was beginning to spread across Macedonia and Thrace, that he could 'hardly believe, that these [Young Turk] activists are very numerous, still less, that they constitute a direct danger [to the throne]'.[35]

The British did not do much better. In the sense that London's relationship with the Porte was less intimate than Berlin's, the lack of good British intelligence on the state of affairs in the Ottoman army is understandable. But the British misreading of the Young Turks is still an instructive episode in the annals of modern diplomacy, because it was such a colossal missed opportunity. Just as repeated appeals for British support from Damad Mahmud and Prince Sabahaddin had been ignored going back to the turn of the century, so now would Turkish army reformers be left in the lurch by the liberal power they most admired. On about 10 July, less than two weeks before Abdul Hamid was forced to accept the constitution, a young CUP officer visited the British Embassy in Constantinople, informing Vice-Consul W. J. Heathcote (perhaps a week or two prematurely) that 'in the course of a day or two a revolutionary movement would break out'. The Young Turk army conspirator then 'asked Mr. Heathcote what the attitude of Great Britain would be towards the movement, and stated that it was the desire of his party to be on friendly terms with that country'. Acting with the utmost diplomatic correctness, Heathcote declined to discuss the matter.[36]

The Germans too were caught off guard by the events of July. At first the reaction in Berlin was hostile, as the Sultan's humiliation seemed to herald the end for Abdul Hamid, the Kaiser's friend and ally. Of particular concern was the fate of Izzet Pasha, the Sultan's notorious secret police chief, regarded by many in the capital as a German tool. The Young Turks were baying for his head, and he was rumoured (correctly, as it turned out) to be hiding in the German Embassy. As Kiderlen-Wächter complained to Bülow on 27 July 1908, 'there reigns here an unmistakable discord against Germany, partly due to our previous good relations with the sultan and the palace, partly due to the fact that any Turk, who can speak any foreign language at all, understands only French and ... the French papers here [are] doing everything possible to incite [hostility] against us'.[37] Luckily for Kiderlen-Wächter, Izzet Pasha skipped town in early August, before the revolutionaries could get their hands on him – escaping on a *British* vessel, which deflected a good deal of political heat away from the German Embassy.[38]

Still, the German position at the Porte remained fragile. Baron Marschall returned to Constantinople at last in late August, and tried to put a brave face on things. As if to welcome back the discredited Abdul Hamid's closest German confidant, Turkish railway workers launched a general strike on 2 September 1908, which hit the Baghdad line hard. Although the strikers were not necessarily all hostile to Germany, they did make a special demand that German managers try harder to accommodate Muslim sensibilities, particularly related to the payment of *baksheesh* (which Teutonic propriety frowned on). Deutsche Bank was called in to help resolve the dispute.[39]

Still more damaging to Germany's reputation in Turkey was her Austrian ally's annexation of Bosnia-Hercegovina on 6 October 1908. Although Austria-Hungary had been administering the province in practice since 1879, the Berlin settlement of 1878 had put Bosnia under nominal Ottoman suzerainty as a salve to wounded Turkish pride after the war with Russia. Making the Austrian annexation even more ominous, it was announced the day after Bulgaria had formally declared its independence from Constantinople, and just days before Crete announced that it would unify with Greece. In less than a week, the new CUP regime had suffered three grave humiliations, each of them a specific repudiation of the Berlin Treaty, theoretically underwritten by Germany, erstwhile ally of the Sultan: and yet Germany had done nothing to stop them. Already the Young Turks had begun talking about annulling the recent Baghdad railway deal, and giving a new concession to Great Britain. As Karl Helfferich, the new Director of Deutsche Bank, observed in December 1908 about the diplomatic revolution at the Porte, Baron Marschall, long referred to by his fellow diplomats as the 'Giant of the Bosphorus', now had 'no weight to throw onto the scales in Istanbul; he was laid completely flat by his Austrian friendship'.[40]

Despite appearances, not all was lost for Germany. Because the key CUP conspirators of July 1908, officers like Major Ahmed Niyazi and Enver Bey, came from the army, they had an almost instinctual respect for Germany, whose own soldiers had helped train them. The Young Turks even invited old von der Goltz Pasha back for another go as the Turkish military's modernizer-in-chief – although, in a curious nod to the pro-Entente inclinations of many of CUP's civilian politicians, they expressly asked the British to approve the appointment.[41]

The Germans were pleasantly surprised to learn that they had admirers even in the new Ottoman parliament. Ahmed Rıza, the longtime leader of the CUP's central committee in Paris, would return from exile in triumph to become Speaker of the Ottoman Chamber elected in early December 1908. On his way back home from France, Rıza petitioned the Kaiser one last time for a meeting: this time, Wilhelm said yes. Despite being rebuffed by and spied on for years by the Germans, Ahmed Rıza was still, improbably, a Germanophile, as the Kaiser, Chancellor Bülow and the Wilhelmstrasse were all astonished to learn.

Evidently it had escaped everyone's attention in Berlin until now that *Rıza's mother was German*.[42] To adapt Bismarck's famous remark about luck in diplomacy, we might say that God reserved a special providence for drunks, fools and the Germans in Turkey.

Ahmed Rıza is an intriguing figure, whose rapid rise and fall in the Young Turk revolution has much to tell us about Turkish Muslims and their conflicted attitudes towards the Christian West. Rıza's father, who had befriended visiting British officers during the Crimean War, was known as 'English Ali', owing to his proficiency in that language, particularly rare in that era. A liberal admirer of Great Britain, Ali had served in the first Ottoman parliament – the one dissolved by Abdul Hamid in 1878. 'English Ali' had fathered Ahmed Rıza in wedlock with a converted Muslim from Munich (she seems to have met 'English Ali' while he was posted to the Turkish Consulate in Prussian Berlin in the late 1850s). It is easy to see where Rıza's cosmopolitan ease with languages came from: born, in 1859, of a famously English-speaking father and a German-speaking mother, he was schooled in French, at the renowned lycée at Galatasaray.[43]

Like most CUP leaders, Ahmed Rıza had oscillated between a genuine admiration for European culture and a resentment at Islamic inferiority vis-à-vis the West. His intellectual development was typical of Young Turk exiles: fluency in French led to a flirtation with fashionable positivism, which produced a kind of political liberalism tinged with a prickly defensiveness about Islam and European designs on Ottoman territory. Rıza became more reactionary after the turn of the century, embracing a kind of aggressive Ottoman nationalism (the 'unionist' position) to counter the open anti-Hamidian treachery of his rival Prince Sabahaddin, who remained the patron saint of Ottoman liberals. In this, too, Rıza was typical of the CUP movement.[44] No matter how hard Young Turks like Ahmed Rıza tried publicly to deny their hostility to Islamic traditions, however, the habits of mind inculcated in them by long residence in Christian Europe could not be hidden for ever. Western attitudes towards women were particularly hard to shed once CUP activists had adopted them, sometimes without even realizing it – and these attitudes were not easily reconciled with the Islamic faith. As a younger Ahmed Rıza had once written to his sister from Paris:

Were I a woman, I would embrace atheism and never become a Muslim. Imagine a religion that imposes laws always beneficial to men but hazardous to women such as permitting my husband to have three additional wives and as many concubines as he wishes, houris awaiting him in heaven, while I cover my head and face as a miller's horse. Beside these I would not be allowed to divorce a husband who prevented me from having any kind of fun, but would be required to submit to his beatings. Keep this religion far away from me.[45]

Staunch secularist, borderline atheist and closet feminist, Ahmed Rıza was not likely to become popular among the Islamic *umma* of Constantinople in his long-delayed return from European exile.

With almost painful inevitability, Ahmed Rıza emerged in the winter of 1908–9 as a potent symbol of everything ordinary Muslims detested about the new CUP government. Contrary to the general impression abroad, the Young Turk revolution had not really ushered in an era of secularism, despite the clear endorsement in the CUP programme of equal rights for religious minorities, which had ostensibly ended the inferior civil status for Christian and Jewish *dhimmis* under Sharia law.* Western press reports about the joyous, multi-ethnic, multi-faith crowds celebrating the supposed downfall of Abdul Hamid in July 1908 had generally failed to note that many of the demonstrators outside Yıldız Palace had actually been cheering him. Even as mutinous army officers promised to bring an end to Hamidian tyranny, the most popular slogan on the streets had been 'Long Live the Sultan!' (*Padışahım çok yaşa!*). Abdul Hamid had not been deposed, after all: after placing his hand on the Koran and swearing an oath to the 1876 Constitution (an oath registered by the *Şeykh-ul-Islam*), the Sultan-Caliph was, to all appearances, more popular now than ever before.

The position of CUP secularists was hardly strengthened by the loss of Ottoman Bosnia and Bulgaria in October 1908, humiliations which

---

* *Dhimmi*, from the Arabic word for 'protected', denotes the inferior status of religious minorities under Sharia law – relating to everything from the payment of special taxes to the exemption from military service. Although legally inferior to Muslims, *dhimmis* still received official 'protection' as fellow monotheists, and the freedom to practise their religion: animists, Zoroastrians and pagan polytheists, by contrast, were inferior even to *dhimmis*, denied the right to freedom of worship under Sharia.

were compounded by the fact that they took place during the holy month of Ramadan. Resentful, revanchist, reactionary, pro-Hamidian Islam made a rapid comeback after its (apparent) eclipse in July: street demonstrations were now directed openly against the CUP, and were 'spearheaded by religious figures – *muezzins*, *imams* and *hocas*'. After a winter lull, the protest movement gathered momentum in spring, with many parliamentary liberals joining with the Hamidian reactionaries in opposing the 'unionist' CUP government. Sparked by the dramatic murder of liberal newspaper editor Hasan Fehmi on the Galata bridge, the riots built up to a crescendo on the night of 12/13 April 1909, when an angry horde of Islamic theological students (*softas*), accompanied by 3,000 mutinous soldiers, many from the Imperial Guard, stormed the parliament in Sultanahmet. Their demands were three: a return to the 'sharia law of the illustrious Mohammed', the restoration of Abdul Hamid's full imperial powers, and the handing over of Ahmed Rıza – so he could be hanged.[46] Just as Abdul Hamid's hated spy chief had been bundled out of town during the July revolution to escape mob justice, so now, in the April counter-revolution, the Speaker of the CUP-dominated parliament was threatened with lynching. In ironic testimony to the enduring strength of Berlin's position at the Porte, Ahmed Rıza, like Izzet Pasha before him, sought Germany's protection – in Rıza's case, not in the Embassy but in a Baghdad Railway Company building.[47] It was enough to produce whiplash: from Hamidian despotism to CUP constitutionalism and back again in only nine months.

The events of April 1909 were not auspicious for Turkish secularists. Although many liberals had supported the opposition movement, it rapidly became clear that reactionary Islam, not liberalism, was the flavour of the hour. Many hard-won gains of the revolution, like civil equality for Christians and Jews, were now summarily swept aside.* On 15 April, the Ottoman constitution was formally suspended and replaced by Sharia law, as wired to every regional governor. As if to

---

* There is a great deal of confusion about when, exactly, religious equality came to the Ottoman Empire, if it ever did. In the sense of freedom of worship, the three monotheistic faiths were always equal. With regard to civil status and tax obligations, talk of civil equality had begun with the Tanzimat. The 'infidel' poll tax (*jizya*) endured, but was transformed, in 1856, into a kind of compulsory duty exempting non-Muslims from military service, which exemption was enforced until 1909. Contrary to the usual

remind non-Muslims of their inferior status as *dhimmis* (Christians in Cilicia, Edwin Pears was told by locals, 'had asserted their liberty and equality with Moslems in terms which were unnecessarily offensive'), reactionary mobs wandered through Anatolian towns, looking for infidels to attack. Twenty thousand Armenians were reportedly killed in Adana alone.[48] An atmosphere of terror prevailed in Constantinople, where 'educated CUP ministers were assassinated, their offices ransacked, and their newspaper presses destroyed'.[49]

It was a moment of truth for the Young Turk movement. Even though the CUP had won the parliamentary elections of 1908, the counter-revolution of April 1909 seemed to reflect genuine public opinion. Mob rule it may have been, but there was no doubt whose side the crowds were on: they wanted the Sultan and Sharia, not European-style 'Union and Progress'. In a sense the events of July 1908 had not changed anything at all. The Sultan's surrender had created the illusion of consensus, in which all factions could see what they wanted in the restoration of the constitution: liberal parliamentary rule and minority rights, a CUP coup, restoration of Sharia law. Abdul Hamid, meanwhile, had remained in place, a symbol of the old ways for those who had never warmed to the new regime. If the revolution were to be completed, perhaps Abdul Hamid would have to be overthrown by the army after all.

This time, there would be no illusion of a popular mandate for the revolution. To regain power, the Young Turks would have to take the capital by force. Regrouping in Salonica, leading CUP officers, including the German-trained Enver and Niyazi Bey, under the command of General Mahmud Şevket Pasha, formed the ominously titled 'Army of Deliverance' (*Hareket ordusu*) to march on Constantinople.[50] Constitutionally speaking, there was good cause: the mutineers of 12–13 April had indeed

---

understanding that the constitution suspended by Abdul Hamid had been 'liberal', however, the 1876 constitution explicitly restored the Holy Law. In this sense the restoration of the constitution in July 1908 was easily interpreted – and *was* interpreted by many imams – as a return to Sharia. Of course, this is not what the Young Turks understood by the restoration of constitutional liberties in the July revolution; but it is easy to see why others did see it this way. For Ottoman Muslims, the idea of the 'Holy Law' was no less sacred than, say, the 1787 constitution is for modern Americans. Politicians, as the Young Turks discovered in 1909, openly traduced it at their peril.

overthrown a legally elected parliament by armed insurrection. On 24 April 1909, the counter-counter revolution commenced, as the Army of Deliverance crashed into Constantinople, taking the city 'after five hours of bloody street fighting', followed by dramatic public executions of mutinous soldiers and Hamidian Islamists. Abdul Hamid was deposed on 27 April and replaced by Mehmed Reshad V, clearly meant to be a figurehead. As if to rub salt in the wounds of the 'Bloody Sultan', Abdul Hamid was exiled to Salonica, where the army mutiny against him had begun. The CUP was in charge.[51]

To what end? Martial law was hardly an inspiring slogan for the new CUP era. To help heal the gaping political breach, Enver Bey organized a public memorial service for fifty unidentified men killed in the battle for the capital, burying them in a common grave. As if seeking to reclaim the moral high ground, Enver alluded – indirectly – to the recent sectarian violence which had followed the Hamidian counter-revolution, proclaiming that here, by contrast, 'Moslems and Christians were lying side by side'. From now on, Enver vowed, Ottoman citizens were all 'fellow-patriots who know no distinction of race or creed'.[52]

It was fine talk. But Enver knew that across-the-board religious equality was anathema to strict Muslims – it was contrary to the Sharia (although not all Muslims minded the lifting of the Christian exemption from military service in 1909). So, too, was the promotion of women's rights, another Young Turk ideal, unacceptable to the *ulema*. Worst of all, the violation of the Sultan-Caliph by Enver's conquering army could easily appear as sacrilege to pious Muslims, some of whom were beginning to suspect that the Young Turk conspirators were not Muslims at all, but likely *Dönme*, or crypto-Jews.* As Baron Marschall noted in an

---

* The *Dönme* were followers of the seventeenth-century Ottoman Jewish Messiah Sabbatai Zevi. To escape the inferior condition of *dhimmis*, they converted, publicly, to Islam, but are said to have retained their beliefs. Because the movement was historically centred in Salonica, it was natural for CUP critics to conflate Young Turks with *Dönme*, the idea being that both groups were secret societies. To this day, the notion persists widely that Djavid Bey, the future Finance Minister, was Jewish, but no one has unearthed any evidence this was true. The claim that the Young Turks were 'crypto-Jews' (or Freemasons) is often tinged with a dose of anti-Semitism. Famously, the British Foreign Office adopted this view of the CUP, which seeped into John Buchan's bestselling novel *Greenmantle*, where 'Enver and his precious committee' are belittled as 'a collection of Jews and gypsies.'

authoritative sixteen-page dispatch from Constantinople in autumn 1909 (forwarded on to every German Consul in Europe), the CUP was treading on thin ice after forcibly deposing a Sultan still popular among the *umma*. 'When Muslims learn,' Marschall wrote with a sense of foreboding, 'that the [newly installed] Caliph is powerless, and is only the puppet of people who are more or less estranged from Islam', then a 'major crisis will be unavoidable.' It was in order to forestall another popular Islamic uprising that, Marschall explained, 'since the catastrophe of 13 April the [Young Turks] have become more careful. Women's emancipation is being put to the side, and once again Sharia law is spoken of. Nevertheless strict Muslims regard the whole [CUP] regime with deep mistrust, if not with outright hostility.'[53]

In order to stay in power, that is, the Young Turks were willing to forgo most of the principles which had inspired them to go into politics in the first place. It was an old, old story, the corruption of power, but in the events of 1909 there was an element of the tragic. For all their faults, most CUP leaders had genuinely wanted to liberalize Ottoman society, by ending Sharia law and bringing civil equality to women and ethnic and religious minorities. True, their motives may have had less to do with altruism than with the desire to modernize the empire so that it could resist European encroachment. But in their willingness (at least before 1909) to work with controversial Armenian organizations like the Dashnaks, and to bring Christians, Jews and ethnic minorities into parliament, the Young Turks had shown real sensitivity to the plight of Ottoman *dhimmis*, and this was truly a revolutionary development in the Islamic world. That they failed to overturn the centuries-old legacy of Sharia law was not surprising – especially considering how little encouragement they received in their efforts to do so from abroad.

It must have been particularly disappointing for the Young Turks that Great Britain, which most of them admired as the world's leading liberal power, so manifestly failed to rise to the occasion. It was one thing to fail to anticipate the Young Turk revolution. It was quite another to misread it after it had occurred. And yet the British Embassy in Pera seemed almost wilfully determined to misunderstand what had happened in July 1908, and even more so the implications of the counter-counter revolution of April 1909. The British Ambassador to the Porte, Sir Gerard Lowther (who, like Marschall, had been absent from the scene in July 1908), fell under the spell of his First Dragoman Gerald Fitzmaurice, a true blue anti-Semite who 'detested the C.U.P. almost from the very outset'. Endorsing every single crackpot popular rumour about the CUP's origins in crypto-Jewish Freemasonry, Fitzmaurice prepared a thorough report for Lowther in May 1910, which was soon adopted as gospel in the British Foreign Office. 'The Oriental Jew,' according to Fitzmaurice and Lowther, 'is an adept at manipulating occult forces', and had thus manufactured the CUP conspiracy in order to seize control of the Ottoman Empire. By 'imitating the French Revolution and its godless and levelling methods', Young Turk internationalists were proving themselves to be enemies of England and all it stood for.[54]

This misreading of the Young Turks was the opposite of the truth. As we have seen, many of the CUP officers who led the original revolution of July 1908 were great admirers of England. Even Enver Bey, who would later become notorious as Germany's man, was still marked by Anglophilia at the time (his formative posting as military attaché in Berlin occurred only after the April 1909 events). After Enver heard in early August 1908 that the Sultan's spymaster, Izzet Pasha, had escaped on a British vessel, he personally sought out the British Consul in Salonica, Harry Lamb, to warn that aiding and abetting this fugitive would 'alienate the natural sympathy for England now entertained by the Ottoman nation'.[55] The political wing of the movement was even more pro-British, to the extent of wanting to annul the German Baghdad railway concession and give it to English firms instead.[56] The biggest Anglophile of all, meanwhile, was Djavid Bey, the Minister of Finance, who went so far as to propose a 'permanent alliance with Britain' in 1911. According to Fitzmaurice and Lowther, however, Djavid was a 'Crypto-Jew' who stood at 'the apex of Freemasonry in Turkey'. Although Winston Churchill, First Lord of the Admiralty, was willing to entertain the alliance idea, the Foreign Office, influenced by Fitzmaurice, said no.[57]

If the British misreading of the Young Turks as 'crypto-Jew' internationalists during the period of liberal constitutional euphoria was at least vaguely plausible, the failure to read the political shift after April 1909 was simply baffling. True, there were widespread rumours about the CUP's 'Dönme' connections following the overthrow of the Sultan-Caliph, which the German Embassy picked up too. But Marschall's interpretation was almost the polar opposite of Fitzmaurice's. The very fact that the CUP was suspected by ordinary Muslims of fronting for Jewish or foreign interests meant, in Marschall's view, that the Young Turks would have to move sharply to the 'right', that is, towards Ottoman-Muslim nationalism. As Marschall wrote to Berlin in April 1911, 'Islamic reactionaries' had 'come to the fore' in the movement. Fitzmaurice's crypto-Jewish bogeyman, Djavid Bey, was even ritually denounced at the CUP congress that month because he *was* suspected of 'fronting for Zionist interests', supporting the 'privileged positions of Jews' in the Ottoman Empire and, not least, of Freemasonry.* All in all, the CUP platform, approved by 180 delegates on 22 April 1911, was, Marschall wrote, 'of a strong Islamic-reactionary character'. As if turning their backs entirely on their origins, the Young Turk committee in the capital even vowed to crack down on 'Judaic-Freemason elements' prevailing in the CUP local in Salonica.[58]

Whether the Young Turks' reactionary turn was just for show or not, it was encouraging for Berlin. Baron Marschall could barely contain his glee in reporting on the April 1911 CUP congress, which seemed to suggest that pan-Islam was back in force, after its temporary eclipse in 1908–9. Abdul Hamid's dramatic fall had turned him into an international martyr of Islam, and an albatross around the neck of the Young Turks who had exiled him. 'Just as the mutineers screamed for Sharia on 13 April,' Marschall wrote, 'so has the parliamentary majority now taken on this slogan as its own.'[59] The German gamble on the 'Bloody Sultan' had not been in vain after all.

---

* Bizarrely, the passionate Anglophile Djavid may have been receiving this anti-Semitic abuse precisely because *The Times* correspondent in Constantinople, reportedly on orders from Fitzmaurice, had told CUP parliamentary deputies that 'serious English capital would only flow into the Ottoman Empire once Djavid Bey was sacked from his position [in the Finance Ministry]'.

In the event, Djavid Bey did not lose his job. One suspects the denunciations at the April 1911 congress were simply for public consumption, particularly for the British Embassy – about whose views the Young Turks seem to have been much better informed than vice versa. Djavid Bey, for his part, agreed to step down so as not to become a focal point for 'anti-Semitic rumours', but the CUP quietly turned down his resignation.

The Germans, we might say, had supported Abdul Hamid for the wrong reasons – and they would now support the Young Turks for the wrong reasons too. It is curious to reflect that the brief period of constitutional rule and religious toleration after the July 1908 events coincided with the eclipse of German power at the Porte. The return to chauvinistic, nationalistic Islamic reaction after the April counter-counter revolution put the Germans right back in the saddle. After a long pause during the political crisis of 1908–9, construction on the Baghdad railway resumed in March 1910. To promote the Baghdad railway, Turcophile journalist Ernst Jäckh then organized a VIP tour of Germany for CUP leaders, and penned a classic primer promoting Turkey to German investors and railway workers, *The Rising Crescent.*[60]

Just as the Germans had come around to support them only after they had jettisoned their ideals, so the Young Turks accepted this aid mostly for pragmatic reasons. Like all successful revolutionary movements, the CUP inherited the same problems which had faced the old regime, and with even less political legitimacy to tackle them. The finances were in even worse shape now than under Abdul Hamid. Where the Sultan had raised import duties from 8 to 11 per cent before the July revolution, the Young Turks would hike them still further in September 1909, to 15 per cent. Even so the pinch remained acute, with revenue so tight that the Young Turks were forced to abrogate all kilometric guarantees in the new Baghdad railway deal, negotiated in 1910. Remarkably, the Germans still took on the concession (through a Swiss front company), despite mounting evidence the Ottoman Empire was effectively bankrupt. Deutsche Bank even fronted a major new loan of 160 million francs to Turkey in December 1910 – after both Britain and France had baulked.[61] German armament firms, including Krupp, also signed huge new contracts with the Porte, worth hundreds of millions of Marks, on which payment was to be laggard.[62]

The difficulties faced by the Ottomans and Germans can be summed up in the ambitious overhaul of the military base at Üsküp (now the Macedonian capital of Skopje). Beginning in June 1912, the German firm of F. H. Schmidt began work on upgrading what was intended as the linchpin of Ottoman Europe. By the end of the year the Porte had ceased payments to F. H. Schmidt as Serbian troops had overrun

Üsküp and Ottoman Europe had substantially ceased to exist. At many different levels, this sort of experience made the Ottoman-German relationship hard to manage.[63] For better and for worse the Germans were in Turkey for good now, and not, evidently, for profit.

Jäckh's *Rising Crescent* was nonsense: in fact the Sick Man of Europe was falling to pieces. Like vultures descending on a rotting corpse, predatory neighbours began lopping off territory left and right from the dying empire. The Italian invasion of Libya in September 1911 inaugurated a decade of nearly continuous warfare, in which the Ottoman Empire fought for its very existence. Although the Turks held out bravely in Libya (where both Enver Bey and Mustafa Kemal saw action), the invasion of the remainder of Ottoman Europe by the Balkan League (Serbia, Bulgaria, Greece and Montenegro) in October 1912 forced the Porte to sue for peace with Italy. By January, with nearly all of Ottoman Albania, Macedonia and Thrace (including the expensively renovated Turkish army base in now-Slavic Skopje) occupied by Balkan Christian armies, rumours swirled around that the Ottoman Cabinet was preparing to surrender even Adrianople (today's Edirne), then holding out under siege. As if to cheat imperial death, CUP conspirators staged yet another palace coup on 23 January 1913, storming the Porte and murdering the War Minister, Nazım Pasha.

The new government, with Mahmud Şevket Pasha installed as Grand Vizier (until he, too, was assassinated in June), vowed to pursue the Balkan war to the bitter end. But the end was not long in coming. By the terms of the London Agreement of 30 May 1913, Ottoman Europe all but passed into the history books, with the new borders of enlarged Christian Bulgaria pressing right up against the beleaguered capital. It is true that the Ottoman army, under Enver's direct command, recaptured the historic former Ottoman capital of Adrianople in July, pushing the borders back some 200 kilometres west. But even this partial recovery was mostly due to the falling out of the Balkan jackal states: Bulgaria had attacked Serbia and Greece in the 'Second Balkan War', leaving its new eastern border undefended. Although it was a great boon to Enver's reputation, the reconquest of Adrianople could not hide the fact that the Ottoman Empire had, by August 1913, lost four-fifths of its European territory and two-thirds of its European subjects.

One might expect that the collapse of Ottoman power in Europe would have disappointed the Germans, who had invested so much time and energy in promoting the *Drang nach Osten*. 'Not a pfennig for a weak Turkey,' the pan-Germans had vowed, hoping that the Baghdad railway would breathe life into the Ottoman Sick Man, harnessing the long-dormant might of Islam against Britain. Whether it was shoring up the sovereign power of Sultan Abdul Hamid, or supporting Young Turk modernizers, the idea, all along, had been to defend the Ottoman Empire against the great Christian powers – and now here were tiny Balkan parvenu states destroying it on their own. It was enough to discourage even Baron Oppenheim, who returned to Germany in autumn 1913 to take up permanent residence in Berlin, as if giving up on his beloved Orient.[64]

There was, however, a silver lining for Germany in Turkey's sad plight. Just as the British bullying of Abdul Hamid in the Aqaba crisis of 1906 had stirred up angry Muslims from Egypt to British India, so now did the death agonies of the Ottoman Empire furnish a *cause célèbre* for the global *umma*. Despite everything the Young Turks had done to weaken the Sultanate, Constantinople was still the seat of the Caliphate, which retained huge symbolic importance in the Islamic world. As German Consul-General Luxburg reported from Calcutta on 16 January 1913, as the Balkan armies were threatening the Ottoman capital, 'a thousand channels flow from here to Constantinople, and if the inheritance of the prophet [i.e. the Caliphate] were in strong hands it could bring forth apparitions, which could seriously shake the equilibrium of this land'.[65] Muslim *medresses* throughout India were raising money from schoolchildren to save the Ottoman Sultan-Caliph.[66] The Turkish reconquest of Adrianople in July 1913 was greeted by Indian Muslims as if it was their own deliverance from oppression. That month, reported Luxburg (now escaping the summer heat, like the British Raj, in the Himalayan hill-station of Simla), 'prayers for the success of Islamic arms were given in all the mosques'. In Lahore, there were 'large public demonstrations which were ... very uncomfortable for the English authorities'.[67] In early August, a mob of angry Muslims in Cawnpore battled British-Indian police, who fired into the crowd, killing eighteen rioters and wounding thirty. There may have been local grievances as well (it was rumoured infidels renovating a mosque had entered its sacred precincts without removing their shoes), but Luxburg believed the real animating passion of the rioters was 'the threat to the existence of Islam evoked by the plight of the Sultan'. The casualties of Cawnpore were now, like the Ottoman Caliph, being fêted all over Muslim India as martyrs to the faith.[68]

By pumping up the Islamic Caliphate, British and German propaganda had created a monster. It was beginning to seem as if the puppet Sultan of the Young Turk regime was a giant voodoo doll of Islam: prick him (say, by sending an infidel army in his general direction) and Muslims halfway across the world cried out in pain. The British Raj, wrote Luxburg from Simla in August 1913, 'must view with a sense of powerlessness how, during Ramadan, the story of the events in Cawnpore is spreading like fire through the bazaars ... disturbing spirits and joining them together'. The 'Mohammedan', as the British were learning, 'forgets nothing'.[69] The global wave of Muslim rage in 1913 reached Britain itself, despite London not being in any meaningful sense a belligerent in the Balkan wars which were the ostensible source of Islamic grievance. Reporting on the tempestuous proceedings of an 'All-India Muslim Meeting' held in London that July, Germany's Ambassador Prince Lichnowsky concluded that 'the recent Turkish war has demonstrated the solidarity of the entire Islamic [world]'.[70]

Just as Oppenheim had predicted, a single *cause célèbre* happening anywhere in the Muslim world could now, thanks to the globalized media, 'send waves across the entire world of Islam'. It did not matter if the news from the war front was good or bad, or who was fighting, or where: all publicity was good publicity. If the tens of millions of Muslim subjects in British India could get this aroused by a war between Ottoman Turkey and a few Balkan mini-states, imagine what they could do if the power threatening the Sultan-Caliph were Great Britain itself. If Germany could conjure up such a war, the waves of Muslim rage could bring the British Empire to its knees. After long years in the wilderness, Baron Max von Oppenheim, the prophet of global jihad, would now take centre-stage.

II
The Prophet Armed

The intervention of Islam in the present war is, particularly for England, a terrible blow. Let us do all we can ... [to ensure] that this blow will be a lethal one!

Baron Max von Oppenheim, 'Exposé Concerning the Revolutionizing of the Islamic Territories of Our Enemies', *c.* late October 1914

4

A Gift from Mars: German
Holy War Fever

*[England] must ... have the mask of Christian peaceableness
torn publicly off her face ... Our Consuls in Turkey and India,
agents, etc. must inflame the whole Mohammedan world to
wild revolt against this hateful, lying, conscienceless people of
shopkeepers.*

Kaiser Wilhelm II, 30 July 1914[1]

We may never know for sure what was said behind closed doors in
Berlin as the European diplomatic crisis heated up in July 1914. The
key German policy-makers, including Chancellor Theobald von
Bethmann Hollweg and Helmuth von Moltke, Chief of the General
Staff, all burned their private papers from the period. Although there
is clear evidence that Bethmann Hollweg (on Kaiser Wilhelm's
instructions) issued a 'blank cheque' inviting Vienna to retaliate
against Serbia on 5 July, the extent to which the Germans deliberately sought to provoke a general European war remains controversial. It was actually a Hungarian diplomat, not a German,
who famously called the 28 June 1914 assassination of Austrian
Archduke Franz Ferdinand a 'gift from Mars'.[2] Of German official
thinking during the July crisis, there remain only snippets of surviving
evidence, notably in the diaries of the Chancellor's private secretary,
Kurt Riezler. Although not quite conclusive on the issue of 'premeditation' – i.e. German war guilt – the Riezler diaries do suggest that
fear of the growth of Russian power convinced Berlin a pre-emptive
war must be fought in 1914, and not several years later, when Russia's
'Great Programme', designed to enlarge her army and expand her
rail network, would make her unbeatable.[3]

If the evidence of premeditation in July is inconclusive, however, the extraordinary war fever which overcame the German government in August can be documented without a shadow of doubt. Audacious plans for world conquest were openly bandied about in once-conservative government ministries. The 'gift from Mars' meant that the gloves were finally off in Germany's battle with Britain for global supremacy. 'So the famous encirclement of Germany,' Kaiser Wilhelm exclaimed on 30 July 1914 after failing to secure British neutrality, 'has now finally become an accomplished fact, despite every effort by our politicians to prevent it. The net has been suddenly cast over our head, and England sneeringly reaps the brilliant success of the anti-German world policy ... against which we have shown ourselves helpless.'[4] Veering instantly from despair to euphoric war lust, Wilhelm vowed to 'inflame the whole Mohammedan world' against the British Empire. 'If we are to be bled to death,' the Kaiser concluded his remarkable outburst, 'at least England shall lose India.' Even Moltke, a notorious pessimist who nearly broke under the strain of the July crisis, succumbed to the fever. After being informed of the secret accord signed between Germany and Turkey on 2 August,* Moltke instructed the Foreign Office three days later that 'revolution in India and Egypt, and also in the Caucasus, is of the highest importance. The treaty with Turkey will make it possible for the Foreign Office to realize the idea and to awaken the fanaticism of Islam.'[5]

Because of the central role the Kaiser's jihad stratagem plays in Fritz Fischer's controversial indictment, *Germany's Aims in the First World War*, it has become customary for Fischer's critics to dismiss these plans as peripheral to Germany's overall war strategy. In a work still considered the gold standard, *Germany and the Ottoman Empire, 1914–1918*, Ulrich Trumpener writes that, although the anti-British holy war idea was 'a recurring theme of the Kaiser's famous marginalia, there is no evidence that Berlin had any coherent action plans on hand when World War I broke out'. Any measures the Germans did take to launch jihad-style uprisings against the Entente powers in August 1914, Trumpener writes, 'bore all the hallmarks of hasty

---

* This treaty will be discussed at length in chapter 5 below.

improvisation'.[6] Those who have followed Trumpener's analysis, such as David Fromkin, have likewise dismissed the importance of the jihad campaign, arguing that it had little bearing on either Turkey's entry into the war or on the way the war was really fought.[7]

To dismiss the importance of pan-Islam in Germany's wartime plans, however, is to fall victim to hindsight. In 1914, if not when they were writing post-war memoirs, Germany's leaders saw in Islam the secret weapon which would decide the world war. Certainly they acted as if they believed this, even if, in some cases, only to honour the Kaiser's own enthusiasm for the idea. For example, Baron Hans von Wangenheim, Germany's influential Ambassador to the Porte, figures in Trumpener's account as a sceptic of the jihad policy, who had to be dragged, kicking and screaming, into supporting it.[8] But there is plenty of evidence to the contrary. Wangenheim, an ambitious diplomat who dreamed of becoming Chancellor, was nothing if not loyal to his Emperor. As he wrote to Bethmann Hollweg from Constantinople in mid-August, 'the revolutionizing of the Islamic world desired by His Majesty is prepared and has been for some time. These measures have been undertaken under strict secrecy.' Enver Pasha, the Ottoman War Minister who consulted almost daily with the German Ambassador, was fully on board, although Turkey had not yet entered the war. According to Wangenheim, Enver had already dispatched agents to spread the word of the coming jihad to Afghanistan, the Caucasus, Baghdad, Benghazi and Cairo. 'Of Enver's good faith in the kindling of the pan-Islamic movement', Wangenheim promised the Chancellor, surely 'there can be doubt'.[9]

Contrary to Trumpener's assertion, there is concrete evidence that Turco-German-jihad action plans were ready to go when the guns of August started firing. According to Wangenheim, a 'commission for the preparation of Islamic Baluchistan', consisting of 'eight tough Armenians', had been dispatched with German funds, in mid-July, weeks before the war's outbreak. Similar German jihad-preparation teams had already been sent to Persia and Russian Daghestan, while the Turks themselves had sent jihad agents everywhere from the Sudan to the subcontinent.[10] On 1 August, the very day Germany declared war on Russia, a mission led by Dr Otto Mannesmann was sent to Tripoli with orders to foment uprisings in French North Africa, intending to use balloons to distribute jihadi pamphlets. Hard on the heels of the British declaration of war on 4 August, the Turkish War Ministry, after decreeing general mobilization, at German insistence ordered the Ottoman Fourth Army in Damascus to begin planning an assault on the Suez Canal.[11] Fortuitously, one of Germany's leading pre-war Arabists, Professor Bernhard Moritz – the Khedivial Library director whom Curt Prüfer had been intended to replace in 1911 – arrived in Damascus on 8 August 1914, overland from the Sinai desert following a scouting trip in Arabia. Moritz gave the Turkish army commanders a thorough briefing on the latest English troop dispositions at Suez, the best routes across the Sinai, the locations of oases and wells (of which there were few), the likely attitudes of the Bedouins, and the availability of camels.[12] 'Hasty improvisation' this may have been, but it was inspired none the less. The Ottoman Empire may still have been officially neutral in the world war, but from Germany's perspective, as Richard Hannay says of his American collaborator in *Greenmantle*, it was 'the best kind of neutrality I've ever heard of'.[13]

Despite the Turks' continued hesitation to enter the war on Germany's side, it was in the heady days of August 1914, while the war of movement continued on both the western and eastern front, that the holy war fever was at its strongest. In those days, everything seemed possible, from the taking of Paris in six weeks (as required by the Schlieffen–Moltke Plan) to the rapid-fire destruction of the British and Russian empires. Here was, as Peter Hopkirk wrote in his great yarn *On Secret Service East of Constantinople*, 'a new and more sinister version of the old Great Game'.[14] If the classic version of the context had been a kind of nineteenth-century Cold War, with only indirect skirmishing between Britain and Russia in Central Asia, the Kaiser's jihad would be a hot war, with the espionage and propaganda struggle punctuated by real battles.

The allure of the new Great Game was extremely seductive. For the most part, the world knows the story through the (largely exaggerated) exploits of Lawrence of Arabia, and from John Buchan's wartime bestseller *Greenmantle*. And yet the British were very slow to cotton on – it was not until 1916 that Lawrence set foot in Arabia and Buchan's novel enraptured British audiences. The Germans, by contrast, were playing the new game in deadly earnest from the first days of August 1914.

It was on Moltke's own instructions, given on 5 August – one day after Britain declared war on Germany – that the German Foreign Office began recruiting spies and agents for the jihad. Moltke wired the Ottoman War Ministry on the 10th, requesting that Enver begin organizing 'Islamic uprisings ... to tie down Russian and English forces'.[15] On 7 August, State Secretary Gottlieb von Jagow instructed the German Consulate in Stockholm to establish contact with the Persian Shah's gendarmerie of Swedish bodyguards, some of whom were conveniently on leave in Sweden. The objective was to promote an Islamic insurgency, targeting Russia from northern Persia and Azerbaijan.[16]

As Jagow's intervention in Sweden suggests, German Consulates in neutral countries were prime recruiting grounds for the global jihad. Many supplicants, particularly in Switzerland, were exiled Egyptian pretenders, Arab sheikhs and Indian princes, manoeuvring to secure German goodwill in case Britain's days were done. The lure of German jihad ensnared European sympathizers too, like Sven Hedin, the world-famous Swedish explorer, who shared his intimate geographical knowledge of Afghanistan and Indian's north-west mountain passes with the German Consul in Stockholm, the idea being to plan an Islamic holy war on British India.[17]

Although there was a great deal of activity in Switzerland and Sweden, the epicentre for recruiting for the German jihad was the Wilhelmstrasse in Berlin. No less than the army, the Foreign Office was beset by volunteers in August 1914, with every German who had ever worked or lived in the Orient eager to get in on the action. Many were the kind of ne'er-do-wells in civilian life who thrive on the racket of war. But Germany's jihad volunteers also included perfectly respectable businessmen, like the Mannesmann brothers sent to stir up jihad in Morocco. Other improbable German jihadists included Albert Ballin, owner of the Hamburg-Amerika shipping line which had recently become active in the Persian Gulf, and Robert Wönckhaus, who owned a smaller shipping company actually based in Basra. Another prominent volunteer was Professor Otto Warburg of the University of Berlin, a scion of the Hamburg banking dynasty which handled German government finances, a world-renowned botanist, and not incidentally chairman of the international Zionist Executive in Berlin.

The brothers Mannesmann, Ballin, Warburg and Wönckhaus all figure prominently in one of the most extraordinary policy papers ever drawn up by a civilized government. This 'Overview of Revolutionary Activity We Will Undertake in the Islamic-Israelite World', written on 16 August 1914 – at a time when the fighting in Europe had scarcely begun – proposed that Germany combine the Kaiser's anti-British jihad with an Israelite-cum-Zionist rebellion in Russia. Once it became clear that the global Zionist movement had the backing of Germany's powerful army, Jews in the Pale of Settlement would, with German encouragement, sabotage grain depots and deliveries, thus starving the Russian army. Once the regime began to wobble, Russian Jews would then lead the way in toppling the Russian Tsar, the greatest enemy of world Jewry.* Meanwhile, Turco-German jihadi propaganda could be distributed via Wönckhaus and Hamburg-Amerika ships to hajj pilgrims coming or going from the Hejaz, which would allow the 'waves of rebellion to spread from Egypt via Mecca to the entire Islamic world as far as India'.[18]

Baron Max von Oppenheim had been born for this moment. Having recently settled down in Berlin after over two decades of travel and study in the Orient, the prophet of global jihad was in the perfect place at the perfect time. Summoned to the Wilhelmstrasse from his Kurfürstendamm flat on 2 August 1914, the same day Germany's secret treaty with Turkey was signed, Oppenheim did not hesitate for a second to serve the Foreign Office which had rudely disowned him only four years ago. Where before the Baron had been kept at arm's length because of his Jewish origins and his questionable, quasi-native lifestyle in Cairo, he was now given the rank of Minister-in-Residence and offered every perk imaginable. The parvenu had arrived.

With the Foreign Office at last behind him, Oppenheim began sketching out an ambitious blueprint. Jihad headquarters would be Berlin itself, where Oppenheim planned to create a pan-Islamic propaganda clearing house to publish anti-Entente screeds in German, French, English, Russian and Dutch, which would also be 'translated into Arabic, Turkish, Persian, Hindustani, Swahili (for German- and

---

* The German Zionist stratagem outlined in this memorandum, and its world-historical consequences, will be discussed at more length in the Epilogue.

British-East Africa) and eventually into the languages of Russian Muslims'. Germany must, Oppenheim wrote to Chancellor Bethmann Hollweg on 18 August 1914, arm the Muslim brotherhoods of Libya, Sudan and Yemen; she must fund Arab exile pretenders (including the deposed Egyptian Khedive, Abbas Hilmi, who had conveniently been trapped in Constantinople during the July crisis); and she must raise the standard of anti-colonial rebellion in French North Africa and Russian Central Asia. Above all, Germany must incite Habibullah Khan, the Emir of Afghanistan, to invade British India at the head of an Islamic army. The Emir, Oppenheim informed the Chancellor, could already dispose of '40–50,000 armed men'. According to Wangenheim, Enver had already agreed to send a Turkish military mission to buttress the Emir's forces, under the command of '20 to 30 German officers'. The signs of visible 'cooperation between His Majesty the King and Emperor [of Germany] and the [Ottoman] Sultan-Caliph in Afghanistan', Oppenheim promised Bethmann Hollweg, would incite Muslims from Cairo to Calcutta to rise and 'shake off the yoke' of British imperial rule. Even if the rebellions failed to materialize (or if the war were over 'too' quickly), Oppenheim assured the Chancellor that the mere threat of an Indian Muslim uprising would 'force England to [agree] to peace terms favourable to us'.[19]

The groundwork for German jihad propaganda in British India had been thoroughly prepared by 1914. As we have seen, Mehmed Reshad V, the Young Turks' puppet Sultan, had become a focus of anxiety for Indian Muslims during the Balkan wars, with every threat to his throne taken as a personal offence in the subcontinent. Ideally, of course, the beleaguered Sultan-Caliph would proclaim a holy war against the British: but long before this happened, German diplomats reported that Muslim rage was surging through India. Cleverly, the Germans had planted the story that the two Ottoman dreadnoughts commandeered in port by the British navy on 31 July* had been 'gifts from Indian Muslims to the Caliph'. Britain's theft of the warships had therefore created 'much bad blood' with Indian Muslims before the war had even begun.[20] Three British officers had already been murdered by Muslim mobs in India,

---

* This story will be discussed at length in chapter 5 below.

where German Consuls reported that 'great unrest is reigning among the Mohammedan population'.[21]

British Egypt seemed no less vulnerable. Although Professor Moritz had advised the Turkish Fourth Army that it would be difficult to storm the Suez Canal by force, reports on conditions in Cairo reaching the German government suggested a military operation might not even be necessary. According to a report reaching the German Consul in Athens, the British, terrified of a jihadi-style rebellion, had already begun disarming Muslim Egyptian army and police officers.[22] Lending credence to British fears, Enver Pasha told Wangenheim on 3 September 1914 that four Turkish agents were already secretly at work in Cairo spreading sedition, having enlisted forty Egyptian army officers in plans for a general uprising. The plan was to create bands of twelve to fifteen armed Muslims in every district in Cairo, each under the direction of a Turkish agent or a mutinous Egyptian officer. These jihad-terror *comitaji* bands, the Germans hoped, would strive to assassinate British officers, and to sabotage key infrastructure chokepoints, like railway depots and telegraph stations. Not to be outdone, the Germans had their own man in the Egyptian police, Robert Mors, a German national who had settled in Alexandria before the war and risen to the rank of lieutenant. Mors had been on leave in Constantinople when the war broke out. He would now develop with Turkey's own agents plans for a general Egyptian police and army mutiny, coordinated if possible with an assault on the Suez Canal. Mors would also look into ways of sabotaging the canal itself, for example by sinking ships in narrow sections to block passage.[23]

As Enver's (exaggerated) early September report on the state of seditious activity in Egypt suggests, the crushing German victory over two Russian armies in East Prussia near Tannenberg (25–30 August 1914) had produced a wave of enthusiasm in Constantinople for the Turco-German holy war. Wangenheim reported to Berlin, 'Enver fears only that the war will be over before the various rebellions [in Entente countries] break out, the preparations for which will take several months.' Enver had just created a special jihad department inside the Ottoman War Ministry, which, Wangenheim said, 'was already working with great enthusiasm'. Even more desperate to join the winning side were the leading sheikhs of Arabia, including Hussein of

Mecca, Ibn Rashid and Ibn Saud, all of whom sent sons to the Porte, bearing gifts for Enver and declaring themselves 'ready to undertake action against England'. Obviously well-informed about Tannenberg, the sheikhs told Enver to tell Wangenheim that 'in all the mosques of Arabia, even in Mecca and Medina, the people pray for Germany's victory'.[24]

With impeccable timing, Oppenheim's holy war protégé from pre-war Cairo, Curt Prüfer, arrived in Constantinople on 3 September, the very day Enver met with the Arab sheikhs, and reported to Wangenheim on Turkish jihad-preparations in Cairo. Prüfer, the former dragoman, was so well regarded in the Foreign Office for his linguistic skills and general expertise on Islam and the Orient that there seems to have been a bidding war for his services. In part this was because there were few other Germans with good working knowledge of Arabic (or Turkish, for that matter). From Prüfer's field correspondence it is clear that he was reporting to Oppenheim's jihad bureau in Berlin,* organized inside the Wilhelmstrasse's Near Eastern Department, headed by Baron Langwerth von Simmern. But Prüfer also answered to Arthur Zimmermann, the Under-Secretary of State who was in overall charge of Germany's notoriously reckless wartime 'Seditious Undertakings Against Our Enemies' (*Unternehmungen und Aufwiegelungen gegen unsere Feinde*), which included everything from the jihad to support for Zionism and Russian revolutionaries, to Zimmermann's famous telegram offering to return the south-western United States to Mexico if the latter entered the war on Germany's side.[25] After arriving in Constantinople, Prüfer was also taken under the wing of Ambassador Wangenheim, and struck up a fast friendship with Captain Hans Humann, the German naval attaché, who had his own jihad agents in the field. After leaving Constantinople later in September, Prüfer would become the indispensable dragoman to Djemal Bey, the former Ottoman Naval Minister ordered to take over the Fourth Army in Damascus.[26]

---

* By way of the Embassy in Constantinople, which did give Wangenheim a look-see on what Oppenheim's agents were up to. Telegraphic embassy communications with Berlin and Vienna went by way of Bulgaria and Romania until autumn 1915, when the knocking out of Serbia also opened up the more direct Belgrade line.

Prüfer's orders from Berlin seem to have been very loosely defined, but it is clear what his overall objective was. By hook or by crook, the Germans wanted to knock the English out of Egypt, or at least to render the Suez Canal inoperable, which would cut London off from India. While the war of movement continued on the western front, the Germans' objective was akin to blackmail: with both France and Russia on the ropes, a serious threat to the canal, it was thought, might convince the British to sell out their beleaguered allies. The bogging down of the German army at the battle of the Marne in France (6–12 September) made it clear that no easy victory was in the offing. Far from discrediting the jihad idea, however, the German retreat to the Aisne river, and the fateful defensive entrenching which followed, made it appear more like military necessity. With a stalemate on the western front, an 'eastern' strategy offered the only way out.

As if he did not already have enough people to answer to, Curt Prüfer's Suez Canal brief was now buttressed by an urgent dispatch from the Chancellor at German army headquarters in Luxemburg. 'We are forced,' Bethmann Hollweg wrote to Wangenheim on 7 September 1914, as the bad news from the Marne was filtering in, 'to exploit every possibility to break the resistance of England.' Despite concern in the German high command about the possibility that Turkey's entry into the war might lead to a British effort to force the Dardanelles and attack the Ottoman capital, the possibility of pushing the British out of Egypt made the risk well worth taking. 'An undertaking against the Suez Canal,' Bethmann Hollweg wrote, 'would be of inestimable value for us.' Wangenheim was to speed up joint planning with the Ottoman War Ministry for an operation against the canal, involving 'from 20 to 30,000 men'. Bethmann Hollweg also authorized Wangenheim to offer Enver all the 'weapons and ammunition' he requested.[27]

Enver did not take long to make his request. For the Ottoman Fourth Army to be sufficiently equipped to take the Suez Canal, he demanded, on 8 September 1914, 'at least 6 rapid-firing field batteries with adequate munition'. Field artillery rounds, Enver emphasized, were much more important than infantry ammunition. Ideally, the Germans would send 10.5 mm Howitzers, with 8,000 shells apiece. Then Turkey, too, would need funds to pay for the operation – Liman von Sanders estimated the cost at 100,000 Turkish lira or pounds (about $500,000, or some $50 million today). On 13 September, Enver's requests were heartily approved at Germany military headquarters – on the understandable condition that Turkey actually declare war on the Entente powers. For his part, Enver assured Wangenheim that he personally was 'ready to enter the war at any time and any price'. Probably at the insistence of Kaiser Wilhelm, who had with characteristic hysteria swung behind the Suez operation as Germany's last chance to win the war, Bethmann Hollweg intervened on 16 September to appropriate the funds for Suez, even without an Ottoman declaration of war.[28]

Despite the Germans' increasing frustration that the Ottomans were dragging their feet in joining the war, this did not preclude active collaboration. Prüfer met Enver for the first time on 7 September, the same day Bethmann's urgent telegram to speed up the Suez operation was dispatched from Luxemburg. Like everyone else, Enver was impressed by the young German dragoman, and the feeling was mutual. The two men were both rising stars in their early thirties, who might easily have been rivals had they not worked for different governments. In his diary, Prüfer described the Ottoman War Minister as 'a man of stone', possessed of 'a trait of unmatched toughness'. Above all, he took note of Enver's ambitious air. 'The man,' Prüfer wrote, as if also describing his own restless nature, 'wants something; it doesn't matter what the "something" is.'[29]

Prüfer was cutting a fine figure on the Bosphorus. But his talents as interpreter and Oppenheim's number-one field man were not best employed in the Ottoman capital, where Wangenheim had plenty of diplomatic staff already hard at work convincing the Porte to declare war. On 13 September, Prüfer had dispatched the Egyptian police lieutenant Robert Mors on a ship to Alexandria, laden down with 'dynamite, detonators, propaganda leaflets, and several Egyptian cohorts' who would assist him in sabotaging the Suez Canal, or inciting a Muslim mutiny in the Egyptian army and police, or just generally making life difficult for the British in Cairo. With the Mors mission now up and running, there was no reason for Prüfer to stay in Constantinople. After a final week of negotiations with Wangenheim over mission protocol, on 20 September 1914 Prüfer at last packed his bags and took a ferry to Haydarpasha station, to board the still-unfinished

Baghdad railway, which would take him as far as the Taurus mountains en route for Damascus.* He was attached as dragoman and
adviser to the military mission of the wonderfully named Bavarian
Lieutenant Colonel Kress von Kressenstein, sent to prepare the
Ottoman Fourth Army for the coming assault on Suez.[30]

The German jihad was getting serious. At the same time as the Suez
mission was heading east from Haydarpasha, another mission aiming
to raise the green banner of holy war in Afghanistan was en route from
the west for Sirkeci station, on the European side of the Bosphorus.
The Afghan mission, led by another Bavarian officer, Oskar von
Niedermayer, who had travelled widely in Persia before the war, was
even larger than the Kress–Prüfer group, involving some thirty German
soldiers and covert agents of greatly varying levels of experience.
Because neutral Romania was honeycombed with Entente spies,
Niedermayer's team had disguised itself as a 'travelling circus'. Unfortunately for the Germans, the ruse was discovered by an alert Romanian
customs officer in Bucharest, whose suspicions were aroused by the
lengthy German wireless station aerials poking out of the baggage car
(labelled on the invoice as circus 'tent poles'). After a stressful week
(and the dispensing of hefty bribes), Niedermayer's group was allowed
to proceed, but not before the embarrassing mishap had alerted the
Allies to the nature of his mission.[31]

Niedermayer and Prüfer had by far the most important German
jihad briefs, targeting British India and British Egypt, respectively.
But they had plenty of company. Otto Mannesmann, sent to Tripoli
in early August with a vague brief to do with raising the banner of
revolt against French North Africa, was later entrusted with stirring
up the Sanussi tribesmen of Libya against British Egypt. Bernhard
Moritz, after advising the Ottoman Fourth Army in Damascus in
August 1914 on the best approaches to Suez, was dispatched on
Oppenheim's orders in October to set up a German propaganda

---

* Although a separate line from Aleppo to Damascus was open, across both the Taurus
and Amanus mountains between Cilicia and Syria huge gaps in the Baghdad railway
remained, which could only be traversed by a mixture of caravan roads and (for armaments and rail supplies) a growing number of narrow-gauge service lines. Wartime
construction efforts on the line will be discussed in more detail in chapter 14 below.

bureau in Medina, the second holiest city of Sunni Islam. Leo Frobenius, Germany's leading African colonial explorer, was sent simultaneously via the Hejaz to conjure up an Islamic holy war in Abyssinia (today's Ethiopia) and the Anglo-Egyptian Sudan. Fritz Klein, a German army captain, set out at the same time for southern Mesopotamia, with orders to win an endorsement of the Turco-German jihad from the leading clerics of the Shiite holy places of Najaf and Karbala, while also securing the oil-rich region around Basra (or sabotaging the wells, if the British beat him to it). It was also decided in October to send an accomplished Austrian Orientalist, Professor Alois Musil, to the desert wastes of central Arabia, to enlist the major tribal sheikhs in the Turco-German jihad (although Musil reported to Vienna, his mission was entirely financed by Berlin).*

Most ambitious of all was the mission of Max Roloff-Breslau, a German who had lived before the war in Dutch Indonesia, where he studied under Snouck Hurgronje, the famous scholar of early Islam. Roloff, whose mission was run out of German military intelligence instead of Oppenheim's bureau, answered to Hans Humann, the naval attaché in Constantinople, who furnished the would-be hajj pilgrim with 200,000 gold Marks. The idea was for Roloff to set sail from Rotterdam in September 1914 for the East Indies, travelling on a Dutch passport. In Sumatra, he would adopt Muslim disguise, just in time to board a Hejaz-bound vessel with other Indonesian hajjis (the first day of the pilgrimage in 1914 would fall on 20 October). Whether or not he reached Mecca (and there was considerable controversy in the Foreign Office as to whether he ever did make it there), Roloff could canvass other Mecca pilgrims for their views on the European war, and spread the good word about Germany, Hajji Wilhelm, and the coming global jihad against the Entente powers to be proclaimed by the Ottoman Sultan-Caliph.[32]

By October 1914, holy war fever was raging high on the Bosphorus. Every day trains were arriving at Constantinople's Sirkeci station full of suspicious-looking characters from Central Europe, along with German gold, guns and ammunition. The Pera Palace Hotel was swarming with Allied spies, whose job was made considerably easier by the

---

* These missions will be discussed individually below.

loose tongues of would-be German jihadis. Niedermayer, who arrived in early October, was forced into damage control almost immediately. 'I cannot strive hard enough,' the Bavarian colonel wrote in exasperation to the Foreign Office, 'to put a lid on the wild stories [being spread] by some of the men here.' The problem, Niedermayer explained, was that the men Oppenheim had selected for him were too enthusiastic about the jihad mission to Afghanistan: they simply could not shut up about it. There were also too many of them, many working at cross-purposes.[33] Wangenheim, too, was increasingly concerned about the Baron's poor vetting of holy war recruits. 'In the future,' he begged Oppenheim on 15 October 1914, 'please send us no more hitherto unknown people for revolutionary purposes.'[34]

Unfortunately for the overworked Wangenheim, Oppenheim was only just getting started. After being frustrated in his designs for years by well-born Foreign Office grandees, the Baron was not about to stop now that he was on a roll. All the frustration and rage against arrogant Albion Oppenheim had bottled up now came rushing out in a white-hot policy paper which may be the single most extraordinary document of 1914. Like his pre-war reports from Cairo, this 'Exposé Concerning the Revolutionizing of the Islamic Territories of Our Enemies' ran to over one hundred pages laced with vitriol. Covering everything from holy war propaganda to the burning of oil wells to full-blown orders of battle for invasions of British Egypt and India, Oppenheim sketched out a blueprint for a global jihad engulfing hundreds of millions of people. With ruthless single-mindedness, Oppenheim consigned religious minorities in Islamic areas across Asia to the dustbin of history, writing off the Armenians and Maronite Christians, for example, as hopeless Entente sympathizers who would be 'of no use' to Germany (*nicht viel nützen können*). The Baron was not entirely heartless: he did reassure the Wilhelmstrasse that his Indian Muslim agents had promised, when jihad came to the subcontinent, to spare the lives of 'women, elderly men and children' (one assumes this means able-bodied male infidels would *not* be spared). The ultimate target of the Indian jihad, of course, was the British Raj. 'The intervention of Islam in the present war,' Oppenheim concluded with a flourish, 'is, particularly for England, a terrible blow. Let us do all we can, let us combine all our forces, that this blow will be a lethal one!'[35]

Like Isaac Deutscher's Trotsky, the prophet of global jihad was armed by the outbreak of the world war with all the might of imperial Germany behind him. So, too, Oppenheim believed, were the hundred million Muslims under British occupation on Germany's side, along with the forty million or so ruled by France and Russia. Had not the Kaiser declared his friendship for all of the world's 300 million Muslims? From reports in the field, Oppenheim assured the Foreign Office that 'not only in Turkey and Egypt' but in British India and 'even Persia' the world's Muslims were all 'praying for the triumph of German arms in the mosques'. It was true, the Baron conceded, that 'Germany was not an Islamic power'. This was why the war on the Entente powers needed to be 'endorsed with the seal of the Sultan-Caliph'. As soon as this endorsement was given, Oppenheim promised, 'the entire world of Islam' would be enlisted alongside the Central Powers in 'the greatest war that has ever erupted on this earth', with Germans and Muslims 'fighting together, shoulder to shoulder, for their very existence'.[36]

It was an intoxicating vision, but there remained a serious problem. Despite the signing of a secret alliance treaty on 2 August binding Berlin to defend the territorial integrity of the Ottoman Empire and notwithstanding burgeoning Turco-German cooperation in military planning and covert operations against British Egypt and India; in spite of the dispatch of German missions to every corner of the Ottoman Empire; despite War Minister Enver's professed enthusiasm for the Turco-German jihad; despite weeks of promises from the Porte of imminent intervention – Turkey was still not at war.

5

The War for the Porte

*The decisive resolution of the 'Eastern Question' will probably
occur in the next few years.*

I. K. Grigorevich, Russian Naval Minister,
7 November 1913[1]

Few decisions in world history have been as fraught with consequences
as Turkey's entry into the First World War. From the closing off of the
Straits for years to Russian commerce – a major cause of the economic
upheaval which led to the Russian Revolution – to the creation of the
modern Middle East out of the wreckage of the defeated Ottoman
Empire, the Turks' decision to fight in 1914 lies at the root of the most
intractable geopolitical problems of the twentieth century, many of
which are still with us today. Although never formally saddled with
'war guilt' for having provoked the conflict, as their German allies
were, the Ottoman leaders who pushed Turkey into the war still bear
a heavy responsibility, in no small part because they took the final
plunge without anything resembling the kind of public support found
in the Western belligerent countries.

In hindsight, it appears inevitable that the Porte would have in the
end been drawn into the burgeoning conflict, as were other neutrals in
the region, like Italy, Bulgaria and Greece. And yet this is to mistake
cause and effect: it was Turkey's entry into the war in 1914 which
ultimately drew the other powers in, by offering up the Ottoman
Empire as war booty. The neutrals were awaiting Turkey's decision
anxiously all summer and autumn, whether out of desire to lop off
more Ottoman territory (Greece), to use Turkish belligerence as a

springboard to settle regional scores (Bulgaria), or out of concern over Turkish jihadi-style disruption of colonial territory (Italy). The Great Powers were also desperate to see which way the Porte would go, with Germany and Austria-Hungary keen to unleash the Turks on Russia to relieve the pressure on the eastern front, the Russians apprehensive of precisely this if Turkey joined the fray (although also sorely tempted by the prospect of conquering Constantinople at long last), and the British and French terrified at the prospect of their beleaguered Russian ally being cut off by sea, and of the colonial rebellions which might follow an Ottoman declaration of war on the Entente.

And yet, despite the Porte having long been under German influence prior to 1914, the truth was that no one knew which way the Ottomans would go in the war, least of all the Turkish ministers themselves. When news of the spiralling war crisis first reached the Porte in July, the diplomatic possibilities seemed almost endless, although every potential decision was fraught with danger. Since the Eastern Question had come to the forefront of European diplomacy a century before, Ottoman sovereigns and their advisers had sought to play the powers off against one another, trusting none implicitly. Following Napoleon's invasion of Egypt in 1798, the British had assumed an unofficial position as lead protector of the Porte, while reserving the right to go the other way when the opportunity might strike, as with the Greek revolt of the 1820s (the success of which was ensured by the British naval victory at Navarino in 1827).

At times, even the Turks' arch enemy Russia had played this role, sending troops to Constantinople in 1833, for example, to prevent the Ottoman Sultan from being deposed by the armies of the reformist Egyptian Khedive Muhammad Ali. France had also taken a hand, teaming up with the British in the Crimean War to defend Turkey against Russian encroachment. The Germans, as we have seen, took their turn under Wilhelm II, but this relationship, too, was tense at times. Tacit German diplomatic support for Austria-Hungary's annexation of Ottoman Bosnia in 1908, and for the Greek seizure of Aegean islands during the Balkan wars, had strained trust almost to the breaking point. Where before 1908 German-Ottoman relations had been buttressed by the personal friendship of Kaiser and Sultan, CUP leaders, with the exception of Enver Bey, had never been particularly friendly to Germany. Nor was Wilhelm himself as fond of the Young Turks as he had been of the unfortunate Abdul Hamid (now whiling away the hours under house arrest in Beylerbey Palace).* During the First Balkan War, the Kaiser had refused to side with the beleaguered Ottoman army, describing his policy as one of 'free-fight and no favour'. For all his enthusiasm for pan-Islam, the Kaiser also loved his sister Princess Sophie, who was, from March 1913, Queen of Greece. Hajji Wilhelm may have dreamed of unleashing the forces of Islam against the British Empire in Asia; but when it came to Ottoman Europe he was of an entirely different mind.[2]

Even before the outbreak of the world war in 1914, the Porte was the scene of frantic diplomatic intrigue, with the Russians in particular on high alert. With Turkey reeling from its losses in the Italian and Balkan wars, seemingly every question was open, from the restoration of Turkish influence in formerly Ottoman provinces in the Balkans and on Aegean islands (or its further eclipse), to partial autonomy in the Armenian-heavy provinces of eastern Anatolia (negotiated by the powers in early 1914), to control of the Straits and even Constantinople itself. The closure of the Straits during the Turkish-Italian war of 1911–12 had devastated Russian shipping, cutting off most of her burgeoning grain export trade, not to mention imports of components desperately needed by Russian industry. In November 1912 and again in March 1913, the Bulgarian army advanced as close to the Ottoman capital as the Russians had in 1877. Bulgaria, a state literally created by force of Russian arms in 1878, now threatened to conquer the 'Second Rome' of Russian Orthodox dreams – without Russia's help. Little wonder St Petersburg began quietly manoeuvring to 'protect' Constantinople just as it had in 1833. As the Bulgarians raced across Thrace in October 1912, the Russian navy put an amphibious landing force based at Odessa on high alert. In a moment of immense drama, Naval Minister Ivan K. Grigorevich (with the apposite patronymic of Konstantinovich) had wired Tsar Nicholas II at 1.30 a.m. on the night of 25–26 October 1912 with a request to place the entire Black Sea Fleet under the command of M. N. Girs,

---

* Abdul Hamid, first exiled to Salonica, had been returned to Constantinople after the city was conquered by Greece in the First Balkan War in 1912.

Russia's Ambassador to the Porte, the idea being that Girs might summon ships and troops to suppress 'anarchy' in Constantinople if the Bulgarians got too close. (Although not ecstatic about being awakened, the Tsar agreed).[3] Although the Bulgarians later retreated and the Turks retook Adrianople in July, Constantinople itself now seemed to be in play. Parallel to the 'Great Programme' launched the same year to expand Russia's army and speed up its mobilization by rail, in 1913 the Russian navy began drawing up a five-year plan to make the Black Sea Fleet strong enough to seize the Straits by force. Grigorevich, optimistic, predicted that 'the decisive resolution of the "Eastern Question" will probably occur in the next few years'. Russia would have to be ready. If all went well, she would be – by 1917 or 1918.[4]

Paradoxically, the closer the Russians came to fulfilling the age-old dream of conquering Constantinople, the friendlier relations became between St Petersburg and the Porte – at least on the surface. In March 1914, as the Russian navy was putting the finishing touches on its expansion plan with an eye to seizing Constantinople and the Straits (the final draft was approved by the Tsar on 5 April),[5] a Russo-Turkish friendship committee was formed with great public fanfare in Constantinople. Although the initiative seems to have come from the Russian side, the Turks actually picked up the tab for the venture, apparently on the instructions of Talaat Bey, the CUP Interior Minister.[6] With the support of Grand Vizier Said Halim Pasha, Talaat was dispatched in early May 1914 on the Sultan's yacht to the Tsar's summer retreat at Livadia, in the Crimea, to meet with Russian Foreign Minister Sazonov and Tsar Nicholas II himself. As if seeking to pre-empt Russia's designs on the Straits, Talaat's stunning proposal was an out-and-out Russo-Ottoman alliance, in exchange for which the Porte would promise never again to close the Straits to Russian shipping. Although refusing to bite, the Russians did not reject Talaat's offer out of hand.[7]

It would be easy to dismiss this exchange as insincere on both sides. On the Russian side, there was certainly a cynical edge to the courting of Constantinople: according to German agents, the Russians were intriguing behind Talaat's back to depose the Sultan and install Enver, the War Minister, as puppet dictator.[8] And yet there were real, if temporary, grounds for convergence between Russian and Turkish interests following the Balkan wars. Although St Petersburg was itself largely responsible for the creation of the monster of anti-Turkish Balkan Slav irredentism, the Russians were losing patience with their clients. The belligerent Bulgarians were getting way too big for their britches, and the Serbs, too, were proving hard to control. The last thing the Russians wanted was for an ambitious Balkan power to seize Constantinople and the Straits, which would put Russia's economy at the mercy of the ungrateful Serbs or Bulgars. Russia was increasingly adamant that Serbia should not be allowed to take over Albania, which would give them a coastline on the Adriatic and Great Power pretensions. In January 1914, Sazonov began intriguing to restore Albania to Ottoman control. In this, the Russians were closer to the Porte than the supposedly Turcophile Germans, who favoured Greek control of Albania – and were unwilling to back down. No wonder both the Austrians and Germans began to worry in spring 1914 that they were losing Turkey to the Entente. Johann Markgraf von Pallavicini, the Austrian Ambassador to the Porte, usually referred to as the 'dean of the diplomatic corps' because he had served there longer than anyone else, concluded in May 1914 that the Young Turks had finally thrown in their lot with the Triple Entente: he advised Vienna to offer the Russians Constantinople in exchange for quieting her Balkan Slav allies, thus to be done with the whole Eastern Question.[9]

It is one of the strangest ironies of the First World War that Turkey's fateful decision to fight alongside Germany came at a time when German influence in Constantinople was again, as it had been in 1908–9, in almost total eclipse. The Kaiser's emotional support for Greece over the Albanian question in 1913–14, coupled with his abandonment of the Turks during the Balkan wars, had all but destroyed the German position at the Porte that Marschall had so carefully established. Marschall's successor, Baron Hans von Wangenheim, faced an uphill struggle following his appointment, with inauspicious timing, in October 1912 – shortly before the First Balkan War transformed the Porte into a palace of paranoia in which every foreign diplomat was suspect. Had Wangenheim arrived on the Bosphorus during the era of Hamidian good feelings between Germany and Turkey, it is likely this 'burly Thuringian' would have been just as smashing a success as Marschall, the original Giant of the Bosphorus. At six feet two inches tall, Wangenheim towered over most Turks – not known for their height – with his 'huge, solid frame, his Gibraltar-like shoulders, erect and impregnable'. And yet in the fevered atmosphere of 1912–14, Wangenheim's imposing physical presence was not exactly reassuring to Turks concerned that their empire was being carved up with the connivance of the European powers. A man of remarkable energy who also suffered periodic bouts of nervous tension, Wangenheim was not dissimilar in spirit to the erratic Emperor he served – with whom he was also personally close (the Ambassador had often been invited to Kaiser Wilhelm's summer villa on Corfu).[10] Prone, like his beloved Emperor, to gusts of enthusiasm and periodic plunges into depression, Wangenheim was peculiarly ill-suited to the profession of diplomacy, and particularly to such a sensitive post as Constantinople.

Contrary to the suspicion in Entente circles that Wangenheim enjoyed favoured access at the Porte, the German Ambassador was mistrusted even by Enver, the biggest Germanophile in the government. Nor did Wangenheim get on well with his own nominal subordinates. Hans Humann, the German naval attaché, intrigued furiously against Wangenheim and accused him, at one point, of 'professional incompetence'.[11] Liman von Sanders, commander of the forty-strong German military mission sent to Constantinople in 1913, despised Wangenheim from the outset – for the understandable reason that the Ambassador had refused even to meet him at Sirkeci station when he arrived. When the Sultan gave Liman command of the Ottoman First Army Corps on 4 December 1913, this put a German national in nominal charge of both Constantinople (and its Embassies) and the Straits defences. That Russia would vigorously protest at this appointment was not surprising, considering the strategic importance of the Straits for St Petersburg. But it is curious that Sazonov blamed Wangenheim for the notorious Liman von Sanders affair, despite the fact that the latter had not even welcomed the German commander to town. In January Wangenheim personally arranged the compromise which saw Liman promoted to General, a rank which rendered him 'overqualified' for the command of a simple army corps – he would now be Inspector-General of the Ottoman First Army, deprived of operational command.[12]

Just as the British shot themselves in the foot through their hostility to Djavid Bey, the greatest Anglophile in the Ottoman Cabinet, the

Russian Foreign Ministry persisted in demanding Wangenheim's dismissal, failing to realize that he was friendlier to their aspirations than either Humann or Liman.* Like Pallavicini, Wangenheim was convinced the Russians were destined to control Constantinople: in his view Germany should concede the Straits in exchange for Russian recognition of German primacy in Asiatic Turkey. Wangenheim's poor relations with Enver also worked right into the Russians' hands. Curiously, the 'Germanophile' Ottoman War Minister did not get on with General Liman either, whether out of personal antipathy or resentment of the German's presumed influence over the Turkish rank and file soldiery (by contrast, Enver had much better relations with Humann, a childhood friend whose naval brief also meant he was not a rival for the army's loyalty). Weakening Wangenheim further was the Kaiser's vocal support for the Greek cause in Albania, which the German Ambassador did his best to counter at the Porte – only to be personally rebuked for his meddling by Kaiser Wilhelm at a summit on Corfu. On the eve of war, Wangenheim was dangerously isolated in Constantinople, mistrusted by all sides. Seeing the German Ambassador shortly after his return from Corfu in June 1914, Pallavicini thought him a broken man.[13]

As the diplomatic fallout from the assassination in Sarajevo reached the Porte in July, it appeared that the Eastern Question had been turned on its head. Russia was now sponsoring the restoration of Ottoman sovereignty over its lost provinces, while Germany was recast as the covetous imperial villain. France, like Russia, had returned to favour. Djemal Bey, the CUP Naval Minister, travelled to Paris in July 1914 to lobby France for the return of Rhodes and other Aegean islands lost to Italy in the 1911–12 war.[14] Had the British Embassy not remained under the spell of Fitzmaurice, London could almost certainly have won broad concessions from the Porte in exchange for even a conditional guarantee of Ottoman territory. So desperate were the Turks for an alliance on the eve of the First World War that they approached *all* the powers, only to be rejected by each one in turn.[15]

---

* The Russians may have been misinformed on this score by Friedrich Pourtàles, the German Ambassador in St Petersburg, who fervently disliked Wangenheim and tried to get him sacked from his post.

It was like a diplomatic game of musical chairs, except that instead of sitting down at the Turkish table every time the music stopped, the powers each tried to remain standing idly by for as long as possible. Even the Germans, who had every reason to try to bring Turkey into the coming war to divert Russian and British strength, continued to baulk. Wangenheim rejected Enver's proposal of an Ottoman-German alliance outright on 22 July 1914. Fatefully, Kaiser Wilhelm, suddenly remembering his enthusiasm for Islam and its possible importance in a global war with Britain, overruled his beleaguered Ambassador two days later, ordering Wangenheim to re-open alliance talks. A Turkish draft of an alliance treaty was duly sent to Berlin on 28 July, only for the Germans to hesitate again, for the understandable reason that they already faced a two-front war and taking on further strategic obligations seemed foolish. On 31 July, the day before Germany declared war on Russia, Chancellor Bethmann Hollweg wired Wangenheim from Berlin that the latter was authorized to sign the Ottoman alliance treaty only if 'Turkey can or will undertake some action against Russia worthy of the name'.[16]

There now ensued an extraordinary episode, first related by David Fromkin. Drawing on the work of Ulrich Trumpener in the German diplomatic archives, and his own cross-checking in the British Public Record Office, Fromkin proposes that Enver Pasha played a clever trick on Wangenheim. If the consequences for the subsequent history of Germany, Russia and the Middle East were not so colossal, the story could easily be played as farce. It seems that Enver knew as early as 1 August 1914 – the day the world war began – that Winston Churchill had detained in port two state-of-the-art dreadnought-class battleships built in British yards for the Ottoman navy (the *Reshadieh*, completed in 1913, and the even more powerful *Sultan Osman I*, just being finished), with the aim of commandeering them for the British navy. Probably informed of the matter by the Ottoman Ambassador to London, who called on Whitehall to protest at the seizure after British crews boarded the ships on 31 July, Enver discussed Churchill's action in the Ottoman Cabinet on 1 August 1914. On the very same day, Enver met with Wangenheim and promised to meet his condition of 'taking action against Russia' by offering 'to turn over to Germany the most powerful warship in the world: the *Sultan Osman*'. Oblivious to the fact that this dreadnought, seized by Britain, no longer belonged to Turkey, Wangenheim agreed to Enver's proposed bargain. In a historic decision, he then affixed his signature on 2 August 1914 to a treaty in which 'Germany obligates itself, by force of arms if need be, to defend Ottoman territory in case it should be threatened'.[17]

Wangenheim had not done his homework. Not only was he probably tricked by Enver into providing the unconditional territorial guarantee which had been the holy grail of Ottoman diplomacy for decades, it seems he may not have read the treaty's fine print regarding Turkey's own obligations towards Germany. In exchange for guaranteeing Ottoman borders 'by force of [German] arms', Wangenheim seems to have thought he had won a pledge from the Porte to enter the war against Russia – to, in Bethmann Hollweg's words, 'undertake some action against Russia worthy of the name'. And yet the draft treaty had been ingeniously worded by its Turkish authors so that the Ottoman Empire would declare war only if Berlin had itself gone to war according to the terms of her own alliance with Austria. Since Germany had proactively declared war on Russia on 1 August, several days before the Austrians had done the same, the treaty of 2 August did not, strictly speaking, oblige the Turks to fight.[18]

It was a brilliant victory for Turkish diplomacy, if a devious one. It was also a brilliant victory for Enver. The young Ottoman War Minister had been turning heads for years in his meteoric rise to prominence in Turkish politics. It was Enver who directed the palace coup of January 1913, which saw the CUP take over the Cabinet directly for the first time. It was Enver, too, who had commanded the Ottoman army which reconquered Adrianople in July 1913, a city of more than strategic significance – it had been the Ottoman capital at the time of the conquest of Constantinople in 1453. Thus draped in the glory of a *ghazi* warrior for Islam, Enver was named War Minister on 4 January 1914 – at the age of thirty-two. There was nothing subtle about Enver's subsequent ascension to the centre of Turkish politics that summer: after marrying the Sultan's niece, he moved into a pasha's palace and travelled about the capital 'accompanied by four or five general officers and aides-de-camp'.[19] Just in case anyone missed the point about Enver's opinion of himself, the young pasha put portraits of Napoleon and Frederick the Great on the wall above his desk.[20] Conspicuously, he wore his elegantly waxed moustache in the style of Kaiser Wilhelm II (which, recalled one lady of Pera society, 'aroused no little amusement among the European colony').[21]

Enver's pretensions of power in pre-war Constantinople were easy to mock, but when the War Minister rode to the eye of the diplomatic storm of summer 1914, few were laughing anymore. The German alliance treaty of 2 August, to be sure, remained a secret to the Entente, but inside the Ottoman Cabinet Enver's triumph was complete. Love him or hate him, the man had just dramatically ended Turkey's isolation. If the Porte did enter the conflict, Enver's power, as War Minister, would be almost limitless. If Turkey stayed out, Enver had still won a guarantee of Ottoman territorial integrity from the country believed to have the world's most powerful army – without giving up a thing.

Buttressing Enver's growing power still more was the dramatic arrival of two German warships in the Sea of Marmara on 11 August 1914. The saga of the *Goeben* and *Breslau*, commanded by German Admiral Wilhelm Souchon, has been well-told before, most famously in Barbara Tuchman's 1962 bestseller, *The Guns of August*. Tuchman, the granddaughter of US Ambassador Henry Morgenthau, actually witnessed the first German-British naval clash of the war from an Italian passenger steamer en route from Venice to Constantinople to visit her grandfather, when the *Gloucester* engaged the German warships off the Greek coast on 7 August 1914. All three ships fired, although 'no hits were scored by anyone'. Just six years old, Tuchman was invited to recount this exciting tale to Wangenheim at the American Embassy. Wangenheim, Tuchman recalled, subjected her 'to a most minute, though very polite, cross-examination'.[22] The German Ambassador had ample cause for concern: the *Goeben* and *Breslau* had narrowly escaped British Mediterranean patrols on three occasions before evading the *Gloucester*'s guns, and had now gone silent somewhere near the Peloponnese, with the British navy giving chase. Souchon was less than two days' steaming from the Straits, where Turkish shore guns guarded entry. Would he be allowed to proceed?

The Porte now faced a fateful decision. If the Ottoman government denied entry to the *Goeben* and *Breslau*, it risked alienating the German government with whom Enver had just signed a far-reaching (though secret) alliance treaty. If, on the other hand, the Dardanelles were opened, Turkey would be violating the laws of neutrality, thus risking war with the Entente powers. It was an agonizing dilemma, in which either choice must necessarily antagonize one side or the other in the European war. It was also, however, an opportunity. If Turkey did not allow the *Goeben* and *Breslau* through the Straits, they would, sooner or later, be blown out of the water by the British fleet. This meant the Turks could name a price for passage. The belligerent Enver, keen to get Turkey into the war, was willing to let the German warships in for free, but fortunately for Ottoman diplomacy he was overruled by the Grand Vizier. Said Halim's asking price was steep: Germany must accept the abolition, in perpetuity, of all the Capitulations which still granted exceptional legal status to Europeans in the Ottoman Empire; she must obtain fair terms for Turkey if Bulgaria or Romania entered the war; she must promise to return former Ottoman islands to Turkey if Greece joined the Entente powers and Germany won; she must promise to adjust Ottoman borders in Anatolia eastwards so as to 'place Turkey into direct contact with the Muslims of Russia'; and last, Berlin must 'see to it that Turkey receives an appropriate war indemnity'. Although predictably offended by the onerous price Germany was being asked to pay to, in effect, turn over two powerful warships to the Ottoman Empire, Wangenheim realized he and Admiral Souchon had no choice. He signed the deal late in the afternoon on 6 August 1914.[23]

In a classic one-two punch, the Grand Vizier had thus completed the job Enver had begun of harnessing the might of imperial Germany to the unconditional support of Turkish interests. What was still more amazing was that Enver and the Grand Vizier had the gall to force Souchon to wait for four more days after agreeing to this deal with Wangenheim before finally wiring permission to enter the Straits. Souchon's boilers had been leaking steam for days, and he was running his ships hard. On 8 and 9 August, unaware that a deal had already been signed at the Porte to approve his entry into the Straits, Souchon holed up in radio silence on Denusa, a small island in the Aegean. While the *Goeben* and *Breslau* took on coal at a furious pace, 'a lookout post was erected on a hilltop to keep watch for the British'. Souchon was unable to use his wireless to communicate with the German Embassy in Constantinople, because doing so would have betrayed his location to the Entente powers. In the drama which followed, the importance of Souchon's own irascible personality and iron will should not be underestimated.

Because of political complications at the Porte, his original orders to reach Constantinople had actually been rescinded by the German Admiralty on 5 August, although Souchon had been left free to determine his own course. As the stubborn commander later recounted, he chose, entirely of his own volition, to make a risky dash through the British screen to Constantinople in order 'to force the Turks, even against their will, to spread the war to the Black Sea against their ancient enemy, Russia'. Now kicking his heels in the Aegean islands, awaiting permission to enter the Dardanelles, Souchon grew impatient with Turkish prevarication and decided to force the issue. On 8 August he dispatched a German support ship, the *Commander*, to Smyrna (today's Izmir) to wire Captain Humann, the German naval attaché, with instructions to tell the Turks that he needed to steam through the Straits immediately on grounds of 'military necessity', and would do so 'without formal approval if necessary'. Continuing his radio silence, Souchon had no way of knowing whether or not his message had gone through until the *Commander* wired him with the Turks' answer. All through the day on 9 August, Souchon awaited news, but none came. Just before dawn on 10 August, he intercepted the wireless signals of the British squadron as it entered the Aegean in hot pursuit. It was now or never. With almost melodramatic timing, just minutes later the *Commander* wired Souchon that permission to enter the Straits had been granted by the Porte.[24]

From both the Ottoman and the German perspective, the fortuitous arrival of the German ships was like manna from heaven. Not only did effective possession of the *Goeben* and *Breslau* give the Porte a serious bargaining chip to use with both sides in the war, it also offered Germany the prospect of 'replacing' the two dreadnoughts commandeered by Churchill.* As Tuchman writes with only slight exaggeration, 'the sudden appearance of the two German warships, as

---

* In operational terms, only the *Goeben* can really be said to have 'replaced' one of the British dreadnoughts: the *Breslau* was a light cruiser about one-fourth its weight. Nevertheless, in propaganda terms, the appearance of two German ships to right the wrong of two ships 'stolen' by Britain was a potent coup for the Central Powers.

if sent by a genie to take the place of the two of which they had been robbed, put the populace in transports of delight and invested the Germans with a halo of popularity'. The British, by contrast, were now in a foul stench in Constantinople, as the arrival of the *Goeben* and *Breslau* only reminded Turks of the outrage they had felt a week earlier on learning on 3 August that London had 'stolen' the *Sultan Osman I* and the *Reshadieh*, both of which, it was shouted far and wide, had been fully paid for.*[25] The British seizure of the latter ship had been particularly galling, in that funds for the *Reshadieh* had been raised by public subscription, such that 'millions of Moslem contributors are personally interested in her fate'.[26] And now here were two warships, which had appeared as if by magic to right the wrong committed by perfidious Albion.

Still, exciting as Souchon's arrival was, it also put Turkey in a delicate position. Even Enver had hesitated at the last moment before allowing the *Goeben* and *Breslau* in, knowing that by thus violating the laws of neutrality he might provoke the Entente powers into declaring war. Although happy to have the ships in hand, the Porte would have preferred Souchon to delay his arrival for as long as possible – the Grand Vizier was at the time negotiating terms with Bulgaria over possible entry into the war, even while keeping the Romanian Ambassador on ice over a proposed neutrality pact. Born in Cairo in 1865, Prince Said Halim Pasha, the grandson of the great Muhammad Ali, was a clever old fox of diplomacy. He was not ecstatic over Souchon's 'premature' arrival, which threatened to force the issue of belligerence before terms had been agreed with Sofia. If Britain, France or Russia declared war on Turkey over the violation of neutrality entailed in the entry of German warships into the Straits, Said Halim complained to Wangenheim on the evening of 10 August, the Bulgarians might 'exploit engagement elsewhere and march on Constantinople' – as they had in both 1912 and 1913.

To pre-empt a declaration of war by the Entente powers, the Grand Vizier proposed that ownership of the German vessels be transferred

---

* This was not in fact true, at least of the *Reshadieh*. On this ship the Porte still owed two years' worth of quarterly payments of £846,400, the last falling due on 14 June 1916.

to Turkey by a 'fictitious sale'. Before even receiving a reply from Berlin, on 11 August 1914 'the Porte unilaterally issued a public declaration that it had "bought" the two German cruisers for "eighty million Marks"' – although no money changed hands. The *Goeben* and *Breslau* were renamed the *Yavuz Sultan Selim* and the *Midilli*, and the (still German) crew members put on Turkish fezzes and ran up the Ottoman colours.[27] The charade about the 'sale' could not have fooled any of the Entente Ambassadors: the British were even told, point blank, that the purchase of the German ships had been conceived in direct retaliation for London's 'detention of the *Sultan Osman*'.[28] Unless they wanted Turkey to immediately enter the war on the side of the Central Powers, however, which would immensely complicate Russia's ongoing mobilization on the eastern European front, there was little the Entente Ambassadors could do but send notes of protest. Nor could the Germans dispute the phoney 'purchase' of their ships without forfeiting their favoured position.

Yet again, Ottoman diplomacy had cornered the Germans. In just ten days, the Porte had won from Berlin an unconditional guarantee of Ottoman borders, agreement to the abolition of all remaining Capitulations, promises to help Turkey regain Balkan and Anatolian lands, as well as Aegean islands, lost in wars stretching back to the 1870s, promises of financial compensation following the conclusion of the war, and one powerful, state-of-the-art warship – the *Goeben* was a dreadnought mounting ten 11-inch guns, capable of making 26 knots – which threatened to make obsolete Russia's entire Black Sea Fleet. In exchange for all this, the Porte had given the Germans vague assurances that Turkey might, just possibly, consider declaring war on Russia.

The Grand Vizier's clever coup illustrated the powerful leverage of neutrality. So long as Turkey refused to be embroiled in the war, she could keep the powers guessing as to her intentions, and name a price for either coming in or staying out. Ideally, the threat of Ottoman intervention would seem real enough to satisfy the Germans and scare the Entente, while not quite tipping over into actual hostilities. To the wily old Prince Said Halim Pasha, Enver was a useful battering ram, whose promises to Wangenheim of imminent intervention, made more plausible by his creation of enthusiastic 'jihad' committees (see chapter 4 above), kept the ball of belligerence in the air. The Grand Vizier and the less belligerent members of the Cabinet could then act as the voice of reason, reassuring the Entente powers that Turkey had no intention of actually fighting. Djavid Bey, the Finance Minister, visited all three Entente summer residences in Therapia in August 1914 to discuss possible terms for securing Turkish neutrality. Djemal Bey, the Naval Minister who had recently made the rounds in Paris, thoroughly charmed British Ambassador Louis Mallet at Therapia on 20 August, even while agreeing on nothing in particular.[29]

These pro-Entente overtures may or may not have been sincere. Djavid Bey, in particular, was keen on reducing Enver's influence in the Cabinet, and thought he might be able to do so if he could get a solid guarantee of Ottoman territorial integrity from the Entente powers, along with their agreement to the abolition of the Capitulations.[30] Theoretically, the Grand Vizier's deal with Wangenheim which had allowed the *Goeben* and *Breslau* to enter the Straits meant that the Central Powers (or at least Germany) had already accepted the abolition of the Capitulations. Still, why not demand acceptance of the same from the Entente powers as well? The longer Djemal, Djavid and the Grand Vizier could keep the powers guessing as to the Porte's real intentions, the higher the asking price of neutrality – or belligerence – could go.

In this bidding war, the Entente powers faced an uphill struggle. As Djavid told Russian Ambassador Girs point-blank on 19 August 1914, to secure neutrality the Entente would have to offer more than the Germans were offering.[31] Enver himself did approach the Russians around the same time, offering a cynical horse-trade in which Turkey would pull back its troops from the Caucasus, allowing Russia to reinforce the western front, in exchange for a Russian territorial guarantee.[32] But this was almost certainly a trial balloon designed to tease out Russian intentions, which predictably led nowhere. The level of cynicism involved on the Entente side was perhaps best expressed by Gaston Doumergue, the recently deposed French premier, who promised Russian Ambassador Izvolsky on 11 August 1914, as the French and Russians were trying to coordinate a response to the arrival of the *Goeben* and *Breslau*, that any Entente territorial guarantee to Turkey 'need not disturb [Russia's claim] on the Straits at the end of the war'.[33] The British, for their part, helpfully informed

Djavid that they 'were prepared, in the event of our beating the Germans, to hand over German railway concessions to Turkey'.[34] The Turks, to their great credit, saw right through these cynical pledges, noting that the Entente powers were prepared to compensate the Ottoman Empire only at *Germany*'s expense. The Capitulations, by contrast, which affected Entente interests directly, remained non-negotiable for France, Britain and Russia.

As it turned out, the Porte did not even need the powers' approval to abolish the Capitulations. With the Entente Embassies tripping over each other to offer bribes to keep Turkey out, and the Germans stamping their feet in frustration over Turkey's refusal to go in – Liman von Sanders was 'talking of challenging both Enver and Djemal to duels' – the desperation of both sides was growing more obvious by the day.[35] In a gesture of defiance which must have been richly satisfying after a century of humiliation at the hands of the European powers, the Porte unilaterally abrogated all remaining Capitulations in the Ottoman Empire on 8 September 1914. As if intentionally to outrage the Embassies, the government shut down foreign post offices and confiscated diplomatic correspondence, discovering much compromising material in French Embassy bags.[36] So accustomed had the European powers become to their privileged legal position in Turkey that all five belligerents (plus Italy) set aside their differences to issue an extraordinary joint communiqué condemning the Porte's action. But the gesture was toothless, and everyone knew it. None of the powers was willing to risk a rupture in relations while the Ottoman government was still deciding whether or not to enter the war.[37]

Yet again the Turks had run rings around the European Embassies which had dominated Ottoman affairs for so long. Accepting an end to the Capitulations would have been the trump card for either side in the war for the Porte, but it was now too late for that: the Turks had played the trump themselves, allowing neither coalition to win. By protesting at the fait accompli, even the Germans had lost, by exposing that Wangenheim's earlier acceptance of the Grand Vizier's terms had been hollow. But the Germans still had Enver, Liman's military mission and the *Goeben* and *Breslau* to influence the Porte. Once the Capitulations were off the table, the Entente powers had no other cards to play.

As August gave way to September, the German position began to look stronger. In part this was because of the great victory at Tannenberg, which, as we saw above, produced a wave of enthusiasm in Constantinople for the Kaiser's holy war idea, if only to forestall the possibility the conflict might be over before Turkey had entered it. But the encroachment of German influence was not just a matter of perception. Quietly, Berlin had been sending arms, ammunition, wireless installations, medicine and even gold to Constantinople by way of the Orient Express. In the last week of August, a special train carrying no less than 700 German sailors and coastal defence specialists was observed passing through Bucharest and Sofia en route for Sirkeci station – and possibly the batteries guarding entrance to the Dardanelles. Liman's original mission of forty had mushroomed in size: there were now nearly 2,000 German military advisers in Turkey. The Porte denied that it had requested German crews to overhaul the Straits defences, but the Entente powers, predictably, were not convinced. Ominously, British Ambassador Louis Mallet reported rumours on 29 August 1914 that German civilians in the capital had begun 'sending away their wives', preparatory to volunteering for the Ottoman army. On 10 September, Mallet reported that 'all German reservists who have not been able to leave Turkish Empire have been instructed to report for enrollment with Turkish troops.' Adding to Mallet's anxiety were mushrooming reports from Alexandretta (Iskenderun), Aleppo and Damascus of ambitious Turkish military preparations. Although the British did not yet know about the military mission of Kress and Prüfer, who left Constantinople for Damascus on 20 September, they were aware that the Ottoman Fourth Army was mustering horses, carriages and – most tellingly – camels, which suggested that an assault on the Suez Canal across the Sinai desert was in the works.[38]

The British would have been more frightened still had they known that Enver and Souchon, the German Admiral who commanded the *Goeben* and *Breslau*, had begun intriguing together to provoke the Russians into declaring war. With the Dardanelles forts reinforced by the new German garrison, Enver felt confident enough to risk war with Russia – which he knew would bring in the British navy. On 14 September, Enver gave Souchon authorization to enter the Black Sea and engage the Russian fleet. The Grand Vizier, however, intervened before Souchon had his chance, forcing the War Minister to rescind his own orders.[39] The Entente powers had dodged a bullet.

Or had they? One of the enduring mysteries of late 1914 is the real attitude of the Entente powers towards the prospect of Ottoman intervention. Girs, Russia's Ambassador to the Porte, had suggested to Sazonov as early as 27 July 1914 that the Bosnian crisis might allow Russia to 'take the initiative herself for war [with Turkey]'.[40] Coming from a man who had been entrusted with command of the Black Sea Fleet, these were not idle words. On 27 August, Girs reported to St Petersburg in detail on Turkish preparations for a naval sortie into the Black Sea. Upon hearing this news, one of the most influential members of the Council of Ministers in Petersburg, A.V. Krivoshein, told British Ambassador Buchanan that 'he personally would be glad if the Turks declared war on Russia, as then the Turkish question would be finally settled'.[41] By October, Girs was talking openly about 'settling accounts' with the Turks.[42]

On the British side, Churchill, at least, was itching for a fight. On 17 August, Prime Minister Asquith noted that Churchill was 'in his most bellicose mood all for sending a torpedo flotilla thro' the Dardanelles'.[43] But Churchill was not in a strong position in the Cabinet: many blamed him for provoking Turkey by seizing her dreadnoughts. Churchill looked even worse after he authorized the British navy on 25 September to search Turkish vessels exiting the Straits, provoking the Porte to retaliate by sealing off the Straits and laying mines two days later. The closure of the Dardanelles on 27 September 1914 could easily have been construed as an act of war, had Churchill's more cautious colleagues not been so keen to preserve Ottoman neutrality.[44]

Inconveniently for the Central Powers, however, Turkey had still not declared war. It is easy to see why the Germans were so frustrated with their Ottoman clients, to whom they had offered everything but the kitchen sink to bring about the Porte's intervention. Souchon, bottled up in the Bosphorus, did not have the seniority to be able to stage proper manoeuvres. The chain of command remained murky: was he a German officer or an Ottoman one? To soothe Souchon's nerves, on 23 September the Porte appointed him a Vice-Admiral in the Ottoman navy, which placed him directly below Djemal Bey, Minister of the

Navy, assuring that no Turkish officer would be able to countermand Souchon's orders. The upshot was that Souchon was now free to stage manoeuvres in the Black Sea. Meanwhile, on the same day Souchon received his new brief, a crisis involving Liman von Sanders had come to a head. For some time Liman had been threatening to leave Constantinople and take his key advisers with him. Although he had given up on fighting a duel with Enver (who had proven himself willing to bring Turkey into the war), Liman was fed up with everyone else in the Ottoman Cabinet. Had the leaders of the German military mission left at this crucial juncture, it would have altered all calculations at the Porte, strengthening the hand of Djavid and the Grand Vizier in their struggle against Enver to keep Turkey out of the war. Yet again, at the critical moment, it was Kaiser Wilhelm II himself who intervened, reprimanding Liman on 24 September and ordering him to stay in Constantinople.[45]

The Austrians, meanwhile, were even more fed up than the Germans over Turkish prevarication. Vienna's frustration was largely a reflection of powerlessness: by October 1914 the Habsburg armies were not only retreating to Cracow and the Carpathians in the face of a general Russian advance, they had failed to subdue even tiny Serbia, over whose complicity in Archduke Franz Ferdinand's assassination the war was ostensibly being fought. Whereas Berlin wanted the Porte to enter the war for geopolitical reasons to do with a global anti-British jihad, Vienna wanted the Turks to divert Russian strength on grounds of urgent military necessity, ideally through an amphibious Turkish landing which could threaten the Russian position in Galicia. The Kaiser's jihad idea was potentially dangerous for the Austrians, who had their own Muslim subjects in Bosnia, and who were terrified that Italy might join the Entente if her colonial interests in Libya were threatened by an Islamic uprising. The Austrian Ambassador Pallavicini was thus in a very delicate position, anxious for Souchon to strike against Russia, even while trying to undermine the Ottoman jihad which was the Germans' primary goal in launching such an attack.[46]

With both the Germans and Austrians decided on unleashing Souchon's warships against Russia, the countdown to war had now begun. All that remained to be determined were the terms of entry. Although Enver had by no means won over the Ottoman Cabinet – the Grand Vizier was still meeting regularly with the Entente Ambassadors to reassure them the Porte was still neutral – this would not matter if Petrograd (as the Germanic-sounding St Petersburg was renamed on 31 August) could be provoked into declaring war. This had been Enver's idea when he gave Souchon authorization to engage the Russian fleet on 14 September, only to be overruled by the Grand Vizier. Although he was still reluctant to provoke an open break with Said Halim, Enver's position was growing stronger by the day. On 8 October, the War Minister pointedly told Wangenheim to disregard the Grand Vizier's 'conciliatory messages towards the Entente', on the grounds that Said Halim was no longer 'in charge of the situation'.[47] Each shipment of German war *matériel* arriving in Constantinople was openly publicized so as to weaken the peace party. Since the end of September, Mallet reported to London on 17 October 1914, 'six thousand nine hundred cases of Mauser ammunition, 540 cases of Mauser rifles, [and] 13 trucks of war material' had arrived from Germany.* A submarine and two warplanes were soon expected, along with two shipments of German gold, each of one million Turkish pounds (together equivalent to about one billion dollars today).[48] No matter how many times Said Halim reassured the Entente Ambassadors that he could keep Turkey out of the war, the visible evidence of approaching belligerence was hard to ignore.

The Porte was the scene of great political drama in October, as Enver conspired against the Grand Vizier to stack the decks for war. Since the publication of Djemal's memoirs in 1921, the world has known of a secret meeting held on 11 October 1914, when Enver, Talaat and Djemal, along with Halil Bey, President of the Chamber of Deputies, agreed on a pro-intervention policy, whether or not they

---

* Because the Serbian section of the main European railway to Constantinople was cut off, the Germans had to improvise supply routes. At this time (autumn 1914) arms were still being sent by barge along the Danube to Rustchuk in Bulgaria, whence they were loaded onto trains (this is the route dramatized in *Greenmantle*). Before long, however, Serbian shelling had rendered this route too risky. There was a longer, partly interrupted rail link through neutral (until 1916) Romania, but Prime Minister Ion Bratianu had closed Romanian railways – in theory – to arms shipments (although he proved not unresponsive to large German bribes). Bulgaria, too, put up obstacles, although in the end Sofia mostly went along (not without selling information to the Russians on what the Germans were shipping to the Porte).

could win over Said Halim.[49]* The price of intervention would be the two million pounds Berlin had already agreed to send – not until the gold was physically present would the Turks risk unleashing Souchon – along with a five million pound loan to be disbursed as soon as Turkey entered the war, with a 'guaranteed subsidy' of 500,000 pounds per month for the Turkish war effort.[50] Further, the Germans promised to help the Austrians knock Serbia out of the war, so a direct rail link could be established to send war supplies to the Porte.[51] From the Turkish operational side, Enver agreed on 25 October 1914, in consultation with Wangenheim and Pallavicini, to unleash Souchon against the Russian Black Sea Fleet, specifically at Odessa, as desired by the Austrians; to mount operations against the Russians in the Caucasus and the British in Egypt; and not least, to the 'proclamation of [Islamic] holy war against all Europeans with the exceptions of Austrians, Hungarians, and Germans'.[52]

While it is true that Enver had formal approval from neither the Grand Vizier nor the Ottoman Cabinet for this action plan, he may even have relished the chance to serve up a fait accompli. As the Maréchal de Saxe once wrote, 'the human heart is the starting point of all matters pertaining to war'.[53] The Ottoman War Minister – and, contrary to common belief, Naval Minister Djemal as well – had already decided on war, with or without full Cabinet support, and war is what Turkey now got.† On 27 October 1914 – six days after the second shipment of German gold had arrived – the Ottoman fleet, commanded by Admiral Souchon, steamed out of the Bosphorus into the Black Sea. Enver had provided Souchon with open-ended orders to engage the Russian fleet if a 'suitable opportunity' came up.[54] (As Souchon mischievously interpreted Enver's orders, he 'would not, so to speak, prevent the cannons from discharging by themselves' if, by some chance, he came across the Russian fleet.)[55] Although the orders were left deliberately vague so that waverers in the Ottoman Cabinet might later have some wiggle room to claim that Souchon had exceeded

---

* The Russians, for their part, knew of this meeting the day after it happened.
† As Djemal wrote on 2 November 1914, 'I believe that it is the Turks' ultimate duty either to live like an honourable nation or to exit the stage of history gloriously.' Remarkably, the Russians knew of Djemal's defection to the war camp a week before the historic 11 October Cabinet meeting, when Djemal and Enver teamed up.

them, in fact Enver, Djemal and Souchon had secretly agreed on a broad list of Russian shore targets, including not only naval batteries but also petroleum and grain depots.[56] In the event, Enver and Djemal left operational decisions entirely in the German's hands, sending 'no radio instructions at all' to the fleet after it entered the Black Sea.[57] Souchon was happy to oblige, mining the approaches to the Bosphorus, sinking a Russian mine-layer, and then shelling the Russian ports of Odessa, Novorossiysk and Feodosia with perfect impunity. At Odessa, Souchon's torpedoes scored direct hits on five Russian warships, sinking the *Donetz* and heavily damaging another, while setting five oil tanks on fire. At Novorossiysk, Souchon's ships sank fourteen grain ships and blew up fifty petroleum tanks.[58]

Not surprisingly, Souchon's offensive, carried out under the Turkish flag without even a hint of Russian provocation, produced an Ottoman Cabinet crisis. The Grand Vizier and Finance Minister Djavid were particularly incensed. But their objections were largely beside the point. Enver even agreed to Said Halim's request to send a note of apology on 1 November 1914 to the Russian government, which was roughly akin to, say, a Japanese apology for the sneak attack on Pearl Harbor in 1941 and about as likely to be accepted.*[59] By inserting a short passage which, absurdly, blamed the Russians for provoking Souchon's multi-pronged naval assault, Enver ensured that Russia would take the bait. Although Sazonov stated himself willing to accept even this obnoxious quasi-apology, provided the Porte immediately expelled all German military personnel from the Ottoman Empire, he must have known this was impossible. On 2 November 1914, Petrograd officially declared war on the Porte, setting in motion the events which would eventually destroy both the Romanov and Ottoman Empires.[60]

---

*There was one major difference between the two world-historical sneak attacks, however. Despite a popular conspiracy theory, there is no documentary evidence that the US government had credible prior warning of Pearl Harbor. The Russians, by contrast, were not surprised in the least by Souchon's offensive, although they still did a rather poor job of defending against it. So well-informed was Girs – he not only had paid informants attending Ottoman Cabinet meetings, but was regularly intercepting Pallavicini's telegrams to Vienna – that the Russian Black Sea naval command was warned on 20 October to expect Souchon's naval assault imminently, following the arrival of the second shipment of German gold. The Russians, to be sure, did not know exactly where or when Souchon would strike – but they did know he was coming.

Further south, there was an important coda to the drama in the Black Sea. While the naval offensive cooked up by Enver and Souchon has understandably received the most attention, the Ottoman army played no small part in the fateful plunge into war. In *A Peace to End All Peace*, David Fromkin expresses surprise that Britain casually slid into undeclared hostilities with the Porte, boarding Turkish ships in the Aegean on 29 October, thus furnishing Enver's faction with yet another pretext for war.[61] But joint German-Ottoman army preparations for assaulting the Suez Canal were well advanced long before Souchon's Black Sea sortie. Robert Mors, the saboteur Curt Prüfer had sent to Egypt to prepare a jihadi uprising to coincide with the Suez offensive, had been captured by the British in mid-October, and promptly spilt the beans. Advised by Mors where to look, Cairo dispatched agents who observed an armed column of Bedouins crossing twenty miles inside the Egyptian frontier on 28 October 1914 – the day Souchon began shelling Odessa.[62] Mallet launched an official protest, only to be told, rather cynically, that the Ottoman Empire did not recognize a border with Egypt.[63] Although the public declaration would have to await the announcement of hostilities, in the field the jihad had already begun. The Kaiser would have his holy war after all.

6

The First Global Jihad: Death to Infidels Everywhere! (Unless they be Germans, Austrians, Hungarians, Americans or – possibly – Italians)

The killing of the infidels who rule over the Islamic lands has become a sacred duty, whether it be secretly or openly, as the great Koran declares in its word: 'Take them and kill them whenever you come across them'.

Translation of German-produced Arabic jihad pamphlet,
c. winter 1914–15, from US State Department archives[1]

Perched atop the fourth hill of the ancient Roman city, the Fatih Sultan Mehmed Mosque towers over the Istanbul skyline as one crosses the Galata bridge from Pera. Although not as beautiful as the Blue Mosque preferred by tourists, nor as holy for Muslims as the older Eyup Mosque further up the Golden Horn, Fatih Camii plays a more important role in the life of the city, anchoring a large complex which once housed a library, sixteen Islamic *medresses*, a hospital and public baths. Although the original structure was damaged in a series of earthquakes, Fatih square has retained its importance as a public gathering place. Constructed on the ruins of the Byzantine Church of the Holy Apostles on the orders of Mehmed II, the Sultan who had captured Constantinople in 1453, Fatih ('the Conqueror') was intended to surpass the Hagia Sofia in grandeur. According to legend, Mehmed cut off the hands of his architect once it was clear that his namesake mosque had failed to attain the height of Justinian's great church. Mehmed's tomb lies menacingly in a mausoleum adjoining Fatih Camii, as if in reproach to succeeding Sultans who failed to live up to the illustrious deeds of the Conqueror.

It was in this mosque rich with historic symbolism that Urgüplü Hayri Bey, the *Şeykh-ul-Islam* of the Ottoman Empire, presented Sultan-Caliph

Mehmed Reshad V with the Sword of the Prophet on 14 November 1914 to sanctify the war against Britain, France and Russia. Coming on the heels of five jihad *fetvas* issued over the preceding week, the ceremony at Fatih Mosque inaugurated the first ever global jihad, in which it would be the duty of Muslims everywhere on earth to wage war on (Entente) infidels.[2]

The Ottoman holy war *fetvas* of 1914 were historic, but not entirely unprecedented. Wars against Russia in the 1770s and 1820s had been declared state 'jihads', as had the war against Greece in 1897 (although not the 1877–8 war with Russia or the recent Balkan wars). Like these earlier declarations, the jihad *fetvas* of 1914 announced that Turkey's war against the Entente was a defensive *farz-ı ayn*, 'an urgent personal obligation incumbent on all Muslims', as distinct from a *farz-ı kifâya*, an offensive jihad in which the participation of some fulfills the duty of all.[3] What distinguished the 1914 jihad *fetvas* was not the terms of the declaration itself but the open-ended selection of targets – including Entente civilians, along with armies – and the pointed exemptions for German and Austro-Hungarian nationals, for which there was no known precedent.[4]

A good deal of this was theologically unsound. According to strict, pre-Ottoman interpretation of Islamic law, jihad was a more or less continuous condition of war between those inside the *Dâr al Islam* and the *Dâr al Harb* not yet converted to Islam, which is to say everyone else. Traditionally, the Caliph, as a kind of 'supreme commander' of Muslims, was duty-bound to carry on this war, or to pause it temporarily so as to gather strength for later battles. The modern Ottoman idea that a special edict of the Sultan-Caliph was needed to sanctify one of Turkey's wars as a 'jihad' was a symptom of the declining power of the Islamic world, as the Porte invoked once formidable powers the Caliphate no longer possessed. It was protesting too much.[5]

The legally problematic nature of the November 1914 jihad declaration is not surprising, when we consider that the impetus behind it came not from Ottoman religious leaders but rather from the German government, which subsidized distribution of the *fetvas* and most of the accompanying commentaries by Muslim jurists.[6] Despite his own holy war promises to Kaiser Wilhelm, in October even Enver had cold feet about issuing a full-on global jihad declaration, for fear the Germans, too, would be ensnared if it were taken literally.[7] The result – a 'proclamation of holy war against all Europeans with the exceptions of Austrians, Hungarians, and Germans' – was something of a mess, neither uncompromising enough for the Germans, nor theologically proper enough to satisfy Muslim clerics.[8] Read literally, moreover, it meant that citizens of neutral countries could be targeted. So, too, could Belgians, who were specifically named in Ottoman jihad decrees, and Serbians.[9] By contrast, US citizens resident in Turkey were specially exempted, along with employees of American missionary colleges.[10]

Pallavicini, Austria's Ambassador, was acutely sensitive to the Pandora's box of problems the Turco-German holy war might open up. Jihadi stirrings in Italy's African colonies could easily propel Rome into the war on the side of the Entente, despite Italy being a nominal ally of the Central Powers. Wangenheim also shared this concern, agreeing privately with Pallavicini that a global jihad, 'aside from the moral standpoint, also for reasons of practicality should not be greatly encouraged'. Moreover, Pallavicini warned, it was a grave mistake to unleash the atavistic passions of Muslims against Christians. Although Ottoman minorities – Armenians, Greeks and Levantine Christians – were not named in the jihad *fetvas*, long-standing precedent suggested that the brunt of Muslim rage would be directed at them, as Enver Pasha himself conceded to his friend Humann, the German naval attaché. Were such massacres to transpire, a great deal of the moral burden of blame must soon 'fall on Germany as the instigator'. This would inevitably create image problems for the Central Powers in neutral countries, making the 'worst possible impression' on public opinion, 'particularly in Italy and America'. On top of all this, any jihad must inevitably target Christians. However selective the list of infidels whom 'all good Muslims are duty bound … to kill as enemies of Islam', most subjects of the Central Powers were themselves Christians. 'We must reckon seriously with the possibility', Pallavicini warned Vienna ominously, that 'the situation will change such that [passions] directed today against Russians, English and French may be brought to bear against Austrians, Hungarians and Germans tomorrow'.[11]

As the (private) dissent of the German and Austrian Ambassadors suggests, the Kaiser's beloved jihad looked considerably different on the ground in Constantinople than it did in Berlin. In a city which had seen so many popular massacres over the centuries, it was not reassuring to even well-protected Embassy personnel when mobs were witnessed marching through the city in early November 'waving large green flags', as 'dervishes howl and wave blood-soaked pieces of cloth'.[12] Seeking to delimit the proper targets of Muslim rage, the Ottoman government organized a public holy war demonstration outside the War Ministry on 14 November, which then proceeded in orderly fashion to the German Embassy. Temporarily overcoming his reservations about the coming jihad, Wangenheim dramatically mounted the Embassy balcony to salute the Sultan-Caliph and his holy war. In a colourful bit of political theatre, Wangenheim was flanked by fourteen Moroccan, Tunisian and Algerian Muslims, several of whom promised (in broken Turkish) to carry the Ottoman jihad to French North Africa. Here was, said the gossips of Pera with a sneer, a *Holy War alla franca*.[13]

The curious *mise-en-scène* at the German Embassy was a typical Oppenheim operation, combining theatrical flair with a bit of hocus-pocus. Ostensibly spontaneous, the appearance of the Francophone Muslims to sanctify the anti-French jihad had actually been planned weeks ago, before Turkey had even entered the war. Karl Emil Schabinger von Schowingen, a German Foreign Office dragoman who had earlier served in Casablanca, Fez and Tangier, was sent by Oppenheim's jihad bureau in October to scour Germany's burgeoning prisoner-of-war camps for captured draftees from France's Muslim colonies. Fearing, understandably, that soldiers only recently having escaped the terrors of the western front may not have been keen on jumping right back into battle (or on committing treason against France), Schabinger did not tell his recruits for what purpose he had chosen them, nor where they were going. Instead, he simply told them that the Kaiser was a great friend of Islam and wanted to reunite them with their Muslim brethren. Once he had assembled fourteen presumably gullible North Africans, Schabinger returned to Berlin to board the train for Constantinople by way of Romania. As if to parody the recent adventures of Niedermayer's Afghan expedition, Schabinger's Muslim POWs were entered in the register as acrobats in a 'travelling circus'.[14]

Schabinger himself seems to have viewed his mission with a healthy dose of cynicism. A true blue-blood, Schabinger insisted on travelling in style, occupying a whole first-class carriage on the Orient Express while his Muslim charges crowded in third. Immediately on arrival in Sirkeci station, Schabinger's fourteen would-be jihadis were taken into custody by the Ottoman police, reappearing again only on the big day at the German Embassy. Schabinger had literally a few minutes to teach his men their lines, which they read with solemn indifference. Following the declaration of the jihad from the Embassy balcony, a kind of holy war train, with Schabinger at its head – carried in a chaise longue – proceeded through the streets of Pera, looting and burning French- and English-owned shops and businesses. Before getting too directly involved in jihadi mischief, Schabinger had his chaise set down in front of his hotel, the Tokatlian. Owned, as the name suggests, by a rich Armenian Christian, the Tokatlian was 'the most beautiful, and expensive, in Constantinople'. With a symbolic flourish, Schabinger's Turkish police escort entered the Armenian hotel and fired a single bullet into the English grandfather clock at the end of the lobby. The German jihad was up and running.[15]

Rumours of impending massacres of Constantinople's huge Christian population were rampant following the Porte's entry into the war. Sirkeci station, gateway to Europe by way of still-neutral Bulgaria, Greece and Romania,* was a 'surging mass of excited and frightened people'. US Ambassador Morgenthau later described the scene as the first wave of refugees tried to depart: 'people were running in all directions, checking baggage, purchasing tickets, arguing with officials, consoling distracted women and frightened children'.[16] Morgenthau was the man of the hour in the European colony of Pera, now staking out a protective position in front of a prominent church or Christian-owned business, now negotiating terms with Turkish officials, now escorting Entente diplomats across the Galata bridge to Sirkeci. The fate of European residents was still up in the

---

* The destination of most of the 'refugee' trains was Dedeagatch, just across the Bulgarian border (now the Greek city of Alexandroupoli). During the world war, Dedeagatch was a thriving hub for diplomats, spies and smugglers serving both sides. From here, the Russians continued on home via Romania, while the British and French generally embarked on Allied ships through Greek ports.

air: would they be allowed safe passage out of the country, or interned en masse as enemy nationals?

Considering that Turkey, like the other belligerents, had legitimate concerns about the fate of its own nationals trapped in Entente countries (and in British Egypt), it was a delicate situation. Morgenthau did all he could to extract promises from Talaat, the Ottoman Interior Minister, and Bedri Bey, the Prefect of Police, that Entente subjects, including Ambassadors and Embassy personnel, would be allowed to leave. Bedri Bey, an ambitious CUP official still keen on advancing in the Ottoman government hierarchy, was reluctant to show weakness. By contrast, Talaat was by now secure enough in his own position to risk a display of moderation. In the first of many clashes to come in Porte policy over the treatment of foreigners and Christians, Talaat overruled Bedri Bey and ordered him to allow diplomatic trains to leave. In the end, Morgenthau himself was forced to intervene at Sirkeci to ensure that Bedri Bey carried out Talaat's own orders, by confirming the identity of departing diplomats and Embassy personnel.

Although most of the diplomatic corps had left safely by mid-November, thousands of Entente nationals remained at risk in the capital. With the Capitulations abolished, they no longer had the protection of Western civil law, and, with their Ambassadors gone, they did not even have diplomatic pressure to fall back on. As Morgenthau wrote with only slight exaggeration, 'there was really nothing between the foreign residents and destruction except the American flag'. To their credit, Ottoman officials like Talaat took pains to mitigate the popular violence unleashed by their own holy war declaration – no thanks to the German army command.*[17] Even Talaat, however, could not prevent Muslims from sacking Aya Stefanos, the Orthodox church built by the Russians in Yeşilköy to commemorate their advance there in 1878.[18] Gradually, the process of expropriating Entente property in Constantinople was streamlined so as to prevent the worst mob excesses. On 18 November, Ottoman police blanketed Pera, taking over

---

* According to Morgenthau, Talaat blamed the holding up of the diplomatic trains on Liman von Sanders, who was 'making a big fuss, saying that we are too easy with the French and English and that we must not let them get away'. While Talaat had every reason to lie, evidence that Germany pushed for harsher treatment of Entente nationals is overwhelming.

'all scholastic institutions and hospitals, religious or laic, English, French, and Russian'. The general procedure was for one policeman to guard the door while the others searched for Entente nationals to deport, and helped themselves to whatever goods were not carried out by the infidels. Those lucky enough to escape with property before their establishments were invaded fled to the US Embassy, which began to resemble a giant refugee camp. Morgenthau and his wife visited as many Entente churches and schools as possible to offer American protection. The presence of Mrs Morgenthau, wrote the French Embassy dragoman, 'has certainly attenuated the brutality of the measures taken against our religious [institutions]'.[19]

Despite these efforts to curtail the violence, it was an ominous beginning for the German jihad. The trouble with even a carefully circumscribed Islamic holy war, as Pallavicini had warned, was that no one knew when or where it would stop. Morgenthau's presence in Constantinople, along with that of CUP leaders like Talaat who worried about neutral opinion, helped ensure that Europeans were afforded some protection from mob attacks, even if many were still deprived of their property. In the provinces, enemy nationals were on their own, with their fate decided largely by the whims of local Ottoman governors – and German officers. Despite Talaat's promise to Morgenthau that 'there would be no concentration camps', no round-ups of enemy aliens, precisely this transpired in Damascus.[20] On 8 November 1914, Djemal, the Naval Minister, sent to replace Zekki Pasha as commander of the Ottoman Fourth Army, announced officially that all English and French subjects would be held as hostages against a prospective British naval attack on Syria's coastline. Just in case the message was lost on the detainees, Djemal promised that he would have 'three English or French' shot for any Muslim killed in a British naval bombardment of the Syrian coastline.[21]

Although Djemal does not seem to have had Talaat's permission for issuing this threat, his policy was wholeheartedly seconded by Colonel Kress von Kressenstein, the German liaison officer charged with organizing the upcoming assault on the Suez Canal. Kress had taken the Kaiser's holy war to heart, working hand in hand with Djemal to sanctify the Turco-German jihad. On 15 November 1914, a holy war procession toured the streets of Damascus carrying 'the flags of Germany and Austria-Hungary alongside the Turkish flag and the green flag of the Prophet'.[22] As if to pre-empt Pallavicini's concerns about any damage which might be done to Germany's reputation through the use of unarmed Entente civilians as human shields, Kress pointedly told the French Consul in Damascus that if, 'as a result of such bombardments [of Syrian ports], enraged Muslims massacre Christians, we decline all responsibility'.[23]

By December, hundreds of English, French and Russian subjects had been interned in Damascus, including consular personnel up to the rank of dragoman and counsellor. The archives and papers of all of the Entente Consulates in Damascus were confiscated, which furnished useful intelligence for the Turco-German war effort, if at the cost of outraging neutral opinion yet again, occasioning a sharp protest from the Americans in particular.[24] Although the rounding up of these unarmed civilians, many of them religious volunteers, teachers, nurses and doctors, was shocking to Western sensibilities, it was within the boundaries of international law: the European powers (followed by the Americans after the US entry into the war) likewise rounded up enemy nationals suspected of posing a security threat because of their presumed sympathy with hostile belligerents. The British did the same with Germans resident in Cairo.[25]

It was quite another thing, however, to use civilian prisoners as human shields and hostages. This practice, clearly forbidden by the Geneva and Hague Conventions signed by all the belligerent powers in the war, was yet central to the German conception of jihad: Koranic passages in holy war pamphlets exhorted Muslims to slay infidels 'wherever you find them' (from Sura 9:5, the 'Verse of the Sword').[26] When the British navy at last threatened the ports of Alexandretta (Iskenderun) and Beirut in mid-December 1914, Djemal thus felt perfectly justified in threatening to execute English hostages in Damascus in retaliation. There was a kind of elegant symmetry in Djemal's threat: Captain Frank Larken of the British HMS *Doris* had issued his own ultimatum prior to shelling Alexandretta, requiring the turning over of Entente subjects detained there.[27] Larken evidently assumed he was dealing with an adversary following the laws of Western warfare, who would either surrender to superior force or engage in a proper battle. However, the open-ended rules of German jihad offered a third option: humanitarian blackmail.

So confident was Djemal of the righteousness of his position that he openly communicated the terms of his blackmail to the British via US Ambassador Morgenthau, who now represented Entente interests in the Ottoman Empire. 'All Englishmen [in Syria] are imprisoned in Damascus,' Morgenthau informed Larken, and Djemal has warned that 'if fire is opened on [the] undefended city of Alexandretta and any Ottoman subjects are killed, he will shoot a number of Englishmen to be determined by him'.[28] After he received Larken's own ultimatum, Djemal's threat grew more specific. 'For every Ottoman [subject] whose blood is spilled,' he warned the British captain, 'the commander in chief of Syria [i.e. Djemal] will have a corresponding number of English subjects shot.'[29] Although this represented a retreat of sorts from the earlier Djemal–Kress promise to execute *three* European Christians for every single Muslim killed, the earlier threat had been issued at a time when very few enemy nationals had yet been rounded up. By mid-December, Djemal informed Captain Larken that he already had more than 500 Entente subjects in custody in Damascus. For good measure, Djemal induced three English hostages to pen a kind of kidnapping-style ransom letter, in which they pleaded pathetically that the British navy not 'take any action against an undefended town as would endanger our lives here'.[30]

In the event, the December 1914 battle over Alexandretta was inconclusive. Ottoman munitions stored there had long since been transported inland beyond the range of British naval guns, leaving only a few defunct locomotive engines as proper military targets. Without troops or authorization from London to attempt a landing, all Larken could do was fire a few ineffectual shells at the railroad, which was a branch line of little strategic significance. Because there were no civilian casualties from these volleys, the hostages in Damascus remained safe. On the other hand, they were not freed, either.[31]

In the impasse at Alexandretta, we can see the possible danger to the Entente powers posed by the Turco-German jihad, but also its strategic limitations. Blackmail was inherently a defensive weapon. Unless the jihad could catch fire among Muslim subjects in the Entente colonies, it would remain little more than an operational nuisance. Nevertheless, the precedent set by the Djemal–Kress blackmail was disquieting. J. B. Jackson, the US Consul in Syria, who had delivered

Djemal's messages in person to HMS *Doris* lying offshore, tried to convince Captain Larken not to take Ottoman hostage-murdering threats too seriously, on the curious grounds that 'the people with whom he was dealing were not acquainted with International Law'.[32] With his own charges (theoretically) protected from Turco-German jihadi violence by the special exemption accorded Americans, Jackson may not have appreciated the dilemma Larken was facing. Nor did Jackson seem aware that the Germans were themselves wholeheartedly behind Djemal's policy of bartering the lives of Entente hostages, nor that Djemal, far from being ignorant of international law – like most of the Young Turks he was well educated and well travelled – may instead have been obeying the higher law of Islam, unrecognized by the Christian powers.

If it was difficult to delineate proper behaviour for Turkish army commanders charged with carrying on the holy war, it was still more difficult to control riotous Muslims looking around for infidels to attack, so far as they knew with the blessing of their government. Incidents of mob violence against Christians were legion in the months following the Ottoman entry into the war, with Greeks and Armenians targeted along with unfortunate Entente nationals. In the town of Develiköy, near Smyrna (Izmir), six Greek men were killed then decapitated in late January 1915. This was the kind of gruesome religious violence which occurred from time to time in the Ottoman Empire, and may not have had anything to do with the jihad *fetvas* issued in November. Still, a number of concurrent incidents in the area, involving English nationals, who had never before been subject to this sort of treatment, suggest that the holy war declaration may have had an effect after all. From Smyrna (Izmir), US Consul George Horton reported that jihadi bands were touring the surrounding countryside looking for *Ingiliz* to attack. One such band opened fire on the house of Mr Abraham, manager of a local mine, wounding his children and killing a servant girl. Americans 'returning from the interior', Horton recorded on 4 February 1915, 'report that there is great hostility to Englishmen among the Mussulmans'. As this feeling was 'something new in the region', Horton concluded, 'and is shown especially by the military, it is doubtless being artificially worked up from headquarters'. Tellingly, the Americans reporting to Horton had themselves been repeatedly harassed by roving jihadi bands because, in both their appearance and their use of spoken English, they had been 'mistaken for British'.[33] As Colonel Stumm warns the neutral American Blenkiron in John Buchan's *Greenmantle*, one needed to be extra careful when speaking English while the world war was on, because the locals 'don't distinguish between the different brands'.[34]

Just as Pallavicini had warned, a selective jihad would not remain selective for long. Many Muslim officials, ignorant of the subtleties of European politics and ignorant of European languages, simply lumped all foreigners together as infidels who were fair game for the jihad. Imams preaching the holy war during Friday sermons similarly made little effort to distinguish between the nationalities of those in the *Dâr al Harb* against whom ordinary Muslims should target their wrath.[35] In Aleppo, resident Austrians were expropriated and deported in the euphoric score-settling of November and December 1914 along with the English and French, despite the explicit exemption granted Habsburg subjects in the jihad decrees.[36] As yet no such indignities had been visited on Germans, perhaps because the presence of ruthless officers like Kress ensured a kind of protection. But the Germans could not remain immune from anti-infidel resentment for ever.

Throughout the Ottoman Empire, European nationals reported similar incidents of harassment. For the most part, we know of this story, like that of the Armenian massacres of 1915, through the reporting of American Consuls in the provinces. These reports, to be sure, are not uniformly reliable, yet because US diplomats were charged with protecting the interests of all Entente nationals in Turkey, they have a special resonance. Everywhere Europeans sought the protection of American officials, in many cases successfully. Morgenthau was not alone in petitioning the Ottoman government for better treatment of Entente nationals: US Consuls in Smyrna, Aleppo, Damascus, Beirut and Baghdad all did much the same. It was Morgenthau's idea to distribute American flags throughout the major provincial cities, to be flown in front of European-owned schools, businesses and consular buildings so as to offer them some protection.[37]

Many Ottoman officials cooperated with American Consuls to restrain mob violence. The Vali of Smyrna, for example, promised Horton that he would do everything in his power to protect innocent

Christians, even while consenting to the 'requisitioning' of European-owned properties for the war effort.[38] Others deeply resented American interference. When the US Consul in Beirut protested at Djemal's use of Entente prisoners as hostages, the latter responded huffily, 'I do not authorize you to meddle with my affairs.' After Morgenthau passed word of this outburst to the Porte, Talaat ordered Djemal to 'liberate all British and French citizens ... unless he had some strong military reasons to the contrary'. Far from reassuring Morgenthau, this rebuke of Djemal, coming on the heels of the earlier clash between Talaat and Bedri Bey over the departing diplomatic trains, seemed to suggest that the Turkish government was 'fast drifting into semi anarchy, [as] promises are made one day and recalled the next'.[39]

It was not an encouraging sign for Christians seeking protection from jihad-style massacres. Talaat and Enver may have repeatedly assured Morgenthau in Constantinople that the holy war was not directed at innocent Ottoman subjects or Entente civilians, but this mattered little in distant provinces where the writ of the Turkish government barely registered. Compounding the difficulty facing Ottoman officials trying to restrain jihadi violence was the fact that the holy war propaganda leaflets exhorting Muslims to slay infidels were independently written, printed and distributed by Germans – not only by Oppenheim's agents, but even by German civilians. As J. B. Jackson reported from Aleppo in April 1915, a certain Frau C. G. Koch, with or without the connivance of her husband (who, Jackson touchingly believed, 'may be entirely innocent'), was witnessed passing out seditious Arabic-language pamphlets which evinced 'a determined effort to cause bloodshed among the civil population'. After receiving terrified complaints from Arab Christians and a Jewish rabbi, Jackson warned Morgenthau that 'the Germans are directly responsible for trying to stir up a massacre here'.[40]

Contrary to Jackson's evident belief that Frau Koch was a dangerous Hilda von Einem figure masterminding a spontaneous local holy war,* the pamphlet he uncovered was of course only one of thousands printed under Baron Oppenheim's direction in Berlin and distributed throughout the Ottoman Empire, primarily along the main routes covered by

---

* Hilda von Einem is the mastermind of the German scheme to unleash a prophet to stir Islam to holy war against Great Britain in John Buchan's *Greenmantle*.

the still-unfinished Baghdad railway. In his 'Exposé Concerning the Revolutionizing of the Islamic Territories of Our Enemies', Oppenheim had asked the German government for 100 million Marks ($25 million, or roughly $2.5 billion today) to finance jihadi propaganda. Although he did not get anywhere near this much, by the end of November 1914 the jihad *fetvas* had already been translated into French, Arabic, Persian and Urdu, with more in the Turkic languages of Central Asia in the works.[41]

If the Oppenheim pamphlet being distributed by Frau Koch was not unique, however, it still provided a precious glimpse into the dark heart of the German jihad. Flush with citations from the Koran and running to over thirty blood-curdling pages, this extraordinary document sketched a detailed vision of what Morgenthau called 'the Kaiser's desire to let loose 300,000,000 Mohammedans in a gigantic St Bartholomew's massacre of Christians'.[42] Lamenting 'the stage of degradation to which the World of Islam has arrived', the pamphlet blamed this state of affairs entirely on European Christians. In India, Egypt and Sudan, 'hundreds of millions of Muslims' had fallen 'into the grasp of the enemies of God, the infidel English'. The countries of the Maghreb suffered the indignity of rule by the French, those 'enemies of God and his Apostle'. From the Crimea to the Caucasus to Central Asia, Muslims were under the Russian jackboot. Even the neutral Dutch were targeted for having 'shackled in the fetters of captivity … forty millions of Muslims'. So, too, were the Italians – not for the general holy war, but in the 'little Jihad' or 'local Jihad' being fought by the Sanussi desert warriors in Tripoli.[43]

For their crimes against Islam, European infidels would now receive a death sentence. Muslims everywhere, Oppenheim's pamphlet proclaimed, 'should know that from to-day that the Holy War has become a sacred duty and that the blood of the infidels in the Islamic lands may be shed with impunity (except those who enjoy the protection of the Muslim power and those to whom it has given security and those who confederate with it)'. Moreover, the 'killing of the infidels who rule over the Islamic lands' – that is, British, French, Russian and possibly Dutch or Italian nationals – was not only justified but 'has become a sacred duty, whether it be secretly or openly, as the great Koran declares in its word: "Take them and kill them whenever you come across them"'.[44]

In case neither right nor duty was enough inducement to Muslims to slaughter infidels, Oppenheim offered them heavenly compensation. 'To whoever kills even one single infidel of those who rule over Islamic lands,' the jihadi screed promised earnestly, 'there is a reward like all the living ones of the Islamic world'.* Still, killing just one Christian was not enough for true jihadi warriors. Going one better than Djemal and Kress, Oppenheim asked that each Muslim believer 'take upon him an oath to kill at least three or four of the ruling infidels, enemies of God, and enemies of the religion' – not in retaliation for the deaths of their Islamic brethren but simply as a matter of course. Here, in a nutshell, was the German contribution to the age-old doctrine of jihad: rather than killing soldiers in the course of wars fought against unbelievers, Muslims were enjoined to slaughter certain named Christians anywhere and everywhere, whether soldiers or civilians – and to kill at least 'three or four' of them.

Oppenheim's instructions, the pamphlet explained, pertained to a different kind of holy war than the traditional 'Jihad by Campaigns' led by the Caliph. This type of holy war would continue, as the Ottoman armies engaged the enemy in battle. But Muslims were also now obliged to deploy 'individual Jihad', by which Oppenheim meant assassinations of Entente officials with 'cutting, killing instruments' (i.e. swords or knives). Perhaps more important still was the 'Jihad by Bands'. Here Oppenheim was referring to the spread of 'secret formations', or jihadi-terror cells, behind enemy lines in places like Egypt, India and Central Asia. These, too, would target government officials for killing, while also striving towards the 'continual annihilation of the commerce of the enemy'.[45]

With this seemingly all-encompassing moral sanction for murder, how could would-be jihadis determine which infidels were friends, and which foes? While Oppenheim's pamphlet hinted darkly that even neutral Christian powers like the Dutch and Italians could be targeted, Germans, Austrians and Hungarians are nowhere mentioned by name. At first glance, this is a bit curious, as one might

---

* Oppenheim's man may have been referring to the notorious seventy-two virgins here, but the pamphlet leaves the nature of the reward to the imagination, perhaps not wishing to sully the sacred cause by speaking of sinful images.

expect that exemptions should have been made as explicit as possible. Rumours being what they are, however, it may have been better not to draw attention to the Central Powers at all. Theologically, it was problematic at best to declare a holy war against some, but not all, Christian powers, and it was better not to go too deeply into the particulars. Still, a jihad would not be a jihad without firm Koranic backing, and so Oppenheim concluded his murderous screed by invoking scriptural authority to sketch out the limits of global jihad. As in the Verse of the Sword, Suras 4:89 and 4:90 exhort Muslims to kill infidels, while yet making clear that not quite *all* of them are to be killed. According to this verse, it is acceptable for the faithful to take on non-believers as 'friends or helpers', so long as these infidels are 'allied with one of your peoples by covenant between you and them'. Other possible allies of Islam might include non-believers 'who come to you, their hearts forbidding them to fight you'. Germans, Hungarians and Austrians were covered in the former case, whereas neutrals were offered protection by the latter. Both, however, must needs be very careful, for if these temporary allies of Islam dared 'turn back' to enmity, Muslims were duty-bound to 'kill them wherever they find them'.[46]

Armed with this somewhat less than airtight immunity from attack, Oppenheim's German jihadis now set off to spread the fires of holy war to the global heartland of Islam in the Middle East.

III
Adventures in German Jihad

I have reports from agents everywhere – pedlars in South Russia, Afghan horse-dealers, Turcoman merchants, pilgrims on the road to Mecca, sheikhs in North Africa, sailors on the Black Sea coasters, sheep-skinned Mongols, Hindu fakirs, Greek traders in the Gulf, as well as respectable Consuls who use ciphers. They tell the same story. The East is waiting for a revelation. It has been promised one ... The Germans know, and that is the card with which they are going to astonish the world.

Walter Bullivant, fictional head of British intelligence in
John Buchan's *Greenmantle* (1916)

7

Parting the Red Sea

The Arab tribes [in Sudan] await the arrival of the green flag that
I am carrying, having smuggled it through customs unseen.

Leo Frobenius, reporting from Massaua,
in Italian Eritrea, 19 February 1915[1]

There was no secret about the strategic objective of the Turco-German jihad in the Middle East. A decisive blow at the Suez Canal would sever the shortest supply line to British India for troop ships and merchant convoys, while seriously damaging English prestige in the Orient. The mustering of men, horses and camels in Damascus had been picked up by British intelligence in October 1914, even before the Porte had declared war, and there had already been some light skirmishing between scouting parties in the Sinai desert near the border. There was no doubt in the War Office in London that a Turco-German assault on the canal was in the works. The only question was when, and at which point along the canal.

Djemal and Colonel Kress, then, did not stand much chance of benefiting from an element of surprise in their drive on Suez. Nor could the Ottoman Fourth Army expect to achieve anything close to parity in firepower against the British, because of the large gaps remaining in the Baghdad railway at the Taurus and Amanus mountain passes, which meant that munition shipments from Constantinople had to be transferred there on to primitive mule caravans, and also as a result of the lack of any good roads or track (or wells for drinking water) in the Sinai desert. If it came to a straight-up battle between British expeditionary forces well supplied with guns and shell from nearby Cairo and lightly armed Turco-German forces exhausted after a long waterless trek, there was little doubt who would win the day.

In the Caliph's November call to Islamic holy war, however, the Germans believed they had a secret weapon. Might not Egyptian Muslim soldiers mutiny, with their civilian brothers rising behind enemy lines in Cairo, if they heard that judgement day for their occupier was nigh? Promoting such mutinies had been Robert Mors' objective, until he had been rounded up by the British authorities in October. Still, the Turks had their own covert agents at work in Cairo, who would be ready to wreak havoc in the capital when Suez was struck. Meanwhile, what about the Sanussi tribesmen of neighbouring Libya, where the Germans had sent Otto Mannesmann back in August, or their brethren in Anglo-Egyptian Sudan? If Turco-German jihadis could stir up enough trouble in Egypt's backyard, British troop strength would have to be diverted from the canal, laying Suez bare for the Ottoman Fourth Army.

The difficulty of staging these diversionary gambits was the same faced by anyone seeking to topple Britain's global empire: the Royal Navy controlled the seas. Mannesmann had succeeded in reaching Cyrenaica in part because he had set sail in the first week of August 1914, before the British naval screen had fully descended on the eastern Mediterranean. Although Mannesmann was able to make contact with Sheikh Ahmad al-Sharif, leader of the Sanussi Islamic order whose tribes roamed the desert hinterland from Italian Libya to northern British Egypt and Sudan, al-Sharif understandably declined to join the jihad unless the Germans could promise sufficient material assistance to justify making enemies of both London and Rome. With the British keeping strict watch on North African ports from Alexandria to Tripoli, such a guarantee seemed out of the question.*

With the Libyan gambit on Egypt's western frontier on ice for now, the best chance of diverting British forces from Suez was to strike somewhere south. Since General Gordon had been killed by the Mahdi in 1885, the British occupation forces in Egypt had kept a watchful eye on Sudan. Kitchener had made his name in conquering Khartoum,

---

* See chapter 15 below.

and yet the British hold on the region remained precarious. Although the Royal Navy patrolled the Red Sea, as it did the eastern Mediterranean, the former comprised a narrow channel between Africa and the Arabian coastline, funnelling down to less than twenty miles at the tip near Aden. More significantly for the Turco-German jihad, the Red Sea abutted the Hejaz, the heartland of the Islamic faith: Mecca itself is less than fifty miles from the shoreline. If the Germans, with Ottoman help, could get some of their jihad agents across the Red Sea, by way of the sacred cities of Arabia, the flames of holy war might be kindled in the Horn of Africa. Given the right inducement, the ferocious warrior tribes of Somalia and Abyssinia (Ethiopia) could be hurled northwards, expelling the British from Khartoum and possibly even Cairo.

It was an ambitious undertaking.*[2] To reach the Yemen, Oppenheim's men would have to travel nearly a thousand miles overland into the Hejaz beyond the railhead at Ma'an, or risk disembarking further south in Medina, the second holiest city of Islam. Another option would be setting sail from Yanbo or Jedda, but as those were the principal Red Sea disembarkation ports for Mecca pilgrims, they were under heavy British surveillance. Travel in the Hejaz was a risky proposition for infidels: to this day Christians and Jews are not allowed to visit Mecca or Medina. A German wartime mission to Abyssinia or Sudan would face a myriad of perils, from marauding Bedouins to suspicious sheikhs, many of whom were reportedly in British pay.

To lead such an operation would require courage, regional expertise and considerable tact. At first glance, Leo Frobenius (1873–1938) was an ideal choice. The son of a Prussian army officer, Frobenius combined the qualities of ruthless discipline and intellectual curiosity in classic German fashion. Founder of the German Inner-African Research Expedition (DIAFE), Frobenius was equal parts colonial adventurer and academic. Blending together elements of the disciplines of archaeology, ethnography and cultural anthropology with a healthy imagination,

---

* Not least because it seems to have escaped the Germans' notice that most Abyssinian tribesmen, particularly in the northern part of Ethiopia bordering Sudan, were Christian and quite hostile to Islam. With revealing vagueness, the head of Oppenheim's mission promised that he would 'make use of the Abyssinians' adventurous spirit (*Abenteuerlust*)'.

BULGARIA

BLACK SEA

RUSSIAN EMPIRE

CASPIAN SEA

GREECE

Adrianople

Constantinople

Batumi

Trabzon

Erzurum

Baku

O T T O M A N   E M P I R E

Smyrna (Izmir)

Konya

Tabriz

Mersin

Alexandretta

Aleppo

Mosul

PERSIA

CYPRUS (British rule since 1878)

MEDITERRANEAN SEA

Damascus

Baghdad

Alexandria

Port Said

Toussum

Jerusalem

Ismailia

Suez Canal

Beetsheeba

Basra

Cairo

Sinai Desert

Ma'an

Aqaba

R. Nile

BRITISH EGYPT

Medina

Yanbo

ARABIA

Jedda

Mecca

Port Sudan

Suakin

RED SEA

Anglo-Egyptian SUDAN

Asir

N

Khartoum

Kassala

Massaua

Eritrea

Sanaa

Ottoman Empire

0   500 km

0   250 miles

FRENCH SOMALIA

Aden (British rule since 1838)

ABYSSINIA (ETHIOPIA)

Addis Ababa

2. The Red Sea region

Frobenius had published four books on human origins, notably formulating a rather curious theory about the mythical lost city of African Atlantis, which purported to explain why remnants of a prior white civilization still existed in Africa at the time of the European conquest – contrary to the then-fashionable colonialist view of the 'barbarous negro' who had never known civilization. In his ideas, too, Frobenius was typically pan-German in the Oppenheim vein, combining affectionate condescension towards native cultures with the seemingly contradictory notion that the other European colonial powers were too racist to appreciate them.[3]

Charged by Oppenheim with heading the jihadi mission to Abyssinia and Sudan, Frobenius attacked the task with characteristic thoroughness. Germany's leading colonial explorer did not travel light – at least when others carried his kit. After arriving incognito in Constantinople on the Orient Express in November 1914, Frobenius began commissioning materials from Berlin for his journey. Along with pistols, ammunition and fifty kilos of explosives, Frobenius requested 40,000 Austrian silver coins for bribe money (the 'Maria Theresa Thaler', originally minted in 1780, was then still the best-recognized and best-trusted coin in the Arab world). Frobenius then asked for six German Imperial Crown Medals to be dispensed as gifts to Arab sheikhs, a 'great number of smaller badges of honour' to flatter lesser tribal chiefs, and of course an elevated title for himself to make the right impression on Arab and Abyssinian notables (Wilhelm duly named Frobenius 'Kaiserlicher Geheimer Regierungsrat', or Imperial Privy Councillor). Completing the picture of a Teutonic Indiana Jones, Frobenius specially requested that his wife send on from Berlin his favourite exploring outfit: khaki trousers and corduroy suit with felt hat, brown shoes and leather belt, spurs and cap. Recognizing a kindred spirit – a man of action, and with style to boot! – Oppenheim gladly obliged.[4]

The next question was personnel. Ideally Frobenius, whose own spoken Arabic was shaky, wanted as many native Arabs as possible in his party to help smooth his path through the Hejaz. For the final leg through the Horn of Africa, Frobenius requested three Somali tribesmen. Because his proposed itinerary would involve passing through Eritrea, Frobenius also needed someone to help grease the wheels with the Italian authorities there. Conditions in Constantinople being what they were, however, after a frustrating month of recruiting, Frobenius was at last forced to settle for, in lieu of Arabs, an Algerian nobleman, Mohammed Said (the nephew of Abdel Kader, hero of the resistance to French occupation in the nineteenth century), and a half-Syrian German Consulate dragoman from Jerusalem named Solomon Hall; in lieu of ferocious Somali warriors, eleven dark-skinned Moroccan prisoners of war; and as an expert guide to Eritrea, a half-Italian philosophy professor named Mario Passarge. Accompanied by one Turkish and four German army officers charged with overseeing mission security, Frobenius' motley crew left Constantinople on 2 December 1914.[5]

Despite having to switch from railway to caravan for the mountain gaps in the Baghdad railway, Frobenius made fairly good time. After stopping over in Damascus to resupply on 12 December, he and his men immediately boarded the Hejaz railway for the trip to Medina, where they arrived on the evening of the 15th. Two weeks from the Bosphorus to the Hejaz was hardly the stuff of German Baghdad railway dreams, but considering the difficulties of the mountain caravan route, it was still quite an achievement, and must have owed something to Frobenius' iron will. Oppenheim seemed to have chosen his man well.

As soon as his mission reached the Hejaz, however, Frobenius' luck took a turn for the worse. Although he carried effusively flattering letters from the Kaiser to tribal leaders in Eritrea, Abyssinia and Sudan, in his haste to reach the Red Sea Frobenius had not taken proper care to court Ottoman officials and German diplomats. His brusque manner had bothered both Enver and Wangenheim in Constantinople, and he scarcely bothered to see Djemal in Damascus, where his men stayed only a few hours. Before they set off south by rail from the Syrian capital, the five Germans and Passarge had all changed into the traditional garb of Turkish Muslims: Frobenius, with the grandest costume, styled himself Abdul Kerim Pasha. Yet without Djemal's permission to visit the holy cities, his men were on shaky ground as soon as they reached the Hejaz railway terminus. Although Frobenius and his fellow German officers had publicly converted to Islam before leaving Constantinople, 'Abdul Kerim Pasha' was not certain they would pass muster as Muslims in Medina, where infidels were not allowed to trespass. Upon reaching the last Hejaz railhead, Frobenius ordered his men to march into the desert immediately, refusing to spend even one night in Medina. Before long they began encountering hostile Bedouins and masses of hungry hajj pilgrims. It was lucky Frobenius had armed his mission so thoroughly, else they might have met their end then and there.[6]

When his mission at last reached the Red Sea coast at Yanbo, Frobenius ran into an unexpected problem. In a case of too many cooks spoiling the broth, another German jihadi agent had beaten him there. Professor Bernhard Moritz, the Orientalist whom Prüfer had hoped to succeed as director of the Khedivial Library in Cairo, had been tasked in October with setting up a German propaganda centre in Medina – Oppenheim had even provided film projectors for the purpose.[7] The Baron, himself fond of photographs, was probably unaware that strict Islamic doctrine forbids pictorial representations of human and animal forms, let alone motion pictures. Moritz, far better informed about Islam than Oppenheim, decided the mission to Medina was a fool's errand, and so set off for Sudan instead, with authorization from Wangenheim.[8] Although Frobenius knew and respected the Professor's work, he fiercely resented the apparent doubling up of his Sudanese brief. Moritz was an accomplished linguist, but Frobenius thought him a poor field man. The famous Orientalist was, in Frobenius' view, 'in his innermost heart a despiser of Oriental peoples (*ein Orientalverächter*), who has no inkling that one must always try to please the people here with elevated compliments'. Moritz's travels in the Hejaz and particularly in Yanbo, Frobenius complained, had left behind 'bitter feelings', winning for the cause of *Deutschtum* 'neither recognition nor respect'. Although Frobenius did not do so well himself in flattering Turkish officials, he was showering Arab sheikhs with medals, and wished dearly that Moritz had done the same.[9]

Still, despite these frustrations, Frobenius was gathering useful intelligence on the Hejaz. The war had thrown the local economy into upheaval. The onerous grain requisitions required by the Turkish army were resented everywhere in the Ottoman Empire, but the impact was felt particularly keenly in the Arabian desert, which depended entirely on imported foodstuffs and was reaching near-famine conditions. Turco-German propaganda, of course, could and did blame food shortages on the British coastal blockade, but this claim could only reinforce the importance of the British navy for the delicate economic ecosystem in Arabia. Hajj pilgrims no longer relied on the old Ottoman caravan routes to reach Mecca: most now travelled as far as Jedda by sea in British-owned vessels. Because the Bedouins lived off the carrying costs and protection money paid by the pilgrims, they too were now effectively at the mercy of the British. British gold, liberally dispensed to tribal leaders like Sherif Hussein of Mecca (who had just ignominiously expelled the Ottoman governor of Mecca), was already eroding Turkish power and prestige, which was 'everywhere weak'. British grain, sent to Jedda to alleviate the impending famine on ships conspicuously mounting the Union Jack, could complete the rout.[10]

The prospects for stirring up a Turco-German jihad in Egypt's rear, then, appeared bleak. But Frobenius was not a man easily discouraged. Touring the Red Sea coast in a small Arab dhow, his team spread black rumours about British perfidy wherever they went. To counter English 'food propaganda', Frobenius put his stash of Maria Theresa Thalers to work, buying up sacks of rice in Massaua, the nearest port city in Italian Eritrea, to distribute on Germany's behalf along the Hejaz coast. It was hard work, not least escaping enemy detection by Entente warships and merchant vessels plying the Red Sea. On 13 February, Frobenius' dhow was accosted by a French steamer, the *Dessaix*, and boarded. Predictably, the Europeans' native disguises proved useless in the crunch: the Germans and Passarge were forced to hide away in a small enclosure in the ship's hull, buried underneath a pile of animal hides and palm straw, while the Algerian nobleman took on the part of a travelling merchant (the sacks of rice were a useful prop). The Moroccans, meanwhile, claimed to be pilgrims returning home from the hajj. In all, the search lasted for over an hour of ever-mounting tension for Frobenius: the French captain even unknowingly brushed against his knee at one point. And yet the North Africans stuck gamely to their parts, rescuing the Germans from captivity with their sangfroid.[11]

Undeterred by the close call with the French, Frobenius grew bolder still. After dispatching a team led by his Turkish liaison officers to sabotage the Port Sudan railway at Suakin, he hailed a merchant ship owned by the Hamburg-Amerika line, and immediately commandeered it for the Turco-German jihad. The ship's civilian captain, Julius

Tutt, seemed almost beside himself with excitement to be enlisted on a secret wartime mission, and rolled over backwards to please Frobenius. Tutt cabled company headquarters in Hamburg, asking for an emergency loan of 20,000 Marks to buy up foodstuffs to win over the bedraggled Arabs of the Red Sea coast for *Deutschtum*. Frobenius used the funds to purchase corn, rice (2,000 tons), beans (75 tons), sugar (1,000 tons), and tea (20 tons). It was inspired improvisation. As yet Frobenius was nowhere near Abyssinia, much less Sudan, but he seemed to have conquered the Red Sea by sheer force of personality.[12]

Clearly, no one could fault Frobenius for his courage. Despite all of their learning, neither Prüfer nor Moritz had yet displayed similar initiative. But Frobenius' heroic exploits had done little to further his core mission. After commandeering several more German merchant vessels, and their men, in port at Massaua in mid-February 1915, Frobenius at last felt his position was strong enough to organize a proper desert expedition inland through Italian Eritrea to Addis Ababa, the Abyssinian capital. With his rear flank secured, his sabotage team en route northwards for Port Sudan, and a secure communications link (via Captain Tutt's merchant vessel) established, Frobenius proudly reported that he was ready to begin the African jihad against Egypt's southern underbelly. 'The Arab tribes [in Sudan],' he wrote from Massaua on 19 February 1915, 'await the arrival of the green flag that I am carrying, having smuggled it through customs unseen.'[13]

It was heady news – or at least it would have been, had Frobenius begun his diversionary jihad several weeks earlier. The battle for the Suez Canal, alas, had been joined in early February, and had already long since run its course. The idea of countering British food propaganda with German charity shipments across the Red Sea basin had been sensible in its way – but it had cost Frobenius several precious weeks. By the time his jihadi sabotage mission was at last on the ground and running, it was far too late to make any difference for Kress and Djemal.

If Frobenius had not succeeded in launching his holy war in time, however, he had won himself a great deal of attention. The French *Dessaix* did not simply happen upon his dhow by accident: every Entente and Italian vessel in the Red Sea was looking for him. Before

Frobenius' field reports had reached Oppenheim in Berlin, his mission's ostentatious arrival in Massaua was already the subject of vigorous discussion in Rome. Despite constant German protestations that the Ottoman holy war was directed only at the English and French, one could hardly blame the Italians for being concerned that a well-armed team of German-Arab jihadis was planning to prowl around the desert hinterland of Eritrea, making trouble. By early March the Frobenius mission had splashed onto the front pages in neutral Italy, where public opinion was swinging sharply against the Central Powers.[14]

It was not only the Italians who were disquieted by Frobenius. With Rome creeping closer to active belligerence and the Austrians in a panic, Berlin pulled the plug on the mission to Addis Ababa. In light of this depressing news, Frobenius' men turned on him. Mohammed Said, the Algerian nobleman who had saved the German's skin, reported after returning safely to Damascus that his master had 'completely lacked the ability to get along with Orientals and Muslims'. Frobenius had been the worst sort of despot, who 'treated everyone like the most menial servants', rationed the mission's food parsimoniously, and did not allow the Moroccans to smoke.[15] Solomon Hall, who escorted nine of the Moroccan prisoners of war back to Jerusalem, chalked up the mission's failure entirely to Frobenius' poor leadership skills.[16]

Worse was to come. Rochus Schmidt, a no-nonsense German army colonel who reported to the Colonial Office instead of to Oppenheim's jihad bureau, was dispatched from Berlin with a small commando team in late February 1915 on a mission to Sudan to clean up Frobenius' mess. After arriving in Constantinople on 10 March, Schmidt gave Berlin a devastating verdict on the Frobenius mission, coloured by Wangenheim's own dislike for the African explorer, whom the latter now judged a 'charlatan'. The most powerful Arab ruler Frobenius claimed to have won over, Sayyid al-Idrisi of Asir, had not been impressed by Frobenius at all. Al-Idrisi, one of the Arab sheikhs who had travelled to Constantinople in the flush of the Germans' victory at Tannenberg the previous year, bearing gifts to consecrate the coming Ottoman holy war against Britain, had changed his tune after meeting Frobenius. The Sheikh now declared publicly that he would 'slit the throat of any German or Turk who set foot on his land'.[17] This declaration may, of course, simply have meant that al-Idrisi had recently been added to the British payroll. Whatever the source of the turnabout, it did not speak well of Frobenius' diplomatic skills.

Still, at least some members of the mission to Abyssinia appreciated their commander's decisiveness. Showing that there was some cultural affinity between the Germans and their Turkish allies, the one man willing to speak up for Frobenius was the Turkish officer he had dispatched to sabotage the Port Sudan railway at Suakin. Abdul Djelil, an Ottoman lieutenant born in Tripoli before it had been lost to the Italians, had led a small team across the Eritrean border into Anglo-Egyptian Sudan, carrying heavy explosives. Unaware that Berlin had recalled the mission, Djelil continued reporting to his esteemed 'Excellence Abdul Kerim Pasha' well into April 1915, long after the would-be Ottoman pasha had returned to civilian life as mere Leo Frobenius. Although his team never quite reached the Port Sudan railway (the British were deploying mobile 'camel-cavalry' command posts to protect the tracks, and had rushed a new detachment of Indian soldiers to Suakin), Djelil was able to tour Sudan's coastal areas, spreading the message of the coming jihad. Interestingly, he observed, in Sudan's coastal villages the Ottoman jihad *fetvas* had already been plastered across town squares and in all the mosques (although, Djelil noted, very few villagers could read). In Kassala, a large market town on the main inland road from Port Sudan to Khartoum, there had even been a serious anti-British uprising, quieted only after the British had bribed the local sheikh, who began 'preaching daily to the people, that they should wait'. Overall, Djelil reported with pride, 'the entire Mohammedan world here is very pleased with the Germans and Turks'.[18] Perhaps the Frobenius mission had not been fruitless after all.

After a great deal of haggling in Massaua, Frobenius himself was finally deported from Italian Eritrea in late March 1915. He arrived in Rome on 2 April, and six days later was shipped back on the night train to Berlin. Frobenius was embittered by the failure of his mission, reported Ambassador Bülow, and the way he had been disowned by the German Foreign Office. Bülow and the Wilhelmstrasse had reason to regret this rough treatment, for Frobenius now took his revenge.

During his sojourn in Rome, the German explorer invited reporters into his hotel room, where he regaled them with tales of his Red Sea derring-do. The drumbeat of anti-German stories now coursing through the Italian press, Bülow noted, 'can probably be traced back to [Frobenius]'.[19] Oppenheim's one-man German jihadi band had not only stirred up a holy war along the east and west coastlines of the Red Sea: Frobenius had helped bring Italy into the war on the Entente side.*

In both his boldness and his blundering, Frobenius was an Oppenheim man through and through. The irritation of neutral powers was probably an inevitable result of the Kaiser's global jihad, but it did not have to happen so quickly. Frobenius' diplomatic vices, like those of Germany, were the mirror opposite of his military virtues: daring, improvisation and speed, in the absence of strict regard for strategic objectives, had conjured up unforeseen dangers. Frobenius' stirring of jihadi unrest in Italian Africa had been damaging to the German cause in the same way that the violation of Belgian neutrality via the Schlieffen Plan had been – the pursuit of a specific goal had thrown up a world of further problems which made the goal unattainable. Germany's forceful man of action had had his chance. Perhaps a subtle Austrian academic could do better.

---

* Of course, there were other factors involved in Italy's decision to declare war on the Central Powers on 23 May 1915, such as greed for Austrian territory and the Germans' smuggling of weapons into Libya that month to arm the Sanussi (see chapter 15). Still, Frobenius did his small part.

8

An Austrian in Arabia

A Bedouin yearns for booty day and night, not so much to enrich himself with it as for the thrill of capturing it; and the greater the danger the more alluring the adventure. As soon as the booty is safe in his hands, it ceases to please him: he gives away what he has captured and plans whither to go after fresh loot. The Bedouins consider fighting as a sport.

Alois Musil, in *Arabia Deserta*[1]

For all his daring along the Red Sea coast, Leo Frobenius had scarcely brushed up against the Islamic heartland of the Hejaz, let alone the vast desert beyond it. This is hardly surprising, when we consider how very few Europeans had penetrated the inner regions of Arabia. Richard Francis Burton, the legendary British spy who had done the first Western translation of Oppenheim's beloved *Thousand and One Nights*, once famously passed unnoticed as a Persian in forbidden Mecca (it helped that he claimed to know the Koran by heart in the original Arabic) but then even this holiest city of Islam is less than fifty miles from the Red Sea coastline. Charles Doughty, Burton's near contemporary, had penned a 1,200-page memoir of his *Travels in Arabia Deserta* between 1876 and 1878; but he too had confined his itinerary to the coastal north-west. The most intrepid 'sand-mad Englishman' may have been Captain William Shakespear, British liaison to the Saud clan of Wahhabis in the central Nejd desert, who was the first Westerner 'to cross the width of the Arabian peninsula from Kuwait to Suez'. Yet Shakespear was something less than an explorer-scholar in the vein of

Burton, Doughty and Oppenheim: he had stuck to the main caravan routes, guided by his Wahhabi hosts.

On the eve of the First World War, the central Arabian desert remained largely *terra incognita* to Europeans. Were the tribal sheikhs, Bedouin warriors and camel dealers of Arabia to be enlisted in the Turco-German jihad in time for the great assault on the Suez Canal, Oppenheim needed a man able to penetrate this inner sanctum of Islam.[2] Fortunately for the Central Powers, the man generally considered in 1914 to be the world's foremost living scholar-explorer of Arabia was a subject of the Habsburg monarchy, Alois Musil (1868–1944). In part due to the friendships he cultivated with a number of Arab sheikhs, Musil had covered some 9,000 miles in his desert travels before the war. Although he was an Austro-Hungarian subject, his geographical expertise on northern Arabia was enlisted by the British government during the Aqaba crisis of 1906, to help draw the border between Palestine and Egypt. Showing that he played no favourites, five years later Musil had also performed survey work for the German engineers building the Hejaz railway.

Alois Musil, second cousin of the novelist Robert Musil, was, at first glance, an unlikely Arabist. The eldest of five children from a peasant family in rural Moravia, his first language was Czech, and his first love the Bible. A devout, if somewhat unorthodox, Catholic, Musil enrolled in the theological faculty in Olomouc, where he developed a passion for the Old Testament which seems to be de rigueur among serious Arabists. Sponsored by the Archbishop of Olomouc, Musil continued his biblical studies at the French Dominican École Biblique in Jerusalem (1895–7) and thereafter at the French Jesuit St Joseph University in Beirut.

Musil's first regional excursions, into Egypt, Sinai and Gaza, were carried out as part of his scriptural studies, but he rapidly succumbed to the romance of the desert. He was particularly drawn to the ancient biblical lands of Moab and Edom, near Madaba in what is now northern Jordan. Since the region was plagued with tribal warfare, Musil sought the protection of Talal ibn el-Fayez, chief of the Beni Sakhr, who were feuding with the Rwala Bedouins. It was under Talal's protection that Musil carried out his first serious archaeological work between 1897 and 1902, studying the ruins of an old Umayyad castle at Qusayr 'Amra. To demonstrate his loyalty, Musil even rode with the Beni Sakhr in one of their raids on the Rwala. Characteristically, however, during a later trip to the region in 1908–9, Musil courted two of Talal's tribal enemies, Auda ibu Tayi of the Howeitat (who features prominently in *Lawrence of Arabia*) and the Rwala Bedouin chieftain An-Nuri ibn Sha'lan. Musil helped to set Auda's wounded arm while the latter was visiting An-Nuri's camp in 1909, thus winning great personal prestige with the Howeitat. The Austrian performed similar wonders for An-Nuri's semi-independent son Nawwaf, to whom he gave several authentic Mauser rifles with 'substantial quantities of original rounds' in 1909. Nawwaf ruled the oases surrounding al-Gawf in northern Arabia, with the help of around 100 personal slaves. Of all these sheikhs, it was An-Nuri who became Musil's closest friend in Arabia.[3]

This was a lucky circumstance for the Central Powers, for An-Nuri ibn Sha'lan was just the sort of man the Kaiser needed for the Turco-German jihad. An-Nuri's Rwala tribesmen, who roamed the Mesopotamian, Syrian and north Arabian desert in a rough triangle bounded by Baghdad, Damascus and the Hejaz railway, were Bedouins of the classic definition, in that they bred and sold camels – desperately needed by Djemal and Kress for the Ottoman Fourth Army's push across the Sinai desert. An-Nuri was notoriously bloodthirsty and combat-ready, a man who 'boasted of having killed with his own hands no less than 120 men'. Credible rumours were also spread that An-Nuri had coolly dispatched two of his own brothers. Musil, who (like Lawrence after him) dressed in the native Bedouin style of flowing white robes, was affectionately called 'Sheikh Musi' by An-Nuri, who came to trust him implicitly and even deployed 'Musi' to negotiate on his behalf with hostile tribal chiefs.[4] It was not unreasonable to suppose that a Musil mission in 1914 might succeed in enlisting An-Nuri's ferocious Bedouins, and perhaps more importantly their camels, in the coming assault on the Suez Canal.

Musil himself, however, was not so sure. The value of this scholar as an intelligence agent for the Central Powers was also his weakness as a jihadi field man: Musil knew the Bedouins too well to rate them very highly as wartime allies. Years of experience had taught 'Sheikh Musi' that Arabia was a seething cauldron of tribal raids, truces and betrayals. An-Nuri's Bedouins feuded not only with the Beni Sakhr, but also with Oppenheim's beloved Shammar Bedouins of Ibn Rashid, who were heavily subsidized by the Turks – Enver had sent Rashid 15,000 rifles, 50,000 Turkish pounds and a luxury automobile in 1913 alone – and therefore thought to be pro-Ottoman.[5] Ibn Rashid's tribe, in its turn, had been at war for years with Ibn Saud. Saud's Wahhabis of the Nejd were the most devout (if extreme) Muslims on the entire Arabian peninsula, and in this sense were the most promising candidates of all for the Turco-German jihad. And yet Ibn Saud was mistrusted by the Turks, who believed him (correctly) to be in British pay. In classically cynical divide-and-conquer style, earlier in 1914 Enver had offered Ibn Saud the unprecedented title of *Saheb ad-Dawla*, or Vali (Governor) of Inner Arabia, despite having just heavily armed Saud's arch enemy, Ibn Rashid. Predictably, Rashid's Shammar Bedouins launched a major offensive against Ibn Saud immediately he returned from Constantinople bearing his new title, in effect using Ottoman arms against the first-ever Ottoman Governor of Arabia. Piling on the anti-Saud bandwagon, Sherif Hussein of Mecca then issued a ban on all Wahhabi tribesmen entering the Hejaz. 'Governor' Ibn Saud and his warriors were now cut off from Syria, the Hejaz and Egypt, leaving only the British-controlled eastern Arabian coastline open for supplies of food, gold and ammunition. Whether or not the Wahhabis had really been loyal to London before, when the world war broke in summer 1914 they were pro-British as a matter of necessity.[6]

Because An-Nuri and Ibn Saud shared a common enemy (in Ibn Rashid), Musil's friendship with the former at least offered the possibility of a reconciliation with the latter – if he could reach him. Geographically, however, the Wahhabis of central Arabia were much too far afield to join the Suez offensive, particularly now that they were unable to travel freely through the Hejaz. Dominating the southern approaches to Damascus, An-Nuri's Rwala Bedouins were, by contrast, close enough to make a difference at Suez – if they wished to. But the Rwala were much less promising as jihadis than the Wahhabis. In the sense that much of their livelihood came from looting Mecca pilgrims, illiterate Bedouins like the Rwala were arguably more hostile than friendly to Islam as such. Their mentality was tribal, not religious. It was with An-Nuri in mind that Musil later wrote, in *Arabia Deserta*, that Bedouins were, at root, thrill-seekers always in search of 'fresh loot'.[7] These were not people who would easily submit to German military discipline.

Musil's doubts about the prospects for the Kaiser's jihad were not confined to the problems of controlling the Bedouins. 'Sheikh Musi' knew that Arabian tribesmen, with the possible exception of the mercenary Ibn Rashid, had little love for the Turks, and Ottoman influence was almost non-existent in the desert. Even important port towns like Aqaba, which guarded the Red Sea approach to the Sinai, were lightly held and poorly equipped. Of the 150 Turkish troops stationed in Aqaba, Musil observed while visiting the town in 1910, 130 were stricken with malaria and fever. Mecca pilgrims stopping over en route from Egypt often brought cholera in their wake. Syphilis, too, was rampant. Because there was no rail link, seriously ill soldiers needed to be carried on camelback to the railhead at Ma'an, to be sent on from there to Damascus. Many died en route.[8]

When the Sultan-Caliph proclaimed his jihad on behalf of the Central Powers in November 1914, Alois Musil thus found himself in the peculiar position of being the most qualified candidate to promote the Ottoman holy war among Arab Bedouins, but also believing that the task was more or less futile. In a quickie book he wrote in August 1914, *Turkey and the European War*, Musil had viewed the Turkish cause as hopeless if the Porte entered the conflict. Arab nationalism, he prophesied, assisted by English gold and propaganda, would split the empire apart. The Porte was backing the wrong man in Arabia: Ibn Rashid was, in Musil's opinion, by far the weakest of the three main warrior chieftains. Instead, the Porte should throw its weight behind An-Nuri and Ibn Saud. Although quite far from an Arab nationalist himself, Musil said he thought Syrian independence was inevitable and should be welcomed.[9]

This was hardly the testimony of a true believer in the Turco-German jihad. Musil was not unaware of the objectives of Oppenheim's bureau in Berlin: the two men had long been friends and corresponded frequently. But it was not Oppenheim who enlisted Musil in the Kaiser's holy war. In fact the initiative came from Musil's friends in Arabia. An-Nuri and Auda both wrote to 'Sheikh Musi' in early October 1914, asking for advice. The English were already throwing gold around Arabia, and had attempted to bribe the Rwala and Howeitat into neutrality, and possible hostility, against the Turks. The Ottoman governor in Damascus had also sent both men gifts, hoping to counter the bad impression left by the huge subsidies sent to their enemy Ibn Rashid. What did the 'Inkliz' want, and why were they fighting Austria? Which way should the Bedouins go? It was in response to these questions that Musil, then teaching at the University of Vienna, approached Count Heinrich von Tschirschky, Germany's Ambassador to Austria, on 14 October 1914 about the possibility of travelling to the Middle East to aid the war effort.[10]

Musil's mission to Arabia was thus undertaken in the spirit of free agency. It was Musil who approached the Germans about supporting his mission, and not the other way around. In his exploratory memorandum to Tschirschky, he proposed that he attempt to quiet the feud between Ibn Rashid and Ibn Saud, winning both over for the Ottoman cause. Assuming he could also count on the loyalty of his friend An-Nuri, this meant that Musil could win roughly 'two thirds of Arabia' to a policy of 'enthusiastic support for the Turkish government'.[11] This was something less than active support for the Ottoman Fourth Army's Suez offensive, but then that was Germany's priority, not Austria's. To ensure that Oppenheim's bureau would give the Austrian the support he needed, Tschirschky made a crucial addendum to Musil's proposal, promising Berlin that Musil would deploy his influence to assure the participation of Bedouin camel warriors from north Arabian tribes in the 'undertaking … against the Suez Canal'.[12]

Thus was born the misunderstanding which would plague the Musil mission from beginning to end. Musil, for his part, demanded and thought he was granted 'absolute freedom of movement in Arabia' and operational control, refusing to be subordinate to either the German or the Ottoman army. The Germans, on their side, thought Musil had promised to recruit Bedouins and camels for Kress's Suez offensive. This was not an unreasonable presumption, considering that Berlin was forced to pick up the entire tab for Musil's expenses after the Austrians refused to pay, fearing (so thought the Germans) that stirring up an Arabian jihad might frighten Italy into declaring war on Vienna. The Porte, which had not yet entered the war, was initially told merely that Musil was on a 'scholarly mission'. Oppenheim himself wanted to meet with Musil to clear up any lingering doubts about his objectives, but the Austrian did not wish to waste time coming to Berlin, and so no such meeting took place. On 2 November 1914, he left Vienna by train, reaching Sirkeci station two days later.[13]

In Constantinople, Musil was somewhat surprised to discover that neither Enver nor Liman von Sanders had been briefed on his mission. Although Liman was friendly and encouraging, in the Ottoman War Minister Musil seems to have run up against serious resistance. Enver knew that Musil was friendly with the enemies of his man Ibn Rashid, and did not trust the Austrian in the slightest. It did not help that Musil openly expressed his contempt for Enver's Arabian policy and for Ibn Rashid. Playing tit for tat, Enver mocked his pretensions of being able to pass for an Arab in Arabia, telling him the Bedouins knew perfectly well he was an infidel. With the Sultan about to issue his jihad *fetva* (this exchange took place between 4 and 8 November 1914, just after Turkey entered the war), Enver had little confidence in Musil's ability to enlist Arabia in the holy war. How likely was it, Enver asked Musil teasingly, that the Caliph of Sunni Islam would 'send a Catholic priest as emissary to fanatical Arab [tribes]'?[14]

Despite his scepticism, Enver was willing to give Musil the benefit of the doubt, if only to placate the Germans. With war raging between the Shammar and the Wahhabis, the Ottoman government had no open lines of communication to Ibn Saud anyway: perhaps Musil might perform a miracle and win the Wahhabis over for the holy war. And so Enver wrote up passports for the Austrian and gave him personal letters of introduction to Ibn Rashid and Ibn Saud, promising great material support to both leaders if they joined the jihad against Great Britain.[15]

Arriving in Damascus on 11 November 1914, Musil was given a hero's welcome by the commanders of the Ottoman Fourth Army, who desperately needed his help in mustering the Bedouins and their camels for the push across the Sinai to Suez. And yet this operational help is precisely what Musil felt unable to promise. While agreeing that Bedouin support would be essential to a successful crossing of the Sinai, Musil told the Germans on 1 December 1914 that he himself would be unable to participate, 'because I must travel to Arabia, to win over the tribes'. To do so he would require weapons, ammunition and bribe money. Kress had just promised another 10,000 Turkish pounds' worth, roughly equal to $5 million today, but more was urgently needed. 'Without the necessary funds,' Musil told the Germans, 'I cannot equip the necessary [Bedouin] battalions.' Even if he were given enough gold, he emphasized that he could not promise success, 'because time is too short and the distances too great'. Pay them and arm them they must, but the Germans must not actually expect nomadic Arab tribesmen to participate in any battles. 'For the push into Egypt and for operations in Syria and along the Red Sea,' Musil wrote, 'the [Ottoman] government should not count on any help at all from the Bedouins.'[16] In this Musil may well have been right, but it was a strange kind of honesty which consisted in disowning one's mission before it had begun.

The Germans would have been more disquieted still had they realized what Musil was reporting to Vienna behind their back. As if to reassure Oppenheim and the Kaiser that he was worth the money the Germans were paying him, the would-be Austrian jihadi promised the Germans in his 1 December report that, 'with Allah's help, I will be able to accomplish a great deal' in Arabia. But he wired Pallavicini at the same time that the Bedouins were everywhere 'fleeing from the requisitions' of the Turkish army and had therefore become 'all but hostile to the government'. Worse, he said that he had sensed 'a strong current of pro-English sentiment' in the Ottoman high command in Damascus (although he did not name names). Kress's orders, Musil continued, were almost never followed by Turkish soldiers, and were often disobeyed.[17]

Musil and Kress do not seem to have hit it off, to put it mildly. As Musil later recalled, the two worked together for sixteen days in Damascus, discussing the best routes across the Sinai to circumvent British surveillance (avoiding Beersheeba and using the al-'Awga oasis instead), the best places to dig wells in the desert, the Sinai Bedouins and where to look for them, and of course how to deal with the camel-breeding Rwala tribesmen of Musil's friend An-Nuri. 'After lengthy discussions,' Musil reported somewhat haughtily on 1 December 1914, 'my recommendations were accepted.'[18] Although going through the motions of helping Kress prepare, however, Musil had little real hope the Suez attack would succeed. Overall, he thought the Bavarian lieutenant colonel was in over his head. Kress's relatively low rank meant he was not taken seriously by Ottoman officers, and his ignorance of the Turkish language completed his isolation. Musil all but pitied the German liaison officer, who had been 'sent into the Syrian hornet's nest ... without knowing the land, people, or language'. To be sure, he recalled, the Turks and Arabs in Damascus were 'full of enthusiasm' for the upcoming assault on Suez, but not out of any interest in the military objective. Rather, the locals were interested only in 'the German gold which had been sent to achieve' it. Everyone in town, Musil wrote, 'knew and spoke of the monstrous amounts of gold Germany had sent to Syria ... in the name of holy war'. This was why the high command in Damascus was beset with volunteers for the Turco-German jihad: not because anyone there cared a fig for Turkey, Germany or the holy war *fetvas*, but simply because the Germans had 'awakened avarice for gold'.[19]

Kress, naturally, remembered his meetings with Musil somewhat differently. Unlike this wandering scholar, Kress was preparing an army for battle, and he wanted straight answers. Although Musil was later somewhat cagey about what exactly he had promised Kress in Damascus, once he had made contact with the Rwala Bedouins in the desert, Musil wrote on 29 December 1914 that An-Nuri would send 3,000 camel-mounted warriors to the Egyptian border – presumably (although he did not explicitly state this) to participate in the Suez attack. Emir Nawwaf had promised to send another 2,000. In all, this meant Musil was offering Kress 'some 5,000 camel-mounted warriors for the support of the [Ottoman] government'.[20] How exactly these Bedouins would support the Turks was left unsaid; but one can hardly blame Kress for believing the idea was that they would participate in the Suez offensive. Asked, several years later, to evaluate the results of Musil's mission to Arabia,* Kress replied that the Austrian had 'failed to fulfil any of his promises to send camels and camel-mounted warriors' to the Sinai. After Musil slipped into the desert from Damascus in December 1914, Kress never saw him again.[21]

If he was not going to help Kress muster men and camels for the Ottoman army's push across the Sinai to Suez, then what, exactly, was Musil up to? Tellingly, he concealed the real objective of his mission from not only the Germans, but even the Austrian government. Back

---

* As a diplomatic sop to their beleaguered ally, the Germans had nominated Musil for the Iron Cross. Needless to say, Kress did not give a favourable recommendation.

on 1 December 1914, the same day Musil demanded more money from Kress and promised (or so it seemed) to muster Bedouins and camels for him, the scholar-explorer had penned a private letter to his sister from Damascus, in which he confessed he had already resolved on ditching the Germans and doing 'scholarly research' instead. Musil was already forty-six years old, and did not know how much longer he would have the health or strength to carry out his field studies. With extraordinary selfishness, given the consequences for the lives of those in the Ottoman Fourth Army, he now resolved to use the funds Berlin had given him to make a grand scholarly tour of Arabia and Mesopotamia.[22]

Still, to justify his salary, Musil had to give the Germans something. And so, after voyaging out into the desert in early December, he salted his field reports with the sort of political gossip which sounded useful, even if it did not contain anything in the way of practical policy recommendations. Ibn Rashid's Shammar Bedouins, he reported from 'somewhere between al-Hegm and al-Bark' on 29 December 1914, though beloved of Enver and Oppenheim, were actively plundering the Howeitat and Rwala, when they were not doing the same to Ibn Saud's Wahhabis. If Musil could somehow cool down Ibn Rashid, then perhaps the Arabs would stop killing each other and develop an interest in killing Englishmen instead. It was not that he really expected that either Ibn Saud or Ibn Rashid, both angling for military suprem-acy in Arabia, would contribute troops to the upcoming assault on the Suez Canal. His idea, rather, was that if they did not stop fighting one another, then they definitively would not help the Ottoman army, and none of the other tribes would either. An-Nuri and Nawwaf, at least, were close enough to the Sinai to send camels and warriors there; but they would only do so if Ibn Rashid, ostensibly with Enver's backing, would stop plundering their caravans. If he could achieve a truce between the Shammar, Rwala and Howeitat, Musil wrote with characteristic vagueness, 'great forces would be made available for the [Ottoman] government'. It was a big 'if', however. English agents were already hard at work courting sheikhs with gold, while oner-ous army requisitions had turned settled Arabs against the Turkish cause. 'If only,' Musil concluded in his usual tone of pre-emptively excusing his failure to produce, 'I had come two months earlier!'[23]

Like Frobenius, Musil had run up hard against the influence barrier wrought by British bribery. His endless requests for more gold and tribute began to grate on the ears of the Germans, who by December 1914 had already given him 50,000 crowns, 10,000 Turkish pounds, and a huge supply of arms and ammunition, and were not at all clear on what they had received in return for this outlay.[24] And what, exactly, was going on with these Bedouins? Why was there, as Musil now reported from the north Arabian desert, 'no sign at all of any enthusiasm for Islam'?[25] Why did Musil keep asking Kress for more bribe money? Was not the whole strategic point of the jihad for Berlin that it was a cheaper way of fighting Britain than using German troops? If you had to pay Arab Muslims to fight, then they were not 'holy warriors', but mercenaries.

The biggest mercenary of all, according to Musil, was Ibn Rashid. The Shammar headman, whom Enver had materially entrusted with virtually his whole Arabian policy (even while pretending to support Ibn Saud), was neither a great warrior for the Ottoman cause nor even a loyal one. Documents uncovered in the French Consulate in Damascus, Musil had informed the Germans on 1 December 1914, showed that Ibn Rashid had been negotiating with French agents for a Syrian protectorate. Fifty thousand rifles, a one-time bribe of 15,000 Turkish pounds (some $20 million in today's terms), a luxury car, and a monthly stipend of 220 Turkish pounds had not been enough to purchase Ibn Rashid's loyalty to the Porte.[26] What it *had* bought, in the wake of Ibn Rashid's renewed attacks on the Wahhabis, was the enmity of Ibn Saud, a real jihadi warrior of Islam who was 'at least twenty times stronger than Ibn Rashid'. The new headman of the Rashid clan, just eighteen or nineteen years old, was, despite being physically strong, a mental weakling and 'almost an idiot'. At the height of the Rashid dynasty's power, the Shammar had controlled some nineteen oasis towns; these were now 'nearly all destroyed'. In all, some 250 members of the Rashidi clan had already fled to join forces with Ibn Saud.[27]

Musil's field reports make for interesting reading. Because he had so little confidence in the Turks' and Germans' regional objectives, Musil made almost no effort to tell his paymasters what they wanted to hear. This infuriated Germans like Kress, of course, but they might have been better off listening to what Musil was telling them. Ibn Saud, for example, may well have been in London's pay, but this did not mean he was London's tool. He took gold, munitions and foodstuffs from the British not because he liked them but because he needed gold, munitions and foodstuffs. At heart, Ibn Saud was a 'full-blooded Bedouin who hates all foreigners' – including the English. More to the point for the Germans, Saud was 'a believing Muslim who hates all unbelievers'. For this reason he would have been happy to do the bidding of the Sultan-Caliph in Arabia, if the Porte could provide him with the provisions he needed. Instead, the Turks had backed Ibn Rashid, a man as indifferent to Islam as he was militarily impotent.[28]

As for the rest of Arabia's tribal sheikhs, from Musil's viewpoint they were not exactly jihad material. Saud Ibn Melhem, headman of the Hsene Bedouins, was rich enough to own several urban properties in Homs, and thus unwilling to risk his worldly wealth by getting involved in the world war. Moreover, Melhem's tribesmen were (of course) feuding with several other tribes, the Fed'an and the Sba'a, and could hardly offer aid to the Ottomans unless a general truce was negotiated first. The same went for the Qmusa, who were fighting with the Sba'a. Musil could do his best to quiet these feuds, but because he was known as An-Nuri's friend and thus anti-Rashidi, pro-Ottoman tribes mistrusted him. 'The friend of the Turks,' he wrote of this frustrating period, 'was then my enemy, the enemy of the Turks were my friends and brothers.'

Besides the incessant feuding, Musil found that the 'moral level' of the Bedouins was 'not terribly high'. By this he meant not simply the taking on of twelve-year-old girls as wives and concubines, but widespread interbreeding with African slaves, the results of which were evident in the 'negroid features of many sons from the best [families]'. With their principal energies devoted to tribal feuding and the pleasures of concubinage, the Bedouins of north Arabia would have little left over for the Turco-German jihad.*[29]

---

* On the issue of sexual morality, at least, Kress and Musil saw eye to eye. Kress also observed that girls were married off at thirteen or fourteen years old. The Bedouins, he later wrote with a shudder, regularly bought and sold women as chattels, with fathers often selling 'pristine young daughters' for proper riding camels or a mature date tree. Widows or divorcees, by contrast, would usually only fetch a pack animal in barter.

In both his unromantic view of tribal life and his cold analysis of Arabian power politics, Musil was on the money. He was that rarest of birds, a genuine scholar who could appreciate the customs of the people he studied without going native. Without condescending to his Bedouin hosts, he saw them for what they were: primitive tribesmen who knew little of the world beyond the desert and did not particularly desire to know more. The Bedouins were not jihad material, as the Germans and then the British would discover in their turn. The one exception to the rule was Ibn Saud, whose Wahhabis alone possessed the single-minded tenacity and discipline to sustain forces in battle. But the Turks had forfeited Saud's support by backing the overmatched Ibn Rashid, whose dynasty was rapidly dying out in the face of the Wahhabi ascendancy.

It should not come as a surprise that Musil, an academic by profession, was in the end much better at gathering intelligence than at making war. Both the Germans and the British could have greatly benefited from Musil's analysis, saving themselves a good deal of gold and grief had they known how little their efforts to recruit warriors on the Arabian peninsula would avail them. Still, however penetrating the Austrian scholar's field reports were, one begins ultimately to sympathize with poor Kress in Damascus, who had not asked Musil for a long-winded ethnography lesson but simply for camels. In the end, the struggle for Suez would not be decided by bribes or the intricacies of Bedouin politics, but by real modern armies and the order of battle.

9

Showdown at the Suez Canal

Out of all the confusion there emerged by and by a completely orderly and picturesque train, which wound slowly up and down the steep hills and the narrow palm-bedecked streets of the old city, between houses decorated with flags and old carpets, towards the Damascus gate. Before nearly every Arab house the headman stood and sprinkled us with rose oil dispensed from antique silver pitchers.

Lieutenant Colonel Kress von Kressenstein, on the passage of the Ottoman Fourth Army through Jerusalem en route for the Suez Canal[1]

For all their colour, the adventures of holy war field men like Frobenius and Musil had remained peripheral to the course of military events. Doubtless a general jihadi uprising in Sudan, or a mustering of Bedouin tribes and camels from Arabia, could have made some small difference in the playing out of the long-planned Ottoman offensive against the Suez Canal. So, too, might have the German efforts to sabotage the canal, including an attempt in mid-August to scuttle a German ship in shallow water to block passage, and the Robert Mors all-purpose sabotage mission dispatched by Prüfer in October. In December Prüfer had also dispatched several sheikhs of the Sanussi order, accompanied by a Hungarian, aboard Red Sea schooners on a Frobenius-style operation to fire oil tanks and dynamite railway bridges in Upper Egypt. All three missions, predictably, had been foiled by the British navy, which since the start of the war had blanketed the approaches to the Suez Canal. These clashes, along with the skirmishing which had already begun in the desert areas near the Egyptian-Ottoman border, ensured that Cairo was on high alert all winter for the upcoming Suez offensive.

These intelligence failures on the Turco-German side were serious, but not necessarily fatal. Sir John Maxwell, who commanded British forces in Egypt, would have known Kress and Djemal were coming across the Sinai to Suez whether or not Mors had been captured. This did not mean, however, that he knew when they were coming, or which part of the canal they would pinpoint. The Suez Canal is roughly 100 miles long, and never wider than several hundred metres across. It was by no means unthinkable that Turco-German forces, if materializing from the desert against a relatively undefended portion of the canal, could win a localized bridgehead before British reinforcements could be rushed in. Of course, it was unlikely that the Ottoman Fourth Army could cross the Sinai desert in strength anywhere near the 70,000 or so troops Maxwell could (by winter) bring to bear across the entire theatre, but a small tactical breakthrough at Suez might be enough to induce panic in Cairo or, better still, a mutiny among the Egyptian and Indian Muslim soldiers under Maxwell's command.

Such, at any rate, was the idea entertained at Damascus headquarters.[2] To be sure, Kress himself would have loved to attack in strength, with a fully equipped army disposing of mobile field artillery, flanked by thousands of Bedouin camel warriors from Arabia. But the weeks of preparation and planning in Damascus had made it clear that nothing of the sort was in the offing. Musil, as noted, had refused even to try to win over the north Arabian tribes for the offensive, or obtain their camels. The only Ottoman munitions factory was back in Constantinople, and even its meagre output was mostly destined to reinforce the Straits defences, which meant that any supplies of field guns, shell, rifles and rounds for Suez would have to be shipped in all the way from Germany. With long Balkan sections of the Orient Express still cut off, owing to Romanian interference and fighting on the Serbian front, and several dozen kilometres on the Baghdad railway near Cilicia still uncompleted, getting guns to Syria was like sending them to the moon. Not for the last time, Kress lamented the dreaded Taurus and Amanus mountain gaps, which had ensured that his forces would be woefully short of firepower at Suez.[3]

If he lacked artillery and Arabian support, however, Kress did have one secret weapon in Damascus: Curt Prüfer. Oppenheim's talented protégé, as we saw above, had set off something of a bidding war when he arrived in Constantinople in September. In a nod to the crucial importance of the Suez offensive, Oppenheim, Wangenheim and Enver had set aside their differences long enough to appoint Prüfer liaison to the Ottoman Fourth Army, which turned out to be an inspired decision. Arriving in Syria towards the end of September 1914 along with Kress, the former Cairo dragoman immediately proved his worth. Djemal, who arrived on 8 December to replace Zekki Pasha as commander of the Ottoman Fourth Army, had good French, but no German or Arabic. Zekki himself, who stayed on under Djemal's command, was actually Kurdish, although with good Turkish. Kress knew a bit of French, which allowed him to talk awkwardly with Djemal, but no Arabic or Turkish (nor, of course, Kurdish). A Turkish captain, Ekrem Bey, who had come in on Kress's train from Constantinople, knew some German, but not French or Arabic. A few of the Arab officers knew some French, but none knew German, and most did not know Turkish either. Virtually none of the Turkish officers, meanwhile, knew Arabic. Compounding the linguistic confusion, Kress later recalled, were the misunderstandings wrought by 'Oriental politeness', which forbade Turks or Arabs from admitting to superiors that they did not understand what was being told them.[4]

In this Babel of tongues Prüfer was the man of the hour. Now helping translate Kress's training orders to Ottoman recruits, now patching up misunderstandings between Turkish and Arab officers, now smoothing over ruffled tempers at high command, Prüfer was the model of the old Ottoman dragoman, who by pivoting between uncomprehending worlds became indispensable to each of them in turn. In any coalition army, the thorniest issue is the chain of command. Kress and Djemal had every reason to be jealous of one another's authority. Prüfer won the trust of both men, which allowed him to establish a rough working relationship between them, in which Kress handled training, logistics and operational planning, while conceding to Djemal the overall strategic command.

The task facing Djemal, Kress and Prüfer was daunting. Before they could tackle the logistical problems of getting men and supplies across the barren desert wastes of the Sinai, there were political complications which threatened to overshadow even a successful operation. To begin with, in whose name exactly was Egypt to be conquered? Although the Ottoman Fourth Army (via its VIII Corps) would be providing most of the soldiers for the offensive, the funding, training, arms and supplies were almost entirely German, while the diplomatic impetus was ostensibly to do with restoring Egyptian independence from British (mis)rule. Or was it? Until London, fearing precisely the Suez attack which was now in the works, finally declared Egypt a British protectorate on 18 December 1914, the country had theoretically been under the Porte's suzerainty. Did the Turks want it back, in the name of the Ottoman Sultan-Caliph who had nominally ruled Egypt since 1517? If so, would they rule directly, or through the legitimate, though recently deposed, Khedive, Abbas Hilmi II? Or would the Khedive rule under some sort of German protectorate? Something of the confusion of the Suez operation was captured in Ernst Jäckh's mock slogan, 'Turkey, a German Egypt'.[5]

Whether Egypt would be Turkish, German or Egyptian, the man chosen as its titular ruler if the British were overthrown would almost certainly be Abbas Hilmi II. But the Khedive was a wild card. Although Abbas had intrigued for years with Egyptian nationalists and pan-Germans like Oppenheim, until 1914 he had been Britain's man, at least in the sense that the British allowed him to retain title to the Egyptian throne. It was in part due to suspicion of Abbas's pro-Ottoman leanings that the British had formally absorbed Egypt into the empire following the Porte's entry into the war. But the Turks did not trust Abbas either, and the feeling was mutual. Somewhat by accident, the Khedive had found himself summering on the Bosphorus when the July crisis broke, and was thus under Enver's thumb as the European war began. The two men had never got on, but tensions were particularly acute following an assassination attempt on Abbas in July, which he blamed, not unreasonably, on the Porte.* Enver, for his part, accused Abbas of taking money not only from London, but from the Italians during the

---

* The assailant had been killed on the spot by Ottoman policemen present at the scene, without being questioned. Abbas Hilmi suspected the Grand Vizier, Said Halim Pasha, who was his cousin and a possible rival to the Egyptian throne.

Libyan war of 1911–12.[6] Making a surprise visit to the German Embassy on 4 September while Abbas was calling on Wangenheim, Enver 'shouted charges of treason at the flustered Abbas and challenged him to demonstrate his loyalty to the Sultan by leading the Turkish columns towards the Suez Canal'. As moral blackmail, this was hard to top. As Frank Weber has written, for the sake of honour Abbas was forced to accept 'Enver's cruel jest', despite the fact that the Khedive was still recovering from the wounds inflicted by the would-be assassin's bullet, and had no military experience anyway.[7]

Complicating the situation surrounding the Khedive still further was the Austrian angle. Vienna had made a devil's bargain with both Berlin and the Porte to get the Turks into the war, hoping for relief against the Russians in Galicia but receiving nothing of the kind. Were Abbas to follow through on his promise to lead a liberating army into Egypt under the auspices of the Turco-German holy war, it might easily tip a terrified Italy over into belligerence on the Entente side. As early as September, long before the Turks had gone in, Pallavicini was sounding alarm bells about the preparations for a Suez attack, going so far as to dispatch his military attaché, Joseph Pomiankowski, to talk down Enver.[8] Although Pallavicini's warning had done nothing to curtail the mobilization of the Ottoman Fourth Army in Syria, the Austrians drew some reassurance from the Khedive's departure from Constantinople in November 1914 – not for the front lines, but for his vacation home in Vienna. His promise to Enver now evidently forgotten, Abbas returned to the world he knew best: high-stakes diplomacy, in which the future of the Egyptian Khediviate was bandied over in the comfort of European chancelleries. What was the Sinai desert, compared to the glittering palaces of Vienna?

The Abbas affair painfully illustrated the conflicting strategic aims of the Central Powers, which were only exacerbated by the prospect of conquering Egypt. Berlin, Vienna and Constantinople were all operating in bad faith to one degree or another. The Germans ostensibly wanted to help the Porte regain control of formerly Ottoman Egypt – but not if it meant the Turks would actually control the place, as Wangenheim confessed at one point to US Ambassador Morgenthau.[9] The Austrians had no wish for either Germany or Turkey to control Egypt, but were not above indulging the Khedive, in whose name the Suez attack was supposed to be joined, by treating him as a head of state: Abbas was given a private audience with long-serving Habsburg Emperor Franz Josef.[10] Enver and Talaat were, if anything, even more Machiavellian in their approach to the question of the Egyptian succession. Neither man trusted Said Halim, the Egyptian-born Grand Vizier, and for this very reason they happily intrigued to get rid of him by promoting his claim to the Cairo Khediviate over that of Abbas Hilmi II.[11]

The Khedive himself was more transparent, but for that reason less effective. Abbas knew perfectly well what the Young Turks thought of him, and so played the Germans straight off against them. Summoning Baron Oppenheim, an old friend from Cairo days, to Vienna in early January 1915, the Khedive demanded that the Germans wring from the Porte a promise to respect Egyptian sovereignty if the British were overthrown. More to the point, Abbas demanded that the Germans guarantee his throne in case the British were expelled from Egypt – and that Said Halim renounce his own claim. In consultation with Wangenheim, the wily old Grand Vizier agreed, not, one suspects, out of deference to his cousin, but rather because he realized that this proclamation would tie Abbas's fortunes irrevocably to the chancy undertaking at Suez.[12]

While the Khedive was carrying on his intrigues in Vienna, the Germans and Turks in Syria were doing the grunt work to win him back his throne – at least in theory. In fact there was little love for Abbas in the Ottoman army command. The Egyptian officers the Khedive had seconded to the Suez mission were sent back to Constantinople soon after they arrived in Damascus, which suggests that Djemal himself had no intention of re-installing Abbas on the Egyptian throne.[13] Turkish officers did not trust Egyptians, nor Arabs in general. As Kress later recalled, 'in every Arab division the majority of the [command positions] were given to Turkish officers, for political reasons'.[14]

The Bedouins were trusted even less. With Musil gone AWOL, there was little chance the great Arabian sheikhs would show up for the fight. As if he did not already have enough to do as all-purpose drago-man, it was thus left to Prüfer to win over the local Bedouins of Syria and the Sinai, and muster camels. Although Prüfer himself lamented his failure to do enough – as always, the nefarious English were offering better prices for camels, making bartering difficult – the dragoman certainly outperformed Musil. After seemingly interminable haggling, Prüfer acquired some 2,000 camels from a Damascus dealer, Bassâm (imported, bragged Bassâm, all the way from Mesopotamia), at the onerous price of some 10 Turkish pounds each (about $50, equal to some $5,000 today). This brought the total number of camels available to Ottoman VIII Corps up to 10,000.

The Bedouins themselves proved more difficult to recruit for the Suez attack. Most demanded huge bribes to participate, which Prüfer liberally dispensed. One local chieftain, Mumtas Bey, went so far as to promise the Ottoman army command that 'he and his Bedouins would either die or raise the Ottoman flag on the Citadel in Cairo'. Mumtas was given enormous sums in gold, whereupon he disappeared into the desert. Not quite reaching Suez, much less Cairo, Mumtas retired his forces immediately he encountered a party of British Indian reconnaissance troops somewhere in the Sinai, never to venture out again. This 'squalid fiasco', Prüfer wrote on 31 December 1914, showed that Bedouin warriors were, at heart, 'cowardly and insubordinate'.[15]

Somewhat more promising were Syria's settled town-dwelling Muslims, who volunteered for the Suez operation in much greater numbers than the Bedouins. At least in the towns, there were some literate Arabs able to appreciate the Ottoman jihad *fetvas*. Judging by the tone of newspaper coverage of the war in Beirut and Jerusalem, even the Christians and Jews were supportive of the Turco-German cause, if only in the interest of self-preservation and to exempt themselves from Muslim wrath.[16]

After the Ottoman VIII Corps moved from Damascus to Jerusalem in December to begin mustering closer to the Sinai, the Turco-German holy war began to take shape in earnest. Rumours of the impending arrival of a holy green flag from Mecca set off stormy demonstrations on 20 December, as 'numerous Muslim clerics, city elders, schools and associations – an enormous crowd, some on foot, some in cars, and some on horseback – gathered by the Nablus gate'. As the horse-drawn wagon containing the green banner approached the gate, recalled Kress, there was an 'indescribable commotion' which rapidly turned 'life-threatening', because 'every believing Muslim wanted to kiss the holy flag'. It was a dangerous moment, not least because the flag-bearer was an elderly sheikh of sixty-five, whose health was precarious. Djemal himself intervened to protect the Mecca holy man, narrowly avoiding a disturbing omen for the jihad.[17]

There now ensued an inspiring spectacle. As the 'orderly and picturesque train' wound through the old city towards the Damascus gate, women and children posed on the balconies in the 'picturesque, colourful garb' of the Orient, while their men blessed the army with rose oil. All in all, it seemed that 'indescribable jubilation and bright enthusiasm took possession of the entire population'. Jerusalem, the city which had so fired the Kaiser's enthusiasm for Islam, had now blessed his holy war.[18]

One can hardly blame Kress for getting carried away in the holy war procession in Jerusalem. After all the frustrations and delays in Damascus, it seemed the battle for Suez was finally being joined. Scouting parties began slipping into the Sinai desert to invest Bedouin watering holes for the arrival of the Ottoman army, dumping supplies and posting sentries. For the long arid stretches in between oases, German sappers and military engineers dug wells at suitable intervals along the proposed marching route. Behind enemy lines in Egypt, Turkish spies distributed jihadi propaganda and spread word of the upcoming attack to prepare the Muslim population to rise. Whether Kress and Djemal were ready or not, the big day was now approaching fast.

With all the holy war fanfare, the Germans and Turks had, in effect, called their own bluff. There were countless reasons to postpone the assault on Suez, from the unresolved political complications with the Khedive, to Musil's disappearance and the subsequent failure to procure enough camels or Bedouin warriors, to the inadequate supplies of everything from howitzers to light machine guns to ammunition. There was even a disastrous holy war omen on the day before Christmas, when the elderly green flag-bearer from Mecca died, the stress of carrying the flag into Jerusalem amidst clammering throngs having evidently aggravated his heart condition.[19] Ill omens or not, excessive delay could also be fatal. As Prüfer wrote from Jerusalem on 31 December 1914, truly adequate munitioning of a Suez offensive would require not only the completion of the Taurus tunnels, but the construction of an entirely new rail line from Ma'an across the Sinai to the canal, which might take three years to finish. If Djemal and Kress wanted to strike in 1915, they would have to do so by March at the latest, unless they wanted to reckon with spring sandstorms, not to mention brutal summer heat to follow. More to the immediate point, if the Ottoman army failed to strike at Suez after the ostentatious preparations in Damascus and Jerusalem, Prüfer wrote, it would 'be tantamount to the total discouragement of the Egyptians, who are cowards anyway'.[20]

If the Kaiser's dream of expelling the British from Egypt were to be realized, it was now or never. On 10 January 1915, the Ottoman VIII army corps set out southwards from Jerusalem into the Sinai desert, accompanied by the holy green banner of Mecca – but without the sacred flag-bearer. The banner itself was something of a nuisance to carry, considering how tight the transport situation was. Most heavy baggage was abandoned at Beersheeba, along with the sick and those too weak to continue. Officers were permitted only fifteen kilograms of kit to reduce the strain on the men and animals, and were forbidden even field beds. There was one glaring exception to the general rule of austerity and common suffering: Ottoman Fourth Army commander Djemal, who, as Prüfer complained in his diary, 'takes magnificent tents, hat stands, commodes, beds etc. into the desert and we sleep in the open!'[21] Even Djemal, however, had to suffer the meagre rations of food (mostly hardtack biscuits, plus a few dates and olives) and 'wicked tasting, barely drinkable' water. The liquid drawn from hastily engineered desert wells was usually salty or muddy, while in other oases it was usually just rainwater stored away in filthy petroleum cans. It was largely thanks to the 'astounding performance' of German medics, Prüfer reported from the field, that only twelve men fell seriously ill during the gruelling march to the Suez Canal.[22]

Kress may not have been much of a linguist, but when it came to moving troops and weapons he clearly knew his business. In the annals of the First World War, the successful Turco-German Sinai desert crossing has to count as one of the greatest achievements. The famous 1917 crossing of the Nefud desert to Aqaba dramatized in *Lawrence of Arabia* involved only some 500 irregular Bedouins, armed with swords and a few guns. The Sinai crossing of 1915 involved a proper army of some 20,000 men and thousands of camels and pack animals, carrying howitzers, shell, heavy machine guns and ammunition stores, medical supplies and German steel pontoons for bridging the canal – all transported across 260 kilometres (160 miles) of near-waterless desert. True, the Turco-German Sinai crossing was made in January, which meant the heat was simply intolerable instead of overtly life-threatening. Even so, the men marched only at night, both to conserve water and to avoid British surveillance. Many of the Turkish soldiers trod the sands barefoot. Somehow, after nearly three weeks of marching seven hours a night or more, Djemal's army materialized just north-east of the stretch of the canal between Toussum and Serapeum. Kress later recounted the scene: 'from atop a nearby sand dune we caught our first glimpse of the Suez Canal. Like a silver ribbon it wound itself through the white sand dunes, here and there widening out into a broad sea and then again disappearing from our sight.' The showdown for Suez had begun.[23]

The men were nearly all exhausted, but many were in excellent spirits and ready to launch the Turco-German jihad. Ottoman Christian and Jewish soldiers had been left behind at Beersheeba, to enhance the quality of a purely Islamic army (although the Germans, of course, remained).[24] Adding to the sense of Islamic solidarity were Tripolitanian *mujāhidīn* veterans of the Italian war, Kurdish and Circassian cavalry units, and to crown them all a special company of Mevlevî whirling dervishes in traditional tall conical hats (this had been Enver Pasha's own idea).[25] At the oasis of Hafif el Auja, Djemal made the rounds before retiring to his tent, hoisting aloft the holy war banner from Mecca. Each Muslim soldier, Kress recalled, was enjoined to swear a sacred oath on the green flag. Djemal, holding the flag in his resplendent pasha's costume, was flanked by several Muslim army chaplains (imams) on horseback, who read out 'fiery speeches of such eloquence', Kress wrote, 'that they made an impression even on the Germans, who understood not a word'. The Muslims, meanwhile, were so overwhelmed by the moment that 'some of them had spells of hysteria and fell into paroxysms'.[26]

Here was the Kaiser's holy war made flesh. To be sure, Kress and Djemal commanded only some 20,000 exhausted, malnourished men against the entire occupying army of Egypt, more than three times as strong (although, as it turned out, only some 35,000 troops had been

posted at the canal), and infinitely better supplied. But there were
Indian, Egyptian and Sudanese Muslims in British ranks, who might
well mutiny if they saw their liberators carrying the sacred green flag
of Mecca. This impression was buttressed by intelligence reports
reaching Kress and Prüfer that the British were disarming Indian
Muslim soldiers manning the canal defences.[27] British fears of pan-
Islamic sympathies undermining army morale were by no means
unfounded: five Punjabi Muslim soldiers in fact deserted on 1 February,
shortly before the battle was joined – and it was Punjabis who held
the line at Ismailia where the attack came.[28] An English reconnaissance officer captured in the desert in late January reinforced the optimism in the Turco-German camp, telling Prüfer that the British had
only Australians, New Zealanders and Indian troops in Egypt, with
few Englishmen, and had 'no heavy guns' along the canal.[29] If this
were true, perhaps a breakthrough was possible, and the Egyptian
jihad would ignite after all.

It would be easy to dismiss the holy war enthusiasm in the Turco-
German camp as foolish optimism, hopelessly out of touch with the
realities of the order of battle facing them at Suez. Most historians
have done so.[30] But then armies march not only on their stomachs,
but on morale. If nothing else, the Sultan's holy war *fetvas*, the theat-
rics with the green banner from Mecca, the whirling dervishes, and the
constant exhortations from Djemal to die for Allah kept the Ottoman
army together on the long march to Suez, and helped ensure that
Muslim soldiers – or at least the Turks – were ready to lay down their
lives when the guns started firing.

As night fell on the canal on 2 February 1915, Djemal and Kress
gave the order to take the western bank just south of Toussum. Had
the German sappers succeeded in laying pontoons across the canal
under cover of darkness, the Turco-German army may well have won
a defensible bridgehead by morning. But hours of valuable time were
lost due to a vicious sandstorm, which ruined visibility and wrought
havoc with the alignment of the eight columns Kress had assembled
for bridging operations. The attack was supposed to begin at 10.30
p.m., but it was not until 3.30 a.m. on the morning of 3 February that
the first steel pontoons were finally lowered into the water. Although
three of the bridging teams did reach the other side of the canal before

being detected, the early dawn light seems to have doomed the operation. Once the British caught a glimpse of the enemy sappers, they poured down murderous machine-gun fire on them.[31]

It was not a fair fight. Sir John Maxwell was much better informed about Turco-German strength than Djemal and Kress were of British dispositions. An aerial reconnaissance report filed on 2 February, shortly before the Suez attack, had estimated 'a total enemy force of 19,000 men and 16 guns ... within 4 to 12 miles from the Suez Canal, extending from Kantara to Suez; additional force known to be pushing forward'. Contrary to the Germans' belief that they were betrayed by the early morning light, in fact the attack had been expected. As Maxwell reported to Kitchener on 3 February, after the first assault had been repulsed, 'the Turks attempted to cross the canal south of Toussum during the night. They were allowed to approach and bring their bridging material right up to the bank, and a completely successful attack was delivered when it was observed that they had begun bridging operations.' Without achieving surprise, the sappers were mowed down one by one, the shooting resembling, as one English officer put it cruelly, a 'grouse drive'.[32]

The battle for Suez was over nearly as soon as it had begun. The British quickly rushed reinforcements overland to Ismailia and Toussum, while bringing an entire naval squadron into the canal nearby for good measure. Although the Turks and Germans were game, continuing to fire on enemy positions all through the day on 3 February and even making a quixotic second attempt to lay pontoons that evening, the Bedouins, followed rapidly by Arab regulars, turned tail almost immediately. This behaviour Prüfer contrasted unfavourably with the heroism of the German Major von Hagen, who had gone down firing, his body riddled with no less than eighteen bullet holes.[33]

For all the inspiring holy war rhetoric, Muslim solidarity was a phantom on a serious battlefield. 'Despite all our agitation, despite the thousands of pamphlets,' Prüfer reported to Oppenheim following the battle, 'we did not have any [Muslim] deserters.' As for would-be Muslim jihadis on the Ottoman side, only the Turks had showed any 'élan': everyone else 'fled at the first opening of machine-gun fire'. Particularly shameful was the behaviour of Arab 'holy warriors' from Medina, who had 'sneaked away surreptitiously before the battle, [carrying] the holy flag with them'. The Bedouins, Prüfer reported, 'scattered immediately the battle began, or went over to the enemy'. Their only contribution seems to have been shouting 'Allahu Akbar' so loudly that they betrayed Djemal's positions to the British.[34] Other holy war volunteers and self-styled 'mujehadin', including Kurds and Druze, 'never appeared at all, instead remaining behind in Palestine'. Even Turkish officers, while displaying courage in battle, had sometimes offered 'passive resistance' to German marching orders. That morale was preserved through the gruelling desert march and the hail of gunfire at the canal, Prüfer wrote, was 'thanks in the main to the admirable calm and assurance of Herr von Kress'.[35]

If nothing else, the Turco-German debacle at Suez provided valuable feedback for German war-planners. Clearly, the makeshift army Kress had led across the desert had not been large enough to threaten the British position in Egypt. Field artillery had been woefully inadequate. The few howitzers Kress had been able to drag across the desert could launch shells only six kilometres, which meant the rail tracks behind British lines, over which reinforcements had been rushed into Toussum, had remained out of range. Expectations of mutinies in the British ranks had obviously been overblown; so, too, Oppenheim's notion of a jihadi uprising in Cairo piggybacking on the Suez attack. British surveillance planes had cost Kress any chance of catching the canal defenders off guard, while Bedouin reports on enemy dispositions had proved exaggerated and inaccurate. To achieve rough parity in striking power with the enemy, particularly in heavy artillery, the Baghdad railway gaps had to be forded as soon as possible, and a new branch line constructed from Ma'an, through Jerusalem and Beersheeba, 'at least as far as Chabra I', an oasis within easy marching distance of the canal. To ensure that orders were followed, Prüfer and Kress concluded, German officers must have unfettered command.[36]

It is noteworthy that Prüfer sent two separate Suez post-mortems from the field on 9 February 1915, one addressed to Ambassador Wangenheim, and the other to his mentor, Baron Oppenheim. To Wangenheim, Prüfer gave a no-nonsense, blow-by-blow narrative of the battle and forwarded Kress's requests for money, *matériel* and infrastructural investment for a renewed attempt to take the canal. For all the acrimony between German and Turkish officers following the rout,

Prüfer noted that a retreat to Jerusalem had been conducted in good order (itself a further major feat), and that only some 800 men were either dead or missing out of an army of nearly 20,000. In strictly military terms, this was hardly a 'catastrophe'.[37]

In Prüfer's report to Oppenheim, by contrast, there is an elegiac note which suggests a coming of age. Without quite saying so openly, Prüfer made it clear that he thought Oppenheim had grossly exaggerated the potential of pan-Islamic propaganda, and misread the Egyptian mentality entirely. Turkish-Arab tension was rife in the Ottoman army, making a sham of the notion of Muslim brotherhood-in-arms. 'The holy war,' Prüfer concluded with a note of melancholy, 'is a tragicomedy.' Having been lightly injured in the Suez battle, Prüfer informed Oppenheim he would be returning to Jerusalem for medical treatment, which meant he would not be able to report again for some time.[38] In fact, this was the last time Prüfer reported to Oppenheim directly.

With the setback at Suez, the Kaiser's anti-British jihad had been dealt a serious blow. Kress and Djemal, both advised by the redoubtable Prüfer, were not about to give up, but it would be at least a year before the Ottoman Fourth Army could mount another attack on the canal. In the meantime, news was trickling in that the Third Army, which Enver had led into a suicidal attack on the Russians in the winter snows of the Caucasus, had met an even more serious disaster in January than had Djemal's army in February. In the snowdrifts of Sarıkamış, those Turks who had not already frozen or starved to death were routed by the Russians, with only some 50,000 typhus-ridden survivors staggering back in headlong retreat to Erzurum out of an army of nearly 100,000.[39] Rumours of British preparations for a naval assault on the Straits were more worrying still. Scarcely had the Turks recovered from the loss of prestige at Suez and Sarıkamış than they were faced with the prospect of losing Constantinople itself.

10

Gallipoli: From Disaster
to Triumph

Those who watched the Turkish gunners at Kilid Bahr on the Gallipoli side of the straits say they fought with a wild fanaticism, an Imam chanting prayers to them as they ran to their work on the gun emplacements. This was something more than the usual excitement of battle; the men were possessed ... with a religious fervour, a kind of frenzy against the attacking infidel.

Alan Moorehead, *Gallipoli*[1]

The small town of Gallipoli (Gelibolu) at the north end of the Dardanelles has never been much to look at. Today, it could easily be confused with any of a thousand other sprawling, nondescript settlements, filled with half-finished cement vacation homes that blight so much of the eastern Mediterranean. The town has grown mildly prosperous on fishing and on the tourist industry, not least as a place where countless Anzac-inspired tourists visit each April.

And yet it was here that the Ottoman general staff directed one of the most crucial battle in Turkish history, out of the fires of which the modern republic was forged. Today Gallipoli may be a byword for bungling, for pointless slaughter and military incompetence (at least from the Allied side), but there is a reason why so many soldiers died on this peninsula, why the battle lives on in the memories of the Turks, the English, Scots, Australians and New Zealanders who took part.*

* This is not to slight the French, who also took part in the fighting. Because so much of the First World War was fought on and over French soil, however, Gallipoli has never really been an essential part of the national story of modern France.

In the first six months of the First World War, almost nothing had been settled on the main European battlefields. The Germans had advanced far into Belgium and France, only to become bogged down in a colossal stalemate, with impassable trenches dug from Switzerland to the English Channel. In eastern Europe the Germans had (mostly) bested the Russians, who had bested the Austrians in turn. Here a different kind of equilibrium reigned, in which Russia's endlessly replenishable reserves of manpower made a decisive German victory impossible, even while Austro-Hungarian weakness gave the Russians every reason to fight on. The British decision to force the Straits was the mirror image of the German jihad plan: a turnaround, to force a decision in the East while stalemate reigned in the West. Just as the Turco-German gambit at the Suez Canal had aimed to split the British Empire in two, an Allied breakthrough at the Straits would bring into play Constantinople itself, the greatest prize of the war, and put a nail in the coffin of the Germans' *Drang nach Osten*. With his dream of an empire stretching from the North Sea to Baghdad and the Persian Gulf shattered, and the Russian Tsar instead inheriting the Second Rome and the Straits, surely the Kaiser would have to sue for peace. This, at any rate, was the British hope.

The Turks and Germans, of course, had other ideas. Just as there was no secret about the designs of the Ottoman Fourth Army on the Suez Canal, so too was the British assault on the Straits expected by everyone in Constantinople. It was the Dardanelles through which the Kaiser's yacht had passed as he made his historic first visit to Turkey twenty-five years before; it was the tense and exciting passage by the *Goeben* and *Breslau* through the same Straits which had won the Germans their position of primacy at the Porte in August 1914; and it was Enver's closure of the Dardanelles in September which had helped make inevitable Turkey's entry into the war, by striking directly at Russia's most vital interests. The Straits are the 'windpipe of Eurasia', through which pass nearly all of Russia's exports – then mostly grain, now mostly oil – the control of which has been fought over for millennia. If the men in Flanders had little sense of the importance of the muddy, barbed-wire strewn encampments for which sake they were dying by the thousands, the same cannot really be said of the Narrows over which Xerxes had erected his Hellespont, nor the heights on the

European side commanding the Straits, over which the Gallipoli campaign was fought. Here was history in the grandest sense: Europe facing Asia, once pitting Greeks against Persians, now ranging European Christians opposite Ottoman Muslims – assisted by their honorary non-infidel European allies.

General Liman von Sanders, who, as overall commander of the Ottoman First Army, was responsible for the capital,* had been hard at work all autumn and winter strengthening the Straits defences. Aside from the obvious targets of an Allied naval offensive – the forts at Silid Bahr and Chanakkale facing the Narrows from the European and Asian coastlines, respectively – Liman had also erected shore batteries along the western side of the Sea of Marmara between San Stefano (Yeşilköy) and Seray Point, and on the Princes' Islands, in case the British navy succeeded in forcing the Dardanelles. Further north, to meet a possible Russian amphibious landing force rumoured to be gathering in Odessa, guns had been placed in the forts along the Bosphorus, ranging all the way to the Black Sea, buttressed by mobile battalions. It is true that adequate shell and ammunition stores were still lacking along all these fronts, largely as a result of Romania's decision to forbid all arms shipments across her territory, which forced Berlin to resort to bribes, subterfuges and ruses to send arms to Turkey. (Shipments by riverboat along the Danube to Rustchuk, meanwhile, had proved impractical, owing to Serbian shelling, a result of Austria-Hungary's chaotic failure to invade Serbia successfully in the war's opening campaigns.) Faced with a probable British attempt to force the Straits, the frustrating diplomacy of Balkan transport in the weeks following Ottoman belligerence had caused a near panic in the German high command. Although it took nearly a year to work through the diplomatic complications with Vienna, on 14 November 1914, just ten days after the Porte entered the war Erich von Falkenhayn, Moltke's successor as Chief of the German General Staff, began planning an offensive to knock Serbia out of the war to open the road to Turkey.[2] Liman, who had inspected most of the Straits batteries in

---

* Von der Goltz Pasha, now a Field Marshal, had arrived in Constantinople in December 1914 following a brief stint as military governor of occupied Belgium and was much Liman's senior; but to avoid friction with Liman over command von der Goltz had been given a mostly symbolic role as general adjutant to the Sultan.

person, was more sanguine about the threat posed by a British naval bombardment. Boldly, he assured Falkenhayn on 7 December 1914 that all necessary precautions had already been taken: the defences would hold.[3]

Liman is an enigmatic figure in the Gallipoli story. It is ironic that this laconic and dull personality occasioned such passionate objections from his many rivals. Partly deaf, Liman's hardness of hearing seems to have greatly accentuated his natural anti-social tendencies. Even Liman's defenders concede that he had little talent for diplomacy and played no role in the social life of Pera. Enver could not stand him, and let everyone know it. Liman's own adjutant, Fritz Bronsart von Schellendorf, spied on him for Ambassador Wangenheim. Wangenheim held Liman in such exquisite contempt that, having failed numerous times to secure his dismissal, he began spreading the rumour in December 1914 that Liman was insane and even asked the German General Staff to send a qualified psychiatrist to examine him. Wangenheim's basically negative assessment of Liman has been adopted by most German diplomatic historians, who ascribe Liman's complaints about ill-treatment at Wangenheim's hands to 'self-pity and paranoia', and his better relations with Pallavicini and Pomiankowski to Liman's need for 'shoulders ... ample to cry on'.[4]

Whether out of genuine sympathy or (as Wangenheim believed) a desire for inside dirt on German-Ottoman diplomacy, the Austrians indeed took Liman on as one of their own. But it was not only Pallavicini and Pomiankowski who grew fond of the taciturn German field marshal. Alois Musil was absolutely taken with Liman, finding him both more intelligent and 'stronger' than Enver and Bronsart, and much preferring the Marshal's company to Wangenheim's.[5] There was something in Liman's abstracted manner, his appearance of being lost in thought, which appealed to the subtle Austrian mind, even while it drove many Germans (and headstrong Turks like Enver) crazy. Liman was nothing if not a systematic thinker, and while prone at times to volatile mood swings, he was basically cautious in his style of command. He thought little of the holy war schemes dreamed up by the Kaiser and Baron Oppenheim, dismissing them as 'obscure fantasies' which distracted the Turks from the imperative need simply to defend their territory. Although he got along well with Musil and Prüfer,

Liman did everything he could to block the missions of Frobenius, Niedermayer and Oppenheim's other sundry jihad field agents.[6] Liman refused Enver's repeated requests that he take on the Ottoman Third Army command in Erzurum, believing Enver's idea of a winter Caucasian offensive stupid. He thought the Ottoman War Minister's larger aim of sending an army across Persia and Afghanistan into India was 'utterly fantastic'. In all these cases, Liman's innate caution would have served the Turco-German cause much better than the inspired scheming of the Kaiser, Oppenheim and Enver.[7]

Following the disaster at Sarıkamış, for which he was personally responsible, Enver was hardly in a position to criticize Liman's preparations. Nevertheless, he did not refrain from doing so. After the long-expected British bombardment of the Dardanelles forts began on 19 February 1915, Liman refused to order emergency measures beyond the preparations already undertaken. Against Enver's express wishes, Liman did not even recall either of the two infantry divisions in the II Corps at Adrianople (Edirne), and had Bronsart charged with insubordination when he tried to do so. This affront so offended Enver's *amour-propre* that he wrote directly to Kaiser Wilhelm, demanding that Liman be cashiered. There is even a rumour that Enver tried unsuccessfully to have the German marshal poisoned at about this time to get him out of the way. Fortunately for the Turco-German forces guarding the Dardanelles, Wilhelm refused to sack Liman, who remained 'curiously unperturbed' by both the Allied naval assault and Enver's intrigues against him.[8]

The closer one looks at the behaviour of the political and military policy-makers in Constantinople during the Dardanelles campaign, the more remarkable Liman's measured conduct becomes. Liman's very caution and calm infuriated those around him, particularly Bronsart and Enver. Wangenheim expressed his contempt for Liman more subtly, but in a manner hardly geared to shoring up confidence in the field: by initiating peace feelers with London, via a British director of the imperial Ottoman bank, even while the Royal Navy was pounding the Straits batteries. If the Allied navy got through 'because of Germany's and Austria's failure to live up to all their promises concerning the supply of ammunition', Wangenheim wrote to Berlin on 8 March 1915, 'the effect on the attitude of the Turks would be incalculable'.[9] Already the beleaguered Ambassador believed that '90 per cent of the Turks frankly hated the Germans'.[10] To save German residents in the Ottoman Empire from the wrath of angry Turks, Wangenheim wanted to stave off the consequences of an Allied victory by surrendering the Straits pre-emptively. So sure was Wangenheim that the Dardanelles forts would fall that as early as January 1915, he asked US Ambassador Morgenthau to take charge of his personal valuables.

Wangenheim's sense of desperation was widely but not universally shared in the diplomatic community in Pera. Pallavicini, too, was hedging his bets, arranging passage for himself and his staff aboard emergency trains which would depart for the interior in case of an Allied breakthrough.[11] Following the bombardments of 19 and 25 February, British marines had landed on both the Asian shore and the tip of the Gallipoli peninsula, 'blowing up the abandoned guns, smashing the searchlights and wrecking the enemy emplacements'.[12] Constantinople was, at most, ten days' steaming from the Straits in case the navy got through. It was little wonder that, as Pomiankowski recalled, a 'regular panic' now descended on the city. Haydarpasha station was mobbed with Turks and foreigners alike, trying to flee to the interior. Wild rumours were afoot that the House of Osman was going to abandon its ancient capital, the sacred 'Red Apple' of Muhammad's eye. More amazing still, these rumours were entirely true. The CUP government, the Sultan and his court with all its furniture, the gold and cash reserves, even the sacred Islamic relics of Topkapı, were all packed up and sent into Anatolia for safekeeping: the government to Eskişehir, the Muslim artefacts to Konya. According to Morgenthau, Wangenheim was afraid to follow the Young Turks into Anatolia, fearing they would hold him as a hostage to negotiations with the Allies.[13]

Liman, by contrast, showed no signs of special concern, even after the Allied bombardment had destroyed the outer Dardanelles forts and reduced the city of Chanak, guarding the Narrows, to rubble. Like Pomiankowski, the Austrian military attaché, and Humann, the German naval attaché, Liman found the idea of an imminent Allied breakthrough incredible.[14] Were there not a hundred guns still trained on the attacking fleet from both sides of the Straits? Had not the downstream sections of the Dardanelles, up to and including the

Narrows, been thoroughly mined? Was not the impregnability of the Straits, once mined, a reason the Central Powers had pushed Turkey into the war, so as to cut off Russia from her Western allies? Had not Liman assured Falkenhayn in December that the shore defences would hold?

All through February and March, as one assault after another was ultimately repulsed by the artillery batteries on shore, Liman remained impassive. True, the British and French naval guns did serious damage, and by mid-March ammunition was growing short. But the Turks, with the aid of stereotypically stubborn German officers, held their ground. As the British navy began its final, ferocious assault on the Narrows on the morning of 18 March 1915, explosions rocked forts on both sides of the Straits. The battle raged on through the day. For the most part the British had the better of the fighting because of the superior range of their naval guns, but this was ultimately to little avail. First the *Bouvet*, then the *Irresistible* and the *Ocean*, ran over a new line of twenty mines laid on 8 March. The loss of three battleships greatly disturbed Admiral John de Robeck, the senior British commander. Although Commodore Roger Keyes, who had organized the minesweeping efforts, was determined to press on, as was First Lord Winston Churchill, de Robeck's superior rank overawed the Cabinet. In a fateful decision which Churchill would rue for the rest of his life, Kitchener and Prime Minister Asquith sided with de Robeck in calling off the naval offensive until ground troops had demolished the Gallipoli forts on shore.[15]

There is no way of knowing for sure what would have happened had the Allied navy pushed on with the minesweeping offensive. There is every chance the British would have passed through the Narrows, albeit with heavy casualties; but even so Liman had fortified the approaches to the city along both sides of the Marmara coastline. True, the long-range guns of the British dreadnoughts would have had free range on Ottoman palaces, not to mention – as Wangenheim feared – the German Embassy. And yet any Allied effort to take the city would surely have met with serious resistance. Panic or no panic, the Çatalca lines had held in 1877, 1912 and 1913. The Red Apple was not easily taken, as invading Arabs, Turks and Slavs had all learned at great cost. From the stout resistance the Ottoman Fifth

Army offered the British and Anzac forces which landed on the Gallipoli peninsula on 25 April, one can hardly credit the idea that the Turks would have given up their capital without a fight.

Whereas the objectives in the Suez and Sarıkamış offensives had remained obscure to many enlistees, there was no mystery at Gallipoli. As at Suez, a company of dervishes strove to strengthen Muslim morale, but this time with far more success.[16] Allied soldiers and commanders were nearly unanimous in praising the fighting spirit of the Turks, who seemed possessed with 'wild fanaticism', whether out of simple patriotism or religious fervour against the infidel invaders.[17]

Here, at last, was a real jihad, the holy war of the Kaiser's dreams. And yet neither the Kaiser, nor Oppenheim, nor any of Germany's far-flung holy war agents had anything to do with it. Mustafa Kemal, who famously rallied the Turkish defenders on the heights of Sari Bair against the Anzac troops landing at Ari Burnu on the historic day of 25 April 1915, did not need Ottoman jihad *fetvas* to convince his men to hold their ground. In one of the most celebrated in a career of memorable lines, Kemal (according to legend) told his men, 'I don't order you to attack. I order you to die.'* More to the operational point, after coming across Turkish soldiers from the 9th Division who were retreating eastwards in the face of the Anzac advance, claiming to have run out of bullets, Kemal 'ordered them to fix their bayonets and lie down. As they did so, the enemy too lay down. We had won time.' With a mixture of courage, audacity and shrewd strategic sense, Kemal won the heights of Chunuk Bair, which today are memorialized in Turkey as 'Kemalyeri', or Kemal's place.[18]

Although no one knew it at the time, Kemal's legendary stand had settled the Gallipoli battle nearly as soon as it had begun. Chunuk Bair and the Sari Bair ridge were the key to the whole southern half of the peninsula. Visitors to 'Kemal's place' today can easily see the

---

* This remark may well have been invented by Kemal after the fact, as the 57th Regiment, to which the order was given, was indeed 'almost entirely wiped out' in this and subsequent engagements, lending the would-be *bon mot* an air of prophecy. Kemal's written orders to the 57th Regiment, later found on the body of a fallen soldier, read instead 'I do not expect that any of us would not rather die than repeat the shameful story of the Balkan war. But if there are such men among us, we should at once lay hands upon them and set them up in line to be shot!'

reason why: from these heights the Turks had a clear field of fire down upon the Anzac cove on the western coast of the peninsula. Although only some 850 feet high, Chunuk Bair also looks down on the Narrows to the south-west. The view from here is one of the grandest in the entire Mediterranean, with Europe on one side and Asia perched invitingly on the other across the Dardanelles. On a clear day one can see water east, west and beyond the cliffs of Cape Helles to the south, with even the most majestic ships plying the Straits looking like little more than 'toys in a pond'. Had the Anzac troops captured these heights in April, the British forces could have dominated the Narrows. As the Ottoman general staff itself admitted in its post-mortem on Gallipoli, if the Anzac advance 'had been extended so as to include the ridges overlooking the straits', 'a serious, perhaps fatal, blow [would have been] struck at the heart of the Turkish defences'.[19]

It was a great stroke of luck for the Turks and Germans that a commander of Kemal's calibre should have found himself atop the Sari Bair ridge that day. Kemal, who then commanded the 19th Division of the Ottoman Fifth Army, had in fact been stationed in reserve at Bigali, near Maydos on the western shore above the Narrows, some five miles east of Anzac cove. Liman himself rushed to Bulair upon hearing news of the landings, at the northern neck of the peninsula facing the Gulf of Saros, falling hard for a British feint. If Liman misjudged the Allied landings, however, he rapidly realized the importance of Kemal's improvisation at Chunuk Bair, awarding him an Iron Cross. Kemal was promoted Colonel on 1 June 1915. Although Enver's jealousy would ensure that Kemal's heroics remained unmentioned in the Turkish press, the seeds of the Atatürk legend had been well planted at Gallipoli.

Liman, too, deserves much credit for the successful Ottoman defence of the Gallipoli peninsula. As in the earlier naval battle, Liman's imperturbability helped to reassure the Turkish and German officers serving under him. His refusal to panic, even after mistakenly reinforcing Bulair, was admirable. While there remained considerable friction between German and Ottoman officers, for the most part the pressing military imperative ensured that discipline reigned.

The relationship between Liman and Kemal was emblematic in this regard. Neither man much liked the other. Kemal's pre-war sympathies for France and antipathy to Germanophiles like Enver were well known to Liman. When the German marshal asked Kemal for his opinion as to why the Bulgarians had still not joined the Central Powers, the latter replied that it was 'because they are not convinced Germany will win'. Asked for his own opinion on the subject, Kemal calmly answered, 'I agree with the Bulgarians.'[20] Liman, for his part, was not happy with Kemal's stubborn resistance to his orders, as in the latter's refusal to give up the Ari Burnu command to take up a new one at Anafarta following the Suvla landings in August. But Kemal's stubbornness was rewarded: Liman ultimately agreed to place six whole divisions under him. Adding another chapter to the growing legend, Kemal personally led a counter-attack on 9 August which recaptured Chunuk Bair, where he had first made his stand in April. Despite his frustration with Kemal's borderline insubordinate attitude, Liman later admitted that the rising star of the Ottoman army had 'put up steadfast and unyielding resistance against constant violent attacks', such that he was 'able to place total confidence in his energy'.[21]

Just as at Suez, Islamic solidarity had counted for much less at Gallipoli than simple military discipline. The only signs of panic on the Ottoman side in the crucial early days following the first British landings were found in the 77th Regiment under Kemal. The 77th was, significantly, composed of Arab conscripts, who fled the battlefield on 26 April – to be replaced within hours by Turkish reinforcements. Although chanting imams and notions of paradise may well have motivated some Muslim soldiers to fight on under heavy British and Anzac fire, for the most part it was simple Turkish grit which won the day, aided by Liman's organizational skill in arranging reinforcements and ammunition where they were needed, and Kemal's battlefield élan.

Had the architects of the Turco-German jihad been paying close attention, they would have drawn the appropriate conclusions from the triumph at Gallipoli. Neither of the two principal authors of the victory put much stock in the Kaiser's holy war. Liman actively sabotaged Oppenheim's missions whenever he could. Kemal, for his part, was so cold to pan-Islam that he would one day completely dispose of the Caliphate in whose name the Kaiser's holy war was being fought. The Ottoman 'sick man' had been saved, once again, from premature death, thanks not to pan-Islam but to military discipline. Here as elsewhere in the First World War, defence had trumped offence, which suggested it would be better for Turkey to hunker down and guard its borders than to waste its limited strength in faraway adventures in jihad. Of course, the Kaiser and his holy war team concluded nothing of the kind.

II

The Blood of the Prophet

[The prophet] must be something extra special if he can put a spell on the whole Moslem world ... He must be of the Blood ... To capture all Islam ... the man must be of the Koreish, the tribe of the Prophet himself.[1]

Sandy Arbuthnot, in John Buchan's *Greenmantle*

The Turks' triumphant stand at Gallipoli did much more than save Constantinople for the Ottoman Empire. Astute military observers may have chalked up the victory to Liman's army reforms, the April arms build-up, and Kemal's tactical brilliance, but to Muslims raised on the ideas of *kismet* and *inshallah* fatalism, the notion of divine deliverance by Allah's will was not to be discounted. While a final Ottoman victory would have to await a British evacuation, the strategic reversal at Gallipoli offered endless possibilities for Islamic holy war propaganda.

With impeccable timing, the prophet of global jihad arrived in Constantinople in April 1915, just in time to have a front-row seat for the drama at Gallipoli. Baron Oppenheim had conceived his propaganda mission in late February and early March, at the nadir of Ottoman fortunes, following the disasters at Sarıkamış and Suez and while the British navy was pounding the shore batteries at the Straits. Characteristically, Oppenheim had chalked up the defeats not to poor generalship or deficiency of arms, but to inferior propaganda. To kick-start the floundering holy war and spread the good word among Muslims about Hajji Wilhelm and the German cause, Oppenheim proposed to tour Asiatic Turkey, setting up jihad propaganda bureaux in Constantinople, Konya, Aleppo, Damascus, Beirut and Jerusalem.[2]

Central to Oppenheim's plans for reinvigorating the Ottoman holy war was the still undefined role of Hussein, the Sherif of Mecca. During the Aqaba crisis of 1905–6, as we have seen, the Sherifiate had become a political football in the new Great Game between London and Berlin, with the British seeking to weaken Abdul Hamid's hold on the Caliphate in favour of that of the Mecca Sherifs, and the Germans countering this by talking up the Sultan's claim as loudly as possible. The pan-Islamic propaganda battle between the rival Christian powers had temporarily gone cold in the wake of the quasi-secular Young Turk revolution, only to resume with even greater urgency following the proclamation of the Ottoman holy war *fetvas* in November 1914. While many British and German policy-makers had forgotten the earlier shadow war over the Caliphate, Oppenheim never did. As early as September 1914, before it was even clear that Turkey would enter the war, Oppenheim had pointed to the danger posed by British efforts to establish a new, Mecca-based Caliphate independent of Turco-German influence.[3] Oppenheim's warning was prescient. With the Ottoman threat to the Suez Canal looming in mid-January 1915, Kitchener wrote to Gilbert Clayton, his man in Cairo, in a letter promptly translated into Arabic and forwarded to Sherif Hussein, that 'it may be that an Arab of true race will assume the Khalifate at Mecca or Medina, and so good may come by the help of God out of all the evil that is now occurring'.[4] If the British won over Sherif Hussein, whose Hashemite clan was indeed widely believed to be 'of true race' – that is, lineal descendants of Muhammad's own tribe, the Koreish, via the Prophet's grandson, al-Hassan ibn Ali – it could deal a serious blow to the already tenuous theological legitimacy of the Sultan's holy war *fetvas*.

Fortunately for Oppenheim and the prospects of the Turco-German jihad, one of Sherif Hussein's sons had agreed to come to Constantinople in May 1915 to iron out the Hashemite family's differences with the Young Turk regime. This was Feisal, the future king of Syria and Iraq, at this time still in the shadow of his older brother Abdullah, Mecca's first representative in the Ottoman parliament and the future king of Transjordan. Ironically in view of Feisal's later fame as Lawrence's favourite Arab, he was deputized as Hussein's goodwill emissary to Constantinople because Abdullah was then more compromised than

Feisal with the British connection, having consorted with Kitchener himself in Cairo early in 1914. Just thirty years old, the dashing Feisal was the very picture of a desert warrior chieftain. Unlike Hussein and Abdullah, both thoughtful men who were gentle in their outward manner, Feisal seemed cut out of central casting for the part of prince of the Koreish blood. Lawrence was to describe him as 'tall, graceful, vigourous, almost regal in appearance'.[5] Here was just the man to carry the green banner of Islam into battle against the British Empire.

Getting Feisal and his father on board the Ottoman jihad, however, would be a tricky business. Hussein was widely reputed to be in British pay, and Abdullah's meeting with Kitchener in Cairo had been no secret in the Turco-German camp. The diplomatic position of the Sherifiate had been immensely complicated even before the war by the globalization of the hajj, which meant many pilgrims now relied on the British navy for safe passage to Mecca. The economy of the Hejaz depended on the annual pilgrimage, which had been disrupted by the war. Ottoman grain requisitions, and the locust plague of 1915, further compounded the desperate situation in western Arabia, now dependent on British food imports. The Bedouins, with few pilgrims to shake down, relied in their turn on British bribes, when they were not double-dealing with the Turks or Germans. On economic grounds alone, the Sherifian family could ill afford an open break with Britain, unless Constantinople could offer material sustenance to match the inevitable losses. Until the mountain portions of Baghdad railway (from which the Hejaz railway branched off to Medina) were completed, this was highly unlikely.

Compounding the diplomatic difficulty with Mecca was the mischief wrought by the Young Turk revolution. Hussein was a Muslim prince of the old school, who saw the CUP's forceful deposition of Sultan Abdul Hamid in April 1909 as something close to sacrilege. The Hamidian emphasis on pan-Islam had been of great benefit to the Sherifiate, both in the increased pilgrim traffic and in the Sultan's promotion of Arabs to high imperial positions. The Sherif had been further alienated by the centralization of political authority under the Young Turks, and by their efforts to introduce secular schools in Mecca and Medina, in which European infidel languages were taught.[6] Relations had hit a particularly bad patch during the Italian war, when Hussein had conspicuously failed to offer support to the Ottoman cause. As the world war began, mutual suspicions between Mecca and the Porte were running at fever pitch, with rumours afoot that the Turks were going to sack the Sherif and replace him with Ali Haidar Pasha, a CUP favourite who headed the dispossessed Zaid branch of the Hashemites.*

With Abdullah already discredited in Turkish and German eyes because of his Cairo connections, Feisal had a better chance of protecting the family business at the Porte. With little or no trust left between his father and the Young Turks, his task was daunting. Feisal, however, had a secret diplomatic weapon in reserve: Baron Max von Oppenheim. Just as the Baron had been used by Abbas Hilmi to promote his case for the Egyptian throne with the German government, so too was Oppenheim potentially a valuable diplomatic asset for Hussein. In the good old days of Abdul Hamid, the future Sherif had wined and dined the impressionable young German social climber in his Bosphorus palace, making a predictably electric impression. The Baron had never forgotten the glamorous Hashemite prince of Mecca, and neither had Hussein forgotten the compliments Oppenheim had showered down upon him on behalf of the Kaiser.[7]

Baron Oppenheim, almost preternaturally favourable by temperament and inclination to all things Arab, was an ideal intermediary for the Sherif with the suspicious Young Turks. To help butter up the Baron, Feisal paid court to the German in Oppenheim's own room at the Pera Palace Hotel, thus reinforcing the Baron's pride of diplomatic placement. Feisal was accompanied to the hotel by his uncle, Sherif Nasser, one of Hussein's brothers, who seems to have been sent along as a check on Hussein's ambitious son. The meeting took place on Saturday morning, 24 April 1915, the day before the widely anticipated British landings at last materialized. The coincidence of timing may explain why so little is known to this day about Feisal's charm offensive in Constantinople: the drama at Gallipoli immediately drowned out any public sensation which might have been produced by a reconciliation between the Porte and the Sherif.

---

* Lending credence to these rumours, following Hussein's revolt in June 1916 the Young Turks did indeed name Ali Haidar the new Sherif, installing him in Medina.

The pressing news from the nearby front notwithstanding, the Feisal–Oppenheim tête-à-tête was still a historic occasion. The prophet of global jihad, the Kaiser's personal envoy to his beloved Islamic world, had finally arrived in Constantinople to take personal charge of the Turco-German holy war, and his first item of business was to win over a true prince of the blood. Feisal was no less attuned to the potential significance of the meeting, seeking to win through Oppenheim's offices Germany's support for Hussein's claim on the Sherifiate, cutting the legs off CUP plans to replace him.

The meeting proceeded with great amicability. Speaking in a mixture of Arabic and French, Feisal and Oppenheim exchanged the usual pleasantries, with Feisal taking particular care to emphasize the esteem in which his father held the Baron. The gushing personal compliments were predictable, but the political compliments were more interesting. 'I thank God,' Feisal told Oppenheim, 'that the interests of Islam are entirely identical with those of Germany.'* It is true, the Hashemite prince conceded, 'that there is a difference in religion between Muslim countries and Germany. But in material interests relative to this world differences over religion should never stand in the way of these reciprocal interests.' Despite Sherif Hussein's outward show of amity with Great Britain, Feisal assured the Baron that 'the current alliance between Germany and Turkey is one for which he prayed'. So sacred was the Turco-German cause to his father, Feisal claimed, that upon witnessing its 'consecration' with the Ottoman holy war *fetvas*, Hussein had told him that 'if I die now I will not have a single regret'.[8]

This was fine talk, but Oppenheim wanted more than assurances of moral support for the holy war. What was needed, he emphasized again and again to Feisal, was a true union of Islamic peoples. Above all, there must be no talk of relocating the locus of spiritual power with the Sherifs in Mecca. 'The Ottoman Caliphate', Oppenheim insisted, 'must remain always the unique and central focus towards which the eyes of all Muslims are directed.' If the Ottoman Caliph did

---

* In a curious and telling parallel, only several months previously Parvus-Helphand, the notorious intermediary between Berlin and the Bolsheviks, had proposed to Wangenheim in a historic meeting at the German Embassy in Pera that 'the interests of the German government are identical with those of the Russian revolutionaries'.

not retain control over the holy places, he warned Feisal, 'England would get her hands on Mecca and Medina, and thereafter on all Muslim countries'. If they took control of the Hejaz, the infidel British would then be in a position to manipulate or suppress the sacred Mecca pilgrimage and, Oppenheim intoned darkly, 'prevent the free exercise of your religion'. It should thus, the Baron declared, be the duty of all Muslims, beginning with the Sherif and his Hashemite clan, 'to fight against English intrigues', to 'follow the commandments of the Ottoman Caliphate', and in this way 'safeguard the force and prestige of Islam'.[9]

Feisal did not disagree with Oppenheim about the deleterious effect of British influence on the hajj and on Islam more generally. But if the two men felt in common fundamental antipathy to Albion, Feisal did not likewise share the Baron's reverence for the primacy of the Ottoman Caliph, particularly now that the institution was a mostly powerless tool of the Young Turk government. The real purpose of Feisal's trip was probably to divine the intentions of Talaat and Enver towards his father, whose spies had unearthed evidence that the Young Turks were planning to depose him.[10]

It was a delicate game between the Porte and Mecca, in which both sides were proceeding with great caution. Hussein had so far refused to publicly endorse the Turco-German holy war, despite a deluge of telegrams and emissaries from Constantinople, ostensibly for fear of inciting the British to blockade the Hejaz and starve his people. The Sherif's passivity was infuriating to Enver and Djemal, but if they sacked him in retaliation it might throw the theological legitimacy of the holy war into question. And so they waited, for now. The Sherif, for his part, did connive in the dispatch of the green banner to Djemal's army in Jerusalem. But this was rather a cheap way of supporting the crucial Suez Canal operation, without sending troops. It was not likely to fool Djemal.

Feisal's charm offensive with Oppenheim was another clever feint from the Sherifian side. Hussein knew perfectly well that the entire holy war idea had been cooked up by the Baron and the Kaiser, with the Young Turks themselves playing along in order to harness German power to Ottoman interests. Feisal implicitly admitted this in his discussion with Oppenheim, in which he heaped bushels of praise on

Germany and the Kaiser, while subtly avoiding the matter of the Ottoman claim to primacy in Islam. In a particularly brilliant man-oeuvre, Feisal glossed over the sore subject of Mecca's lack of support for the Porte during the Tripoli war by chalking up Sherifian passivity to the 'despair' his father had felt following the Italian invasion, because the misbehaviour of this erstwhile member of the Triple Alliance had, it seemed then, ruined the dream of an alliance between Germany and Islam. Missing this elision of Sherifian treachery entirely, Oppenheim replied by chastising his own government for failing to condemn the Italians. The conversation then shifted on to the subject of Entente perfidies against Islam, on which ground Feisal could not possibly get into trouble.[11]

Oppenheim himself was easy for a Hashemite prince to please, but to win the trust of Enver and Talaat, Feisal would have to do better. And so he dropped hints throughout his conversation with the Baron that the Sherif would be turning over a new leaf. It was not that Hussein was reluctant to join in the jihad, rather that he would only do so if the Turks themselves took a more serious approach to the holy war. Going on the offensive, Feisal reminded Oppenheim that the CUP had corrupted the purity of the holy places by establishing secular European-style schools in Mecca and Medina. Instead of teaching the languages of infidels to Arabs and visiting hajj pilgrims, the Ottomans should proselytize the cosmopolitan population of Mecca to join the jihad.[12]

It was a clever counter-argument to the Ottoman charge of disloy-alty. But to win over the Young Turks, Feisal would have to offer more than rhetorical tricks. What would the Sherif bring to the table? Care-ful as ever not to entrap his father by assenting to concrete obliga-tions, Feisal told Oppenheim that Hussein was prepared to 'raise an army of Arab cavalry and other Bedouins to participate in [a future] attack on the Suez Canal' – without specifying the size of this would-be striking force, nor the time frame in which it would be organized. Still vaguer was Feisal's promise to send emissaries to promote the jihad in Somalia and Sudan (where Muslim followers of the Sheikh Marghani, he claimed dubiously, would display 'total obedience to the moral authority of my father'), and further afield in British India.

Sceptical for once about these promises of the impending outbreak of Islamic holy war, Oppenheim asked Feisal to describe how, exactly, these jihad emissaries would cross the Red Sea, much less the Indian Ocean, without provoking unwanted attention from the British navy. Here, too, Feisal was slippery. The Red Sea was easily traversed every day, he told the German, by Arab dhows too small to be detected. In this way, he explained, 'we can easily communicate with Egyptian Sudan'. As for the more challenging voyage to India, Feisal said that his father's holy war emissaries would simply board ordinary British vessels at Jedda disguised as 'adherents of various reform societies'. These jihad agents would be careful not to carry incriminating documents, but would rather transmit the Sherif's holy war commands orally to Indian Muslims. Asked by Oppenheim to evaluate the potential of such an operation for raising the green banner of revolt in British India, Feisal replied, with characteristic evasion, that 'we will do our duty and will then leave to Allah's will the question of our success'.[13]

It would be easy to dismiss Feisal's performance at the Pera Palace as merely a cynical ploy to buy time for the Sherif in his struggle to stay on his throne. Oppenheim was notoriously susceptible to the charms of clever Arab chieftains, and he was clearly quite taken with Feisal. The Baron was not stupid, however, and he insisted that Feisal repeat his promises more formally to the far more suspicious Enver. Simply to arrange an audience for the Sherif's son with the Ottoman War Minister was a substantial achievement, for which Oppenheim deserves credit. Feisal and Enver met twice in the last week of April 1915, to iron out the outstanding differences between Mecca and the Porte. From the Sherifian side, Feisal asked the War Minister for money and weapons, and specifically to cease favouring Ibn Rashid on the Arabian peninsula. Enver may not have trusted in the good faith of his negotiating partner, but he did take time to put down instructions to Sherif Hussein in writing. To illustrate the Sherif's loyalty, Enver demanded the seconding of one of his sons to the Ottoman Fourth Army, the idea being that a member of the Sherifian family must personally participate in the next assault on Suez. In a similar way, Hussein was enjoined to send Hejaz and Syrian Bedouins into action by making clear that it was their sacred duty to join the Ottoman jihad against Britain. As for Feisal's promises to send jihadi emissaries to Somalia, Sudan and India, Enver demanded detailed progress reports sent to the Porte on a week-by-week basis.[14]

The Sherif's real intentions at this point in time remain murky. It is true that Feisal had met with nationalist Arab officers in Damascus while en route for Constantinople, suggesting that the future Arab revolt was in genesis as early as March 1915. Yet there is no reason to believe Feisal was not genuinely interested during his visit to Constantinople in divining the Porte's intentions towards the Sherif, nor that Enver had already resolved on deposition. If nothing else, Feisal's meetings with Oppenheim, Enver and the Grand Vizier forced him to think seriously about what Sherifian support for the Ottoman holy war would look like. As Feisal told the Baron at Büyükdere on 30 April 1915, Mecca was a natural recruiting centre for would-be jihadis, not simply because of its sacred importance to the faithful but because it offered perfect cover for espionage. Just in the last five years, he told Oppenheim, the number of Sudanese nationals resident in the Hejaz had quintupled, to nearly 30,000: if merely a fraction of these could be sent back home to foment jihad, the British authorities in Khartoum and Cairo would have a serious problem on their hands. As for British India, the more thought Feisal devoted to the problem, the more convinced he was that Mecca was the ideal launching pad for a serious jihadi uprising there. Beyond the annual pilgrims, there were thousands of British subjects living more or less permanently in the Hejaz, who could all be recruited. Feisal proposed an ingenious propaganda ploy: these Indian Muslims would be sent back to the subcontinent to spread the story of mass starvation in the holy cities, which could of course be blamed on the British blockade. It was true, Feisal admitted, that the British had docked four huge grain ships on the coast since the outbreak of war in 1914, helping feed almost the entire Hejaz population – but Muslims in India did not know this. Mecca pilgrims and emigrés, repatriated as if innocently aboard English merchant ships, could keep silent until reaching home, where-upon they would begin spreading gruesome tales of deliberate mass starvation in Mecca to fire the flames of an anti-British holy war. All this, Feisal promised Oppenheim, would be done – if only the Porte would provide the necessary funds.[15]

It was a big 'if'. Considering his father's continued reluctance to express public support for the Ottoman holy war, Feisal did not expect to receive serious material support from Enver's War Ministry for jihadi propaganda, nor the arms his father would ostensibly use to raise Bedouin battalions for a renewed assault on the canal. Even Oppenheim, by nature an optimist in all matters related to the Kaiser's holy war, was not entirely convinced that the Sherif would get seriously into the game. In his own post-mortem on his meetings with Feisal, Oppenheim claimed to have achieved one undeniable 'positive result': to have prevented 'a calamitous break between the Caliphate and the Sherifiate during the war'. Of course, the Baron was dying for Hussein to endorse the Turco-German holy war, which alone would give it the sacred imprimatur it seemed – thus far – to be lacking. The Sherif's public backing of the jihad *fetvas* would help to unify 'all Muslims under the banner of the Sultan-Caliph', not least by taking away the stigma of the 'partiality of a European power' – i.e., Germany – in the proclamation of holy war. Washed in the sacred blood of the Prophet's own clan, the holy war would be cleansed and purified of the taint of the infidel.[16]

With the ruler of the holy city of Mecca at last promising to get on board, the Kaiser's jihad was now ready to roll on into British India. There remained, however, one serious problem. While nearly all Indian Muslims professed the same orthodox Sunni variant of Islam as the Turkish Sultan and the Mecca Sherifs, the shortest path from Asiatic Turkey to India lay astride the Shia-dominated regions of southern Mesopotamia and Persia. Here the imprimatur of the Sultan-Caliph, the Ottoman *Şeykh-ul-Islam* and the Sherif counted for little. To secure the road to India, the endorsement of the Ottoman holy war *fetvas* by Shia clerics would also be required.

12

The Shia Stratagem

Here, in the middle of a desert wasteland on the lower Mesopotamian plain, near the site of ancient Babylon, was located one of the most sacred shrines of Islam, the Mecca of the Shiites, the tombs of Hassan and Hussein, the sons of Ali, Mohammed's nephew.

Hans Lührs, German archaeologist and secret agent[1]

The British cottoned on quite late to the new Great Game launched in 1914 with the declaration of holy war by the Sultan-Caliph. Kitchener, it is true, perceived the importance of Islam as early as December 1914, but then his famously clumsy intervention with Hussein of Mecca gives the lie to British worldliness and competence. Kitchener's offer of the title of Caliph to the Sherif showed that he had mistaken a position of political power in the world of Islam for a merely spiritual office. Among Kitchener's more important oversights was the Sunni–Shia divide in the world of Islam, which assured that even the most legitimate Ottoman Sultan-Caliph could never be recognized as a spiritual authority by Shia Muslims, let alone a Sherifian pretender.[2]

Since the martyrdom of Muhammad's nephew and son-in-law Ali, slain while praying in a mosque in 661, 'Shiat Ali', or Ali's followers, have believed that only Ali's descendants can be true Caliphs – with the implication that the Umayyad, Abbasid and Ottoman Caliphs recognized by orthodox Sunnis were never accepted as such by Shia Muslims. In most of the Islamic world, Shias have remained a small minority sect, which helps explain why they were largely invisible to Western policy-makers like Kitchener, whose own experience with Islam was confined to Sunni-dominated British Egypt and India.

Shiites were not invisible, however, in southern Mesopotamia, where Ali's son and heir, Hussein, was slain and gruesomely decapitated at the battle of Karbala in 680. Contrary to common belief today, Persia was never the symbolic centre of Shia Islam, with most of the lands comprising today's Iran won over for the Shiat Ali only under the Safavid dynasty in the sixteenth century. Iraqi Karbala, not Iranian Tehran, Qom or Meshed, is the second Mecca of Shia Muslims. Just as Sunnis must, if physically and financially able, make the hajj to Mecca once before they die, so, too, are the Shia faithful expected to make the 'Karbalajj' to the tomb of Hussein in lower Mesopotamia. Much like Mecca, Karbala remained a sleepy backwater well into the twentieth century, although greatly enlivened (and enriched) by the pilgrim trade. The elegant mansions of Karbala, most of which had been built by wealthy Indian Shia Muslims to house incoming religious brethren, were powerful testimony to the importance of the Karbalajj in global Islam. Until British vessels took over Indian hajj traffic in the modern era, it was much easier for Shias from the subcontinent to make a sacred pilgrimage to Mesopotamia than for Sunnis to reach the distant Hejaz. With Persia perched in between Karbala and India, Shias dominated the shortest land route between Asiatic Turkey and the subcontinent.

Little wonder, then, that Oppenheim's jihad bureau organized a secret wartime mission to win over the Shia clerics of Karbala in 1914. Whereas many British statesmen in London remained oblivious to the binary cleavage of the Islamic world, Berlin was well up to speed. The Baron was by no means the only German explorer with pre-war experience of Mesopotamia. While the Niedermayer mission had a great deal of trouble finding German nationals who knew Afghanistan or India intimately, when it came to the lands of present-day Iraq and Iran Oppenheim had much better people at hand. An entire team of German archaeologists, including Hans Lührs, Conrad Preusser, Paul Maresch and Walter Bachmann, had just finished a major excavation in Mesopotamia when the July crisis broke in 1914. Lührs in particular was a gem of a field agent, having established excellent relations with tribal leaders, in large part due to his good spoken Arabic. He was also a fine writer, whose account of the Mesopotamian operation deserves much greater renown in the genre of First World War memoirs, not only for its literary elegance but for the grandeur of the subject matter.* As Lühi recounted years later, 'our mission envisioned nothing less than an effort to smooth over the ancient, smouldering dispute between Shiites and Sunnis and win over Shia Muslims for the "holy war" proclaimed by the *Şeykh-ul-Islam* of the Sunnis'.[3]

The secret mission to Karbala in which Lühi participated was headed by Captain Fritz Klein. Klein, like Lühi, was an inspired choice. As military attaché in both Cairo and Tehran in pre-war days, Klein had travelled widely in the Middle East, and even participated in military operations against a Kashgai uprising in southern Persia in 1913. Like Kress, Klein had all the ruthless can-do spirit of a good German officer, but, unlike Kress, he had diplomatic skills too. These last would be essential, not only in dealing with tribal headmen in lower Mesopotamia, but in securing the blessing of the (Shia) Grand Mufti of Karbala for the (Sunni) Ottoman jihad *fetvas*. Although there was every reason to think that Shias would welcome the destruction of the British and Russian empires which had cynically carved up much of Persia into 'spheres of influence' in 1907, this did not mean they had any greater affection for Germany. Still less did the Shiat Ali love the Turks or their Sunni Sultan, who had warred with Shiite Iran for centuries. In recent years the Persian-Ottoman conflict had grown quiet, but the age-old sectarian feud between Sunnis and Shias had never been doused entirely.

The Klein mission evolved somewhat haphazardly in winter 1914–15. Although Oppenheim's jihad bureau oversaw the mission from beginning to end, Klein's original brief was more in the line of sabotage than cultural diplomacy. Among the far-flung goals of the holy war initiative outlined in both the August 1914 Foreign Office 'Overview of Revolutionary Activity We Will Undertake in the Islamic-Israelite World' and Oppenheim's more detailed October 'Exposé Concerning the Revolutionizing of the Islamic Territories of Our

---

* Hans Lühi, *Gegenspieler des Obersten Lawrence* (1934). Because it was published shortly after Hitler came to power, Lühi' memoir may have been dismissed with the taint of Nazism by English-language publishers: it was never translated. However obliquely Lühi' recollections of wartime heroism may have served the Nazi cause, the memoir was clearly not conceived in a propagandistic vein. Outside the introduction penned by Dagobert von Mikusch, contemporary politics do not intrude on the narrative.

Enemies' was the capture of the Abadan oil tanks and refineries in the Karun region at the head of the Persian Gulf. Under Churchill's far-sighted leadership, the British navy had recently begun the transition from coal-to oil-fired engines, and the German navy wished to follow – if Berlin could find a reliable source of oil. Albert Ballin, the owner of the Hamburg-Amerika shipping line which in recent years had developed extensive interests in the Persian Gulf, wrote to the Wilhelm-strasse in early October 1914 that occupying the Karun region along the Shatt-al-Arab waterway would win Germany 'an oil source of unending wealth ... of the greatest value for the Reich naval office'. Oppenheim, characteristically, was less interested in the constructive potential of the Abadan tanks and refineries than in the prospect of denying them to Britain. Initially the Ballin objective of seizing the oilfields intact won out in the German general staff, only for the dispatch of a British Indian expeditionary force to the Gulf in November to rule out any realistic possibility of capturing Karun. Instead of trying to occupy and hold Abadan, Klein was to take up Oppenheim's original plan, to set the oilfields aflame by conjuring up a local jihad.[4]

To spread the fires of Ottoman holy war to the Persian Gulf, Klein would have to pass through the Shia heartland of southern Mesopotamia. So, too, would Niedermayer's mission to Afghanistan have to pass through Shia-dominated Persia. Sooner or later, then, Germany's holy war field agents would need to confront the sectarian divide hanging like Damocles' sword over Oppenheim's global jihad. Because the shortest route from Baghdad to Karun would require passing almost directly through Karbala, it made sense to entrust the Shia charm offensive to Klein instead of Niedermayer, who, to avoid British surveillance, would try to stay as far north of the Persian Gulf as possible.

Klein's diplomatic mission to Karbala thus began as something of an afterthought. As British reinforcements poured into the Gulf, however – some 12,000 Indian army troops were ashore by the end of 1914, including light artillery – the Shia stratagem began to seem more pressing than the increasingly unlikely prospect of sabotaging the oilfields. Oppenheim therefore seconded to Klein some of his most experienced Middle Eastern hands, such as Lührs, Preusser, Maresch and Bachmann. In the classic fashion of the new Great Game, these archaeologists, like the hero Richard Hannay in *Greenmantle*, were plucked from the obscurity of the trenches to join Klein's mission to Mesopotamia. Unlike Hannay, however, who was initially reluctant to go because he had been 'happy in his soldiering', Hans Lührs, at least, was ecstatic to trade in the mud of Flanders for the mystical Land of the Two Rivers. Like Oppenheim, Lührs had been enraptured by the Orient and jumped at the chance to return to the scene of happy pre-war memories.

Despite the spiritual importance of the Shia stratagem, the Klein mission was quite small, encompassing just six Germans, a Persian translator, one Persian nobleman who was a distant relation of the Shah, and a smattering of Arab servants. If Klein lacked the numbers which he would have needed to attack the British in force at the Gulf, however, the modest size of his jihadi band was ideally suited to the subtle task at hand. Whereas Niedermayer would need to produce as many armed men as possible to impress the Emir of Afghanistan with the might of Germany, Klein's aim required more diplomatic finesse than brute strength. To send a German army into Karbala would be just as grossly offensive as an infidel invasion of Mecca. Sheikh Ali el Irakein, the Grand Mufti of Karbala, would surely not sign a jihad *fetva* at gunpoint. Even if he did so, it would carry little legitimacy then for Shia Muslims.

As the Klein party wound its way southwards from Baghdad in January 1915, Lührs was struck by the contrast between the dramatic historical resonance of the landscape and its barren condition he saw. It was a land of ghosts, where the dead seemed more real than the living. Although the all-pervasive 'solitude and solemnity of this vast deserted plain' was sometimes interrupted by a passing caravan or two, it was not enough to 'awaken the impression of an inhabited world'. Even the caravans had the air of death about them, as nearly all of them included at least one or two caskets of deceased Shia Muslims, carried from as far away as India and China to be buried in the sacred ground of southern Mesopotamia. Lührs had caught a whiff of the puritanical grimness of the Shia world, with its all-pervasive cult of martyrdom and suffering. Overall, an eerie stillness prevailed in the region which had once been the beating heart of the Assyrian, Persian and Abbasid empires. 'The clanging of the bells round the necks of the pack animals and the rumbling of the wagons,' Lührs recalled, 'made a melody of nothingness against the exalted silence of the landscape.'⁵

After the bleakness of the landscape south of Baghdad, the first sight of the holy city came as a profound relief. 'Here, in the middle of a desert wasteland on the lower Mesopotamian plain, near the site of ancient Babylon,' Lührs writes, the Germans at last glimpsed, just over the horizon, the blue tiled dome of the world's most sacred Shia mosque, framed by a smattering of palm trees and the flat roofs of 'mysterious Karbala'. For the residents of the holy city, the sight of the strange party of European travellers, clothed in a motley mixture of 'half German, half Turkish army uniforms', must have been equally striking. Barely had the Klein party approached the city limits before they were surrounded by 'a swarming mass of Oriental peoples: Arabs, Persians, Afghans, Indians ... and a whole flock of half-naked children, who all greeted us spiritedly and with more or less astonishment'.⁶

In Karbala, as in Mecca, worlds collided every day, and never more so than on this one. A party of German soldiers and archaeologists, representing (in theory) the Turkish Sultan-Caliph, working through Persian and Arabic translators, had come to petition the Grand Mufti of Shia Islam to embrace the Ottoman jihad *fetvas*. Naturally, Sheikh Ali, although intrigued when he heard of the arrival of this party bearing mysterious gifts and promises, was in no hurry to make any decisions. After sending a long stream of low-ranking emissaries to meet the infidel visitors, Ali at last dispatched his brother to invite them to his home. The Germans were amazed to discover that the Grand Mufti lived in an ordinary Arab-style dwelling. Ali was also simply, if elegantly, dressed in classical Arab robes, crowned by a white turban 'no different from those worn by other imams and Mullahs'. The great Sheikh was very obliging to his German guests, laying out a giant spread of Persian pilaf and ensuring that they received the best morsels of meat. After the meal the Germans were treated to coffee, cigarettes and ritualized conversation in the Arab-Persian manner, in which the pleasant stream of small talk and gushing compliments made it seem impolite to raise matters of business – including the reason the Germans had come to Karbala.

It was the first of many frustrating encounters for Klein and the Germans with the Mufti. In the Orient, what one said mattered less than how one said it. As Lührs explains, what seemed to count with the Mufti were the little things, 'how one spoke, gestured, smoked one's cigarettes, how you slurped your coffee'. Slowly, subtly, and with evident enjoyment, Sheikh Ali was sizing up Klein and his companions as men, to see if he could trust them. In between elegant repasts, he showed them the sacred shrines of Karbala, the mosque, the graves of Hassan and Hussein, the tombstones erected by wealthy Indian pilgrims. Just as Lührs had suspected from the death rattle of the caravans, burying the dead was the principal industry in Karbala. The most desirable real estate for pilgrim tombs was that surrounding the mosque, near the grave sites of Hassan and Hussein. Burial there was a mark of real honour and distinction for Shia Muslims; only the rich, mostly from British India, could afford it. Perhaps to appease their conscience, many of the wealthiest Indian pilgrims had endowed large guesthouses for less fortunate pilgrims to stay in while paying their respects to Hassan and Hussein.[7]

The prominence of British Indian Muslims in Karbala seemed to offer a promising opportunity for German jihad propaganda, but it also presented a problem. Just as the Royal Navy now effectively held the Mecca hajj hostage through its control of the Hejaz coastline, so too did British influence increasingly overshadow the Karbalajj. When Klein at last broached the delicate subject of the world war with the Mufti, Sheikh Ali was just as evasive as Hussein had been with Enver and Feisal with Oppenheim. To be sure, the Mufti deeply resented the Anglo-Russian accord of 1907, which had humiliated Persia and outraged Shia Muslims everywhere. And yet, he informed Klein, the salaries of all the clerics of Karbala were paid out of funds contributed by Shia Muslims from India – and these funds were transmitted to Karbala by way of the British Consulate in Baghdad. Were he to consecrate a jihad *fetva* against Britain, the Grand Mufti of Karbala would forfeit his entire income. For this reason he demanded 50,000 Marks to endorse the Ottoman holy war.

Although it had taken many frustrating weeks, Klein's men were in business. After a bit of haggling over terms of payment – the Mufti insisted the 50,000 Marks down-payment be repeated at the same time every year, in perpetuity, as a kind of tribute – Sheikh Ali el Irakein wrote up a jihad *fetva* on a sheet of 'heavy parchment', stamped with the embossed seal of Karbala, in which Shia Muslims everywhere on earth were enjoined to wage holy war against England and Russia. The Mufti also gave the Germans an official letter to the Shah of Persia, inviting him to join the jihad against the Entente powers.[8]

It was a stunning victory for the German holy war planners in Berlin. Whereas Kitchener, Enver and Oppenheim had all so far failed to win over Hussein of Mecca, Captain Klein had received the unconditional endorsement of the Turco-German holy war from the world's leading Shia cleric. Winning over the Grand Mufti of Karbala had not been inexpensive, but to the Germans it was cheap at the price. For taking on an annual subsidy of about $12,000 at 1915 rates, Berlin had summoned up the messianic fury of Shia Islam to destroy British power in Persia and open the land road to India. With the Niedermayer mission en route for Afghanistan, the new Great Game was on.

13

To the Gates of India

There is a dry wind blowing through the East, and the parched grasses wait the spark. And the wind is blowing towards the Indian border.

Sir Walter Bullivant, fictional head of British
intelligence in *Greenmantle*[1]

However stunning its success, the German Shia stratagem would have been of little account had not an even more ambitious jihad offensive been underway. Klein had in fact been attached, as far as Baghdad, to Oskar von Niedermayer's larger mission to Afghanistan. Although the oil refinery at Abadan and the Shia shrines of Karbala were important objectives in their own right, southern Mesopotamia was mostly of interest to the Germans as a potential land bridge to British India. Because the Royal Navy so thoroughly dominated the Persian Gulf and Indian Ocean, there was no way the Germans could send war *matériel* to would-be Afghan holy warriors or Indian revolutionaries by sea. Unfortunately for Oppenheim and the holy war planners in Berlin, there were no railways between Baghdad and the subcontinent either. Niedermayer and his men would therefore have to cross the Persian desert in the age-old manner of the horse and mule caravan, the speed of their progress at the mercy of animal power and human exhaustion.

The physical challenge of the journey to India was only the beginning of Niedermayer's problems. The Afghan mission had been plagued by diplomatic complications almost as soon as it had been conceived. As mentioned in chapter 4, a prying Romanian customs officer had nearly deprived Niedermayer of the portable wireless equipment

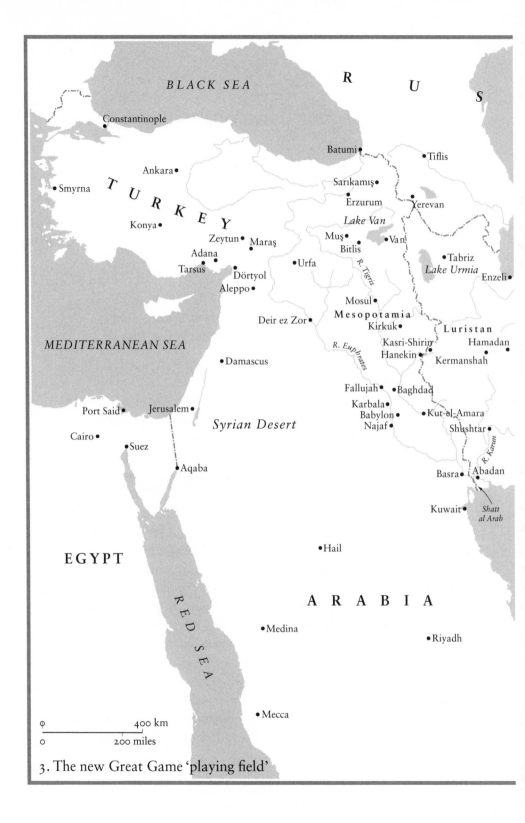

3. The new Great Game 'playing field'

(the aerials disguised as circus 'tent poles') he would need to maintain communications in the field. The loose-lipped bragging of his men in Pera had destroyed any element of surprise he might have enjoyed in leading an offensive through the mountain passes into India, alerting British spies as early as November 1914 that a German Afghan initiative was in the works.

More troublesome still was the complex internal diplomacy of the mission itself. Although Enver was generally supportive of Oppenheim's idea of an Afghan jihad against India, the pan-Turkish Ottoman War Minister had his own ambitions in Asia and was unwilling to subordinate them to the Germans'. As early as 14 August 1914, or nearly three months before Turkey had deigned to enter the world war, Enver had insisted to Wangenheim that any German agreement with either Habibullah of Afghanistan or the Muslims of British India must be 'maintained only through Turkish officers'.[2] To this end Enver had already dispatched his own emissaries bearing greetings from the Sultan-Caliph to the Afghan Emir, both overland and via the Suez Canal aboard neutral ships.[3]

Enver was not the only one staking a claim on Kabul. By the end of August, Oppenheim had selected as the Kaiser's official envoys to Afghanistan Oskar von Niedermayer and fifteen of his fellow officers, with specialties ranging from artillery and explosives to bridge-building, along with military doctors and a Persian-born translator.[4] They would carry with them an officially embossed letter from the Kaiser to Emir Habibullah, along with imperial medals and special state-of-the-art German gift rifles.[5] The German Consulate in Stockholm, meanwhile, was recruiting Swedish members of the Persian Shah's gendarmerie then home on leave, hoping to second them to the mission to Afghanistan. Sven Hedin, Sweden's leading explorer, had volunteered to serve as geographical consultant on India's mountainous north-western frontier.[6] Meanwhile, Oppenheim had begun assembling an 'Indian revolutionary committee' of Hindu, Sikh and Muslim exiles in a three-storey building on Berlin's Wielandstrasse. Their task was nothing less than to infiltrate the British army in India and unleash a nationwide mutiny, with or without a Turco-German-Afghan invasion.[7]

It was a classic case of too many cooks threatening to spoil the broth. So alluring was the planned Turco-German mission to India, the romantic notion of retracing the steps of Alexander's army, that everyone wanted a piece of the action. Turks, Germans, Swedes, Persians, Sikhs, Hindus and Indian Muslims were all itching for the glory of toppling the British Raj. From one perspective, this embarrassment of jihadi riches was a nice problem for Oppenheim to have. And yet working out an unambiguous chain of command in this multinational sabotage operation would be nearly impossible. To cut through red tape and overawe rivals and pretenders, a man of iron will and determination would be needed. Fortunately for the Germans, such a man was available, and willing.

If one were to draw up the perfect curriculum vitae for a jihadi field agent tasked with spreading the fires of holy war to India, one could hardly do better than that of Oskar von Niedermayer (1885–1948). A classic Teutonic type, Niedermayer combined the ruthlessness and precise mathematical discipline of a German artillery officer – he was also an accomplished mountaineer, huntsman and swimmer – with an astonishingly broad liberal education. In 1907, while garrisoned at Erlangen, Niedermayer began attending classes in geology and philology at the renowned local university, where Fichte and Feuerbach had once taught – and where coincidentally, the year before, Curt Prüfer had completed his doctorate in Egyptology. Like that fellow Orientalist-turned-jihad-agent, Niedermayer was taken in by Georg Jacob, a philologist of Semitic cultures who also taught modern Turkish, Arabic and Persian. Although not quite a linguist of Prüfer's calibre, Niedermayer devoted great energy to language study, picking up fairly fluent English and Russian, passable Arabic and Turkish, along with modern Persian.

Islam was Jacob's real intellectual passion, and it would become Niedermayer's as well. Jacob's scholarly studies in the years of Niedermayer's enrolment at Erlangen concerned the Bektashi order of Sufi Islam, who had played a significant role in Ottoman history as founders and leaders of the Janissary corps, until both the order and the corps were banished in 1826. Some Bektashi practices, like confession, even recall Christianity. Yet the Bektashis are better described as Muslim mystics than Christians *manqué*, having absorbed the millenarian elements of Shia Islam, such as intense reverence for the martyred Ali and the belief in the Twelve Imams of the Muslim succession, the appearance of the last of which, Muhammad al-Mahdi, is ever imminent.

It was all heady stuff for the young Bavarian artillery officer. To be sure, there were many other bright young things taking up Islamic studies in this, the golden age of German Orientalism – even King Ludwig II had picked up the fashion, festooning his Bavarian Alpine castle, the Linderhof, with oriental kitsch. What made this young army lieutenant a special kind of student was his colossal energy, ambition and wanderlust. In September 1912, as war clouds were beginning to darken over the Balkans, Niedermayer asked for and was granted a two-year research furlough from his unit, the 10th Bavarian artillery regiment. His stated goal was to carry out excavations and study Islamic practices in Persia, but it is hard to believe the army did not have military intelligence in mind when they gave Niedermayer two years of paid leave. Whatever the real justification for his trip to Persia, it offered the budding young soldier-scholar a precious opportunity to pursue his Orientalist passion at leisure – and on full salary.[8]

Niedermayer's itinerary was perfectly tailored as training for the new Great Game against Great Britain. Accompanied by an Austrian scholar, Ernst Diez, he set out from Vienna on 8 September 1912 for the Caucasus, by way of the Ukraine and south Russia. After a brief stopover in the Georgian capital of Tiflis (Tbilisi), Niedermayer and Diez boarded a Caspian steamer at Baku for the trip to northern Persia. Next came a romantic three-day journey by horse-drawn wagon to Tehran, where the pair gathered supplies and maps for exploring nearby ruins. Like Oppenheim in Syria and Musil in Arabia, Niedermayer fell in love with the grandeur of the desert landscape of Persia. The adventurous Bavarian lieutenant added a personal touch with his love of climbing, setting off on his own in November 1912 on a two-month odyssey through the highlands of northern Persia, accompanied only by pack animals carrying his supplies. Here he came into his own as an intelligence officer, sketching the first serious relief maps of the sparsely populated area between Tehran and the Caspian.

Fascinating as ruins and mountains were, they were not the reason Niedermayer had been given a research furlough. In the spring of 1913, he at last reached Asterabad, the spiritual centre of the Bektashi order in Persia, and of the Baha'i, a Bektashi-style brotherhood founded in the nineteenth century. Like the Bektashi, the Baha'i had adopted a syncretistic blend of Christian and Islamic ideas, including respect for the rights of women and children, with an overlay of the 'eschatological spirit of the Shiites'. It was this last which could be of use to the Germans, if the messianic energy of the Shia brotherhoods of Persia could be stirred up against Britain and Russia. Niedermayer also paid his respects at the grave of Imam Reza in Meshed, the third holiest city of Shia Islam, behind only Karbala and its sister city of Najaf. He spent nearly five months there that summer, compiling a huge dossier on Shia practices for German intelligence.[9] According to Sir Percy Sykes, Britain's own super-spy in pre-war Persia who met Niedermayer in Meshed in May 1913, the Bavarian claimed to have entered the forbidden Shia shrine in nearby Jagharq by disguising himself as a Persian. Sykes, whose assistance Niedermayer was forced to call on in September after his surveying equipment was stolen, did not believe his cover story – that he was in Persia to carry out geological and anthropological studies – for a minute.[10]

As if to confirm Sykes's suspicions that he was spearheading a German Great Game offensive in Muslim Asia, Niedermayer's travels took him next to Isfahan, the holiest Shia city in the British-dominated south, and to Bushire on the Persian Gulf. Here, in February 1914, the Bavarian lieutenant was debriefed by the German Consul, Wilhelm Wassmuss, who was so impressed by Niedermayer that, six months later, he would recommend him to Oppenheim to head the Afghan mission. After talking shop with Wassmuss, Niedermayer set sail for India. Scarcely bothering any longer to conceal the real purpose of his voyage, he toured Bombay and Calcutta, Darjeeling, Madras and Ceylon, taking care all along to make careful notes on the people, the landscape and particularly the rail network. For the most part, he was impressed with British strength in the subcontinent and thought it would be difficult to dislodge the Raj from the throne. To complete his Great Game tour, Niedermayer next took in Cairo by way of the Suez Canal, stopped over in Jerusalem, boarded the Baghdad railway at Damascus, paid homage to the whirling dervishes of Konya, and finally returned to Europe in May 1914 by way of the Orient Express from Constantinople.[11]

Oppenheim could not have asked for a better man to lead the holy war mission to Kabul. More even than Klein and Lührs, Musil and Prüfer, Niedermayer gives the lie to the claim that Germany could not conjure up field men of the calibre of Lawrence – who was himself rather indifferent as a linguist and scholar. As Wassmuss wrote to Oppenheim on 4 September 1914, following recent travels in Persia the Bavarian soldier-scholar now had 'friends in every town – even in India – and wealthy, influential friends at that, he speaks Persian and Russian and knows the borderland near Afghanistan intimately'. Niedermayer even had British friends, such as Sir Percy Sykes, to whom he had recently sent two specially engraved, autographed portraits of the former Bavarian King Ludwig II.[12]

When he received Oppenheim's call to join the Turco-German jihad in early September, Niedermayer's field artillery regiment was pounding away at French lines near Nancy, under the German Sixth Army command of Bavarian Crown Prince Rupprecht. Although much more of a soldier than Hans Lührs, Niedermayer was just as pleased as Lührs to hear the news that his special talents would be put to use in the war. It helped that Oppenheim had sent an impressive emissary to recruit him: imperial dragoman and blue-blood Schabinger von Schowingen (the same who would shortly be carried in a chaise longue during the holy war procession in Pera). Niedermayer insisted only that he be allowed to bring along trusted companions for the long trip, such as Erich Zugmayer, a Bavarian zoologist who had recently travelled in Baluchistan, the region abutting southern Persia, Afghanistan and British India, his adjutant Hans Jakob, and his brother Fritz, a doctor. With these and other requests readily granted by Oppenheim, Niedermayer set off on the Orient Express for Constantinople in late September 1914.[13]

As soon as the Niedermayer party reached the Bosphorus in early October, the troubles began. The knottiest issue surrounding the mission, predictably, concerned the chain of command. Although Turkey was still not at war, Enver insisted on overall military control – on the pretence that, if the Ottoman Empire ever did declare war, a substantial Turkish armed detachment would accompany Niedermayer and the other Germans across Persia. Whether or not this came to pass, Enver was adamant that all details of the group's travel itinerary be cleared with the Ottoman general staff. As Niedermayer complained to Oppenheim shortly after arriving in Sirkeci station, 'it seems that the Turks mistrust us'.

Things were not much more promising with the Germans in Pera. Wangenheim, according to Niedermayer, showed himself utterly indifferent to the Afghan mission, declining all responsibility. Although the German Ambassador went through the motions of helping Niedermayer recover his equipment from Romanian customs, he showed little enthusiasm for the task.[14] Wassmuss, who had proposed Niedermayer as military leader of the expedition to Kabul, had arrived in Constantinople earlier in September, and promptly staked his own claim as political leader of the mission to Afghanistan. Although the Bavarian lieutenant did not mind deferring to his Foreign Office sponsor in matters of diplomacy, Wassmuss's insistence on precedence in mission rank bothered many of Niedermayer's own men. Hermann Consten, a civilian seconded to Niedermayer's staff because of his travel experience in the region and his linguistic skills – Consten knew French, English, Russian, Yiddish, Mongolian and Swahili – complained that Wassmuss was bossing everyone around, and dealing with Enver behind Niedermayer's back.[15] As if to pre-empt the possibility of a collision in the chain of command, Wassmuss slipped quietly out of town with several loyalists en route for Aleppo on 28 September, just days before Niedermayer's arrival. As the Bavarian complained to Oppenheim about this unexpected stab in the back from Wassmuss, the man whose recommendation had plucked him from the cosy confines of Crown Prince Rupprecht's Bavarian-dominated Sixth Army, 'Wir sind doch Deutsche!' ('But we are Germans!').[16]

It was not an auspicious beginning for Niedermayer. In a sense, however, Wassmuss's stubborn display of initiative boded well for the Germans. Reporting from Tarsus in early October after crossing the Taurus mountains, Wassmuss gave his own side of the story. He addressed his dispatch to Chancellor Bethmann Hollweg, by way of Wangenheim (whom he had apparently taken into his confidence, which may explain why Niedermayer found such a contrastingly cool reception with the German Ambassador). Wassmuss's quarrel, as he told it, was not with Niedermayer at all, but with Baron Oppenheim, whose endless committee meetings in Berlin he blamed for the delays in getting the mission's supplies to Constantinople. Hermann Consten, whom Oppenheim had tagged as leading regional adviser to Niedermayer's team, was supposed to arrive in Pera in mid-September with maps, munitions and the Kaiser's letter to Emir Habibullah: instead, he had arrived only on the 25th, with nothing in tow 'except the verbal order, that he was to be supplied in Constantinople'. Wassmuss had therefore decided to abandon the floundering Oppenheim operation, offering as justification 'that there was no organization to speak of, and that I was the only one who had taken initiative in the furtherance of the mission'. Like Frobenius and Musil, Wassmuss would create his own jihad in the field, with whatever materials were at hand.[17]

Niedermayer, by contrast, was an organization man. Although no less courageous than Wassmuss and Frobenius, he was a soldier through and through: he had his orders and he would stick to them. There were merits to Wassmuss's improvisatory bravura, as we shall see below,* but so too was there something to be said for getting properly organized before crossing the Persian desert. Although it took almost two months, Niedermayer gradually assembled the equipment he needed to proceed to Afghanistan. In the early morning hours of 5 December 1914, he and his men took the Galata ferry to Haydarpasha station to board the Baghdad railway. After crossing the Taurus mountains by caravan, they reached Alexandretta (Iskenderun) eight days later, where they were, somewhat to their surprise, reunited with the Wassmuss party. Finding the Turkish Vali in Alexandretta to be of little help, the Germans set out for Baghdad by caravan on 21 December, entering the fabled city via its western gate some three weeks later. Showing that he bore Niedermayer, at least, no ill will, Wassmuss then conceded full control of the Afghan mission to him, setting off southwards from Baghdad on his own by riverboat on 18 January 1915 in the direction of the Persian Gulf.[18]

It was a dubious honour. Baghdad proved to be even more of a hornets' nest for Niedermayer than Constantinople had been. Consul Wassmuss, a shrewder politician than the Bavarian, had perceived quickly that the Germans had walked right into the middle of a CUP power struggle. In December, Emir Habibullah had replied to Enver's offer of a military alliance in the affirmative, without reference to the Germans (although his message, confusingly, was communicated to Constantinople via German telegraph and wireless stations). In his reply, Habibullah asked Enver if he should direct his fire against the

* In chapter 16.

Russians or the English.[19] Considering that Enver had expressly promised the Germans he would enlist Habibullah's armies against British India, the Emir's query may have reflected his own hesitation before incurring British enmity – by doing so he would forfeit his annual subsidy from Great Britain of £400,000 sterling (which would be increased by a further £25,000 in 1915 to counter German bribes).[20] But it was likely that Habibullah was also receiving separate entreaties from one of Enver's CUP rivals, Colonel Huseyin Rauf Bey (Orbay). Somewhat improbably, Enver had appointed Rauf back in October to head the Ottoman mission to Kabul, despite the fact that Rauf was a naval officer who did not even know where Afghanistan was.* Enver may, of course, have meant simply to dispose of a dangerous rival such as Rauf, a naval hero of the Balkan wars who had distinguished himself with numerous raids on the Black Sea, Aegean and Adriatic coastlines. Thus Enver gave Rauf the illogical title of 'Commander-in-Chief of Southern Persia', an area occupied not by Turkey but by Great Britain.[21] Rauf, a passionate Anglophile who would end his career as Turkish Ambassador to London after the Second World War, had no intention of dislodging the British from the Persian Gulf, much less India. It was probably Rauf's own emissaries who suggested to Emir Habibullah that he direct his wrath against Russia, Turkey's traditional enemy, rather than Britain, until recently her protector against the Tsar. Rauf himself had set up shop in Baghdad, having no interest in running Enver's fool's errand. When the Niedermayer party arrived there in January 1915, Rauf not only refused to help, but confiscated the Germans' weapons and all of their personal belongings.[22]

Complicating Niedermayer's situation still further were reports that 10,000 Ottoman troops had crossed into Persian Azerbaijan from Mosul in January. The Turks even briefly occupied 'Russian' Tabriz, where local jihadis had torched the largest Russian bank, temporarily putting the Russian officers who commanded the Persian Cossacks there to flight.† The Turkish commander of this operation, Omer Fevzi Bey, had reportedly threatened to march all the way to

---

* When asked by Enver to head the mission to Kabul, Rauf Bey reportedly objected, 'All I know about Afghanistan is the name. How does one get there? By way of America?'
† After capturing Tabriz without a fight, the Turks held it for nearly three weeks, until, on 30 January 1915, the city was occupied yet again by the Russians.

Tehran if the Russians and English did not withdraw their forces from Persia.[23] At a war council held at the Porte on 11 February 1915, Enver confessed to the Persian Ambassador that his troops had indeed crossed the border and entered Tabriz, although he promised that Persian Azerbaijan would be returned to Persian control – after the war was over. This news was hardly reassuring to the Persian Ambassador, nor to Niedermayer, who already had British and Russian surveillance to look forward to in Persia, and would now have to reckon with the possibility that Turks and Persians would come to blows.[24]

Had Niedermayer been the resentful type, he would certainly have blamed Wassmuss for leaving him alone to deal with the Turks. Without Consul Wassmuss, Niedermayer did not even have a ranking diplomat on hand to negotiate with the stubborn Rauf Bey, who had impounded his mission's entire kit, nor would he have anyone qualified to negotiate a treaty with the Afghan Emir. But Niedermayer was not a man easily discouraged. Concluding that an armed Turkish escort would not be forthcoming, he wrote to Wangenheim that he and his men would set off alone through Persia – as soon as they got their gear. Although initially sceptical of the Afghan mission, the Ambassador now backed Niedermayer when it came to the crunch, insisting to Enver that Rauf Bey relent. Although Enver (perhaps unaware of Rauf's disloyalty) blamed Niedermayer's poor diplomatic skills for the impasse, the Germans were given back their equipment. On 28 March 1915, Niedermayer left Baghdad at last, glad to see the back of Rauf Bey.[25]

Despite the frustrating tangle with Rauf, Niedermayer's time in Baghdad had not been entirely wasted. Like Frobenius and Wassmuss, he was not afraid to improvise when he ran into difficulty. Knowing that he would face surveillance in Persia not only from Russian and British intelligence, but also from Rauf Bey's spies, Niedermayer split his men into small parties which could more easily avoid detection. Wassmuss himself had got this ball rolling, setting off on his own to set up a communications and sabotage base for the Germans in Shiraz, just north of the Gulf port at Bushire. Professor Zugmayer, accompanied by Fritz Niedermayer, artillery officer Walter Griesinger and dragoman Eduard Seiler, was dispatched to Isfahan in south-central Persia. Max Otto Schünemann, a former employee of the German Consulate in Shiraz who had worked more recently as a Persian carpet trader, was tasked with setting up a German base at Kermanshah, on the main route from Baghdad just inside the Persian border. Another team, led by Peter Paschen, was sent north-east to Russian Turkestan, the idea being to establish communications with German and Austro-Hungarian prisoners of war held there. Niedermayer himself, travelling incognito, led a small team to Tehran.[26]

These precautions, it soon emerged, had been entirely necessary. In Kermanshah, Niedermayer observed while en route for the Persian capital, 'an extensive British espionage network had started operating'.[27] Rauf Bey had blanketed the disputed areas of Persian Azerbaijan with troops, and seized the border town of Kasri-Shirin, between Baghdad and Kermanshah, in early April. The Russians had troops and agents all over northern Persia. Following the brief Turkish incursion in January the Russians were in firm control of Tabriz, with their garrison there supplied by a direct rail route to Tiflis. Another possible danger was posed by the Armenians, who, along with Kurds, lived in great numbers in the north-west regions of Persia abutting the Caucasus. 'Numerous Armenians,' Niedermayer reported shortly after reaching Tehran on 25 April 1915, 'have been armed by the Russians and seem all but ready to take action against the Germans.'[28] Complicating the task of evading hostile surveillance still further, Wassmuss had been captured by pro-British tribesmen in the desert near Shushtar on 5 March. Although the wily German escaped from his captors, he left behind a good deal of secret correspondence and, more crucially, his diplomatic codebook, which allowed the British to read cipher no. 3500, the one used by German Consuls in the Ottoman Empire – and by Niedermayer, whose telegraphic communications from Tehran were now regularly intercepted by British intelligence.[*29] The British had the

---

* In a fascinating, and often misunderstood, postscript to the Wassmuss episode, Admiral Hall of British naval intelligence later claimed the capture of his codebook had helped his team decipher the notorious Zimmermann telegram in 1917 which was so instrumental in bringing America into the First World War. This story has wound its way firmly into the historical literature, from Barbara Tuchman's bestselling *Zimmermann Telegram* (1958) to Peter Hopkirk's 1994 popular yarn *On Secret Service East of Constantinople*. From Hall to Hopkirk, the story has been embellished to the point where Wassmuss went into 'transports of rage over the seizure of his pamphlets', but somehow failed to report the loss of his codebook to the German government. As Hopkirk writes, 'Why Wassmuss had so signally failed to warn Berlin of its loss is mystifying . . .' In fact

Swedish codes as well, which came in quite handy in foiling German efforts to mobilize the Swedish-dominated Persian gendarmerie.[30]

The new Great Game in Persia was getting serious. Although the Germans were, it seemed, isolated and mistrusted by all sides, the very fact that they were being pursued by Armenians, Turks, Russians and Englishmen gave Niedermayer's men a patina of legitimacy with Persian natives. So, too, did the colossal sums of bribe money the Germans began spreading around, particularly after £100,000 sterling were transferred to the German Embassy in Tehran via an Amsterdam bank in May 1915.[31] Following the return of German Ambassador Prince Heinrich Reuss to the Persian capital in early May 1915, Niedermayer was able to enjoy at least some diplomatic protection. Despite her territory having become ground zero in the espionage wars between Germany and the Entente powers, Persia was still ostensibly neutral, after all. And yet using diplomatic immunity to avoid trouble was not really Niedermayer's style. Instead the Bavarian, as one of his rivals later complained, travelled around Tehran 'in various disguises under assumed names ... carrying out espionage and sabotage in grand style'. Having given up, for the time being, on the quixotic mission to Kabul, Niedermayer had decided instead to flood Persia with German jihad propaganda, gold and arms, setting up covert smuggling networks (mostly German pharmacies) for the purpose. He also instructed his men in Isfahan and Kermanshah to share information on Russian and British transports leaving town carrying gold and silver, so that he could pass it on to friendly tribesmen. The bank sabotage campaign seems to have been kicked off by the assassination of the Russian director of the Banque d'Escompte in Isfahan in mid-May 1915. Whether or not the Germans were behind this murder, or the attempt later that month on the life of the British Consul in Isfahan (which killed one of his servants), there was little doubt in the Entente camp that Niedermayer and Wassmuss were behind the wave of bank heists and transport hold-ups which began sweeping through Persia that summer, causing

---

Wassmuss informed Berlin of the loss of his codebook as soon as he reached Shiraz. While Hall's men may well have made some use of Wassmuss's codebook, it cannot have been decisive in the deciphering of the Zimmermann telegram, which was encrypted with an entirely different cipher, no. 0075.

all sorts of havoc with British and Russian finances. Warming to his new role as all-purpose saboteur, which he was clearly enjoying, Niedermayer wired Berlin on 18 June 1915 that he needed explosives to blow up bridges and roads used by the Russians to supply their troops in Persia from Central Asia.[32]

Left to his own devices, Niedermayer may well have continued on in this vein, becoming a kind of all-purpose Robin Hood for Persians angry at the Russian, British and more recently Turkish troops who had turned their country into a playground of the powers. By summer 1915, Niedermayer's sabotage gambits had forced British Consuls to flee from Kermanshah, Shiraz and Isfahan, and German influence was said to be peaking in Tehran as well (although not, as yet, the British zone in southern Persia, much more vital to lines of communication with India). All of this was not necessarily welcome news to Ambassador Reuss, who had to put on a straight face nearly every day and deny to his British, French and Russian counterparts that Germany was behind the latest terrorist outrage. On 4 July 1915, Reuss pointedly reminded Berlin that Niedermayer's brief was to enlist Afghanistan in the Turco-German holy war against British India, not start a one-man jihad in Persia. Niedermayer, Reuss complained, had installed rival 'Consuls' in cities like Isfahan (Zugmayer) and Shiraz (Wassmuss), which had created insubordination to his own authority as Ambassador and 'dangerously compromised' his position vis-à-vis the officially neutral Persian government. Rather like Enver getting rid of Rauf Bey by packing him off (so he thought) to Afghanistan, Reuss asked the Foreign Office to order Niedermayer to proceed to Kabul without delay. Wangenheim passed on Reuss's request to Captain Humann, the naval attaché in Pera, who issued the order on 14 July 1915 – copied, for insurance, to Bethmann Hollweg. Niedermayer duly began preparing his men for the desert march into Afghanistan, although not without issuing a note of protest to the Chancellor. The race for Kabul was on.[*33]

---

* Interestingly, once German military headquarters learned of the successes of Niedermayer's destabilization-and-sabotage campaign, as reported in Niedermayer's protest to the Chancellor, a secret directive was sent to the Wilhelmstrasse on 25 July 1915, informing the Foreign Office that the military wished 'in no way for [Niedermayer's] Persian operations to be interrupted'. By this time, however, Niedermayer had already left Tehran en route for Isfahan and the Afghan border.

Niedermayer may well have done serious damage to the Entente position had he stayed in Persia, but the timing was auspicious for a diplomatic offensive in Afghanistan. Since the dramatic Turkish stand at Gallipoli had staunched the bleeding away of Ottoman strength, things had begun to look much brighter for the Central Powers in the world war. Although Italy's entry into the war on the Entente side on 23 May 1915 did appear to threaten the already beleaguered forces of Austria-Hungary, by summer it was Russia which was reeling from the German breakthrough at Gorlice-Tarnow in May. June saw the fall of Lemberg and Przemysl as the Russians fell back from the Carpathians. In August, after wheeling north, the Germans took Warsaw and Brest-Litovsk. The downfall of Russia was in sight, which furnished a golden opportunity for anti-Entente holy war propaganda in Persia, Afghanistan and India. If a small team of German jihadis could reach Kabul with credible news of Russia's imminent collapse, the Emir might indeed join the war against the Entente. The ultimate prize was now in reach for Niedermayer.

Any glory in the Kabul adventure, however, would have to be shared. Shortly before Niedermayer's departure, Werner Otto von Hentig, a former Legation Secretary from the Tehran Embassy, had arrived in Isfahan with orders to replace the departed Wassmuss as diplomatic envoy to Afghanistan. Although there was some friction at first over the question of mission protocol, Wangenheim intervened with a compromise which saw Niedermayer retain operational control as far as Kabul, even while Hentig was given 'political autonomy' to negotiate a treaty with the Emir.[34] Accompanying Hentig was a Turkish lieutenant, Kasim Bey, seconded by Enver, and two leading Indian opposition politicians. These were Mahendra Pratap, a Hindu prince friendly to Nehru and Gandhi, and (more significantly for the Germans) Mohammed Barakatullah, a notorious Muslim revolutionary exile who claimed to be friendly with Nasrullah Khan, the ferociously anti-British (and pro-German) brother of Emir Habibullah and possible heir to the Afghan throne.* Barakatullah, holed up in San Francisco when war came in 1914, travelled to Geneva in neutral Switzerland, hoping to interest the Germans in his schemes to bring

* In 1912, Barakatullah had written that 'In case of a European war, it is the duty of Muslims to be united, to stand by the Khalif, and to side with Germany.'

(*left*) 1. Otto von Bismarck,
German Chancellor and
'anti-Orientalist'

(*below*) 2. Kaiser Wilhelm
II and Chancellor Bernhard
von Bülow entering
Jerusalem, 1898

3. Sultan Abdul Hamid II

(*above*) 4. Damascus. The tomb of Saladin, which so moved Kaiser Wilhelm II during his 1898 visit

(*left*) 5. Baalbek. Jupiter Temple with dual inscription in German and Ottoman Turkish marking the Kaiser's visit

6. Cairo. Max von Oppenheim in European formal wear

7. Cairo. Max von Oppenheim in Arab-style headdress

(*left*) 8. Am Djirdjib. The Sheikh of the Shammar tribe with two relatives

(*below*) 9. Shammar beduins, 1913

10. Cairo. Professor Bernhard Moritz, Max von Oppenheim and German Vice Consul Breiter

27. Wilhelm Wassmuss

28. Lawrence 'of Arabia'

29. Max von Oppenheim at his work desk in Tell Halaf

down the Raj. Scooped up with predictable alacrity by Oppenheim's jihad bureau in Berlin, Barakatullah now found himself in Hentig's train, passing through Tehran en route for Afghanistan and, he hoped, India.[35]

Indian revolutionaries were not all Hentig brought to Niedermayer's table. In part because of the haste with which the original jihad team had been assembled in late 1914, Niedermayer had never been given proper letters of introduction from Kaiser Wilhelm to the Emir, nor the full panoply of presents he would need to make an impression on an oriental potentate. Hentig brought all this, and more, including elaborate imperial greetings to Habibullah from both the German Emperor and the Ottoman Sultan, along with twenty-seven letters signed by Bethmann Hollweg and addressed to Indian princes rumoured to be estranged from the Raj, 'sumptuously bound in leather and written in the recipient's own vernacular'. Most lustrous of all were the gifts for Habibullah and his retinue, which included 'bejewelled gold watches, gold fountain pens, gold-topped canes, hand-ornamented rifles and pistols, binoculars, cameras, compasses, a cinema projector and – the very latest thing in German inventiveness – a dozen radio alarm clocks'.[36]

As if to confirm their sense of incipient rivalry, Hentig and Niedermayer split apart at Isfahan, each leading a multinational party of some 90 to 100 men across the eastern Persian desert to the Afghan border. Breaking up into smaller parties made good operational sense. The British and Russians were setting up an 'East Persian Cordon' to prevent Niedermayer from crossing the Afghan border. Because the ragged frontier was hundreds of miles long, tracking the Germans would come down to guesswork, aided by intelligence gleaned through bribing local nomads and tribesmen. Niedermayer and Hentig hoped to throw the Russian and British sentries off the scent by throwing up feints and diversions, and by planting false rumours of their intended routes.

Although thousands fewer men and far less war *matériel* was transported than in the Kress-led crossing of the Sinai the previous winter, Niedermayer and Hentig made their own crossing at the height of summer, under 'the terrible fire of the Persian sun', with temperatures typically topping 50 degrees Celsius (122 Fahrenheit). Travelling mostly by night, the men somehow made stages of 40 to 50 kilometres a day. Apart from the heat and punishing thirst, the men were menaced by poisonous snakes, 'giant scorpions', and 'armies of insects of every kind'. After reuniting with Hentig's group at Chehar Deh, 200 miles from the border, Niedermayer sent off two small decoy parties. Before crossing the last serious obstacle with his main team, the north–south caravan road from Meshed to Birjand, Niedermayer jettisoned some of the heavier gifts for the Emir, along with piles of jihad pamphlets, to lighten the load for a mad dash to the frontier. On the night of 20–21 August 1915, seven weeks after they had left Isfahan, Niedermayer and Hentig entered Afghan territory. The British cordon had failed to hold. [37]

The very perilousness of the journey served to bind together Niedermayer's men, and to strengthen his own authority. Although Hentig was by no means lacking in courage or fitness himself, he conceded that it was only due to the Bavarian's ruthless determination and leadership that the men reached Afghanistan. 'In terms of physical performance and direct military consequences,' the mission's diplomat later wrote, 'Herr Niedermayer's achievement must rank among the most memorable of the entire war.' Niedermayer, for his part, thanked Hentig in his first dispatch after crossing the Afghan border for having 'supported him in the best manner; between us reigns the most complete harmony'.[38] After enduring nearly unceasing hardship in the desert, the entire party felt the profoundest relief when they were ushered into the lush and fertile valley of Herat by an official delegation from the Governor. Here was an oasis out of an oriental storybook, made all the more overwhelming by the contrast between the merciless sun-baked world they were leaving behind. Received as honoured guests in Herat, the exhausted men were ushered into the courtyard of the Governor's palace, where they relaxed by the cool flowing water and refreshed themselves with exotic fruits. 'With the intoxicating scents from the garden,' Niedermayer later wrote, 'it was like a fairy tale.'[39]

After passing two pleasant weeks in Herat, Niedermayer and Hentig mustered their men again for yet another challenging journey over the mountains to Kabul. Although there were no more British and Russian patrols to evade, the Afghan capital lay some 650 kilometres to the east – almost as long as the distance the men had covered between Isfahan and the Persian frontier. The path to Kabul wound over forbidding mountain ranges, which posed their own set of challenges. Amazingly, Niedermayer had crossed the Persian desert without losing any of his men, aside from a few local guides he had shot for treasonous contacts with the enemy. The four-week trek across the mountains of central Afghanistan, by contrast, claimed the life of Niedermayer's trusted adjutant, Hans Jakob, who was buried on a hillside above Kabul. After the euphoric reception in Herat, Jakob's death was a discouraging omen.

On 2 October 1915, or almost exactly one year after Niedermayer had arrived in Constantinople from Berlin, the Germans at last entered the Afghan capital. It was a heady time in the war for the Central Powers. Russia had conducted its 'great retreat', abandoning Poland to the Germans. The combined Austro-German-Bulgarian assault on Serbia, which would at last open an uninterrupted rail connection through the Balkans to Constantinople, was about to begin. The *Drang nach Osten* was in full swing, and its leading edge was now in Kabul, just 200 kilometres from the Khyber Pass and the North-west Frontier. It had taken much longer than Oppenheim had hoped, but after all the delays and tribulations the German jihad stood at the Gates of India.

There now followed one of the most dramatic encounters of the First World War, made yet more dramatic by the Emir's delaying tactics. Twenty-four days came and went as the Germans kicked their heels under a kind of house arrest in a local merchant's house, each one as pointlessly idle as the last. On 26 October 1915, Niedermayer and Hentig were finally picked up in Habibullah's Rolls-Royce – the only car in Afghanistan – and chauffeured in style down the paved asphalt road (likewise the only one of its kind in the country) to the Emir's palace. Habibullah's first words gave Niedermayer a taste of the Emir's elliptical diplomacy. 'Because you have been already six months underway [on your journey],' the Emir assured the Germans with an evident lack of contrition, 'these several weeks' delay could not have amounted to much.'[40]

The audience which followed was just as frustrating for Niedermayer as the Emir's dismissive opening remarks. Although he was impressed by Habibullah's elegant manners and sharp mind, it was precisely these which allowed the Emir to put the Germans in their place. Habibullah was loath to reveal what he was thinking, listening carefully to German offers and demands while saying little. The Emir received Niedermayer, Hentig, and later the Indian representatives, for almost daily meetings throughout November and December 1915, without committing himself to anything. He reacted strongly to only one member of the party: Pratap, the Hindu prince and would-be revolutionary, who incurred the Emir's displeasure immediately.[41] While evincing no outward dislike of Hentig or Niedermayer, Habibullah treated the Germans as if 'we were businessmen with various goods [to sell], from which he wished to determine which would be good or useful to him'. 'Everything,' Niedermayer later recalled of the Emir with exasperation, 'seemed like mere business to him. This gave long faces to our Muslims with their earnestly propagated lectures on the holy war.'[42]

Habibullah's caution was wholly in character. He had not survived as sovereign of his realm for fourteen years in between the British and Russian empires without learning how to play the powers off against one another. Far from the provincial tribal Islamic headman the Germans had imagined him to be, the Emir was European in both his dress and his manners, and evidently well informed about the world war. Habibullah's October waiting game had probably been concocted not only to torture the Germans, but to see which way the battle for Serbia would go. Similarly, the sudden and surprising melting of the Emir's resistance to German demands in late January 1916 almost certainly reflected his receipt of the news that the British had evacuated Gallipoli (the last troops left on 9 January).

The treaty signed in Kabul on 24 January 1916 was a tremendous achievement for Niedermayer and Hentig. Although Habibullah was no less reliant on British subsidies than the Sherif of Mecca – in fact his annual subsidy of £400,000 sterling dwarfed the Sherif's – the Emir of Afghanistan, unlike Hussein, hereby put his name to paper as a willing ally of the Central Powers in the war against his own sponsor. True, Habibullah did so only under strict conditions, and at a colossal price: to replace the British tribute, which would vanish if his forces invaded India, the Emir demanded from Berlin a lump sum of £10 million sterling, the equivalent of some $5 billion today. The

Germans were also enjoined to guarantee the independence and territorial integrity of Afghanistan, and of course to send as many arms and advisers as the Emir deemed necessary to break through British lines on the North-west Frontier.[43] Still, unrealistic as these conditions appeared, by agreeing to an alliance treaty at all the Emir had implicitly recognized the superiority of German arms and had sanctified the Turco-German holy war.

Or had he? The closer one looked at the Germans' precarious position in Kabul, the clearer it became that Emir Habibullah was playing them. The treaty terms had, in effect, called Niedermayer's bluff. If the Germans really were capable of paying a subsidy of £10 million sterling and dispatching serious quantities of arms to Afghanistan – implying that they could transport all this safely to Kabul – then it must mean they had completed the Baghdad railway, or somehow seized control of the seas from the Royal Navy, which could only be true if Britain had already lost the war. At the Gates of India, no less than at the chokepoint of Suez, the British Empire was guarded by the Taurus and Amanus mountain gaps in German communications. But why was it taking so long to conquer the mountains? It is time to take a closer look at the Baghdad railway.

IV
Boomerang

[Ottoman Muslims] treat Christians with mildness and friendliness, as long as their religious fanaticism is not urged on.

Wilhelm von Pressel, the 'Father of the Baghdad Railway',
c. 1876

14

Trouble on the Baghdad Railway

The Sultan gave his promise to [Ambassador] Marschall von
Biberstein, sworn on the Koran, that the great Baghdad railway
would be built.

German Foreign Office dispatch from Berlin to
Constantinople, 15 October 1915[1]

In Kabul, as at Karbala and Mecca, the Germans had discovered
that the price of Islamic holy war was much higher than Oppenheim
had promised. A global jihad, it turned out, was not something to be
conjured up with magic beans. First one needed the *fetvas*, which
sounded inexpensive enough in theory – but turned out to be anything but. If we judge by the Porte's diplomatic terms for entering the
war, the Şeykh-ul-Islam's holy war declaration itself had required a
down-payment of some £2 million worth of gold, a loan of £5
million more, plus massive shipments of arms on credit.[2] And yet
the Ottoman *fetvas* proved insufficient to stiffen Muslim spines in
Syria or Arabia, which led to the Kress–Prüfer avalanche of gold in
Damascus and the Baron's lavish courting of Feisal in the Pera
Palace. That Klein and Lührs had to shell out 'only' 50,000 Marks
annually to win the endorsement of the leading Shia clerics to
smooth the path to India was small comfort, considering how much
the Afghan Emir was charging at the other end of the Persian desert.
Habibullah's particularly steep asking price came from the acute
bidding war for his loyalty with Great Britain, but was in spirit
not so different from what the Young Turks, Hashemites, Bedouins,
and Syrian and Mesopotamian Arabs had all demanded in their turn.

What was going on? Were not holy warriors supposed to fight for Allah alone, out of religious duty? Where were the *ghazi* warriors of legend, storming citadels and city walls, striking fear into the hearts of infidels? Islam had always been a fighting creed, expanding through the sword from the days of the Prophet to the conquest of Constantinople and the Balkans. Had the decline of the Ottoman Empire in the modern era so dampened the fires of jihad that only pay-to-play mercenaries remained?

Considering how much blood, arms and treasure the Germans had invested in summoning up the ancient spirit of Islamic holy war to bring down the Entente empires, one can understand the creeping sense of disappointment after each successive failure of Oppenheim's jihad to ignite. But a true scholar of Islam could have told the Germans exactly what to expect. As infidels themselves, the Germans could hardly summon up a holy war on their own. In terms of Islamic jurisprudence, the notion of selective jihad against some, but not all, Christians, as we saw in chapter 6 above, is nonsensical. On the other hand, the practice of infidels paying for protection – as the Germans, in effect, were doing each time they asked Muslims to spare them while attacking other Christians – is firmly established in Islamic law. The theological grounds for this *jizya*, or compulsory tax paid by non-Muslims, is explained clearly in the Koran, Sura 9:29: 'Fight those who believe not in Allah nor the Last Day, nor hold that forbidden which hath been forbidden by Allah and His Messenger, nor acknowledge the religion of Truth (even if they are) of the People of the Book [i.e. Christians and Jews], *until they pay the* Jizya *with willing submission, and feel themselves subdued*' (emphasis added).[3] German requests for Islamic *fetvas* and jihadi uprisings against the Entente powers may not have been conceived in Berlin as *jizya* offerings, but that may have been just how they were interpreted by many Turkish, Arab and Persian imams and clerics. For infidels in the Islamic world, there was no such thing as a free lunch.

Still, unfair as the ever-mounting jihad-*jizya* fees seemed, if Oppenheim's holy war ever did catch fire at Suez or in the subcontinent, they would be well worth the price. Compared to the colossal sums laid down on the killing fields of Europe – total German expenditures on the war of 1914–18 have been estimated at over 200 billion Marks, some $47 billion, or the equivalent of nearly $5 trillion today – even the onerous price tag of an Afghan jihad against British India sanctioned by the Emir was a mere trifle in comparison.[4] In addition, the amount of ammunition that would be needed to overwhelm British lines on the North-west Frontier was little more than was expended in a typical day's shelling on the western front. The problem facing Oppenheim in Berlin was not finding £10 million sterling for the Emir (about 200 million Marks, or scarcely more than the cost of a day or two of fighting on the war's main battlefields), or weapons for the Afghan army. The trouble was, instead, how to get all of this safely to Kabul.

Whether it was Frobenius on the Red Sea coast, Musil in Arabia, Kress at Suez, Klein in lower Mesopotamia, or Niedermayer in Persia and Afghanistan, the complaint was the same: more men, money and war *matériel* were desperately needed. The root cause of the supply problems was no mystery. Despite all the hard work of German financiers and engineers, buttressed by an enormous multinational labour force, fifteen years after the historic concession of 1899, the great trunk railway to the Near East was still nowhere near complete. For most of 1915, this was true not only of the difficult sections in the Taurus and Amanus mountains, but of the Balkan stretch as well. Neutral Romania continued to place obstacles in the Germans' path, erecting yet new barriers in May 1915 against shipments of explosives.[5] Not until Serbia was knocked out of the war in November was the European section of the Orient Express fully operational.[6]

East of Constantinople, the daunting mountain passes remained, along with nearly the entire 623-kilometre section from the foot of the Amanus mountains to Baghdad, of which only a tenth part had been finished before the war. The Mesopotamian flats presented their own problems, most euphemistically listed under the heading of 'security'. Then, as now, Iraq was not terribly friendly to foreigners. So dangerous was the eastern bank of the Euphrates that the railway company, at great expense, had to house employees inside fortified station compounds to protect them from marauding nomads. As Karl Figdor reported in *Vossische Zeitung* in May 1914, 'a continuous barbed wire fence encircled the compounds ... only the windows and doors facing the protected interior courtyard could be opened ... the stations situated in the most dangerous areas had no windows at all, only angled

4. The Baghdad railway in 1914, with gaps and projected development

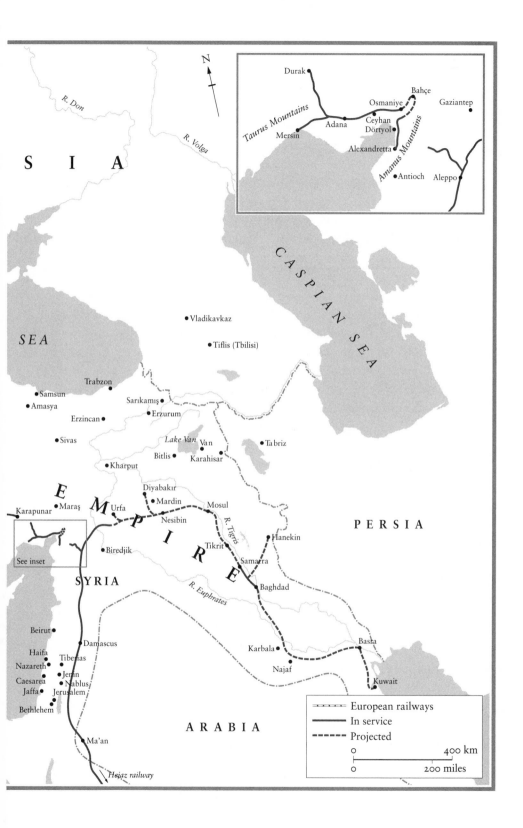

Durak

Taurus Mountains

Bahçe

Osmaniye

Gaziantep

Adana

Ceyhan

Mersin

Dörtyol

Alexandretta

Amanus Mountains

Antioch

Aleppo

N

R. Don

R. Volga

A S I A

C A S P I A N   S E A

Vladikavkaz

Tiflis (Tbilisi)

S E A

Trabzon

Samsun

Sarıkamış

Amasya

Erzurum

Erzincan

Sivas

Lake Van

Van

Tabriz

Bitlis

Karahisar

Kharput

E

Diyabakır

Mardin

M

Urfa

P

Nesibin

Mosul

Karapunar

Maraş

I

R

Tikrit

R. Tigris

Hanekin

P E R S I A

See inset

Biredjik

E

Samarra

SYRIA

R. Euphrates

Baghdad

Beirut

Damascus

Haifa

Karbala

Basra

Tiberias

Nazareth

Jenin

Najaf

Caesarea

Nablus

Jaffa

Jerusalem

Kuwait

Bethlehem

ARABIA

Ma'an

====== European railways
—— In service
- - - Projected

0   400 km
0   200 miles

Hejaz railway

slits in the walls to protect the station against Bedouin bullets'. It was not only European Christians whose lives were at risk in Mesopotamia: even Kurdish and Turkish workers were billeted in station compounds and 'escorted daily to the [work] sites under armed guard'.[7]

Although the precarious security situation in Iraq was frustrating, the most serious barrier in railway construction remained the forbidding mountain ranges. One tunnel alone, at Bahçe in the Amanus mountains between Adana and Antep (Gaziantep), threatened to torpedo the Baghdad railway all by itself. Here, the line ran smack into Gâvur Dağı, or Infidel Mountain, composed almost entirely of solid quartz 'hard enough to cut glass'. Figdor reported in April 1914 that boring machines were being literally ground down by Gâvur Dağı, which tore up over 2,000 drill bits a day. It was enough to drive men mad, and in many cases it did. The site, according to Figdor, 'reported one disaster after another, including robberies, murders, explosions, and fatal accidents'.[8]

Although not every tunnel was as punishing as Gâvur Dağı, it is easy to see why progress in crossing the mountains cost the Germans so much time. All of the drill bits and explosives had to be imported, along with the skilled engineers who knew how to blast away rock and bore tunnels. But then this problem was hardly confined to the mountain sections. Apart from wood and (mostly unskilled) labour, virtually everything required for the construction of the Baghdad railway had to be transported in from abroad at great expense. Steel rails, ties and plates were imported from Düsseldorf, bolts from Hagen, bolt plates from Osnabrück, clamps from Bruckhausen. Some 50,000 tons of German lime and cement were shipped to Turkey every year. In the more barren areas even foodstuffs were imported to feed the workers. German medicines were also required in tremendous quantities, particularly following a series of cholera epidemics which hit the line in 1910 and 1911. Because there were few proper roads to speak of, most of these bulky materials had to be trundled into worksites by mule caravan from the nearest port (Constantinople, Mersin, Alexandretta (Iskenderun) or Beirut), or shipped along narrow-gauge rail service lines which had themselves to be first supplied and built from scratch.[9]

Despite the myriad difficulties, following the renewed Baghdad railway concession of 1911 the Germans had made good progress.

Unlike in the earlier period, when Abdul Hamid's political suspicions had required sequential work on one section at a time, from west to east, in 1911 and 1912 construction proceeded simultaneously up and down the line, from Bulgurlu to Baghdad (from which station the line was now being built 'backwards', or east to west). Blasting was under way at last in both the Taurus and Amanus mountains. Recruitment stations in Germany and Turkey alike were flooded with applicants. The operation took on a truly international flavour, with Germans, Austrians, Italians, Slavs, Greeks and Armenians dominating the skilled positions – blacksmiths, carpenters, engineers, explosives experts and pyrotechnicians, masons, mechanics, tunnel borers – while local Turks, Kurds, Arabs and Albanians handled most of the unskilled manual labour. By April 1912, over 16,000 workers were on the payroll of the Baghdad Railway Company, which now dominated Ottoman economic life across huge swathes of Anatolia, Syria and Mesopotamia.[10]

There was something inspiring about the cosmopolitan nature of this German-led endeavour, one of the last great flowerings of the first era of globalization. Like the other multinational enterprises of the time, however, the Baghdad railway was viable only so long as the precarious international equilibrium held. The very romance of the Orient Express was also its potential undoing, as the line wound its way through some of the most unstable political real estate of the *fin de siècle* world. The Italian and Balkan wars of 1911–13, predictably, caused severe disruption on the Baghdad line, interfering with shipping, while causing price spikes in crucial commodities and freight. Although construction did not cease entirely, at times progress slowed to a crawl, particularly on the capital-intensive mountain sections. When tunnel-boring had begun on the Amanus section in summer 1911, engineers estimated it would take two years to reach the plains on the other side. After three years of on-again, off-again blasting, the same engineers predicted in December 1914 that tunnelling the Amanus would take – another two years.[11]

The Italian and Balkan wars eerily foreshadowed the problems the Germans would have working the Baghdad line during the First World War. The Tripolitanian war of 1911 had produced a forced exodus of Italian workers, mostly skilled masons difficult to replace. Local labour too began to be scarce, as Muslims were called up into the Ottoman army – along with Christians, whose exemption from military service was lifted following the counter-counter revolution of 1909.[12] It was a taste of things to come.

The Great Power conflict which erupted in 1914 was more disruptive still. On the crucial Taurus and Amanus mountain sections, Ottoman mobilization caused the number of employees to drop from nearly 12,000 in August 1914 to just 1,650 in September – and that was before Turkey entered the war in November and the British began blockading the Ottoman coastline. Little wonder the gaps were not closed in time to make a difference at Suez. As Kress and Prüfer complained to Berlin, there was simply no way to meet the British at the canal in strength without an uninterrupted rail connection at least as far as Aleppo, and ideally all the way into the Sinai peninsula.[13] Von der Goltz Pasha, now serving as the Sultan's general adjutant, seconded Kress, adding that completing the Baghdad railway could bring the world war to a 'worthy and decisive conclusion' by making possible the conquest of India.[14] Despite the difficulty of finding money, men and *matériel* while fighting raged in Europe and at the Straits, these pleas were taken very seriously in Berlin. Beginning in February 1915, the German high command convened a series of high-level meetings to speed up construction on the line, with Falkenhayn himself attending, along with Zimmermann from the Foreign Office, the Turcophile journalist Ernst Jäckh and Karl Helferrich of Deutsche Bank (which was expected to pay).[15]

The initial reports from the field were not encouraging. A series of floods in November and December had devastated whole sections of the line in the low-lying coastal areas. Lieutenant Colonel Böttrich, liaison officer between the Ottoman army and the railway company, reported to Falkenhayn in March 1915 that it would be best to concentrate on either the Taurus or Amanus tunnels, as not enough men and materials were available to bore full-time on both sections at once. Because it was easier for caravans to cross the Taurus through the old Cilician Gates than via the comparatively undeveloped Amanus, he recommended that the Baghdad Railway Company concentrate exclusively on tunnelling the latter range, which might then be completed by early 1916. The Taurus, Böttrich concluded sadly, would take another three years at least.[16]

The Germans, however, were not about to give up on the Kaiser's dream railway. Despite the labour and materials shortages, there were encouraging signs from the field. Motivation was not hard to come by as the Turkish fronts in the world war began heating up. By the end of 1914, the Baghdad railway had passed the halfway mark, with 1,104 of the total 2,190 kilometre distance between Konya and Basra in service.[17] Even as the bad news trickled in from Sarıkamış in January 1915, a Taurus tunnel nearly two kilometres long was completed at Bilmedik. In April, the first steel bridge across the Euphrates was opened, a fine feat of German engineering, especially considering the precarious security situation in Mesopotamia. Also in April, Falkenhayn, backed by State Secretary Jagow, intervened, ordering that intensive tunnelling begin forthwith, on *both* the Taurus and Amanus mountains, regardless of cost – at least up to forty million Marks.[18] Theoretically, this was the amount of credit Berlin would open up for the Ottoman government via Deutsche Bank; but based on past precedent the outlay was more like a down-payment. Turkish extortions had bitten Berlin once move: the 'credit' of forty million Marks would soon grow to 360 million, which Deutsche Bank would never see again.[19]

Inexpensive it was not, but in strategic terms the new investment in the Orient Express paid off handsomely. With a nearly unlimited budget, the Baghdad Railway Company could hire whomever it wanted in Turkey, while attracting serious talent from Germany (not least because the project offered an escape from the terrors of the front lines in Europe). In June, engineers at Bahçe finally won their battle with the quartz, tunnelling all the way through Infidel Mountain.[20] Substantial gaps in both the Taurus and Amanus remained, but as spring turned to summer it appeared possible that the tunnelling might be completed by early 1916, in time to turn the tide of the war.

Just when light was beginning to appear at the end of the Baghdad railway tunnels, however, the line was hit by the greatest crisis yet. Under the strains of the war, inter-ethnic tensions in Asiatic Turkey had been ratcheting up to dangerous levels. Although there has been endless acrimony over interpretation and casualty figures, there is broad agreement that the atrocities committed during the Armenian deportations* of 1915 were unprecedented in scope, going well beyond levels of violence seen in 1894–6 and 1909. Turkish historians, while acknowledging that thousands of innocents died in the course of the deportations, have tended to emphasize alleged Armenian treachery at Sarıkamış, Van, Cilicia and elsewhere, which convinced the CUP government it had a fifth column on its hands. Armenian writers, by contrast, while conceding that some of their co-nationals were involved in partisan activities, argue that they merely provided the Ottoman government with a convenient pretext for what was actually a deliberate, premeditated act of genocide.[21]

In a sense, the entire region was on a wartime footing long before Turkey entered the European conflict in November 1914. For centuries, the Ottoman, Persian and Russian empires had struggled to control the contested border region where eastern Anatolia (or Turkish Armenia, as it was then sometimes called) meets the Transcaucasus, northern Mesopotamia and Persia. Although the Armenian question dominated the high-level diplomacy of the time, in many ways it was Kurdish nomadic tribes who were really the prime movers in the region, as they wrought havoc and mayhem on the settled population of Armenian, Nestorian, Syriac and Assyrian Christians, along with those Muslims who worked the land or served as Persian or Ottoman government officials. In Van, the lakeside settlement near the Russian border which features so prominently in the tragic drama of 1915, Kurdish depredations had become so severe by 1913 that the city, reported Russian Consul Olferiev that April, was turning into an armed camp. The Dashnaks were smuggling arms in via Persia, and 'all the Armenian merchants were stockpiling guns in their stores'.[22] In nearby Bitlis, Kurdish tribesmen put Ottoman troops to flight in March 1914, which left the (mostly unarmed) local Armenians at the mercy of a reputedly bloodthirsty Kurdish chieftain, Mullah Selim. Although Selim personally vowed not to harm Christians, few Armenians trusted his promise, and those who could barricaded themselves inside

---

* Legally speaking, the Armenians in question were forcibly 'relocated' inside the Ottoman Empire, not 'deported' beyond its borders. Because 'relocation' has the air of a euphemism, I use 'deportation' and 'relocation' interchangeably here.

the Russian Consulate for safety. One can hardly blame them: the Mullah openly declared the aim of his anti-Ottoman revolt as the restoration of Sharia law, which was not reassuring for Christians still hoping to attain the ever-elusive civil equality the CUP had promised them in 1908.[23]

Even for those with long experience in the region, disentangling the loyalties and intentions of the different ethnic players in these conflicts was difficult. In the Van unrest of spring 1913, Turkish government efforts to confiscate arms from Armenians in April did not prevent some 500 Armenian Dashnaks from pursuing the fleeing Kurdish bandits who had molested the city – alongside Ottoman troops.[24] The Armenians were more like innocent bystanders in the Bitlis battle of March–April 1914, caught in the crossfire as the Ottoman army called in reinforcements to crush the Kurds. True, the Bitlis Armenians had asked the Ottoman Vali for guns to defend themselves against the rebels as they threatened the city (using the reasonable logic that they would help him 'defend the constitution' against the Sharia-spouting Kurdish Mullah), but this request was predictably denied.[25] In a fittingly confusing climax to the battle of Bitlis, as soon as the Turkish government had re-established control over the city, Mullah Selim and two of his main rebel collaborators fled to the Russian Consulate – to the great surprise of the Armenians who had gone there to escape them. Remarkably, the Kurdish Mullah was still hiding in the Russian Consulate months later when Turkey entered the world war.*[26]

As the Bitlis story suggests, hovering over all the confusing episodes of ethnic violence in eastern Anatolia in 1913, 1914 and – even more so – 1915, was the Russian factor. Like a giant elephant in the room, imperial Russia had its trunk in everyone's business. With Ottoman and Persian power in rapid decline, more or less everyone

---

* Some of the Armenians of Bitlis had already left the Consulate by 5 April 1914, the day when Mullah Selim and his Kurdish rebels arrived, but many remained. The episode nearly blew up into a major diplomatic crisis, not because the Russian Consul was protecting Armenians – but rather because he was sheltering the Kurdish ringleaders of the Bitlis uprising. Alas, the Russian Consul does not tell us if the Kurdish and Armenian refugees slept in the same room, or what, if anything, they found to talk about.

in the region expected the Russians to take over. Even as Kurdish tribal chiefs bought arms from the Russians, their Armenian, Assyrian, Nestorian and Syriac Christian targets sought Russian protection. So, too, did *American* Christians, who were increasingly numerous in the Protestant missions now dotting Turkish Armenia. As the Kurdish bandits threatened Van in spring 1913, Dr G.C. Reynolds, the Secretary of the American Mission Board in Turkey, with (he claimed) the approval of the Woodrow Wilson administration, 'arranged with the Russian government to assume a general protectorate of American interests in eastern Turkey'.[27] Even as he was offering protection to American religious missions, the Russian Consul was receiving deputations from Armenian revolutionary organizations like the Dashnaks, who had given up on the once-promising CUP government and decided to throw in their lot with the Russians, despite, as one Dashnak told Consul Olferiev, 'hating the imperialist' Tsarist government. Overall, the 'mood of Armenians' in Van vilayet, Consul Olferiev reported to Ambassador Girs during the Kurdish disturbances of spring 1913, was 'one of complete Russophilia ... the Dashnaks are completely on our side'.[28] It was against this backdrop of increasingly pervasive Russian influence that the European diplomatic campaign to 'reform' and bring autonomy to Turkish Armenia gathered steam in February 1914 – just as the Kurdish crisis in Bitlis was coming to a head. It is hardly surprising that the Ottoman government saw this whole reform campaign as scarcely concealed camouflage for Russian imperialism.

Even before the July crisis, Turkish troops had blanketed the Persian border area, in pursuit of pro-Russian Kurdish bands. In Tiflis, the Russian Caucasian command was looking into arming Ottoman Kurds and Armenians to take on the Turks as early as August 1914, long before the Porte's entry into the war. Prompted by none other than Foreign Minister Sazonov – who himself saw Turkey's entry into the war as inevitable, and took it upon himself to instruct Tiflis command on 26 August 1914 on the need to enlist 'Armenians, Kurds and Assyrian Christians' in the upcoming struggle against the Turks – three days later Lieutenant General Nikolai Yudenich submitted a detailed memorandum on the 'Arming of Ottoman Armenians' (*O snabzhenii oruzhiem' turetskikh' armyan'*). In the classic logic of the self-fulfilling prophecy, the Yudenich report predicted that the Ottoman government would inevitably 'suppress and brutalize the Armenians' as disloyal subjects if Turkey entered the war. To prevent the 'expulsion' and/or 'annihilation' of Turkey's Armenians as a fifth column, Yudenich proposed sending 'at least 20,000 rifles' and 2 million rounds of ammunition to Turkish Armenians so that they might serve Russia as a fifth column.*[29]

If one reads between the lines of Sazonov's astonishing intervention and the resulting Yudenich report, one begins to grasp the nature of the ineluctable tragedy unfolding in Turkish Armenia in 1914–15, eerily parallel to the concurrent saga of Gallipoli. The root cause of both Entente disasters was the enormous gap between Russia's foreign policy aims and her means. Sazonov, sensing the potential danger of unleashing ethnic rebellions behind Turkish lines prematurely, asked Yudenich expressly to recommend that Armenian rebels 'not undertake anything without our instructions' (*nichego ne predprinimat' bez' nashego ukazaniya*). Likewise, Yudenich cloaked his August 1914 memorandum in humanitarian terms – the idea, he says again and again, is to funnel arms to Turkey's Armenians so that 'they will be able to defend themselves' – against both the Ottoman army and Kurdish marauders. In a less guarded moment, Yudenich explained the real reason the Armenians would have to arm themselves: Russia was too weak to protect them, having diverted nearly all her military strength to the western front against Germany.[30] Just as countless young Anzacs, Frenchmen and Englishmen died at Gallipoli because of a strategic dream which Petrograd had not the naval or amphibious capacity to fulfil itself (for fear of the SMS *Goeben*'s guns the Russian fleet was barely a factor at Gallipoli), so would the beleaguered Armenians of eastern Turkey fall on the sword of Russian imperial ambition, as the would-be 'liberees' of an army unable to liberate them.

The April 1915 Armenian uprising at Van, still the subject of ferocious controversy, provides a perfect microcosm of the Armenian tragedy. As we saw above, local Armenian merchants had been stockpiling

---

*This is the same Yudenich who would later spearhead the White offensive against Petrograd in 1919, famously repulsed near Tsarskoe Selo by Trotsky's Reds.

arms long before 1914, and for very good reason. All through the first months of the European war, Russian headquarters in Tiflis plotted ways of getting arms to Armenians in Van, without ever quite figuring out how to evade Turkish border patrols. Instead, beginning in September 1914, Tiflis command began organizing and arming partisan bands on the Russian side of the border, composed of Caucasian Armenian volunteers and thousands of Ottoman army deserters who had made their way over to Russian lines.[31] Rough (in other words unencrypted) telegraphic communications with the Dashnaks in Van were established: rough enough that Dashnak requests for Russian arms were intercepted by Ottoman military intelligence.[32]

Whether, as Armenian historians have long claimed, the April rebellion was a kind of preventive 'Warsaw uprising' of self-defence against imminent Turkish plans for murderous mass expulsions, or instead (as the Turks claim) itself the cause of the subsequent deportation campaign, it was undoubtedly a bloodbath in and of itself. On or around 13 April 1915, Armenian partisans succeeded in expelling government forces and throwing up barricades around Van. That they were well armed seems indisputable, considering that they held the city for nearly four weeks against three Ottoman Jandarma (i.e. police) battalions, the First Expeditionary Force and Kurdish 'Hamidiye' militiamen. That the Armenian rebels established communications with the Russian command in Tiflis during the uprising is also indisputable, although this was not telegraphic: instead three Armenian partisans crossed Turkish lines and contacted the Russians via Azerbaijan on 6 May 1915.[33] Six days later a fourth Armenian messenger smuggled a letter from the leader of the Van resistance 'in the lining of his clothes', in which he informed Yudenich that the Armenians of Van were 'expecting Russian help every day' (*Ezhedevno zhdem' Russkoi pomoshchi*).*[34] The Cossacks, accompanied by as many as 10,000 Armenian deserters acting as guides, did indeed arrive just four days later – although it was not soon enough for many

---

* This letter was proudly forwarded by the Russian Foreign Office to Paris and London for distribution inside the Entente governments – after the elimination of one, possibly explosive, word. As read by the French and English, the Armenian plea from Van spoke of 'the help we are waiting for every day' – but not *Russian* help.

Armenian civilians living outside the town barricades. In retaliation for atrocities they were told Armenians had committed against Muslims inside the city, Ottoman infantrymen and Kurdish militiamen had 'reportedly acted under orders to kill all Armenian males twelve years and older' in the area. Inside Van, the Armenians showed little more mercy. Although initial Ottoman claims that 120,000 Turkish Muslims had been slaughtered in Van are grossly inflated, there is no denying that terrible atrocities were committed by both sides. As one Cossack observed after securing the area, 'the Turks and Kurds took no Armenian prisoners, and the Armenians took no Kurds or Turks prisoner'.[35]

Reading contemporary accounts of the Van uprising, one is struck by the sense of inevitability about the collision. Tensions had been building for months, stirred up not only by Russian agitation but by aggressive (and likely cynical) Ottoman efforts to enlist local Armenians in the army, which produced predictable mass resistance and widespread desertions.[36] As against the somewhat stale scholarly arguments one sometimes reads today about fifth columns and loyalty issues, at the time there was absolutely no secret about widespread disloyalty, draft resistance and desertion among the Armenian population in eastern Turkey, nor that the Ottoman government had anything but the worst intentions towards these Armenians. Nor was the idea that Van had been delivered to the Russians by the Armenian rebels the least bit controversial: Armenian newspapers in the Caucasus boasted openly about this throughout 1915 (with, it is true, the possibly distorting motive of convincing Russia that Turkey's Armenians were worthy clients, deserving of their own state).[37] The Armenians had every possible reason to arm themselves for protection, and to seek Russian aid and arms: but in doing so they inevitably invited the very repression they feared.[38]

The ultimate Ottoman overreaction to these perceived threats is not surprising, when we consider how precarious the Turkish hold on eastern Anatolia was – not least because, as we saw above in chapter 2, Russian diplomatic pressure had derailed Abdul Hamid's dream of building a railway there. With the final routing of the Baghdad line getting nowhere near the Caucasus, to reach the Third Army supplies had to be carried more than 900 kilometres past the nearest railhead at Ankara – or roughly the distance Niedermayer had travelled from Isfahan to the Afghan border. True, there were two 'macadamized all-weather roads', one between Sivas and Erzurum, the other further south between Diyarbakır and Van, but this was hardly the stuff of twentieth-century logistics. With few motor vehicles to hand, the Third Army's logistics trains relied on much slower, animal-drawn wagons.* During and after every battle, these overworked roads had also to accommodate wounded men travelling west or south for medical treatment, even as reinforcements and war *matériel* were rushed in the other direction.

In eastern Anatolia, then, supply lines were precarious. To function at all, the Ottoman Third Army required 'continual replenishment' of its stocks of food, fodder and ammunition, all transported on only two all-weather roads, both easily sabotaged.[39] The army was itself overstretched, with the Erzurum lines in the north thinly held after Sarıkamış, while further south the Bitlis–Van area was retaken from the Russians only in August 1915, with heavy casualties – not least among the Armenians in Van, of whom, Vanakh Dadrian claims, over 50,000 were summarily massacred in revenge for their (alleged) role in delivering the city to the Russians in May.[40] Some Armenian historians even take justifiable pride in their co-nationals' resistance in eastern Anatolia – which, one claims, tied down no less than 'five Turkish divisions and tens of thousands of Kurds, who therefore were not able to fight the Russians on the Caucasus front'.[41] Whether local insurrections tied down five divisions or, as Ottoman military files suggest, only three, it is clear that the Third Army took the Armenian threat extremely seriously.[42]

In Cilicia, the vulnerable communications lines of Djemal's Fourth Army in Syria and the question of Armenian loyalty were painfully intertwined. A glance at the map is enough to explain both the grounds for the Armenian deportations from the area and the reason they went so badly awry. Many of the areas where notorious massacres took place during the deportations of 1915 – Adana and environs, Dörtyol on the Mediterranean coastline north of Alexandretta – were either directly located on the Baghdad

---

* As Richard Hannay and co. discover to their chagrin in John Buchan's yarn *Greenmantle*, after their car breaks down en route from Ankara to Erzurum.

railway, or near its vulnerable choke points. Other notorious flashpoints of violence and repression included Maraş and Zeytun in the highlands above Osmaniye, which, while a bit further from the railway itself, sat astride the southern supply route for the Ottoman Third Army. Had the Armenians not been perceived as a security threat, of course, the geographic accident of their residency in areas near these lines should have been of no concern to the Ottoman government and army: in fact it was greatly to the advantage of the railway company, which relied heavily on Armenian skilled labour.

In the first year of the world war, however, evidence began to mount that the Armenian population of Cilicia might pose security problems after all. Just as the Dashnaks of Van had sought arms from the Russians, so did Cilician Armenians establish contact with Tiflis command – not simply for 'self-defence' but with the avowed aim of severing Ottoman army communications to help the Entente powers. As Vorontsov-Dashkov, the long-serving Viceroy of the Caucasus, reported from Tiflis on 20 February 1915, a 'representative of the Armenians in Zeytun' had come to him, 'declaring that 15,000 Armenians were ready to pounce on Turkish communications [lines] but for lack of guns and ammunition'. Like Yudenich, Vorontsov-Dashkov was eager to comply, 'in view of the location of Zeytun alongside communications lines to the Turkish army at Erzurum', but was unable to promise anything, lacking both adequate arms and a reliable route for smuggling them in. Instead, he proposed to Sazonov that Petrograd lean on the British and French to arm the Zeytun rebels by way of an amphibious landing at Alexandretta, or through some sort of covert weapons dump along the coast.[43]

The British bombardment of the Syrian coastline in December 1914 had indeed raised the spectre of an Allied landing somewhere on the eastern Mediterranean coastline, which might easily sever the Baghdad line the Ottoman Fourth Army relied on for nearly all of its supplies, along with the mountain roads relied on by the Third Army. It was Abdul Hamid's old nightmare all over again: not for nothing had he insisted repeatedly that his great trunk railway be routed as far away from the sea, and thus British naval guns, as possible. Despite the Sultan's protestations, the final routing indeed wound, at one point, within ten kilometres of the Mediterranean at Ceyhan, just north of Dörtyol.

Just as the Armenians of Van and Zeytun sent messengers to Tiflis, Armenian exile organizations openly petitioned the British with offers to sever the Baghdad railway. In March 1915, for example, Dashnaks in Sofia 'proposed to land twenty thousand Armenian volunteers in Cilicia' – half from the Balkans, and half from the United States. Closer still, the Armenian National Defence Committee in Cairo approached Sir John Maxwell in July 1915 with a plan to land 'a force of 10,000 to 12,000 fighters to occupy Alexandretta, Mersin, and Adana'. These, the Cairo committee promised, could join up with the '25,000 Armenian insurgents in Cilicia' and more from 'nearby provinces', to produce a 'formidable force of close to 50,000'.[44] Another Armenian revolutionary organization, the Hunchaks, had put together partisan bands in Maraş, Zeytun and even Aleppo, who promised to place themselves at Russia's disposal – so long as Tiflis command, or failing that the British command in Egypt, sent them arms.[45]

To be sure, the British declined to take up most of these Armenian proposals, and the Russians could no more get weapons to the rebels of Maraş and Zeytun than to the Dashnaks in Van – although not for lack of trying.[46]* The failure of these covert weapons-smuggling networks to coalesce gives the lie to the Turkish claim of large-scale collaboration between Ottoman Armenians and the Entente powers. And yet, even small groups of saboteurs could easily disrupt the Baghdad line, by blowing up key bridges or tunnelled sections which would be expensive and time-consuming to rebuild. Confirming the worst possible fears of the Ottoman military, in early March 1915 Armenian agents, carried on British warships (probably from Cairo), were indeed witnessed coming ashore near Dörtyol, presumably to organize a resistance movement. Even more ominously, on 17 April an Ottoman army raid on an Armenian house adjacent to a Baghdad

---

* Perhaps not wishing to pull the Russians' chestnuts out of the fire again as they prepared to bleed and die to open the Straits at Gallipoli, both the British and French refused to smuggle arms to the Armenians in Zeytun – to the Russians' profound disappointment.

railway bridge at Ceyhan 'netted the authorities 50 kilos of dynamite'. At about the same time, according to one of Djemal's staff officers, 'armed attacks by Armenian guerrillas using guns and bombs began in the rear areas of the 4th Army'.[47] Russian arms or no Russian arms, the Armenian partisans of Zeytun rose anyway in April, just as the Van rebellion was getting serious. More 'bloody clashes' (*krovavaya stolknoveniya*) between Armenian partisans and government forces erupted that month in Muş, Bitlis and Erzurum, as well as a general 'insurrection in Cilicia' (*vozstanie v Kilikii*), as reported gleefully (and perhaps over-optimistically) by Russian military intelligence.[48]

Compared to the overall scale of Ottoman military operations on the Caucasian and Middle Eastern fronts, it is true that these incidents of Armenian insurrectionary activity remained relatively isolated. With the benefit of hindsight and years of research into all aspects of the problem, it appears that the Turks exaggerated the real security threat in eastern Anatolia and Cilicia by an order of magnitude. But this should hardly come as a shock, considering the timing. A glance at the timeline of the deportation orders – beginning with Enver's 24 April 1915 decree that the Armenian population in problem areas must be reduced to less than 10 per cent, and culminating with Talaat's infamous 'relocation' order of 30 May 1915 covering the six eastern provinces – shows that they coincided almost exactly with the Allied landings at Gallipoli and the simultaneous two-pronged Russian invasion from the Caucasus in the direction of Erzurum and Van.[49]

It is sometimes forgotten that Greek Christians, too, were deported from Gallipoli in April 1915, prior to the Allied landings – for almost identical reasons as were invoked to justify the Armenian 'relocations' from eastern Anatolia in the face of a Russian advance. (In fact, there was far more popular anti-Greek than anti-Armenian sentiment in the Turkish press in 1915, mostly because of the unfolding drama at Gallipoli.)[50] In both cases, the security threat was real, even if overblown and used indiscriminately, enveloping the innocent along with the guilty on the principle of collective guilt. As for Cilicia, although the real danger was probably much smaller than Djemal thought, one can hardly blame the Fourth Army commander for being paranoid about his supply lines, dependent as they were on a fragile railway which was not only incomplete, but potentially harassed at multiple points by small guerrilla bands. It is no coincidence that Talaat's 30 May 1915 order specified that Armenians 'who are living near the war zones' be resettled in villages and towns 'at least 25 kilometres away from the Baghdad railroad and from other railroad links'.[51] Although murderous in execution, the Cilician deportations, like those from eastern Anatolia, were initially undertaken for reasons of logistics security.

In a classic escalatory spiral, the crackdown in Cilicia motivated Armenian guerrilla groups to swing into action, which provoked yet more brutal counter-measures. In July, a new wave of Armenian uprisings swept through the region, with major incidents in Antep, Antioch, Karahisar, Maraş, Urfa and Zeytun. Three whole Ottoman army divisions were now assigned to counter-insurgency operations in the area, along with local police units. Although casualty figures are hard to come by, it is clear that 'thousands of insurgents were killed', along with thousands more innocent Armenians caught in the crossfire.[52] The July escalation also furnished a pretext for the extension of the relocation drive to a number of towns well behind the front lines, such as Mersin, Samsun, Sivas, Trabzon and Urfa. The Armenian relocation policy was never extended universally in Anatolian Turkey. Most (but not all) Armenians in Ankara, Constantinople and Smyrna were allowed to remain in their homes, and Talaat granted specific exemptions – in theory – to women, children, elderly men, soldiers and their families, and certain irreplaceable artisans, along with Armenian Catholics and Protestants.[53]

But these exemptions were often ignored, and with the extension of the zone of deportation in July beyond the front lines, the relocation campaign began to take on the air of generalized retaliation and ethnic cleansing, rather than targeted pre-emptive resettlement of a suspected fifth column from danger areas.[54] When Pomiankowski called on the Grand Vizier in August to discuss rumours that Armenians were being slaughtered en masse, Said Halim told him it was 'not a question of massacres', but of the 'removal' (*Übersiedlung*) of Armenians to make room for the never-ending wave of Muslim refugees from the Balkans and Tripoli.[55] The wholesale removal of the Armenian population of eastern Anatolia in 1915, whether pre-meditated or carried out in the opportunistic fog of war, had an important strategic dimension for the

Porte. The Armenian presence, as the Turks had been reminded in 1877, 1894–6, and again in 1912–15, gave the Great Powers an excuse to intervene. Whatever the government rationale for the deportations, the human consequences were horrendous. No one knows the exact number of Armenians who perished at the hands of execution squads, from wounds, or through starvation and thirst in 1915 and 1916: estimates range from 500,000 to as high as 2 million. The end result was the extirpation of the Armenian people in much of Anatolia.

Far from solving the strategic difficulty of securing the army's supply lines, however, the burgeoning scale of the relocation campaign threatened to overwhelm the Baghdad line – not least because the railway itself was used to carry many of the deportees to Syria, Mesopotamia and Arabia. These Armenians were, of course, the lucky ones: and they paid for the privilege of sharing space in 'overcrowded cattle cars' with pack animals and war supplies. Those unable to afford rail passage were forced to march hundreds of kilometres, through desolate and largely waterless territory. The situation was particularly bad at Bozanti at the foot of the Taurus mountains, where even those Armenians lucky enough to have purchased railway tickets were forced on to a roundabout detour of nearly forty-seven miles on foot (the main caravan road was reserved for wagons and lorries carrying essential military personnel and supplies). Here, an American businessman observed, 'there seems to be no end to the caravan which moves over the mountain range ... throughout the day from sunrise to sunset, the road as far as one can see, is crowded with exiles'.[56] Those hardy enough to survive the Taurus passes had still to reckon with the Amanus range, and the desert on the other side. One traveller on the Syrian line estimated that he had seen '1,000 dead Armenians during the daylight hours of his journey, lying by the railway at various points'. The adjacent caravan roads were an even more terrible sight, as by summer 1915 whole stretches were 'littered with decomposing bodies'.[57] Although accurate numbers are hard to come by, in addition to tens of thousands killed in well-documented massacres, many hundreds of thousands of Armenians perished of hunger, thirst or disease on this 'route of horrors' across the Syrian desert – often cruelly within sight of the railway most were unable to travel on.[58]

Far from securing Djemal's supply lines, by late summer 1915 the Armenian relocation campaign threatened to choke them off entirely. Bedraggled Armenian refugees, both alive and dead, now blanketed the roads and rail stations, clogging up communications. From a narrowly logistical perspective the catastrophe also had an unintended impact on line construction. Armenian employees of the Baghdad Railway Company were not, at first, granted any special exemptions from the May deportation decrees, and many were swept up in the general wave of expulsions. On 29 August 1915, the same day Talaat issued a decree which (theoretically) brought an end to the relocation campaign, an order was wired to all Ottoman military commanders instructing them to 'protect Armenian [railway] employees and their families'.[59] Just as Talaat's cease-and-desist order was honoured mostly in the breach, so too did the new exemption for railway workers seem only to invite persecution. 'Our people,' Deputy General Director Franz Günther wrote to Berlin headquarters on 1 September 1915, 'primarily Armenians and Greeks, are trembling for their lives'. Many, he observed, had visible injuries showing they had been 'cruelly man-handled', although they were reluctant to explain why and by whom, for fear of incurring further reprisals.[60] In Bahçe, home of Infidel Mountain, head engineer Dr Winkler complained on 16 September 1915 that the local Kaimakam was trying to expel 'all of our Armenian personnel and their families'. Because so many of the local Armenians occupied crucial skilled positions on the line – as artisans, blacksmiths, locksmiths, mechanics, stokers – Winkler warned that if the deportations were carried out, 'we will be forced to stop all work on the line immediately'.[61]

In Adana, the situation was even more dire. The problems began in early August 1915, when the entire Armenian population of the nearby port of Mersin, comprising some 1,800 people, was deported to Adana following rumours that guerrilla bands were operating in the area, ostensibly in preparation for an Allied landing. Because Adana was located inland from the Mediterranean coast, it seemed 'safer' than Mersin: for this reason Adana had been exempted at first from the deportation decrees. Adana was also, however, the regional headquarters of the Baghdad railway, and one of the main way-stations for deportees coming from elsewhere in Anatolia. In May, several hundred Armenians had been briefly expelled from Adana, before being allowed to return, although under heavy surveillance. Following the arrival of the Mersin deportees, the flagship Baghdad railway station in Adana began to resemble a giant refugee camp. Tensions were running high when, on 29 August 1915, Talaat's cease-and-desist decree came in over the wires. Here, as elsewhere, the Interior Minister's order to stop the relocation campaign produced precisely the opposite of the desired effect. Between 30 August and 11 September 1915 (when provincial insubordination to his 29 August decree prompted Talaat to issue yet another cease-and-desist order), according to the US Consul, more than 6,000 Armenians were summarily deported from Adana, 'without any special regard for the exemption given to Catholics and Protestants'. The Vali of Adana, the German Consul reported on 2 September, 'declared that the orders of the ministry meant nothing to him; he alone was going to decide what to do with the local Armenians'.[62]

The Vali's threat was not reassuring to the Germans. As Winkler wrote to Berlin on 16 September 1915, 'the disdain for orders coming from the central authorities is growing ever stronger'. Rather than calming down tensions in Adana, Talaat's attempt to call off the Armenian deportations had served as a provocation to Turkish officials there. By mid-September, Winkler reported, 'Adana and [nearby] Tarsus have been completely emptied of Armenians, and thus of half their population'. It was not just the rail line which was punished by an exodus of skilled workers: deprived of its artisan population of 'builders, carpenters, plumbers, shoemakers', Adana was now 'utterly deserted, lifeless, without [street]lights'. Conditions were so bad that in recent days the Turks had also begun fleeing from Adana, literally emptying the city of people. In a classic, and utterly deserved, case of retribution, the Vali of Adana, who had expelled his Armenian subjects, petitioned German BRC officials to house his own family, who were now refugees just like everyone else.[63]

With the still-uncompleted mountain sections of the Baghdad line swarming with refugees, many among them their own, irreplaceable skilled railway employees, the Germans at last swung into action. Using the Adana Vali's concern for his family as leverage, Winkler tried to negotiate with him an exemption list of 848 skilled railway workers he wanted to save from deportation for at least forty-eight months. The Vali, at first, held firm, offering only a four weeks' exemption for Armenian BRC employees.[64] But Winkler would not give in. In October 1915, the German field engineer wound his way higher and higher up the political food chain, enlisting Deputy General Director Franz Günther, Ambassador Wangenheim, Arthur Gwinner of Deutsche Bank, and finally Falkenhayn himself. On 3 November 1915, the Chief of the General Staff and Commander-in-Chief of the German armies sent a telegram to the Ottoman War Minister, politely worded yet offering a strong implied rebuke to the Armenian relocation policy. 'I request your support,' Falkenhayn enjoined Enver, 'in making easier the retention of skilled personnel by the [Baghdad Railway Company], which would be greatly endangered through the deportation of Armenian [employees] during the war.'[65]

Falkenhayn's intervention clearly refutes the oft-repeated claim that the Germans did nothing to halt the Armenian deportations. And yet it hardly speaks well of German foreign policy that this rebuke was not delivered until November 1915, by which time the relocation campaign had been under way for six months, and hundreds of thousands of Armenians had already lost their homes and lives. Nor does it speak well of the Germans that this high-level intervention was occasioned not by humanitarian concern over the fate of the Armenian expellees, but instead by the strategic impact of their expulsion on the Baghdad railway. The damage was done: it was time for damage control. The timing of Falkenhayn's telegram seems to have been closely linked to a burgeoning scandal surrounding the German BRC liaison officer Lieutenant Colonel Böttrich, who had foolishly affixed his signature to a 3 October 1915 communiqué which referred to the Armenian deportations in a manner implying consent. Predictably, the Germans tried (but failed) to destroy all copies of this notorious document.* Falkenhayn, although concerned that his officer's communiqué would

---

* In his *History of the Armenian Genocide*, Dadrian calls Böttrich 'a high-ranking German officer who ordered the deportations of the Armenians, and placed his signature on that order'. This is misleading. In the document in question, Böttrich simply passes on without comment an Ottoman order that the relocation policy must be pursued 'gradually and in orderly fashion'. Ironically, this document, dear to Armenian historians, was preserved by the Turks, who used it to blackmail the Germans.

blacken the German army's reputation, refused to cashier Böttrich in wartime. With surprising naïveté, Falkenhayn insisted that his telegram to Enver had eliminated any moral liability on the part of the army in case the Entente sought to blame the Germans for anti-Armenian atrocities.[66]

Far from dying down, of course, the controversy over the deportations, and German complicity in them, was only just getting started. Much of the commentary on the subject from the Entente side, to be sure, was crude and not terribly convincing. 'I will help the Zionists,' Wangenheim is made to say in Henry Morgenthau's not-always-reliable memoirs, 'but I shall do nothing to help the Armenians.'[67] The German Ambassador almost certainly said nothing of the kind. Morgenthau himself admits that Wangenheim lodged a formal protest against the deportations with the Grand Vizier on 4 July 1915. And yet Morgenthau touches a real nerve here. Whether because of the strain of the Gallipoli campaign or the diplomatic nightmare surrounding the Armenian deportations, Wangenheim had suffered a nervous breakdown in June 1915, which caused him to disappear from Constantinople for most of the summer. When Morgenthau saw him for the first time in months in early October, just as the scandal caused by the Böttrich communiqué was breaking, Wangenheim looked like 'the perfect picture of [Wagner's] Wotan': he had a black patch over one eye, his face was perpetually twitching, and 'he seemed unusually nervous and depressed'. Several weeks later, on 24 October 1915, Ambassador Wangenheim died of a stroke. His passing, although not entirely unexpected, cast a dark pall over the diplomatic community in Pera.[68]

While Morgenthau's jibes at the German Ambassador's callousness can easily be chalked up to Allied war propaganda,* the story of Wangenheim's breakdown is amply confirmed by his own diplomatic allies at the Porte. While Pallavicini had often had disagreements with his German counterpart, he considered him a friend and was sad to see what happened to him in 1915. Wangenheim's 'neurasthenic' tendencies, the Austrian Ambassador reported to Vienna on

---

* By 1918, when Morgenthau's memoirs were published, the United States had joined the Entente side in the war. They are thus properly read as war propaganda, even if America had been neutral for most of the period covered in Morgenthau's narrative.

24 June 1915, had been greatly exacerbated by the strain of the Gallipoli landings and the unfolding humanitarian disaster in Turkish Armenia, producing, in Pallavicini's interpretation, a kind of manic depression, with violent mood swings following in rapid succession. At the root of the problem, Pallavicini believed, was the gnawing sense of guilt Wangenheim felt for helping bring Turkey into the war. The German's breakdown, Pallavicini wrote, had most likely resulted from 'the feeling of great responsibility pressing heavily on his shoulders'.[69]

Several weeks after Wangenheim's death, Pallavicini went deeper into the matter. Connecting the Armenian tragedy, as Morgenthau later would, to the unleashing of a holy war in Ottoman Turkey, the Austrian Ambassador produced a withering critique of Oppenheim's jihad stratagem. In global terms, Pallavicini concluded, the Ottoman holy war *fetvas* had only 'succeeded in exposing to the world, that the Caliph no longer has the esteem of Islamic believers as in past times', thus dealing a possibly fatal blow to the prestige of the Sunni Caliphate and of the Ottoman Empire itself. Rather than bring forth armies of Islam, the declaration of holy war by the Sultan had merely encouraged fanatics like Enver and Talaat to indulge further their latent 'xenophobic Muslim-nationalism'. 'If the war lasts much longer,' Pallavicini warned, 'the Armenian persecutions, which are already taking on the character of a general anti-Christian campaign, will ultimately affect the living conditions of all foreigners in Turkey.' Whether because of Wangenheim's death, or the unfolding nightmare on the Baghdad railway, it was clear that 'the Germans are now beginning... to fear that they can no longer exorcize the spirits, that they themselves called forth.'[70]

The Germans had ridden the tiger of Islamic rage and resentment a long way – across the Red Sea into Eritrea and Somalia, into the inner sanctum of the Arabian desert, then winding through Mesopotamia, Persia and Afghanistan to the North-west Frontier – but the tiger was now chafing and clawing wildly in all directions. The Germans were losing the last semblance of control over the animal beneath them.

15

The Reluctant Mahdi

*The form which Sanussism has taken today in Africa is closely
intertwined with Mahdism: the Sheikh of the Sanussi is viewed
by his followers as the expected Mahdi they were promised.
According to the old prophecy the 'true Mahdi', the Rightly
Guided, shall be preceded by the false prophet. So do the
Sudanese of the Upper Nile view the chosen Mohammad
Ahmad.*

Baron Oppenheim to German Chancellor Bernhard
von Bülow, April 1902[1]

You never know what will start off a Jehad!

Sandy Arbuthnot, secret agent and would-be Muslim
prophet, in John Buchan's *Greenmantle*[2]

For all the blood and treasure the Germans had spent conjuring up
Baron Oppenheim's holy war, in some ways they had barely scratched
the surface of possibility. It was all well and good to court the Sunni
Sultan-Caliph and *Şeykh-ul-Islam*, the Sherif of Mecca and the Shia
Grand Mufti of Karbala, as endorsements of the Turco-German cause
from these authorities certainly counted for something in the Islamic
world. And yet it would be stretching the truth a great deal to say that
any of these *fetvas* had kindled the flames of a real jihad in the field.
Certainly the declaration of holy war had done nothing to advance
the cause at Sarıkamış or Suez. Gallipoli was a different story, but
there, too, the impregnable morale of the Turkish defenders probably

had as much to do with patriotism as with Islamic fervour. With Arab detachments in the Ottoman army, as we saw at both Suez and Gallipoli, the paraphernalia of jihad had proved essentially useless.

Here and there, however, there were signs of a more substantial earthquake in the Islamic world. Musil's field reports from the Arabian desert, although generally ignored by their recipients, suggested a historic power shift was under way, as the Hashemites of Mecca and Ibn Rashid's Shammar Bedouins were losing ground to Ibn Saud. Had the Germans appreciated the potential magnitude of this development, they could easily have leaned on the Porte to throw its weight behind Ibn Saud, particularly considering Enver's notorious antipathy to the Hashemites. British gold, as Musil explained, had not really bought Saudi loyalty: the Wahhabis were using London, and not the other way around. Enver, too, would have been hard pressed to expect unconditional loyalty from Ibn Saud, but at least the Ottoman War Minister was a fellow Muslim, and were Enver to give the Wahhabis the honour of protecting the holy places, Ibn Saud would have had every reason to support the Porte in turn. If Saudi power had been thus entrenched in the Hejaz, it is not a great leap to imagine fanatical Wahhabi warriors providing just the spark Kress and Djemal had needed at Suez.

The closer one looks at the order of battle in the Near East, the more surprising it appears that the Germans did not devote their energy in the theatre more exclusively to a renewed Suez Canal offensive.*[3] Without control of the seas or a fantastical extension of the still-uncompleted Baghdad railway into Persia, it is impossible to come up with a realistic scenario in which the Germans could have transported enough arms to Kabul to make a frontal assault on the North-west Frontier worth the while of Emir Habibullah. Taking Suez, by contrast, was well within the realm of possibility. True, the Sinai desert remained a major obstacle, the Ottoman Fourth Army was short of planes and heavy guns, and the Bedouins had proved a bust in the winter 1915 Suez campaign. But Kress and Djemal had reached the canal in force – with nearly

---

*Or, one might think, send German troops to do the job themselves. But this would never have been approved by the Turks. Enver, despite his reputed Germanophilia, made sure that the numbers of German troops serving in Turkey always remained at non-intimidating levels, increasingly modestly from 2,000 in autumn 1914 to about 10,000 by summer 1916, before peaking at about 25,000 in 1918.

20,000 men. It had not proved enough, but this may have been as a result of the failure of Frobenius and Musil to stir up sufficient trouble in Egypt's southern underbelly to tie down British forces. Then, there was the disappointment surrounding Otto Mannesmann's overtures to the Sanussi tribesmen of Libya, whose headman, like Habibullah in Afghanistan, had refused to join the jihad on the grounds that the Germans would not be able to supply him with arms.

While the Arabs seemed by late 1915 to be a lost cause for the Turco-German holy war, the Sanussi were more of an enigma. Founded as a kind of 'fraternity of mystics' in 1837 by a Moroccan named Muhammad ibn Ali al-Sanussi, by the turn of the century the Sanussi had grown into a powerful Islamic brotherhood based in the desert of present-day Libya. Although his followers were mostly illiterate Bedouin nomads, Sheikh Muhammad al-Sanussi inspired them to take Islam seriously, offering up a blend of Sufi mysticism and the severe asceticism of the Wahhabis of Arabia (he forbade the use of tobacco and coffee, along with the usual prohibitions on alcohol and pork). Al-Sanussi was a prophet in the classical vein, imposing his version of Islam on his followers not by theological argument but through the force of his charismatic personality.

It was al-Sanussi's son, Muhammad al-Mahdi, however, who turned the brotherhood into an international phenomenon following his father's death in 1859, with its tentacles reaching westwards across the Sahara desert from Libya and Sudan, and eastwards into the Hejaz to challenge the religious primacy of the Mecca Sherifs. No one really knew how many members there were in the Sanussi order at the peak of its influence in the early twentieth century. British authorities in Egypt thought it might have encompassed 'four or five millions', although this was a wild guess. The religious nature of the movement was even less clearly understood in Cairo, apart from a generalized fear of the Sanussis' 'burning hatred of Christians'.[4] The founder's son had been named al-Mahdi, or 'Rightly Guided One', the long-awaited redeemer who, according to variants in both Sunni and Shia eschatological tradition, will appear at the end of days to combat unbelievers and usher in global Islamic dominion. And yet Muhammad al-Mahdi never seems to have claimed himself to be 'the' Mahdi. When, in 1881, the Sanussi Sheikh's contemporary,

Muhammad Ahmad of Dongola province in Sudan, did declare himself 'the' Mahdi in order to raise the banner of revolt against the Egyptian occupation of Sudan, Muhammad al-Mahdi refused to sanction the Dongolan's millenarian claim, or to join his jihad against Cairo. Complicating matters still further, the self-declared Dongolese Mahdi died in 1885, not long after his men had toppled the British garrison in Khartoum and famously taken the life of General Gordon ('sword in hand'). And yet Mahdism survived the Mahdi's death, in the form of his appointed successor, 'Caliph' Abdullah, who ruled Sudan in the name of millenarian Mahdism for thirteen years, until Kitchener finally crushed the rebellion at Omdurman in 1898. The 'real' Mahdi was dead in 1885, but Mahdism had lived on, and Muhammad al-Mahdi too. Through it all, the Sanussi order endured.

When the Sanussi Sheikh himself died in May 1902, the mystery surrounding the relation (if any) between the order and Mahdism only deepened. To begin with, no one was entirely sure he *had* died. According to a member of the Sanussi order who visited Baron Oppenheim's Cairo mansion the following spring, al-Mahdi's death had been greeted in the traditional tribal manner, with the freeing of one hundred slaves and the ritual slaughter of thirty camels (and 'numerous sheep and cows'). Al-Mahdi's nephew, Ahmed al-Sharif, was proclaimed his successor and greeted by acclamation. But there was a bad omen almost immediately, when over a hundred tribesmen were struck down with disease. Because so many of those present at al-Mahdi's death were now themselves dead, rumours began to fly that perhaps 'the Mahdi' was not dead after all. Nearly a year later, al-Mahdi had still not been buried – or at least no one knew where.[5] In death, even more than in life, the Sanussi Sheikh had become 'the expected Mahdi of hundreds of thousands of Muslims'.[6] Mahdism, only recently extinguished by Kitchener at Omdurman, now lived again in the desert hinterland surrounding Egypt.

What made the Sanussi variant of Mahdism more portentous than the Dongolese version, from the European perspective, was the geographical breadth of the order. With members spread as far afield as Arabia, Sudan and northern Africa, the Sanussi straddled the Ottoman, British and Italian empires. They were also numerous in the Wadai, in present-day Chad, east of Lake Chad, recently claimed by the French in their colonial push from the Congo. Beginning in

1901, Sanussi tribesmen waged guerrilla warfare against the French for almost ten years, with this low-boil colonial conflict dying down only when the Italian invasion of Libya put another European infidel enemy in Sanussi crosshairs. If millennial Mahdism ever truly caught fire among the far-flung desert tribesmen of the Sanussi order, it would threaten the interests of no less than four major powers, the Turks no less than the English, French, and now the Italians.

Little wonder, then, that Baron Oppenheim took on the Sanussi as one of his favourite causes in pre-war Cairo. Germany, after all, had no colonial interests in any of the regions roamed by the order. Where the Egyptian Khedive and his British backers were terrified of a repeat of the damaging Sudanese rebellion of 1885–98, Oppenheim looked gleefully at the prospect. 'It is indeed due to the fact that so many now regard the deceased head sheikh as the Mahdi,' the Baron wrote to Chancellor Bülow in April 1903, 'that the [Sanussi] order now again threatens to burst into the flames of fanaticism.' The English, he reported with characteristic *Schadenfreude*, 'have been trying for years, entirely in vain, to develop friendlier relations with the order'. Even Sultan Abdul Hamid had failed to check growing Sanussi power, receiving no endorsement from al-Mahdi of his claim to the Caliphate.[7] Because 'the Mahdi had forbidden the pilgrimage to Mecca', pilgrim traffic from Sudan by 1903 had slowed to a crawl, squeezing the Hashemite Sherifs hard. Of course, Oppenheim himself had no answers to Mahdism either. All he knew was that the British were terrified of 'the Mahdist idea', which was now 'the greatest danger' threatening the equilibrium of Egypt. It was, therefore, in Germany's interest to cultivate the movement however it was possible to do so.[8]

When war came in 1914, therefore, Oppenheim had great hopes for the Sanussi. If a single Dongolese prophet could knock the British out of Anglo-Egyptian Sudan for thirteen years at a time when peace reigned between the powers, just think what Mahdism might do if it spread through the international Sanussi order while British forces were tied down in Europe. As Oppenheim noted in his October 1914 'Exposé Concerning the Revolutionizing of the Islamic Territories of Our Enemies', during the Turco-Italian war the Sanussi irregulars had very nearly expelled the invaders single-handedly, despite the Italian blockade of the Libyan coastline. Enver himself had established excellent relations with the new Sanussi Sheikh, Sayyid Ahmad al-Sharif, and with the tribesmen, who erected a mosque in Enver's honour where his tent had stood.[9] Enver's prestige in Libya, Oppenheim believed, could be exploited to embroil al-Sharif's tribesmen in a new jihad against British Egypt. Enver, Oppenheim assured the German Foreign Office, had already 'told the Grand Sanussi to prepare for war against England'. If al-Sharif came through as promised, diverting troops westwards from the canal in time for Djemal's Suez offensive, Oppenheim predicted with his characteristic gush of ungrounded optimism, the British would 'suffer the fate of Gordon Pasha'.[10]

What Oppenheim had missed were the mixed signals emanating from the Sanussi. It was true that Enver had cut a fine figure in the Libyan desert during the Tripolitan war, but the Sanussi desert warriors had not entirely forgotten how he had left in November 1912 – making excuses for the Porte's peremptory surrender to the Italians. True, the Turks had given up the fight only because of the October assault by the Balkan League, which brought their capital under threat just weeks after the First Balkan War began. But this was hardly the fault of the Sanussi tribesmen, who had in effect been sold out to the infidel Italians for reasons of state. As a sop to Sanussi pride, Enver had left behind in Libya – in clear violation of the terms of the treaty ending the Turco-Italian war – a small number of officers, including his own brother, Nuri Bey. On 18 October 1912, the day the Turks surrendered to Italy, Nuri, as if to cheat defeat, raised the Ottoman flag in the Sanussi oasis of Jaghbub, to suggest that Turkey would return to avenge her humiliation. Al-Sharif was not impressed by Nuri's gesture: he ordered Enver's brother 'to take the flag down at once'. With this insult, the Sanussi Sheikh put Enver on notice that his loyalty was not easily won.[11]

It is not surprising, then, that al-Sharif rebuffed Mannesmann's envoys in August 1914. Mannesmann, although reporting directly to Oppenheim's jihad bureau, had been sent to Tripoli under full-blown diplomatic cover, as German Consul in Libya. The Sanussi Sheikh knew that Berlin was formally allied to Rome and thus tacitly supported the Italian occupation of Libya, even if Italy had not actually entered the war on the side of the Central Powers. He thus had plenty of reason to be suspicious of entreaties coming from a German diplomat – and rightfully so, as the Germans were at pains to reassure Rome that Cyrenaica was 'off limits' for the jihad.[12] Even if the Germans had been able to get the Sanussi the arms they needed, they would have forbidden their use against the Italian occupiers of Libya – a struggle which was still al-Sharif's main priority. Because the Sanussi, like the Hashemites in the Hejaz, depended on English-controlled shipments of foodstuffs for sustenance, al-Sharif was reluctant to antagonize the authorities in Cairo.

The Ottoman declaration of holy war did little to alter these calculations. Al-Sharif even told British envoy Leopold Royle on 22 November 1914, as if to reassure Cairo he would not be taking up the Sultan-Caliph's recent call to global jihad, that he 'cared nothing for Turks or Germans'. Acknowledging British generosity in allowing food to reach his tribesmen, al-Sharif asked Royle if they might also send money, guns and ammunition. Reluctant to antagonize Italy into belligerence, the Cairo authorities predictably declined the Sheikh's request, but made every effort to assure him of their benevolent intentions. Royle secured from al-Sharif a vow that he had nothing but 'friendly intentions' towards British Egypt. The Sheikh also gave him 'an elaborate Arab robe' as a symbolic peace offering.[13] Less sanguine than Oppenheim about the promises of Islamic warrior chieftains, the acting Consul-General in Cairo, Milne Cheetham, reported to Sir Edward Grey on 7 December 1914 that Sanussi neutrality was assured only so long as 'the [military] situation remains favourable to the British cause'. It was not personal diplomacy and mutual flattery but the course of the world war which would help the Sanussi decide when and in which direction to strike. Should the war in the East turn against the Entente, Cheetham warned Grey, 'we must be prepared for a quite different attitude on the part of the Sheikh and his followers'.[14]

Like Feisal and Hussein – or the Young Turks themselves in 1914 – al-Sharif was willing to play all sides to drive up his asking price for belligerence in the world war. Before Italy herself joined the Entente powers in late May 1915, it was by no means clear which way the Sanussi would go, even if they did join the fight.* As autumn turned to

---

* Although the Ottomans had signed a treaty with Rome in 1912 acknowledging the Italian claim to Libya, the Sanussi had never recognized this claim and continued to resist the occupation.

winter in the first year of the world war, al-Sharif received emissaries from Berlin, Constantinople and Cairo alike, and brushed off each one in turn with similar pledges of friendly neutrality in the war. Because they, unlike the British, were willing to send guns and ammunition to the Sanussi, the Turks and Germans had a leg-up, of sorts; but it was a rather hollow advantage so long as they could not get the arms to the Libyan desert. Enver's first envoy, Süleyman al-Baruni, a colourful Berber veteran of the 1911 war who had vowed not to cut his hair until the Italians left Libya, had done no better than Mannesmann in enlisting the Sanussi in the cause. Aside from his elaborate mane of hair, al-Baruni had nothing concrete to offer al-Sharif, who liked him even less than he liked Nuri Bey and in January 1915 he had al-Baruni arrested. Still, although the Porte had made no headway, the Germans agreed to let the Turks lead the way in courting al-Sharif, the idea being that, as an orthodox sheikh, he would take Islamic emissaries more seriously than infidels. And so Nuri was dispatched to Libya on behalf of Enver's notorious 'Special Organization' (*Teşkilat-ı Mahsûsa*), accompanied by an Arab Muslim officer, Ja'far al-'Askari.[15] The emissaries arrived in the Sanussi camp in February 1915, carrying small quantities of arms and ammunition purchased in Athens. Although Nuri and Ja'far were not arrested like al-Baruni, the timing of their arrival was not fortuitous. Al-Sharif had just received news of the Turco-German debacle at Suez, and was not about to join the losing side.[16]

Just as Cheetham had predicted, the British reversal at the Straits and at Gallipoli that spring led Sheikh al-Sharif to reconsider the possibility of joining the Ottoman holy war. As the Allied offensive ground down in the trenches of Cape Helles and Anzac cove, Alexandria, the nearest major city to the Libyan borderline, began to resemble 'an enormous hospital camp of sick and wounded'. The stench of defeat now hung over British Egypt.[17] At the Sanussi camp, Enver's brother Nuri was the man of the hour, his prestige rising every day the British remained bogged down at Gallipoli. It was just a matter of time, Nuri reported to Enver, before the Sanussi would strike England: the Sheikh needed only to secure his Italian flank.[18] Just four days after the Allied landings at Gallipoli, a Sanussi raid near Misurata destroyed an Italian column of 4,000 soldiers.[19] When Italy declared war on the Central Powers on 23 May 1915, this made al-Sharif a belligerent in all but the strictest legal sense. The trick for the Turks and Germans was to turn Sanussi fire away from Italian Libya, and towards British Egypt.

While not impossible, it was a tough sell. Nuri's growing prestige, and his family ties to Enver and, by extension of Enver's marriage, the Sultan-Caliph, ensured that the Sanussi Sheikh would have to proclaim at least lip-service to the Ottoman holy war with his followers, lest Nuri accuse him of neglecting his Islamic faith. But it was one thing to attack ineffectual Italians, and quite another the more formidable British. The Sanussi had never fought with the latter before, and al-Sharif had a healthy respect for the power of the Royal Navy. To risk his reputation by attacking British Egypt, he would require arms, ammunition and – of course – money to make it worth his while.

The bidding war for the Sanussi had now begun in earnest. While al-Sharif continued sending messengers regularly to the British garrison at Sollum, by April 1915 the Porte had opened a reasonably reliable communications line to the Sanussi as well, by way of Athens. Each shipment of arms, ammunition and gold from the Aegean would further strengthen Nuri's hand – so long as it actually reached Libya. The cause was not helped when, on 16 June 1915, the French navy intercepted the *Olympia*, a Greek vessel carrying seven Ottoman officers and 5,000 Turkish pounds in gold, along with holy war letters from the Kaiser and Sultan to the Sanussi Sheikh.[20] The Germans, meanwhile, had their own man in al-Sharif's camp, a soldier of fortune named Otto von Gumppenberg, who had fought for the Sanussi in the 1911 war and thus had his own local prestige. When Gumppenberg promised, at one point, to secure 100,000 German rifles for the Sanussi, Nuri complained to Enver that his own authority was being undermined.[21] It was not that Enver did not want the Germans to send weapons to the Sanussi, of course. In July, he authorized a shipment of 40,000 Mauser rifles–on condition that his brother could take all the credit.[22] At Enver's insistence (he told the Germans that Gumppenberg was a 'fantasist'), Nuri's German rival was recalled from Libya on 11 July 1915, only to be captured by the Royal Navy that very day – doubtless to Nuri's satisfaction.[23]

Unfortunately for Nuri Bey, Gumppenberg was not the only German threatening to undermine his authority by offering the Sanussi more than the Turks ever could. Otto Mannesmann, although recalled from

his consular post in Tripoli in March 1915 after the Italians had intercepted a letter in his name addressed to al-Sharif, had returned to Libya
in late May 1915 incognito, disguised as a salesman. In early July, just
before Gumppenberg's departure, Mannesmann reached the Sanussi
camp, receiving a hero's welcome. Al-Sharif presented him with 'a holy
robe lined with sable, such as only senior Sanussi sheikhs are allowed
to wear'.[24] It was a clever act of flattery, coming with the usual reciprocal price. To win over the Sanussi for the Turco-German holy war,
Mannesmann now reported to Berlin, he needed to supply al-Sharif with
eight machine guns with adequate clips, two quick-firing field artillery
guns with shell, shrapnel and grenades; 30,000 rifles with 500 rounds
each, 4,000 carbines with 300; at least two million rounds for heavy
guns; cars and motorcycles; 500 kilograms of explosives; along with
12,000 water bottles, 12,000 pairs of sandals and 8,000 field jackets.[25]
Not least, al-Sharif needed money: not the measly sums in Turkish
pounds Enver and Nuri Bey were offering, but English paper money.
Gold coins, the Sheikh explained to Mannesmann, were much too heavy
for Bedouins to carry – at least in the colossal quantities he required.[26]

As in Mecca, as in Kabul, jihad fees were mounting for the Germans.
The confiscation of the holy war funds aboard the *Olympia* in June
gave occasion for gleeful *Schadenfreude* to the British (who, oddly,
were not informed of the matter by the French for two months).
'Sayyid Ahmad Shari Es Senussi might not think it necessary to return
the 4000 [pounds] in gold, the scimitars, and other presents,' a leader-
writer for the *Standard* gloated on 31 August 1915, 'but there seems
no particular reason why he should wish to carry on a correspondence with the Kaiser.' Hazarding a guess that 4,000 lira would be only
a modest down-payment, the *Standard* opined that 'it would require
more treasure than is left in the German war chest to persuade more
than a few followers of the Prophet that his mantle has descended on
the self-elected Sheikh of Potsdam'.[27]

The British had good reason to be wary of al-Sharif's greed.
Each time their envoys reached the Sanussi camp in the western
desert hinterland of Egypt, he repeated his pledges of neutrality –
while hinting that perhaps, just to be safe, the Cairo authorities
should begin subsidizing him. Some on the British side were willing to consider the possibility. After some worrisome skirmishing

with Sanussi warriors near the border post at Sollum, George Hunter 'Pasha', Director-General of the Egyptian coastguard, suggested on 18 November 1915 that the British attempt 'to buy the good will of the Sanussi outright not by driblets of insignificant sums, but a sum of money which would make all hope of competition on the part of any German or Turkish agent ... hopeless'. As if reading Hunter Pasha's mind (Sanussi spies may have got wind of the growing pro-appeasement sentiments in the Egyptian coastguard), al-Sharif offered, on 20 November, to expel Mannesmann from his camp (but not Nuri Bey, who was a Muslim) in exchange for 'a guarantee of one million pounds paid in instalments, also a supply of rifles'. To add a hint of menace to this extraordinary piece of blackmail, the Sanussi headman stipulated that 'First sum should be forthcoming before Sanussi leaves for Jaghbub. He says we must act quickly. Germans have promised unlimited supplies.'[28]

Al-Sharif must have been thoroughly enjoying himself. Just two weeks before demanding £1 million ($5 million then, the equivalent of some half a billion dollars today) from the British, the Germans had delivered him 300,000 rifle rounds, 80 belts of machine-gun ammunition, and 120,000 francs.[29] Evidently unable to procure English paper money, Mannesmann was doing his best, using his family business connections to wire French francs via a network of Swiss banks, mostly based in Basel.[30] On 12 November 1915, or about a week before the Sanussi Sheikh blackmailed Britain for £1 million, Mannesmann was asking Berlin to send him Greek drachmas, preferably in large notes of 500, to find weapons for the Sanussi on the black market in Athens.[31] The game could go on and on like this for ever, as the asking price for Sanussi belligerence spiralled higher and higher. Given another year, it is likely that the Sanussi jihad blackmail fee to the British would eventually rival the £10 million Emir Habibullah had demanded of the Germans in Kabul.

Unfortunately for al-Sharif, however, the British, Germans and Turks alike were beginning to tire of the game. Mannesmann had already tried to force the Sheikh's hand on numerous occasions, leading a Sanussi party to the Libyan coast to fire on a British submarine on 16 August 1915, and orchestrating, from the cliffs above Sollum, a German submarine assault in early November which sank several

British vessels, including the HMS *Tara*, from which ship ninety-two survivors were brought ashore as prisoners. Not to be outdone, on 17–18 November Nuri Bey led a Sanussi raiding party across the Egyptian border, cutting British telegraph lines and skirmishing near Sidi Barrani. By all accounts, Sheikh al-Sharif was unhappy with these manoeuvres, going so far as to send Ja'far to Sidi Barrani to assure the British of his peaceful intentions. It was following this curious peace parley that the Sanussi headman made his astonishing blackmail demand.

The British, however, did not bite. Even if the Sheikh expelled Mannesmann, Nuri would still be there egging on his men to join the Ottoman holy war. Although al-Sharif did not know it, in August British intelligence had intercepted 'a packet of letters from him to Muslim potentates and journalists all over Arabia and India, inciting them to Jihad and informing them that he is the representative of the Caliph in North Africa'.[32] Little wonder, then, that General Maxwell put little faith in al-Sharif's latest conditional pledge of neutrality on 20 November 1915, refusing to pay his ransom. Instead Maxwell ordered reinforcements, while abandoning the forward post at Sollum. Two days later, the Sanussi struck Sidi Barrani again, in sufficient force that 135 Egyptian soldiers, including fifteen officers, deserted to their side. The Sanussi war was on.[33]

With the British now engaged in serious fighting on Egypt's western frontier, the Oppenheim jihad stratagem looked to be bearing its first strategic fruit. According to Muhammad Idrisi, the Sanussi representative in Egypt later debriefed by the British, Mannesmann openly gloated, following the opening of hostilities in late November 1915, that Baron Oppenheim himself 'would be accompanying the new expedition invading Egypt from the east.'[34] Oppenheim had indeed been in Damascus for much of summer 1915, meeting with Kress and Djemal to discuss the latest plans for a renewed Suez offensive. The Baron had even declared his intention of travelling undercover into his beloved Cairo, to prepare the covert groundwork for a native uprising to greet the canal attack. All year, Meissner Pasha – the famous builder of the Hejaz railway – had been hard at work laying hundreds of kilometers of single-gauge rail tracks from Nablus (just south of Jenin) towards the Sinai desert, reaching Beersheeba by October 1915. At one point, the British were actually building their own Sinai line parallel to Meissner's, only 130 km away.*[35] Kress, Oppenheim reported in August 1915, was looking at 1 January or 1 February 1916 as possible attack launch dates.[36]

It was not to be. Between August and November 1915, the Armenian deportations and the subsequent crisis on the Baghdad railway had so damaged Ottoman Fourth Army communications that there was no possibility of provisioning another Suez offensive that winter. Oppenheim himself, whether feeling cold feet at the prospect of risking capture by the British or because Djemal was sick of his company (the Turkish commander, the Baron reported, had 'ordered' him back to Constantinople to debrief Enver), left Damascus in mid-October 1915, en route not for Cairo but for Constantinople and, he hoped, his jihad bureau in Berlin. By the time the Sanussi invaded Egypt in late November, the Baron was bucking up his flagging spirits by the Bosphorus, having been ordered by Zimmermann to stay on there indefinitely as a kind of holy war liaison to the Pera Embassy.[37]

If the Sanussi invasion of Egypt did not quite fit Oppenheim's dream scenario, however, it certainly terrified the British. As the British field commanders considered whether to abandon Sollum in mid-November 1915, Kitchener of Khartoum himself, now War Minister, intervened. Already under strain as the bungled Gallipoli campaign – for which he would take much of the blame – was winding down, Kitchener was in a flat panic about his beloved British Egypt which he had served so long. If the 'forward' strategy of defending Cairo at Sollum, the Sinai and so on were now abandoned, Kitchener feared that 'in Egypt we should have to face certain hostility all along the Western frontier, which would extend to Tunis, Algiers and Morocco; serious unrest and disturbances throughout Egypt and the Sudan'.

---

*This gauge, the same as used in the Hejaz railway, was much smaller than the 1,435 mm gauge used on the Baghdad line, which created yet another problem for through traffic from Constantinople. The reason, in the first case, was that Meissner Pasha had had to import his rolling stock and equipment for the Hejaz line in from Beirut over the existing 1,050 mm French lines in Lebanon and Syria, which they had to fit. In the rush to build across the Sinai in 1915, there was another reason for using the French gauge: Meissner actually ripped up the French rails to use them for the Jenin–Beersheeba line.

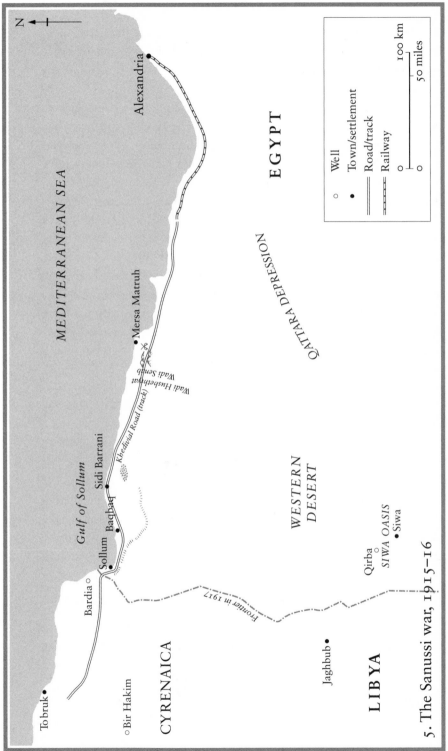

MEDITERRANEAN SEA

Alexandria

Gulf of Sollum

Mersa Matruh

Tobruk ●

○Bir Hakim

CYRENAICA

Bardia ○

Sollum ●
Baqbaq ●
Sidi Barrani ●

Khedivial Road (track)

Wadi Husheibiyat
Wadi Senab

**WESTERN
DESERT**

QATTARA DEPRESSION

EGYPT

Frontier in 1917

Jaghbub ●

Qirba ○
SIWA OASIS
● Siwa

LIBYA

N ←

○	Well
●	Town/settlement
═══	Road/track
┄┄	Railway

100 km
50 miles

5. The Sanussi war, 1915–16

It was like a nightmare rerun of the Mahdist rebellion, only this time involving the far-flung Sanussi order and supported by a European power, the Germans, whose machinations must inevitably now force 'a withdrawal from [Egypt] and from Sudan within a measurable time'.[38]

Considering the run of early successes in the Sanussi invasion of Egypt, Kitchener was not entirely wrong to be paranoid. Commanded by Nuri and Ja'far, both experienced Ottoman officers, the Sanussi quickly overran Sollum, Sidi Barrani and Baqbaq in early December, and threatened the British garrison at Mersa Matruh, only 175 miles from Alexandria. Further south, smaller Sanussi units captured the oasis towns of Dakhla, Kharga and Farafra, 'within easy reach of the Nile'. Following these attacks, even the 'normally imperturbable' Maxwell took fright, reporting to the War Office in London that 'it would take but little enemy pressure [to incite the local inhabitants to holy war] which when started would spread rapidly'.[39] It had not taken much to spread the Mahdist rebellion in the 1880s, which had ultimately toppled the Sudanese government and claimed the life of Gordon Pasha. This time, Egypt itself seemed ripe to fall, if Sanussi millenarianism could spread among the native population, helped along by Turco-German jihad propaganda – and by the Allied withdrawal from Gallipoli that January, which came at terrible cost in prestige to the British garrisons in Alexandria and Cairo.

Strangely, despite extremely favourable conditions, the Sanussi holy war never quite got off the ground in Egypt. It was not that the cause was without inspiration and a patina of glamour: the coastal campaign on the Libyan frontier produced some of the most colourful scenes of the entire war, pitting elegantly robed Sanussi noblemen against bearded Sikhs, Royal Scots, Australian lighthorse, with cavalry charges interspersed with advances by twentieth-century-style motored columns. Casualties were fairly light by First World War standards, but by no means insubstantial: about 45 British killed and 350 wounded in the main battles of December and January, as against some 600 killed and more than 500 wounded on the Sanussi side. As if to crown the campaign's aristocratic overtones, the Duke of Westminster made an appearance, commanding a 'Light Armoured Car Brigade' which included 'six armoured Rolls-Royces mounted with machine guns'.[40] The Sanussi war, from the aesthetic point of view, had it all.

The one thing it did not have, however, was the Sanussi Sheikh himself. As the inevitable British reinforcements gradually ground down the enemy's strength, the two Turkish commanding officers, Nuri and Ja'far, began slinging mud, seeking to blame one another for the mounting series of defeats which saw the British recapture Sidi Barrani and Sollum and rescue the *Tara* prisoners by March 1916. It seems to have occurred to neither man to blame al-Sharif himself, who never once appeared alongside his followers in the entire coastal campaign, nor Otto Mannesmann, who had left Libya shortly after the desert war he had done so much to provoke had begun.*[41] Perhaps disappointed that the onset of hostilities had denied him his longed-for million-pound ransom from Cairo, or possibly wishing to keep his options open for future British bribes, the mysterious Sanussi Sheikh remained missing in action the entire winter. After all the crazed speculation about the revival of millenarian Mahdism in northern Africa, Oppenheim's would-be prophet proved to be a reluctant jihadi, who had to be dragged by the Turks and Germans, against his will, into his own holy war.[†]

Despite a promising beginning, the Sanussi war had turned into yet another disappointment for the Baron and his jihad bureau in Berlin. Mannesmann had done everything he could to incite the Sanussi to jihad against British Egypt, finally attacking the English enemy himself, when the Sheikh proved unwilling. If the Kaiser's beloved Islamic holy war were to make any difference at all in the Near Eastern theatre, perhaps the Germans would have to force the action themselves.

---

* Mannesmann had been reassigned by Berlin to organize the long-awaited push against French colonial forces in the Maghreb. According to Muhammad Idrisi, the German left camp on 23 November 1915, following the Sanussi seizure of Baqbaq, en route for the Maghreb. Mannesmann's departure had been planned at least two weeks in advance, judging from a telegram Falkenhayn sent to Enver on 11 November 1915. It follows that Sheikh al-Sharif already knew the German was preparing to depart when he made his 20 November 1915 blackmail demand of £1 million sterling to the British – with the Sheikh's only vow of good faith in exchange for this colossal bribe being his promise to expel Mannesmann, who, as he knew, was already leaving.

† Al-Sharif, unsurprisingly, lost his claim to the Sanussi succession, following his poor showing against the British in 1915–16, to his cousin Muhammad Idrisi, who would become King Idris I of Libya after the Second World War (until he was deposed by Qaddafi in 1969).

16

Iranian Implosion

What I could accomplish here with ammunition and a bit more money!

Wilhelm Wassmuss, from somewhere in
southern Persia, 8 January 1916[1]

November 1915, the month which saw the Sanussi invade British Egypt, brought the high-water mark of the war for the Central Powers, when the downfall of the Entente powers was in sight for the first time since the heady days of August 1914. Russia was reeling, having lost Poland and even her Galician position, now that German officers had restored discipline to the Habsburg armies. Following Bulgaria's entry into the war in October on the Turco-German-Austro-Hungarian side, Serbia was quickly overwhelmed, which opened an uninterrupted rail link for war *matériel* between Berlin and Constantinople. As the British understood well, this marked the death knell for the Allies at Gallipoli, and might also herald a renewed Ottoman Fourth Army assault on the Suez Canal. In Mesopotamia, although a British-Indian force of nearly 15,000 men led by General Charles Townshend had advanced up the Tigris to within 100 miles of Baghdad, a devastating counter-attack by the Ottoman Sixth Army on 22 November 1915, near the ruins of ancient Ctesiphon, pushed Townshend back downstream to Kut-el-Amara, where his men remained under siege for months. Niedermayer and Hentig, despite the terrors of their journey, were by November safely in Kabul, the honoured guests of Emir Habibullah, whose Afghan warriors were itching for an excuse to invade the North-west Frontier and attack the English. On the other side of the Khyber Pass, a German-directed Indian revolutionary conspiracy was in motion, which aimed to incite an 1857-style mutiny in Calcutta on Christmas Day 1915, which would be used as a springboard for the Afghan invasion. Crowning all these coups, the Germans hoped, would be the entry of Persia into the war on the Turco-German side, which would seal the fate of the British Raj.

Just as the Kaiser's Hamidian diplomacy had been ruined in the very flush of triumph in July 1908, however, it was in the euphoric days of late 1915 that the German *Drang nach Osten* crashed and burned even as the end was in sight. While the Orient Express was finally on track in the Balkans, the Armenian deportations had gummed up the works in Cilicia and Syria so badly that the renewed attack on Suez would have to wait until 1916 – which gave General Maxwell just the breathing space he needed to crush the Sanussi invaders in the western desert. While Emir Habibullah was prevaricating in Kabul, meanwhile, the Christmas Day plot was thoroughly snuffed out by the Raj, with some 300 conspirators arrested in Calcutta and Burma, even while the British ramped up subsidies paid to Islamic tribesmen in the North-west Frontier to ensure their loyalty in case of an Afghan invasion. But the real death blow to German hopes of toppling the British Empire was dealt in Persia, the crucial landbridge to Afghanistan and India, where months of planning went up in smoke in just a few fateful November days.

While Niedermayer's iron will had stamped out personal rivalries to produce a successful mission to Kabul, back in still-neutral Persia there were far too many Germans mucking about independently of one another to allow a coherent policy to emerge. The general idea, to raise the banner of Persian holy war against the hated British and Russians who had carved the country up in 1907, was fairly simple. But was it to be a ground-up operation, a guerrilla war to sabotage Entente Consulates and assets (particularly those of the Anglo-Persian Oil Company)? Or should Ahmad Shah, the young eighteen-year-old nominal ruler of the country, be persuaded to become a formal belligerent, and to raise a proper army which might expel British and Russian troops and personnel – or even join up with Emir Habibullah's Afghan troops to invade India?

Part of the problem faced by the Germans in Persia was that the country's borders were so nebulous, and the government's control over the territory within them even more so. The Anglo-Russian Convention of 1907 had divided Persia up into two roughly equal zones of influence, with the British watching over the south and Persian Gulf ports like Bushire, and the Russians controlling the northern stretches abutting the Caucasus, the Caspian and the Central Asian steppe (there was also a much narrower 'neutral' zone in between). While most of the friction between the old Great Game rivals had been smoothed over in Persia, particularly at the Afghan frontier, where British and Russian forces together had erected an 'East Persian Cordon' to prevent the Germans from setting up lines of communication with Kabul, the border areas with Ottoman Turkey were hotly contested. 'Persian Azerbaijan', at the foot of the Caucasus, was eyed greedily by Rauf Bey in Baghdad, whose Sixth Army troops, as we saw above, had crossed the ill-defined frontier in January 1915 and briefly occupied Tabriz. In the south, 'Persian Arabistan' (today called Kuzistan), the area north of Abadan and Basra, drained by the Karun river, had turned into prime strategic real estate following the British discovery of oil there. By 1914 it had become a British protectorate in all but name, with the local Bakhtiari tribesmen on the payroll of the Anglo-Persian Oil Company (later British Petroleum or BP), so as to protect both the oilfields and the pipeline running down to the refinery at Abadan. The British Indian Army had also taken both Kuwait and the (theoretically) Ottoman port city of Basra firmly in hand, so that the entire area at the head of the Persian Gulf, drained by the lower Tigris, the Shatt-el-Arab waterway and the Karun river, was now under the rule of the British Raj, although nominally the territory was still Ottoman and Persian, respectively.

The Turco-German command in Baghdad thus found itself in the awkward position of needing to invade Persian Arabistan to dislodge the British from Ottoman territory (or just to sabotage the oilfields and pipelines leading to the Abadan refinery, on which the Royal Navy was heavily dependent). Making the operation still more awkward was the smouldering dispute between the Turks and Germans over who would control the Abadan refinery if it were taken. British reinforcements rushed into the area in winter 1914–15, as we saw in chapter 12 above, rendered this prospect remote enough that sabotage seemed the only viable option. In a sabotage operation, at least, the Turks and Germans could work together – but they would still have to violate Persian territory to carry it out. Although they never did reach the Abadan refinery, two Turkish regiments, assisted by Hans Lührs and four other Germans from Klein's original unit, did succeed, in February–March 1915, in blowing up multiple stretches of the Anglo-Persian oil pipeline totalling nearly twelve miles. The line was not fully repaired until June, so that the Royal Navy was deprived of some 70 million gallons of oil.[2]

Although Russian troops had not yet entered Turkish Mesopotamia from the north-east as the British had from the south, Russian forward positions in Persian Azerbaijan (and, claimed Rauf, pro-Russian Kurds there) put Baghdad under threat.[3] Rauf Bey's logic, of establishing his own forward position, thus made good strategic sense – but then he, too, was violating Persian territory, as even the Germans complained after the Turks sacked the border towns of Hanekin and Kasri-Shirin. Friedrich Sarre, German liaison officer to the Ottoman Sixth Army, reported to Berlin in April 1915 that Rauf's brutality had 'destroyed the sympathies of Persians for Turks, such little as they were, and done great harm to our position in Persia, as we are allies of the Turks'.[4]

Coming from the Germans, who were doing everything possible to embroil Persia in the world war, this was a bit rich. And yet Sarre had a point. The political advantage of the German position in Persia was that the Germans had a small footprint. This had been the pretext of the entire Oppenheim jihad stratagem, embodied in the Kaiser's vow that he would be the protector of 'three hundred million Muslims': with her own hands clean, Germany must needs be regarded as the only real friend of the Islamic world. Unlike the British, Russians and Turks, the Germans did not have troops on the ground in Persia, and they therefore had plausible deniability regarding the accusation local patriots hurled at all the other powers – that they sought to rule the country. Even the Swedes, whose officers commanded the loyalty of some 12,000 mostly Persian gendarmes, could claim to have more active forces at their disposal in Persia than the Germans.

The problem with having a small footprint, of course, was that it was a small footprint. The reason Niedermayer and Wassmuss alike resorted to the low-cost methods of guerrilla warfare in Persia was that they *were* low cost: the Germans had neither the men, nor the weapons, nor the money, to do more. Two shipments of German cash and gold did reach Persia in 1915. A credit line of £100,000 sterling in paper was wired to the German Consulate in Tehran in May.[5] Another 80,000 Turkish pounds in gold coin arrived by caravan in October. But this was small potatoes. The Robin Hood- style heists and hold-ups which so terrified the British and Russians in summer 1915 reflected not German strength, but German financial weakness. As Hans Lührs confessed, the reason he and his fellow officers robbed banks was that they needed gold and silver coins to bribe tribal head-men and pay soldiers' salaries, even those of the Swedish gendarmes who had thrown in their lot with the Germans.[6]

Another disadvantage of a small imperial footprint was that German political strength in various areas in Persia was at the mercy of fickle local tribes, or the mostly Swedish-controlled gendarmerie, which was the only real armed force in the country (other than those of the British, Russians and Turks). With the Baghdad railway still cut off in the Balkans until November 1915, and from August 1915 over-whelmed by the Armenian disaster in Cilicia and Syria, the Germans simply had no way of bringing serious quantities of men or war *matériel* to Persia. Sabotage and bank robberies of Entente institutions in Persia were fine up to a point, but they would hardly put the fear of God into the distant British Raj. Even were Prince Reuss, the German Ambas-sador, to somehow lure Tehran into the world war on Germany's side, it would be of little account so long as Persia did not have an army. Quietly, Reuss was working to expand the Persian gendarm-erie, aiming at an effective strength of 30,000 men, which he hoped to supply with German arms and artillery. Until this was done, Reuss wanted to corral the freewheeling jihadi adventures of Niedermayer, Wassmuss and the other German 'Consuls' and agents swarming over the country, which might provoke the Russians into occupying Tehran before the gendarmerie was ready.[7]

By summer 1915, the notion of 'Persian neutrality' in the world war had turned into something of a joke. Rather than staying aloof from the conflict, the beleaguered Persians had walked right into the middle of it, with their country overrun in all directions by the belligerents – and even by 'neutral', pro-German Swedes in the gendarmerie. The anti-German East Persian Cordon had served as pretext for the extension of

British and Russian forces over a 1,000-kilometre stretch of territory running north to south from the Kara-Kum desert to Baluchistan. Rauf Bey's Turkish troops were wreaking destruction on the main caravan route from Baghdad to Tehran, reaching Karind just miles from Kermanshah in June. In August, the Russians landed 25,000 troops at the Caspian port of Enzeli, from which they could easily strike Tehran. The British still held Persian Arabistan, along with Bushire and Shiraz, but Wassmuss was now making all sorts of trouble with Tangistani tribesmen in their rear. In Kermanshah, Max Otto Schünemann, the former carpet trader, single-handedly chased the Russian Consul out of town by leading a theatrical procession of armed tribesmen to the Consulate.[8] In Isfahan, Eduard Seiler and Erich Zugmayer had mustered up a jihadi army of some 300 gendarmes and Kashgai tribesmen, which assaulted the British Consulate in mid-September, killing fifteen to twenty British officers.[9] Understandably, the British and Russian Consuls in Isfahan both fled in terror. Even the British stronghold at Shiraz nearly fell that month, after nearby tribesmen, spurred on by Wassmuss and seeking to avenge a series of foiled attacks on the garrison at Bushire, murdered the British Vice-Consul.[10] In the mountains of Luristan, in north-western Persia between Tabriz, Tehran and Kermanshah, meanwhile, the Swedish-Persian gendarmerie, working with German agents (including Lührs), an Austrian-trained popular militia, and horse-mounted Lur warriors, was preparing to strike the Russians, with or without Rauf's nearby Turkish troops.[11]

By October 1915, Persian public opinion was strongly anti-Entente, with fiery jihad sermons read out in mosques all over the country.[12] The main sticking point in Berlin's courtship of Tehran, Rauf's reign of terror in western Persia, was taken care of in late September, when, after months of German lobbying, Rauf was finally recalled to Baghdad, where he was to be subordinate to a new unified Sixth Army Turco-German command under von der Goltz Pasha.*[13] The Germans were

---

* Enver half-heartedly asked Rauf to go to Kabul, but he seems to have known this would not happen. Staking out a stubborn path as he usually did, Rauf proceeded neither to Baghdad nor Kabul but to Kirkuk in northern Iraq, where he did not have to take orders from anyone. This appears to have suited Enver fine, as his real wish was that Rauf should not return to Constantinople.

playing every card they had to bring in Tehran – some of which, unfortunately for Berlin, cancelled out the others. Prince Reuss was trying desperately to put the various local German jihad operations on ice long enough to win over the Shah before the Russians had an excuse to intervene – and he was failing miserably to do so. The terms of the pending treaty which would bring Persia into the war, negotiated between Reuss and the Shah's government in August and September, were similar to those which had brought Turkey in, with a predictable pledge that 'Germany would provide a large loan and guarantee Persian integrity and independence'. Following some foot-dragging over the particulars, a Persian draft was dispatched to Berlin, arriving on 9 October. Although the Kaiser and the German Chancellor agreed almost immediately to the Shah's terms, communications were so slow that Reuss was not able formally to notify the Persian government of this until 27 October 1915.[14]

Although the Russians were by then threatening to land more troops at Enzeli and occupy Tehran, all indications suggest that Ahmad Shah was keen to sign on with the Germans, even if it meant abandoning his capital. Certainly the Germans were optimistic. From Kabul, Niedermayer proposed in early October that the Afghan army be hurled north-west against the Russian sector of the East Persian Cordon, instead of over the Khyber Pass into British India.[15] It is true that the Shah badgered the Germans for guarantees and for ever-greater sums of money, but this sort of hard bargaining is hardly surprising in a Muslim sovereign, nor unreasonable considering that as yet none of the promised German funds had actually arrived in Tehran. Still, according to Lührs, by November 1915 the Shah's family jewels had already been dispatched south to Isfahan, which was safely in German hands, suggesting that the Shah was fairly serious about throwing in his lot with Berlin.[16] That plans were seriously advanced is implied by the departure from Tehran, on 15 November, of many leading Persian government officials, and nationalist and Democratic parliamentary deputies, along with Reuss and the German and Austro-Hungarian diplomatic personnel. Most went to Qom, which gave rise to the colourful rumour that the Germans were going to have the young Shah 'perform a *hejira*, or ceremonial exodus from the capital to the holy city of Qom', just as Muhammad had once tactically abandoned Mecca for Medina.[17] Qom would have made a fine spiritual setting from which the Shah could proclaim a Persian holy war against the hated British and Russians, who had cynically carved up his country between them.

It was not to be. Just as the Sanussi Sheikh had failed to show up for his own holy war, so young Ahmad Shah got cold feet just as history's stage beckoned. A whiff of legend surrounds the Shah's last-minute climb-down: he is said to have 'called for his horse' for the journey to Qom before at last deciding to stay put.[18] Whatever the truth of this story, the Shah's decision is easy to understand. For months the Germans had been promising him that they would soon shower his country with vast quantities of gold and guns. All that had arrived in Tehran so far, however, were small consignments of paper money, a few crates of obsolete rifles for which ammunition was lacking, and bales upon bales of holy war propaganda. Eighty thousand Turkish pounds in coin were just then en route for Tehran from Baghdad overland, but this German gold caravan, improbably led by a classics professor named Schroeder, did not reach Kermanshah until 14 November 1915, whereupon half of the gold was commandeered by a local German jihadi team for its own use.[19] The gaps in the Baghdad railway had tripped up the Germans yet again. Without a reliable rail link to Ottoman Mesopotamia, there was simply no way to get supplies to Persia in time.

Against German promises of tasty carrots which never quite arrived, the Entente powers offered Tehran the stick of boots on the ground. Just in case young Ahmad Shah had not received the message when the Russians landed more troops at Enzeli on 7 November 1915, on the same day the Russian garrison at Kazvin had begun marching on Tehran.[20] With the Cossacks approaching the capital, the Russian and British ministers laid down the law to Ahmad Shah. 'We gave him to understand in unmistakable language,' the British Ambassador reported to London, 'that if the Persian government did not act against the Germans, then Russian troops would undertake the task, and that if Persia allowed herself to be driven to war against us, the results to Persia and to himself would be disastrous.'[21] As diplomacy goes, it was not subtle. But it was effective.

The Shah's November betrayal marked the beginning of the end for the Germans in Persia. Outside Tehran, there were a few small victories for the anti-Entente cause. In Shiraz, the pro-German gendarmerie overwhelmed the British Consulate on 10 November 1915, taking the Consul, Major Frederick O'Connor, hostage, along with six other employees. Taken into custody by the Tangistani tribesmen who were loyal to Wassmuss, the O'Connor party would remain prisoners for nine months. By the time a barter deal was arranged in August 1916, however, the German position was so weakened that only Tangistani tribesmen were exchanged for the British hostages, although by then many Germans were in Entente custody, whose release Wassmuss was unable to secure.[22] In the mountains of Luristan, the multinational force Hans Lührs had somehow conjured into being captured Hamadan in November 1915, plundering a British-owned bank there, and defeated the Russians at Kangavar pass, which guarded the mountain entrance to Kermanshah – and Baghdad beyond. But the victory was short-lived. By February 1916, the passes were retaken, and the Russians were carrying all before them in Persian Azerbaijan.[23] Elsewhere the news was still worse. Isfahan and Shiraz both fell quickly back into the British orbit. Seiler, Griesinger and Zugmayer, who had all set off on a wave of holy war euphoria in November 1915 to join Niedermayer in Kabul, did not make it far. Seiler was robbed by hostile tribesmen before he reached the Afghan border. Zugmayer and Griesinger, too, had to give up on Afghanistan. They were ultimately captured by the British south-east of Kerman, in Persian Baluchistan.[24]

The lesson in Persia, as everywhere else where the Kaiser's beloved holy war had come to grief, should have been obvious to the Germans. The notion of global Islamic solidarity behind the Ottoman Sultan-Caliph was a fantasy, particularly in the Shia world. Rauf Bey's incursion across the border had reignited centuries-old hostility between Sunni Turks and Shia Persians, very nearly pushing Persia into war – against the Ottoman Empire. As Count Georg Kanitz, the German military attaché, reported from Baghdad (en route for Tehran) in July 1915, Persians and Germans alike were aghast at the 'wretched tragedy of plunder, arson, the defilement of women, and senseless bloodbaths' which had come in the wake of the Turkish invasion. Reports were filtering in from Karbala and Najaf that the Shia clerics, horrified by Turkish misdeeds against their co-religionists in Persia, were reconsidering their earlier endorsement of the holy war, and preparing to make their peace with the British invaders. All in all, Kanitz concluded, 'it was a miracle, that Persia had not long since declared war on Turkey'.[25] With this in mind, simply keeping Tehran *out* of the war (as in securing the recall of Rauf Bey) must count as something of an achievement for the Germans, even if a hollow one.

Nor, contrary to Oppenheim's fondest beliefs, did jihad propaganda alone count for much in the Islamic world, however lovingly prepared and translated. To be sure, the rabble-rousing holy war rhetoric of Persian clerics and imams, which reached fever pitch by autumn 1915 as the Germans were preparing their great push for Persian belligerence, won the rapt attention of Entente officials, particularly the British. When Wassmuss had been (briefly) captured by the British back in March, the London *Times* reported, with a note of grave concern, that 'among his effects was a box containing several thousand violently inflammatory pamphlets in the English, Urdu, Hindu, Punjabi and Sikh languages …'.[26] But such rhetoric could only be dangerous if the men to whom it appealed could be given guns, ammunition and explosives. The Germans had promised to deliver all of these things, in great quantities, to Persian tribesmen, as they had to Emir Habibullah in Kabul. Almost certainly, there were thousands of angry young Muslim men in Persia who would have loved to have settled scores with the English and Russians, had they been given the means to do so. It was because of their failure to deliver more than small quantities of 'inferior weapons of poor quality', Hans Lührs concluded, 'that we lost the trust of the Persians. Their enthusiasm for the Persian-German alliance slowly ebbed away.'[27]

To their credit, many Germans in the theatre do seem to have understood the reasons for their failure in Persia. Prince Reuss felt betrayed by the jihadi freelancing of Niedermayer, Seiler and Wassmuss. Even so, after being recalled from his post he put up little protest.[28] Von der Goltz Pasha, who arrived in Baghdad in December 1915 to take over the Ottoman Sixth Army – at the ripe old age of seventy-four – did cross the Persian border to visit Kermanshah, where he was briefed by Kanitz and Lührs. Convinced that the Persian situation was hopeless, von der Goltz recalled Lührs and other Germans from the Hamadan front and concentrated his strength on the ongoing siege at Kut-el-Amara, which offered the possibility for a much more substantial Turco-German propaganda victory than anything on tap in Persia.

Townshend's original force of nearly 15,000 British and Indian troops had been whittled down to scarcely 10,000 following the battle of Ctesiphon and the gruelling winter siege, but they were still well provisioned and heavily armed. There was also relief on the way, in the form of nearly 20,000 troops under General Aylmer dispatched up the Tigris in January 1916 to break the siege. After Aylmer's force proved unable to break through Turkish lines, another 10,000 troops, under General Gorringe, arrived in March. One attack after another was beaten off by the Turks, who, under the joint command of von der Goltz and Khalil Pasha (Enver's uncle), had constructed an impenetrable network of siege fortifications. Casualties, although not on the scale of Gallipoli, dwarfed those at Suez: the British attackers lost some 23,000 killed or wounded, the Turkish defenders over 10,000. By spring everyone was suffering from the brutal heat with temperatures sometimes topping 60 degrees Celsius (140 F). Von der Goltz himself fell victim to typhus on 19 April 1916. Just ten days later, Townshend surrendered his entire garrison of some 8,000 emaciated troops, giving the Turks a propaganda triumph nearly as great – and as damaging to British prestige in the Near East and Asia – as the Allied withdrawal from Gallipoli.[29] It was a classic Turco-German victory, embodying German discipline and Turkish tenacity. And it had almost nothing to do with Islam.

There was one German in Persia, however, who apparently did not get the memo about the hopelessness of the holy war. The exploits of Wilhelm Wassmuss, before and after the German meltdown of November 1915, quickly became legendary. For reasons just as mysterious as their cavalier dismissal of Germany's other jihad field agents, British officials and chroniclers became enamoured of Wassmuss, with his biographer Christopher Sykes famously anointing him 'the German Lawrence'.* Inspired largely by Sykes's account (itself based largely on British consular and intelligence gossip), the Wassmuss legend has

---

* Rather a peculiar comparison, considering that Wassmuss operated entirely in Persia, never once setting foot in Arabia during the war. A far more apt 'Lawrence' on the opposing side is Alois Musil, who really did see himself as Lawrence's rival for Arab Bedouin affections (and spent much of his later life lamenting the latter's superior access to bribe money, to which he attributed Lawrence's success, such as it was).

grown over the years, with a key element being the German's clever use of a phoney wireless set to ostentatiously communicate with 'Hajji Wilhelm' in the presence of gullible tribesmen. This effective 'proof' of the German Emperor's conversion to Islam (along with Wassmuss's own) was, supposedly, an effective selling point with the Tangistanis, who menaced the British garrison at Bushire.[30]

Now, some or all of this charming story may be true. But Wassmuss's own field reports suggest that he saw himself as far more Teutonic guerrilla warrior than holy war ventriloquist. Whether or not Persia had declared war on Britain, Germany certainly had, and Wassmuss counted up English casualties in Persia in the same way Falkenhayn did on the western front. Under his command, Tangistani warriors and local pro-German gendarmes attacked the British garrison at Bushire repeatedly, on 12 July, several times in August and on 9 September 1915. This last assault, Wassmuss reported proudly (and with dubious accuracy), had been a 'bloody battle. The English lost over 1,000 men, 8 officers dead, the Persians 54 dead and 50 wounded.'[31]*

Wassmuss was by no means discouraged by the political fallout of November 1915. A true field man, he knew that Tangistani warriors cared little whether the Kaiser had converted to Islam or Tehran had become a formal belligerent. What the Tangistani needed, on the other hand, was ammunition for their 7mm Mauser rifles (model 88), which they had been using for years. It is telling that in Wassmuss's request for millions of these Mauser rounds, sent to Sarre in Baghdad via Shiraz in January 1916, he did not once mention Islam. What made the Tangistani 'the best raw material [for guerrilla warfare] you can possibly imagine' was their toughness: they were 'mountain and desert people, accustomed to difficult climates, able to live off bread and dates'. From years of raiding coastal settlements along the Persian Gulf, the Tangistani had become adept at 'warfare in the modern sense'. Were he given the ammunition to load their guns with, Wassmuss promised Berlin, 'I can raise an army of 10,000 men'. Of course, he needed money to pay them too, as not even the most blood-thirsty tribesmen ever fought for free. 'What I could accomplish here,'

---

* While there was undoubtedly a skirmish of some kind at Bushire in September 1915, I have been unable to confirm from British sources that a battle of this scale indeed took place.

Wassmuss concluded his plea with something less than conviction that his demands would be met, 'with ammunition and a bit more money!'[32]

Although his requests, predictably, were never fulfilled, Wassmuss was on the right track. It was not loyalty to the Ottoman Sultan which counted in the tribal hinterland of Shiite Persia, any more than it counted with the Sunni Sanussi in North Africa – or the Hashemites in the Hejaz. What mattered was superior force in theatre, pure and simple. This was the true lingua franca of the Islamic world, as young Baron Oppenheim had once learned after being accosted by a robber chieftain in the Maghreb (but apparently later forgotten). The Sultan-Caliph, now as ever before, was not respected because of his spiritual office: instead, he enjoyed that office because of his politico-military power. If the Sultan could not back up his claim to supremacy in the Islamic world with an army capable of protecting the holy places and the pilgrim routes to them, then he was not really a Caliph at all. The Germans were about to pay a heavy price for calling the bluff of Ottoman supremacy in the Sunni heartland of Arabia.

17

Betrayal in Mecca

Then the Union and Progress rejected God's word, 'A Man shall have twice a woman's share', and made them equal. They went further and removed one of the five corner-stones of the Faith ... by causing the soldiers in garrison in Mecca, Medina and Damascus to break their [Ramadan] fast for new and foolish reasons ... They made weak the person of the Sultan, and robbed him of his honour, forbidding him to choose for himself the chief of his personal Cabinet. Other like things did they to sap the foundation of the Caliphate.

Proclamation of the Sherif of Mecca, calling Arab
Muslims to sacred rebellion against the impious
Ottoman government, June 1916[1]

Despite the disappointments in Libya and Persia, much of the news was good for the Turco-German alliance in winter 1915–16. Both the humiliating British withdrawal at Gallipoli and the entrapment of Townshend's Indian army troops at Kut-el-Amara did much to soothe faltering Ottoman morale after the defeats at Sarıkamış and Suez. By knocking Serbia out of the war and thus opening the Balkans, the Central Powers had become a truly unified geographical entity for the first time along the axis of the Orient Express. True, the fallout from the Armenian deportations, and never-ending logistical difficulties in the mountains and Mesopotamia, continued to plague the Baghdad line. But Meissner Pasha had performed wonders in the Sinai, providing a rail link as far as Beersheeba. As spring dawned in 1916, it seemed only a matter of time before the Germans could get enough men and *matériel* through to Damascus to mount a devastating second strike on the Suez Canal. Jihad or no jihad, the Germans' *Drang nach Osten* had some life in it yet as the war entered its third calendar year.

Unfortunately for Berlin, however, the Entente powers were at last beginning to cotton on to the new Great Game over Islam. The double blows of the Sanussi invasion of Egypt and the Iranian implosion in November 1915, coupled with the impending retreat at Gallipoli, set jihad alarm bells ringing in London, Petrograd and Paris simultaneously. The French had thus far escaped the worst terrors of Oppenheim's holy war, but this was mostly because the Maghreb was much less strategically significant in Germany's bid for world power than Egypt and India. Not until he had succeeded in unleashing the Sanussi warriors against the British garrison at Sollum in late November 1915 did Mannesmann finally set off for Tunisia to rouse native Muslims there against the French occupiers. But it was far too late. After watching North Africa become flooded with Arabic-language jihad pamphlets from Oppenheim's jihad factory in Berlin for over a year, the French were by winter 1915 on high alert for 'pan-Islamic emissaries, who would try to infiltrate themselves into our colonies'.[2] Had Mannesmann succeeded in reaching the Maghreb, he would almost certainly have been rounded up immediately by colonial authorities on the lookout for him. As it happened, the French did not even need to bother: in April 1916 the German spy was murdered somewhere in the Libyan desert.[3]

With the jihadi threat to their North African colonies under control, the French now turned the tables on Oppenheim and went on the offensive. Since the start of the war there had been talk of building a mosque in Paris at government expense as a gesture of solidarity with the North African Muslim troops fighting on the western front. Now the French government decided to go one better, appropriating 500,000 francs in December 1915 for the construction of two grand hotels in Mecca to house hajj pilgrims from the French Maghreb.[4] To counter the Turco-German use of the green flag of the Prophet, meanwhile, the French and British jointly sponsored the annual dispatch of a sacred carpet from Cairo to Mecca during the autumn 1915 hajj, going so far as to rename the ship carrying the carpet the *Kingsmere* (its actual name, SS *Lindenfels*, sounded Germanic). In an impressive display of Entente diplomacy, the Anglicized vessel was escorted by a French ship, whose captain compiled (in broken English) the official report for London. 'Knowing the great importance the Mussulmen attach to the ceremony of the Carpet,' wrote Contre-Amiral Huguet, 'the English and French were glad to accompany [the Carpet] here with great ceremoney [*sic*] to do it honour, and add to the brilliancy of the ceremony, and to bear witness to or respects for the Mussulmen religion which is that of so many peoples in countries occupied by the French and British.'[5] Not for the last time, Western infidels singled out by jihad *fetvas* as legitimate targets for sectarian murder by Muslims responded by rushing to demonstrate their fidelity to Islam.

The Russians, too, went on the attack following the Persian crisis of November 1915, but in their own inimitably blunt fashion. Not for Grand Duke Nicholas and the Army of the Caucasus the theatrical Islamic charm offensives of Paris, London and Cairo. Instead of apologizing for any possible offence caused to Islam by Entente colonialism, the Russians responded to Turco-German manoeuvres in Persia by sending the Cossacks into Tehran. For good measure, the Russians also occupied Hamadan, Kermanshah, Isfahan and Qom. Just in case Persian and Turkish Muslims did not get the message about who was the real boss in the region, on 11 January 1916 Tiflis command launched a frontal assault on the Ottoman Third Army from Kars. With his own men much better clothed, supplied and provisioned than Enver's had been at Sarıkamış, the Grand Duke's assault was lethal. Whether because of superior firepower and morale or – as John Buchan suggests in *Greenmantle* – a stolen staff map of Ottoman fortifications, the Russians took the heretofore impregnable fortress of Erzurum on 15 February 1916, pitching the Ottoman Third Army into headlong retreat towards Ankara.* It was a bitter blow to Turco-German prestige. Any chance Niedermayer still had of inducing Emir Habibullah to launch an Afghani holy war against British India most likely perished in the snows of Erzurum.[6]

The most serious threat of all to the Turco-German holy war, however, would come from the Arabian peninsula. Trouble in Mecca had been brewing since the start of the war, stirred up not only by the British

---

* The Caucasian front will be discussed in chapters 18 and 19 below.

intrigues with the Hashemites but also through the war's disruption of the annual hajj and the entire economy of the Hejaz which depended on it. Still, despite mounting rumours of Sherif Hussein's fundamental disloyalty, so far an open breach had been avoided. Baron Oppenheim would have loved to claim credit for this, following his lavish court-ship of Feisal in the Pera Palace Hotel. But there were plenty of reasons for Hussein himself to wish to avoid openly joining the Entente pow-ers. True, the Hashemites were now receiving tribute from the British residency in Cairo, but then the Porte was funding them as well, sending 50,000 Turkish gold pounds to Hussein as late as spring 1916.[7] Besides, the Baron had a point about the need for solidarity behind the Ottoman Caliph, however much he exaggerated the importance of the office. The Young Turks may have been jealous of the spiritual primacy of the Mecca Sherif and his blasphemous refusal to sanction their holy war, particularly considering the shaky religious legitimacy the CUP regime had endured ever since forcibly deposing Abdul Hamid in the counter-counter revolution of 1909. But blasphemy cuts both ways. If the Hashemites rebelled openly against the current Sul-tan, they could themselves be accused of sacrilege. However much they suspected each other of treachery, the Young Turks and the Hashemites remained wedded together in mutual fear of being unmasked by the other in the eyes of the global *umma*.

As marriages go, it was a reasonably successful one in the first two years of the war. Enver schemed to replace Sherif Hussein with Ali Haidar Pasha, in effect blackmailing Hussein into remaining loyal. Similarly, by courting Cairo the Sherif fired a warning shot over Enver's bow, letting him know that Mecca had another possible patron in tow. Meanwhile, the Germans sought to counter English influence over the Sherif by promising Hussein they would keep Enver in line. This was how the game was played: so long as neither side fired first, the dance between the Sherif and the Young Turks could go on like this indefinitely, to their mutual benefit.

If one had to gamble on which marriage partner would break his vows first, it certainly would not have been Hussein. As local guard-ian of the holy places of Islam, the Sherif was in an ideal position to benefit from the bidding war which surrounded any neutral party in the world war. As the Ottoman Grand Vizier (though not Enver) had understood in 1914, as did Emir Habibullah and the Sanussi Sheikh in 1915, the key to driving up the asking price of belligerence was patience. The longer Hussein could keep both sides guessing as to his real intentions, the more sincere his pledges of support to both, the higher the subsidies would mount. Ideally, like the Afghan Emir, Hussein would have waited out the entire war, both to drive up the tribute paid him by the warring coalitions and to ensure he would not back the wrong horse. Whether it was Germany or Britain, either would-be global hegemon would, it seemed, have equal need of the blessing of the Sherif of Mecca to legitimize its rule over Islamic subject populations.

Unlike Kabul, however, Mecca was not so geographically removed from the theatres of war as to remain inviolable. Nor did Hussein possess an army to unleash on to the field of battle. All the Sherif had was his title, and the authority which either did, or did not, inhere in it. For Hussein to declare open rebellion against Constantinople would be to call his own bluff. If Ottoman Muslim soldiers did not desert to him, then his own spiritual authority would prove just as illusory as that of the CUP's puppet Caliph.

Hussein was playing a very delicate game. Although the Young Turks had, as yet, no written proof of treason, they knew perfectly well that Hussein was intriguing with conspiratorial Arab officers, and the British to boot. It was no doubt with the Sherif's disloyalty in mind that Enver, accompanied by a retinue including the German and Austrian military attachés Bronsart, Humann, Lossow and Pomiankowski, embarked on an inspection tour of Syria, Palestine and the Hejaz in February 1916. Lavishly entertained by Enver and Djemal in Beirut and Damascus, the Christian officers were treated to a tour of Jerusalem, Bethlehem and Beersheeba, before being left behind as Enver and Djemal went on to Medina (on whose sacred Islamic ground infidels were not allowed to tread). Here, on 29 February 1916, in the second holiest city of Islam, the Sherif of Mecca assured Enver and Djemal in person of his loyalty to the Ottoman Sultan.[8] Hussein's son Feisal, meanwhile, spent most of winter and spring 1916 in Damascus, meeting with Djemal and German Consul Loytved-Hardegg on an almost daily basis to reassure the Turks and Germans alike about Hashemite intentions.[9]

Hussein had reason to be nervous. In August 1915, Djemal had executed eleven Arab nationalists in Beirut (ten Muslims and one Christian), and sentenced another forty-five to death *in absentia*. Some of those convicted had been in contact with Feisal earlier that spring, and could easily have betrayed Hussein. As the Sherif must have known, the protest telegrams he dispatched to the Porte that autumn could be used against him. So, too, could Hussein's suspicious request, wired to Djemal in January 1916, that the Young Turks guarantee 'my independence in the whole of the Hejaz and create me a hereditary prince' (i.e. formalize the dispossession of the Zaid branch of the Hashemites from the Mecca Sherifiate).[10] In April 1916, Djemal issued notice to Hussein that he was dispatching 3,500 men through the Hejaz to help a German team led by Major Ottmar von Stotzingen set up a propaganda centre in Yemen.* Later that month Djemal ordered a new wave of arrests, which culminated in the gruesome spectacle of twenty-one public executions on 6 May 1916.[11] If the Sherif was to strike first, it was now or never.

Only Hussein himself knows why he made the final, fateful plunge into revolt against the Ottoman government. But Djemal's latest crackdown on Arab nationalists in Damascus must have been near the forefront of his mind. The Fourth Army commander had no less guile than Hussein and Feisal, and there was good reason to suspect he had his own plans for Mecca and Medina which would not include them – for which Ali Haidar Pasha of the dispossessed Zaid branch of the family might have been the vehicle. Why, for instance, was Djemal sending an army through the Hejaz, if not to assert his own claim there? Adding to the Sherif's suspicions was the fact that Djemal, in his persecution of Syrian nationalists, seemed to be singling out Arab Muslims (who made up seventeen of the twenty-one executed in May 1916) despite more plentiful evidence of disloyalty among the Christian population.[12] This was indeed curious, considering that back in December 1915 Djemal had dispatched Curt Prüfer incognito to canvass public opinion in Lebanon and Syria. Intriguingly, Prüfer dismissed the Arab nationalist threat entirely, claiming it had been brought under control by the 'just and severe measures of the government'

---

* This mission will be discussed in chapter 18 below.

(i.e. the August 1915 executions), whereas 'the Christian population is nearly unanimous in its support for the Entente'.[13] That Djemal did the opposite of what Prüfer recommended, ostentatiously bludgeoning the Arab nationalist movement to death in Damascus, suggests the Fourth Army commander had his own agenda. What was it?

Of the CUP triumvirate ruling the Ottoman Empire during the war, Djemal remains something of an enigma. By reputation he was the most pro-Entente of the three, with particular affinity for the French (whose language he spoke well). And yet it was Djemal who had bartered the lives of British hostages in Damascus in the first winter of the war, only to be rebuked for his cruelty by Talaat, the Interior Minister. With the Armenian deportations, the two rivals seem to have switched sides, so to speak, with Talaat generally being assigned most of the blame for the horrors of 1915 by Armenian historians, while some, like Dadrian, are willing to credit Djemal with having 'tried to resist and discourage the attendant massacres'.* There is good evidence this is true: Walter Rössler, the German Consul in Aleppo, reported in April 1915 that Djemal had threatened anyone who molested Armenians with court martial; and he later carried out this threat even against two Ottoman army officers for their role in the murder of two Armenian parliamentary deputies.[14] Both Kress, who worked closely with Djemal at headquarters, and the Habsburg military attaché Pomiankowski, who inspected the Fourth Army on several occasions in 1915 and 1916, insisted that Djemal unequivocally condemned the deportations.[15] It may be that the Fourth Army commander tried to distance himself from the Armenian massacres in order to make himself viable as a negotiating partner with the Allies. According to an Armenian Dashnak conspirator, Dr Hakob Zavriev, Djemal made a secret peace offer to the Entente in December 1915. The idea was to create a new Turkish state comprising Anatolia, Cilicia, Syria, Palestine, Mesopotamia, Arabia and an autonomous Armenia, and for 'Djemal to be proclaimed Sultan, with heredity from father to eldest son'. In exchange for Allied acceptance of these terms, Zavriev told the Russian Foreign Office, Djemal had agreed to give

---

* Not that this saved Djemal from Armenian retribution for the atrocities of 1915: he was assassinated in Tiflis, Georgia, on 25 July 1922.

up Constantinople and the Straits – after conquering them with substantial Entente *matériel* and logistical support – and to 'undertake forthwith to take measures for the safety of Armenians and for providing them with food till the end of the war'.[16]

To date no one has unearthed evidence confirming that Zavriev spoke on Djemal's authority.[17] Still, it is possible that Djemal himself encouraged rumours that he was going to cut some sort of deal with the Allies on the basis of protecting the Armenians, in order to tease out Entente intentions towards Syria and Lebanon – which territories Djemal now regarded as something of a personal fiefdom. The case Djemal had built against the Arab conspirators was mostly based on documents he had discovered in the French Consulate in Damascus. Despite his own affinity for the French language and literature, Djemal had concluded by 1916 that there was 'not the slightest doubt that the Arab revolutionaries were working under French protection'.[18] Considering that it was the French, not the British or Russians, who rejected his (quite probably mythical) peace offer in March 1916 – on the grounds that they did not want to give up their claim on Cilicia, Syria and Lebanon – Djemal's suspicions of Paris were sensible.[19] The Ottoman Fourth Army commander, despite his Francophile reputation, was, as Kress intuited, 'neither pro-German nor pro-Entente, rather he was a Turk, filled with a burning sense of Turkish patriotism'.[20]

Hussein was therefore not wrong to fear the wrath of Djemal. This was only, however, because the Sherif really was guilty of treasonous contacts with the enemy. Even though the Young Turks had not yet presented a case against him, they may only have been waiting for a smoking gun to emerge. As Djemal himself later recalled, before the Arab revolt he had possessed 'no documentary evidence of the criminal designs of these people', adding that if he had, he would have immediately 'sent a Turkish division in hot haste to Mecca'. The 50,000 pounds in gold Djemal dispatched to Mecca in April 1916, accompanied by enough rifles to equip the 1,500 Bedouin warriors the Sherif had promised for the Suez offensive, amounted to a test. If Hussein used Turkish gold and arms to attack the Ottoman army, it would be hard for him to deny the claim of treason.[21]

What was Hussein waiting for? The Sherif had been assuring the British all year that he was ready, even promising in mid-March that he would strike in June.[22] By May 1916, the pressure to act was mounting. The Stotzingen mission had arrived in Damascus in April, and was gathering strength for an imposing march across the Hejaz to Yemen. Djemal and Kress were in furious preparations for a renewed assault on the Suez Canal, to be launched some time in the summer, ostensibly with Sherifian support (although they were careful not to tell Feisal the date). The bloodbath of 6 May 1916 must have made a serious impression on Feisal, who, according to Djemal, was made to agree the sentences had been just after being shown the evidence. It was when Feisal requested permission to return to Medina a week later – to organize the Bedouin striking force for the Suez attack – that, Djemal later claimed, he first suspected something was brewing in Mecca.*[23]

To beat Djemal to the pass, Hussein at last resolved to act. With his father's permission, Feisal dumped his Turkish military escort as soon as he reached the Hejaz in late May, helping himself to 5,000 Turkish gold pounds and 5,000 Maria Theresa silver Thalers.[24] On about 5 June 1916, Sherif Hussein, as legend would have it, then 'thrust a rifle through the window of the palace and fired a single shot at the Turkish barracks opposite'.[25] It was less baroque than the shot which had launched the Ottoman holy war – fired into an English grandfather clock – but no less effective as political symbolism. Mecca, site of the hajj pilgrimage required of all Muslims, home to the Kaaba and the most sacred square of worship in all Islam, had now declared war on the Ottoman Sultan-Caliph.

It has become customary for historians to dismiss the significance of the Sherifian revolt. With British naval support, the Arabs did take Red Sea port cities like Jedda, Yanbo and later (famously) Aqaba from the Turks. But the holy city of Medina, supplied via the Hejaz railway from Ma'an and Damascus, remained in Turkish hands until February 1919. The most famous achievement of Feisal's Arab Bedouin irregulars, the storming of Damascus dramatized in *Lawrence of Arabia*, never took place at all (the myth of Arab conquest was concocted by the British in order to deny Damascus to the French).[26]

* As Enver explained to his friend Humann, Djemal deliberately kept Feisal in Damascus as a hostage to ensure his father's loyalty.

If it was something of a dud in military terms, however, the Arab revolt was inarguably an event of major politico-religious importance for Islam. Owing largely to the continued influence of the *Lawrence of Arabia* myth, the popular notion persists that the Sherifian revolt was rooted in a kind of secular Arab nationalism. But that is certainly not how Hussein portrayed his own rebellion. In his June 1916 proclamation, the Sherif accused the Young Turks not of suppressing Arab political aspirations, but rather of violating the sacred tenets of Islam. Bringing back all the bad blood born of the 1908 revolution, Hussein reminded Muslims everywhere that the CUP, despite its opportunistic embrace of Islam since 1909, had begun as a European-style reform party estranged from Muslim traditions, and had never really changed its spots.

It was propaganda, to be sure, but many of Hussein's claims hit home. The Young Turks really had tried to proclaim equal rights for women and religious minorities, and to set up European-style secular schools in Mecca and Medina. They had deposed the great pan-Islamist Abdul Hamid with malice aforethought and appointed a weak puppet Sultan in his place. Try though they did to invoke the majesty of the Caliphate to launch a holy war against the Entente powers, since 1909 the institution had been moribund at best. Had the Turks and Germans been able to extend the Hejaz railway to Mecca, they may have succeeded in resurrecting the Sultan's lost spiritual authority. Because they had failed to do so, the holiest city in Islam was now effectively under British, not Ottoman, suzerainty. The Royal Navy, through its selective blockade of the Arabian coastline, now controlled the global hajj and supplied the Hejaz with food-stuffs, funds and arms.

Although Kitchener's ill-thought-out promise to bequeath Hussein the office of what his deputy Reginald Wingate called a 'holy Arabian Koreishite Khalifate' did not quite come off, the Ottoman Caliphate itself was now in serious jeopardy.[27] The House of Osman, of Turkic origin, had never been able to claim descent from the Koreish tribe of Muhammad. It was only military supremacy in Arabia and control of the holy places of Islam which allowed Sultans to claim the title of Caliph. With Mecca now outside Turkish control, this was no longer possible. True, Hussein himself had conquered no more than his own city and a few coastal towns in the Hejaz – which made his own claim to military supremacy in Arabia no less spurious than the Sultan's (although this would not prevent Hussein from laying claim to the title of Caliph after Kemal formally abolished the office in 1924).[28] In this sense the Arab revolt was a kind of double bluff: by destroying Islamic unity in the Ottoman Empire, Sherif Hussein also destroyed the pretence underlying the institution of the Caliphate, which would never recover.

While the failure of Hussein to rally Muslims under the banner of Islam was disappointing to the British, it was still a major blow to the Kaiser's beloved jihad. Curt Prüfer, who had himself long since given up believing in the holy war, spared a thought for his mentor: 'Poor Oppenheim,' he wrote in his diary after hearing the news.[29] The global publicity generated by the Arab revolt rendered absurd the Turco-German claim that the Islamic world was united behind them. Turning the tables on Oppenheim's jihad propaganda factory, the British and French now flooded Arabia with leaflets vowing that under their watch, 'not a single scrap of territory on the Arabian peninsula, which contains the holy places of Islam, will be annexed by us or by any other government'.[30]

The military imperative in the Near East also now shifted in Britain's favour. Djemal's long-awaited second strike at Suez was repulsed with ease at Romani on 4 August 1916, with the Turks beating a hard retreat into the Sinai desert barely twenty-four hours after the attack had begun, having suffered some 9,000 casualties to less than 1,000 in the Egyptian army. By 1916 the British had begun building their own railway across the Sinai (which, in a bitter blow to the Germans, would soon incorporate sections and pilfered materials from Meissner's own Sinai line), in preparation for the conquest of Palestine.[31] Far from establishing a bridgehead for a renewed Frobenius-style offensive in the Horn of Africa, the Stotzingen mission was cut off by the Arab revolt in Yanbo, hundreds of miles short of Yemen.[32] In Arabia and Palestine, it would now be the Entente powers riding the tiger of Muslim rage, with the Germans in its line of sight.

This was a mixed blessing for the British. Part of the reason Lawrence became so famous is that he was the first English soldier given permission to voyage into the Hejaz from the Arabian coast-line to meet Hussein's sons (other than Abdullah, who had been to Cairo). This was because the Sherif, despite his utter dependence on British food, funds and arms, 'would not allow Christian British military units to move inland'. One might think that the £11 million sterling London contributed to subsidize Hussein's revolt – the equivalent of nearly $5 billion today – would have purchased British subjects at least the privilege of visiting Mecca.[33] But that was not how things worked for infidels in the Islamic world. As Lawrence himself later confessed, 'the foreigner and Christian is not a popular person in Arabia. However friendly and informal the treatment of yourself may be, remember always that your founda-tions are very sandy ones.'[34]

The Germans could have sympathized. It would now be London instead of Berlin which would have to pay the ever-mounting fees of an Arab Muslim jihad, as Hussein's monthly retainer rose from 50,000 pounds in gold to 200,000 in just the first six months.[35] English agents could try their own luck cutting deals with conniving tribal leaders, their military plans at the mercy of fickle Bedouins who might, or might not, show up on the field of battle. Before long, Lawrence him-self would be questioning the wisdom of taking on such expensive obligations in the Islamic world (particularly in the hornets' nest of Mesopotamia).*[36] And yet he remained perversely loyal to his beloved Hashemites, whose jihad fees were the highest of all, requiring not just money, weapons and supplies but entire kingdoms to be created and administered for them.

All this, however, still lay in the future. In the meantime, the Central Powers were hanging desperately on to an increasingly precarious position in the Near East. As the *Drang nach Osten* swung into reverse, it was not only German pride and prestige which suffered. With the jihad exemption granted by the Ottoman holy war *fetvas*

---

* As Lawrence wrote in the *Sunday Times* in 1920, 'Our government [in Mesopota-mia] is worse than the old Turkish system. They kept fourteen thousand local con-scripts embodied, and killed a yearly average of two hundred Arabs in maintaining peace. We keep ninety thousand men, with aeroplanes, armoured cars, gunboats and armoured trains. We have killed about ten thousand Arabs ... We cannot hope to maintain such an average ...'

now lifted in Arabia, it was only a matter of time before Turkish Muslims, too, would begin to look askance at the Christian infidels who had brought death, misery, ruin and now Arab sedition to the Ottoman Empire. Just as Pallavicini had warned, the 'passions directed today against Russians, English, and French' were easily turned against other Christians, whether Armenians, Greeks, or subjects of the Habsburg and Hohenzollern empires.

18

The Holy War Devours its Children

For a party of Germans to travel through Medina and Mecca,
even under Turkish escort, would be impossible. No one could
possibly give a guarantee that they would not be killed along
the way.

Enver Pasha to German military attaché General
Otto von Lossow, March 1916[1]

Following the collapse of the Turco-German position in Arabia, the
Caucasus, Persia and the Sinai in 1916, it was obvious to everyone in
Constantinople that the Turkish goal of restoring the old Ottoman
borders, let alone expanding the empire further, was a pipe dream.
Even the surrender of Townshend's garrison at Kut-el-Amara had
merely slowed down the Anglo-Indian advance into Mesopotamia.
Barring a miracle, retaking Basra and southern Mesopotamia was out
of the question. Whether or not the Sixth Army could keep the British
out of Baghdad, there was no prospect of dislodging them from the
oilfields and refineries of the Persian Gulf, nor from Suez, the Sinai or
the Hejaz coastline. Just as Clemenceau liked to remind the French that
'les Allemands sont à Noyon' – only sixty miles from Paris – so, too, could
critics now chide the Young Turks that their puppet Sultan-Caliph of
global Islam no longer ruled even Mecca.

Compounding the sense of crisis was the fact that Turkey, unlike
the other belligerents, had been fighting, in one way or another, since
1911. Where the Great Powers were entering a third painful year of
mobilization and mass carnage in summer 1916, the Ottoman Empire
was entering the sixth year of its own ongoing war of survival. It had

been partly to regain the territories lost in the wars of 1877 and 1911–13 that Enver and Djemal had thrust their countrymen back into war in 1914 after scarcely a year's pause. The Germans may dream of a *Drang nach Osten*, or of sabotaging the British Empire with Islamic unrest. But thus far the Kaiser's holy war had brought Turkey only heartache and the loss of yet more territory to the infidel. What was in it for the Turks?

When we look at the order of battle following the Sherifian revolt and the repulsion of the second Suez offensive in summer 1916, the wonder is not that the Turks held on to Medina and Baghdad, but that they fought on at all. The country's manpower had been utterly spent after a half-decade of continuous warfare. In the first year and a half of the world war, the Ottoman army lost in all some 500,000 men to death, disease and desertion, or nearly a third of its effective strength. As the draft was netting only some 90,000 conscripts per year, in another two years Turkey would literally run out of soldiers if casualty and desertion rates continued at this pace.* Inconsistent treatment of minorities, and a cynical buy-out clause for sons of the rich (who could purchase an exemption for 50 Turkish pounds, equal to $250 then or some $25,000 today), continued to plague Ottoman recruiting efforts. Despite the lifting of the Christian exemption on military service in 1909, in practice a double standard was still applied, with most Greek and Armenian boys shunted into civilian forced labour battalions instead of the front lines in the great mobilization of 1914. The Armenian deportations, among their other awful human consequences, also deprived the army of tens of thousands of potential draftees.

It was a sign of the army's growing desperation that Enver, in April 1915, finally eliminated the last remaining draft exemptions for ethnicity and religion. Perhaps to compensate for the dilution of the Islamic character of the army with the resulting influx of Christians, later in 1915 another new conscription law targeted foreign nationals of Muslim origin, from Albanians and Bosnians to Egyptians, North Africans and Persians. In yet another blow to the holy war ideal, most of these Islamic expatriates turned out to be rich enough to purchase

---

* By 1922, when the Turks repelled the Greek advance at Sakarya, so few enlisted men were left in the army that Sakarya is known to posterity as the 'officers' battle'.

exemptions, and they did so without the slightest hesitation. On the bright side, the buy-out clause did provide the Porte with some desperately needed revenue. No fewer than 20,000 Persian merchant families, for example, paid the get-out-of-jihad bribe in 1915, which raised the astonishing sum of 1 million Turkish pounds – the equivalent of nearly half a billion dollars today. But indulging this latest form of jihad fundraising did nothing, of course, to put bodies into the Turkish army. By 1916, Ottoman draft boards were scraping the bottom of the barrel, enlisting men as old as fifty-five.[2] So desperate was the Porte for soldiers that a group of Chinese Confucian travellers were impressed as 'foreign Muslims', to the amusement of the Austrian military attaché.[3]

As it was the Germans who (with assistance from Enver) had done most of the pushing to get Turkey into the war, it was only natural that the pent-up resentment in the Ottoman army would be directed at them. The feeling was mutual: tensions between German and Turkish officers had been present from day one, not least because of awkward age differences. In part as a result of CUP influence but also simply because the Turks had already been at war for so long, ranking officers in the Ottoman army during the First World War tended to be of astonishingly tender age compared to their German counterparts. Kemal made general at thirty-five; in Germany he would have been lucky to be a major at that age. The upshot was that many proud German officers found themselves taking orders from 'young Turks' several decades their junior. The colossal battles between the thirty-three-year-old War Minister Enver and General Liman, his sixty-year-old subordinate, nearly split the alliance apart in the lead-up to Gallipoli. As the number of German soldiers seconded to Turkey grew by 1916 to over 10,000 – the vast majority of them highly trained specialists, who invariably knew more about the latest weaponry and tactics than Turkish officers who often outranked them – friction was inevitable.[4]

Relations between Kress and Djemal in Damascus were generally better than those between Liman and Enver: it doubtless helped that the age difference between them was only two years (Kress was forty-four when the war began, Djemal forty-two). Still, Kress had had all kinds of trouble with Turks of lower rank, because of both the language barrier and the peculiarities of Ottoman military culture. Many Turkish officers who had come up in the Hamidian era could not shoot properly: so paranoid was the Sultan about assassination that he had not allowed training with live ammunition. Most Ottoman field artillery officers could neither read nor write, which made instruction in the use of the latest Krupp guns rather difficult (although happily it also rendered moot the issue of whether Kress needed to order translations of German instruction manuals). Curt Prüfer had done much to smooth over the language barrier before the first Suez offensive, but even he was grumbling about Turkish recalcitrance and laziness after the canal attack was repulsed. The Turks, for their part, deeply resented the arrogance of German officers and NCOs, many of whom, even Kress admitted, lacked the tact required to get on with men from a different cultural and religious tradition, whether of higher or lower rank.[5]

In southern Mesopotamia, where the British Indian expeditionary army sent to the Gulf in November 1914 had put the Turco-German forces on the defensive almost as soon as the war began, cross-cultural friction was more serious. The German mission to win over the Shiite Grand Mufti had deeply offended the Turks, particularly after Rauf Bey heard that Major Klein had tried to pass himself off as a Muslim in Karbala. Before long, Enver was complaining to the German high command that the Shia Muftis had been forced to undergo a three-step ritual cleansing of their hands after learning that the Germans who had kissed them in greeting were not really Muslims.[6] Whereas the Germans complained that Rauf's invasion of Persia had forfeited them the Shah's sympathy, Rauf blamed the Iranian implosion on undiplomatic German behaviour. The 'harsh martial bearing' of the officers Berlin had seconded to Baghdad, Rauf reported to Enver, 'was equally insulting to Turks and Persians. Everywhere they go they display the same utter lack of tact and discretion.'[7] Rauf might have been referring to von Blum, a junior German officer shot by Hikmet Bey, an Ottoman staff officer, for which offence the latter was executed in May 1916. Hikmet Bey would not be the last.[8]

Complicating Turkish-German relations in the field further was the Arab factor. Many Arab officers and enlistees, out of antipathy to their Turkish masters, sought to cosy up to the Germans, just as Feisal would later win over British Arabophiles like Lawrence by playing on their anti-Turkish prejudices. Baron Oppenheim aside, however, Arab charm was generally lost on the Germans. Unlike Lawrence, field agents like

Musil and Lührs were fluent enough in Arabic to understand Bedouin culture as it existed on the plane of reality, rather than in the romantic Oxbridge imagination. And Lührs, for one, was often more horrified than fascinated by what he saw. Far from being loyal to the cause of Islamic holy war, Arab irregulars attacked whomever they felt like, generally those offering possibilities for plunder and who were least able to resist. After the British repulsed the Ottoman assault on the Karun region on 18 April 1915, the Bedouins attached to the Turco-German striking force turned tail and began picking off wounded stragglers from their own side. As Lührs recalled with a shudder, 'the Arabs stripped those fallen in action completely, leaving them naked and unburied, often desecrating their victims as well, according to their warrior customs and their primitive understanding of Islam, which told them that a dead enemy, particularly a non-believer, was unclean'.[9]

Like Prüfer before him, Lührs learned that the notion of pan-Islamic solidarity on the battlefield was a sham. Shortly before the Turks abandoned Amara to the British, Arab irregulars began hunting down Turks separated from their units during the fighting. Lührs himself, along with a small party of German officers, fled into the countryside. Before they reached Baghdad, the party had been robbed by half a dozen different Bedouin tribes, cheating death only because they were liberally supplied with gold, guns and other Western-made trinkets to barter for their lives. It helped that several of the tribal chieftains offering 'hospitality' looked greedily at the prospect of selling their prisoners to the English. The flight to Baghdad turned into a kind of Mesopotamian striptease: every warrior tribe Lührs and his men encountered asked for another item of clothing, until they were down to their underwear. One pro-Turkish tribe did outfit the Germans in new robes, only for these, too, to be pinched in turn. By this point, the men could only laugh. Counting their blessings, Lührs pointed out to his half-naked companions that there was nothing left on them to steal. 'Woe unto us,' he joked, 'if we had gold teeth!'[10]

A shared dislike of Mesopotamian Arabs might easily have worked to alleviate the strain between Turkish and German officers. But contempt for the locals was hardly a healthy basis for a long-term strategic relationship. Rather than making them fonder of the Turks, the creeping disgust many German officers felt for Arab soldiers simply made them more eager to go home. 'The differences of opinion between Turkish and German officers,' Alois Dandini, the Austrian Consul in Aleppo, reported to Vienna as early as March 1915, 'are, despite denials from both camps, beginning to take on the character of an insurmountable antipathy.' As acrimony engulfed the Fourth Army following the failure of the first Suez attack, a large group of German officers in Syria had 'taken a resolution to return to Germany'. Ironically, it was Liman, who had threatened to leave on two occasions in 1914, who now intervened to convince the men to stay on.[11]

In Baghdad, things were worse. The antagonism between Rauf and Niedermayer gravely undermined the Germans' Afghan mission, which had finally to be undertaken without a Turkish military escort – not to mention a good deal of the kit the Germans had brought with them. Niedermayer may have been happy to see the back of Rauf Bey, but Rauf was happier still, greeting the Germans' departure with undisguised *Schadenfreude*. One of Rauf's aides laughed heartily when recounting to Alois Musil in May 1915 how Rauf had taken one million Marks in gold from Niedermayer, along with 'a great quantity of machine guns', before hauling the Bavarian before a military tribunal. Speaking on condition of anonymity, the officer justified plundering the Germans because of their 'arrogance and unsociability' – not Niedermayer in particular, but all of them. Worse even than the haughty officers were the increasing numbers of German civilians who, despite never having served in the army, were now 'parading around Turkish provinces pretending to be German-Turkish officers and treating the Turks like barbarians'. So universal was the prejudice in Baghdad that one young Turkish colonel, upon hearing Alois Musil speak German, 'made no secret of his hostility to the Germans', and, thinking poor Musil to be one of them, 'placed all possible obstacles in my path'. Just as Americans sometimes needed to watch their English lest they be confused by would-be jihadis with British subjects, so too, following the disasters at Suez and Sarıkamış did Austrians in Turkey need to be careful speaking German.[12]

Far from alleviating inter-alliance tensions, the British withdrawal from Gallipoli and the successful Ottoman siege of Kut-el-Amara seemed to give them new wind. In the euphoria of victory in winter 1915–16, no less than following the run of defeats the previous winter, long-simmering Turkish resentment of outside interference in Ottoman affairs sought release against foreigners, without regard to nationality. In Baghdad that January, hundreds of Christians and Jews were interned as British spies, although Ladislaus von Tahy, the Hungarian Consul, suspected the individuals had actually been targeted for having been seen in the company of Germans and Austrians. Tahy's request for the release of the 'spies' was greeted with a blanket denial, followed by the officially sanctioned looting of Austrian shops in Baghdad. In Palestine at about the same time, German soldiers complained that they had been 'deliberately denied wine and fresh fruit by merchants on orders of the Committee' (i.e. the CUP government). Things were getting so bad that on 30 January 1916 Count Wolff-Metternich, Wangenheim's successor as Ambassador, wrote to Chancellor Bethmann Hollweg that German subjects should henceforward 'be discouraged from travelling in the Ottoman Empire'.[13]

It was sound advice. In the months following Wolff-Metternich's warning, one German jihad agent after another disappeared from sight as the holy war went off the rails. In Persia, following the Russian occupation of Tehran it was clear to bribe-seeking Muslim tribesmen which way the wind was blowing. Seiler, Zugmayer and Griesinger, who had all failed to break the East Persian Cordon at the Afghan border, were arrested by the Persian authorities and turned over to British custody in April 1916. Not wishing to be sold by Emir Habibullah as hostages to the British Raj, Niedermayer and Hentig left Kabul in May. Once more, the rivals split up to lessen the risk of capture, Niedermayer heading back via Persia, while Hentig made a dash for China. Although Niedermayer did make it back to Berlin by autumn, it was not before he had been abandoned in the desert by his Turcoman escorts, having been robbed, beaten and 'left dying of thirst and starvation'. Stubbornly, the hardy Bavarian staggered on to Baghdad on foot, begging all the way.[14] Otto Mannesmann was also relieved of his money and clothes by his Bedouin escorts in the Libyan desert in April 1916, although unlike Niedermayer he did not live to tell the tale. Making his death more shocking, Mannesmann's murderers were the very Sanussi warriors whose holy war he had personally organized and financed since August 1914.[15]

More serious still was the growing number of assaults by resentful Turkish soldiers against German officers kicked off by the von Blum incident in Baghdad in May 1916. According to a rumour picked up and gleefully spread by Russian intelligence, an anti-German pamphlet was making its way around the Ottoman army ranks, exhorting Turkish soldiers not to give their lives 'in order to turn our country into a German colony'. Enver Pasha, the notoriously Germanophile War Minister, was himself assaulted by a bitter Muslim soldier during the Kurban Bayramı that spring, although he escaped relatively unharmed.[16] There were 'persistent rumours', picked up by British intelligence in Cairo, 'of German officers being killed by Turkish soldiers both south of Beersheeba and on the Tigris'.[17] The 'fragging' crisis had grown so serious by June 1916 that twenty-four Ottoman officers were court-martialled for mutinous anti-German incidents. Desperate to deprive angry Muslims of further grounds for assaulting German officers, Enver sent a deputation of Ottoman officers to Potsdam to plead with the Kaiser personally to instruct his officers to show more tact in Turkey.[18]

Small wonder, then, that Enver was not terribly keen on Oppenheim's latest bright idea, that of sending a team of German jihadis through the Hejaz into Yemen to set up a pan-Islamic propaganda centre targeting Sudan and East Africa. 'For a party of Germans to travel through Medina and Mecca,' Enver told the German military attaché on 11 March 1916, 'even under Turkish escort, would be impossible. No one could possibly give a guarantee that they would not be killed along the way.'[19] As if to tempt the holy war fates, Oppenheim assigned as expert adviser to the Stotzingen mission one Karl Neufeld, whose principal claim to fame was having once been captured by the Mahdi in Sudan and held prisoner for eighteen years.* Remarkably, both Neufeld and Stotzingen survived the Arab Bedouin raid which aborted their mission somewhere inland from Yanbo in June 1916, although just about everyone else in their party was killed in the ambush. Another group of German sailors were massacred about the same time somewhere north of Jedda.[20] Licking his wounds in

---

* Neufeld furnishes a fascinating example of what has come to be known as the Stockholm syndrome. Freed by the British at Omdurman in 1898, the famous 'prisoner of the Mahdi' later devoted his life not to taking revenge on his fanatical Islamic captors, but to stirring up Muslim fanaticism to destroy the empire of his rescuers. To crown his new identity as Islamic holy warrior, Neufeld married his eighteen-year-old Kurdish concubine in a traditional Muslim ceremony in Damascus to publicize his conversion to Islam before setting off for Yemen by way of the holy cities of Medina and Mecca. Djemal was not amused.

Damascus in July, Stotzingen conceded that Enver had a point about the Hejaz being unsafe for foreigners – although he blamed the security situation on the impotence of the Ottoman government there, which had been cruelly exposed by the Sherifian revolt.[21]

It is curious to reflect that rumours of the imminent Teutonic take-over of Turkey began to swirl in the Entente camp just as the Germans themselves began to feel the ground shaking underneath their feet. In *Greenmantle* (1916), John Buchan chalked up the Ottoman Empire's surprising resilience in the war to the Germans, whose promotion of Islamic holy war had saved the secularist CUP from the wrath of the Muslim populace. 'It is not a case of Enver and the rest carrying on their shoulders the unpopular Teuton;' Buchan's would-be prophet Sandy Arbuthnot declares, 'it is a case of the Teuton carrying the unpopular Committee'.[22] Buchan had it backwards: by promoting pan-Islamic resentments of infidels the Germans had, inevitably, become targets themselves.

At its mildest, the increasingly xenophobic mood in Turkey mani-fested itself in language reforms. In the first year of the war, censors had begun by shutting down English- and French-language publications. Next to go were advertisements and street signs in Entente languages, which had disappeared from the capital by 1915. In 1916, Talaat began cracking down on public usage of German as well, followed rapidly by Armenian and Greek. Gustav Stresemann, the future Chancellor sent by the Reichstag to investigate the state of the German-Ottoman alli-ance, noticed in March 1916 that German lettering on public signs in the capital was one-third the size of written Turkish.[23] One by one, the old multilingual street and municipal signs of European Pera were replaced with new ones in Ottoman lettering, which few people could actually read.* A group of German advisers were told they would have

---

* Until 1928, Turkish was written in the Arabic script, which suited the language poorly. Whereas Arabic has essentially only one vowel, Turkish has eight. Many Arabic letters have therefore to do double, triple, or even quintuple duty in Ottoman, which makes deciphering texts riddled with guesswork: a single group of letters can literally mean several different things, or indeed nothing at all if one does not know the 'code' of how a particular word is written. Making Ottoman stranger still, one of the more pleasing aural features of Ural-Altaic languages (like Finnish, Hungarian and Turkish) is vowel harmony, which is difficult to render clearly in an alphabet nearly devoid of vowels.

to conduct all official business in Turkish, which was unfortunate, as none of them knew the language. German professors at the University of Istanbul were now required to master Turkish and to wear the fez in the classroom. In Baghdad, German officers were being told they must wear Turkish uniforms so as not to become targets of popular rage.[24] Enver and Talaat were insisting that Berlin and Vienna formally recognize the abolition of the Capitulations, which would remove the last legal protections for foreign nationals in the Ottoman Empire. By spring 1916, wrote Harry Stuermer of the *Kölnische Zeitung*, 'a light had at last gone off' for German civilians in Turkey, who were now leaving the country in droves.[25]

Of course, there was nothing inherently unreasonable about the new requirement that foreigners working in Turkey master the Turkish language. Certainly, knowledge of German was expected of foreigners in Germany and Austria (at least in Vienna), English in England, French in France, and so on. In this, as in their insistence that their own allies finally recognize the long-overdue abolition of the Capitulations, the CUP government was simply insisting on equality of treatment. That the Wilhelmstrasse continued holding out, for fear of losing legal exemptions for German religious and educational institutions on Ottoman territory, was deeply offensive to proud Turks like Enver and Talaat. Were not the Turks and Germans equal as brothers-in-arms?[26]

Still, Berlin had legitimate grounds for concern about the abolition of the Capitulations in an atmosphere of xenophobia and increasingly strident Turkification. There was a long history of popular anti-foreigner riots in Constantinople, particularly in wartime. In late November 1912, as tensions were rising during the First Balkan War, a German restaurant in Pera had been vandalized and looted by Ottoman soldiers, who made a point of desecrating the German imperial flag which had been hung above the entrance to indicate a protected foreign establishment.[27] As food shortages began to bite during the second winter of the world war, it was easy to imagine a repeat episode. As Wolff-Metternich complained in January 1916, high meat prices were being blamed in the press on the Germans – the idea being that cows and sheep were being exported to Germany. The shortage of lamb, something close to sacred in Islamic cuisine (as in the ritual slaughter during the upcoming Kurban Bayramı), could easily spark mob rioting. In the Muslim quarters of Constantinople, Wolff-Metternich warned, 'it was being shouted far and wide, that we should do with the Germans what we did to the Armenians'.[28]

Making the lifting of the Capitulations still more difficult for the Germans to swallow were the Porte's increasingly extortionate financial demands. Was a relationship on equal terms really logical when one alliance partner was picking up nearly the entire cost of the war? As an initial condition for belligerence back in October 1914, Djavid Bey had insisted on a loan of 5 million Turkish gold pounds.[29] It was the first in a long line of insistent financial requests, as Berlin came to be treated like a piggybank by the CUP government.* By the end of 1915, direct German outlays on the Turkish war effort had reached 2 million Turkish pounds a month – and this did not include indirect subsidies such as Deutsche Bank's subvention of the Baghdad railway.[30] In January 1916, a fourth major German gold loan was disbursed to the Porte, worth 20 million Turkish pounds (akin to $10 billion today), intended to back the issue of some 30 million in paper.[31] So assiduously were the Germans supporting the Ottoman Treasury with gold that the Mark was now tumbling against the Turkish lira, dropping from 18.5 to the pound to 24.5, as Matthias Erzberger, another Reichstag deputy on official tour, noted in February 1916. 'There cannot be another example in history,' Erzberger lamented, rivalling 'the way the Turks have taken advantage of us in this war'.[32] During a visit to Vienna in January 1916, a CUP emissary told German Ambassador Tschirschky that even all this generous support was not nearly enough. To appease the 'hostile mood of the Turkish people', the envoy warned, 'some lavish gesture by the German government might be necessary' such as the 'installation of municipal lighting systems and trolley lines throughout the Ottoman Empire at German expense'.[33]

As they awakened with a hangover from the shattered dreams of Oppenheim's holy war, it was beginning to dawn on the Germans that their colossal investments in the Ottoman Empire might indeed go up in smoke even if the Turks won the war. Wolff-Metternich warned

* Asked by an aide, towards the end of the war, why Turkey had made the fateful decision to fight alongside Germany in 1914, Djemal responded, 'so we could pay your salary'.

Berlin in September 1916 that there was little chance Turkey would pay back any of its wartime debts, or honour its obligations to the Baghdad Railway Company.[34] The 'Turkification' of the Baghdad railway was already happening on the ground, in part because so many German employees were leaving. The rail company itself was nearly bankrupt – in fact it already was bankrupt, according to German corporate law (although Deutsche Bank subsidies, underwritten by Berlin, kept it afloat). Periodic Turkish threats to nationalize the railway, although disturbing to German generals and diplomats, began to seem sensible to the moneymen, who wished to wash their hands of the undertaking before they lost everything. In order to stop the bleeding, in October 1916 BRC Director Arthur Gwinner 'urged the Deutsche Bank to cut its losses and turn the entire operation over to the Turks'. Had the line then been complete, Gwinner's offer would probably have been accepted by Enver and Talaat. Because the Taurus and Amanus mountain gaps remained, the Porte demurred, asking that the BRC complete the job. Despite the usual promises – Enver explicitly 'promised the BRC that the Porte would cover the BRC's operations costs for the railway south of the Taurus' – in the end the Germans, of course, paid for everything. Between 1914 and 1918, German banks had raised 250 million Turkish pounds of capital to finance railway construction in the Ottoman Empire (over one billion dollars then, or about $125 billion today). The Porte, for its part, had paid a grand total of 41,000 lira to the BRC, or less than 1/6,000 of the sunk cost – and even this was scraped together from 'other low-interest German loans'.[35] Turkish extortions had bitten Berlin yet again.

One can hardly blame the Germans, then, for feeling under-appreciated by their allies. But the Turks were in no mood to be generous. No matter how much Berlin was paying, the fact remained that Germany, for its own reasons of *Realpolitik*, had helped push the Ottoman Empire into the war – and the war was going badly. The Sherifian revolt killed off any final hopes for the holy war: the Stotzingen mission was the last in a long series of Oppenheim's failures. A far more serious threat to the empire was posed by the Russian advance into Anatolia. In the battle of Erzurum in February, the Turks had lost 327 guns and 15,000 men, nearly half the effective strength of the Third Army. One infantry division, the 34th, had been 'literally annihilated'.[36] At headquarters, there was talk of falling back as far as Amasya and Samsun, or nearly as far west as Ankara – only a short rail journey from the capital. It was like a horrible replay of the 1877 war, as the Erzurum road was clogged with Muslim refugees from the Caucasus.[37] But this time there was no Bismarck or Disraeli to call a halt to the Russian advance. On 18 April 1916, Trabzon fell to the advancing Army of the Caucasus, which cut off one of the capital's main Black Sea ports of supply. By August, the Russians had occupied Muş, Bitlis and Erzincan, threatening Sivas and producing even greater panic in Constantinople than seen when the Allied fleet arrived in the Straits. The British navy was one thing: the Cossacks quite another. The ancient enemy of the Turks was now sweeping through the heartland of Anatolia, living out the worst nightmare of every Ottoman government for centuries.

A search for scapegoats was inevitable. Unsurprisingly, reports trickled in from Cilicia and Syria of another round of Armenian atrocities. In November 1916, the discovery of weapons in an Armenian cemetery in Smyrna prompted a new relocation decree (although Liman soon intervened to stop these deportations).[38] Closer to the line of the Russian advance, there were reports of massacres of Pontic Greeks along the Black Sea coast near Trabzon, which heralded a new deportation campaign. In all, some 100,000 Ottoman Greek Christians were expelled to Greece during the war, mostly from Gallipoli (in 1915) and the Black Sea region (in 1916), while another 50,000 or so were resettled away from war zones in Anatolia. Thousands of Kurds, too, were deported from areas in the line of the Russian advance in 1916 and 1917, for similar reasons.[39] Although Kurdish irregulars had played a notorious role in the Armenian massacres in 1915, many Kurdish tribal leaders had been taking bribes from Petrograd for years. With the Third Army 'all but destroyed' by the Russian offensives of 1916, the Porte was taking no chances with possibly disloyal minorities, even Kurdish Muslims.[40]

As principal sponsor and cheerleader of the Ottoman war effort, Germany took the lion's share of the blame for the catastrophe of 1916. According to a British agent, Turkish officers in Constantinople were 'exasperated' that 'all the best houses and hotels in Pera and on the Bosphorus have been requisitioned by German officers'.[41]

And these luxurious buildings where Germans lived and worked, reported a Russian agent in June, were now defended by German machine-gun units from the wrath of the Muslim mob.[42] Following the dramatic Russian advance in August, German civilians in the capital were issued hand grenades to defend themselves from angry rioters.[43] From Sivas, Karl Werth, the German Consul, reported that Russian and Turkish officers had been seen fraternizing in Erzincan, with talk of a separate peace to be lubricated by the Turks turning over German officers as a prize – or better yet, by slaughtering them.[44] In Sivas itself, one of Werth's informants had attended a dinner with thirteen Ottoman officers who had spoken openly of the need for German soldiers to leave Turkey immediately to avoid 'a frightful massacre'.[45]

Werth's warning was almost certainly exaggerated.* But German nationals really were on increasingly shaky ground in the Ottoman Empire. It was common in school lessons for Germany to be blamed for inflicting the horrors of the world war on Turkey.[46] German propaganda had turned into a farce. Oppenheim's jihad bureau in the Pera Embassy was a laughing stock after the story broke that his lead holy war writer in the Turkish press, 'Mehmed Zeki Bey', was actually a Romanian Jewish conman who had recently done a turn running a bordello in Buenos Aires.[47] German cultural outreach fared no better. Turks, it turned out, did not have a great deal of interest in German light opera, even if it was up to the standard of the Stuttgarter Hoftheater.[48] The arrogance of a new highbrow initiative dreamed up by Ernst Jäckh, which brought academics, lecturers and German-language periodicals to Turkey to counter the preference of Ottoman elites for French, offended even Enver, who complained to Field Marshal Hindenburg in November 1916.[49] As Humann, the German naval attaché, wrote to his friend Jäckh, 'Germany and Turkey do not understand each other at all any more, I believe, neither the statesmen, nor the people.'[50]

Of course, the root of Enver's bitterness had little to do with high culture. As Enver lamented to Humann in November, 'we have lost

---

* Because Werth was of Levantine Christian stock, his reports were generally dismissed at the Wilhelmstrasse on grounds of anti-Muslim bias.

seven provinces, hecatombs of our people have been sacrificed, and our economy has been utterly ruined'. And Enver, Humann warned Berlin, actually liked Germans, unlike nearly everyone else in Turkey. To salvage what remained of the German position in the Ottoman Empire, Enver told Humann that Berlin needed to make a 'grand gesture'. What he had in mind was German acceptance of the abolition of the Capitulations – in perpetuity – along with the abrogation of three hated treaties which limited Ottoman control over the Straits and Christian communities in the empire: Paris (1858), London (1871) and Berlin (1878). Only if the Wilhelmstrasse dramatically freed Turkey from 'these last shackles of international oppression', the Ottoman Foreign Minister told German Embassy counsellor Wilhelm von Radowitz in November 1916, could Germans win back the Turks' trust.[51]

Although the German government did finally sign off on the abolition of the Capitulations in January 1917, the decision was clearly taken under duress. Theoretically, the agreement put the wartime allies on a footing of 'mutual equality'.[52] This did not mean, of course, that the Porte would start paying the war's costs. By way of celebrating the new relationship between 'equals', Djavid proposed, while visiting Berlin, that following the war Germany should embark on an aid programme to revamp the moribund Ottoman economy, showering their ally with 'German capital, German machines, and German engineers'.[53] To make it work, Djavid suggested Berlin put up about 150 to 160 million Marks annually for ten years.[54] In view of the rather poor return the Germans had received on their investments to date, Djavid's 'offer' was less than overwhelming. A German Foreign Office study conducted in March 1917 concluded that by the end of the year, Berlin would have sent to the Porte three billion Marks' worth of gold and war *matériel* since 1914 (equal to $800 million then, or some $80 billion today).[55] Before considering new loans or investments, the Germans decided at an inter-ministerial conference in April 1917, a Deutsche Bank-led consortium must receive concrete concession guaranties to Turkish coal, copper, iron and phosphate deposits – and not least Mesopotamian oil.[56]

If the Turks had reason to resent Germany for pushing them into a war which had cost them so much territory and manpower, the Germans were also hard pressed to see what they had so far gained for their colossal outlays on the Turkish fronts. Had the February Revolution not cut the legs out from under the Russian war effort in 1917, the Army of the Caucasus might have crashed into Constantinople, ending the war right then and there, and putting paid to the German *Drang nach Osten*. Relief at the Porte was short-lived, however. As if relieving a tired football player as he left the pitch, the British resumed their Mesopotamian offensive in January, retaking Kut-el-Amara in February and storming up the Tigris. Considering the symbolic importance of the city, both in Islamic history and German imperial dreams, it is astonishing that Baghdad was taken without a fight after the Turks evacuated the city on 10 March 1917.*[57]

Only Khalil Pasha, von der Goltz's successor as Sixth Army commander, knew why he ordered the fateful retreat from Baghdad. But he may well have given up the city because the Germans had left him in the lurch. As the chargé d'affaires of the Austrian Embassy reported a week before the British reached Baghdad, the Turks were complaining that there were no German troops left in Mesopotamia. Worse, word from provincial Consulates was that Germans were reacting to news of Turkish defeats with 'unconcealed *Schadenfreude*'. Now that 'the Turks had repelled German cooperation with loathing', the German refrain went, 'the Turks would have to rely on themselves, and it was self-evident, that it would end badly'.[58] A week after the fall of Baghdad, Pallavicini reported that German prestige had been seriously damaged by the belief that they had deliberately chosen to abandon Mesopotamia in order to spite the Turks. Whether or not the rumours were true, the Germans were not making any effort to refute them.[59]

Worse was to come. A new round of stories spread through the press in August 1917 that the Germans were deliberately starving the Turkish people. So worried were German officers about an impending massacre that they leaned on Erich Ludendorff, the Quartermaster General who was, in effect, military dictator after Chancellor Bethmann Hollweg's resignation that July, to intervene.[60] The soldiers' concern was not idle: just days later, a German officer, Philipp Schultz, was

---

* As if wishing to sweep the whole episode under the rug, news of the fall of Baghdad was suppressed in Constantinople – and successfully too, for nearly a month. Predictably, when the news finally filtered down to the Muslims of Stambul in mid-April 1917, a wave of anti-German rioting swept through the city.

lynched in Mesopotamia.[61] Because of elaborate security measures, and the flooding of the capital with German troops – there were 20,000 in Constantinople alone by 1918, even as the Mesopotamian front had been emptied of Germans – the anti-German mood in the capital did not claim more lives that autumn.[62] But the mob may have found a better target for its rage. On 6 September 1917, a terrible fire raged through Haydarpasha station, producing a tremendous explosion as artillery rounds and explosives were caught up in the conflagration. So strong was the blast that it 'blew out windows in homes in Pera', the European colony on top of a high elevated ridge on the other side of the Bosphorus, nearly five miles away. With the Mesopotamian terminus already in British hands, it was a fittingly apocalyptic end to the Kaiser's Berlin-to-Baghdad dreams.[63]

If three billion Marks had not been enough to conjure up a holy war strong enough to fell the British Empire, however, the closure of the Straits brought about through Turkey's entry into the war had still wrought serious damage in Russia. The February Revolution had bought precious time for the Ottoman armies, which, despite the endless run of bad news from Anatolia, Mesopotamia and Palestine, were still in the field. Meanwhile, another covert campaign cooked up by the German Foreign Office was just now coming to maturity.* If Lenin and the Bolsheviks succeeded in knocking Russia out of the world war, perhaps Germany's *Drang nach Osten* could resume after all, without the Turks who had resolved on sabotaging it. With their hearts broken by the fall of Baghdad, German war-planners now set their sights on the oilfields of Baku.

---

* And another was blowing up in the Germans' faces: the Zimmermann telegram of 16 January 1917 promising Texas, Arizona and New Mexico to Mexico if she declared war on the US. The telegram was intercepted and decoded by the British, who (very carefully) brought it to Washington's attention, thus giving the Wilson administration a *casus belli* to enter the war against Germany.

19

Consolation Prize?
The Race for Baku

> *Enver's demand, that we should win back for Turkey her 1877*
> *borders in the Caucasus [at the upcoming negotiations at*
> *Brest-Litovsk], is to me just typically extortionate Oriental*
> *haggling ... Baldly stated, [Turkey] is nothing more to us now*
> *than a political, military, financial and moral burden.*

Count Bernstorff, German Ambassador to the Porte, to State
Secretary Richard von Kühlmann, 17 December 1917[1]

Among their other world-altering consequences, the Russian Revolutions of 1917 opened up a critical caesura in the history of the First World War. Those few historians who have tackled the complexities of the Eastern Front tend to round out their narratives in 1917, when the breakdown of morale in the Tsarist armies brought serious fighting there to a halt.[2] Although histories of campaigning in the Middle Eastern theatre do devote considerable attention to the British offensives of 1917–18 in Mesopotamia, Palestine and Syria, concurrent developments on the Turkish-Russian front lines – in eastern Anatolia, Transcaucasia and Persian Azerbaijan – receive short shrift, if they are mentioned at all. In the official history of the world war prepared by the Turkish General Staff, the entirety of 1917 merits only twenty pages out of 1,660, or about 1.5 per cent; and even these mostly concern the British, not the Russian, sector.[3]

Considering how poor the literature on Russia's performance in the First World War remains generally, it is not surprising that we know so little about the Caucasian front. The Soviet government, perhaps in order to conceal the origins of the Bolshevik regime in a humiliating surrender to Russia's enemies in the Great War, never got around to publishing a history of the conflict: to this day no official chronicle has appeared. Western historians have not done much better on the Caucasian theatre, in part owing to a near-exclusive focus on the Armenian question, which has drowned out serious discussion of military developments in eastern Anatolia. Those few histories of the region which do go beyond the Armenian controversy treat the world war and the Russian Revolution in classic 'before and after' fashion, with little connecting thread to weave together the two stories. After surveying the literature as it exists today, one could be forgiven for concluding that there was a victorious Russian army occupying eastern Anatolia in 1916, which, sometime in 1917, grew so exhausted that the men all decided to declare defeat, pack up and go home.[4]

How could this happen? To penetrate the mysterious collapse of Russia's victorious Army of the Caucasus, we must pay careful attention to both geography and chronology. Whereas the 'Kerensky' offensive of June 1917 on the Galician front, and the successful German counter-attack which repulsed it in July, exposed deep cracks in Russian army morale, we must not forget that these men were facing Germans. However formidable an enemy the Turks had proved while entrenched at Gallipoli, in the mountain snows of eastern Anatolia it was generally the Russians who had had the better of the fighting. In 1916, as we have seen, the Army of the Caucasus had the run of eastern Anatolia, and could quite possibly have pushed on to Ankara, had the order come from above. The Ottoman Third Army, by contrast, had been wrecked by the Russian offensives of 1916, and was haemorrhaging deserters. Overall Ottoman losses on the Anatolian front from disease, desertion and deaths to date numbered over 100,000 men, leaving behind only shattered remnants of the army Enver had sent to Sarıkamış. By the time of the February Revolution, the Ottoman Third Army was at breaking point, preserved from annihilation only because of the severity of the winter, which had prevented the Russians from resuming the eastern Anatolian offensive.[5]

Little wonder, then, that the Russians held their lines at Bitlis, Erzincan, Erzurum, Muş and Trabzon through summer 1917 even as the Russian Eighth Army was breaking in Galicia. The Russian *muzhiks* who had taken these formidable fortress cities were proud heroes of their country: why would they wish to turn tail and surrender? Pride in the victories of 1916 must explain why, despite the resignation of Grand Duke Nicholas from his Caucasian command following the Tsar's abdication in March, the February Revolution did not greatly disturb discipline in the Grand Duke's army. Nicholas was immediately replaced by General Yudenich, who, as Chief of Staff, had been the real mastermind of the defence of Sarıkamış and the sack of Erzurum. (Yudenich would later distinguish himself as White commander of the North-western Army which nearly captured Petrograd during the Russian Civil War.) Although soldier 'soviets' spread through the Caucasian army as everywhere else in Russia, the heroes of Erzurum proved, in the main, to be more patriots than pacifists. As Yudenich himself reported in March 1917, 'the membership of the [soldiers'] committees is generally favourable in the sense of the inclination to strengthen law and order and to conduct the war to a victorious end'. At a soldiers' congress held in April in Tiflis (Tbilisi), a ranking general was even elected chairman, a development inconceivable in the mutinous northern garrisons which had cracked in the face of the German advance.[6]

It was not only the lingering afterglow of Erzurum which accounted for the resistance of the Caucasian army to the mutinous spirit of 1917. Outside Baku, which, as a result of the oil boom, had acquired a large urban proletariat receptive to Bolshevism – and where the large Azeri Turkish population tended (for obvious reasons) to be less supportive than others of the war against Turkey – Bolshevik defeatism was nowhere to be found in the Caucasus. Tiflis, where the army command was located, was dominated by the Mensheviks and Kerensky's party, the Social Revolutionaries (SRs), both of which favoured continuing the war – a popular position on a front where the Russians had so far been unambiguously victorious. Caucasian Armenians, in particular, were ferociously committed to winning the war with Turkey, so as to avenge the massacres of 1915. Despite their ostensibly revolutionary credentials, Dashnak leaders were so obsessed with defeating the Turks that many were now giving speeches celebrating 'Russian imperialism'.[7] Although the Bolsheviks strove all spring and summer to create party cells in the Caucasian army, with the exception of the 2nd Grenadier Division and a few regiments in the First Caucasus Division, they made little headway against the regional tide of pro-war sentiment.[8]

It was not until news of Lenin's seizure of power reached the Caucasus in November that mutinies began at last to sap the strength of the Caucasian army. For those who persist in viewing the October Revolution as a genuine 'proletarian' uprising, the connection between labour upheaval in Petrograd and the disintegration of the Caucasian army thousands of miles to the south must seem perplexing. But of course the 'revolution' in Petrograd was nothing of the kind. The takeover of the Russian capital during the night of 24–25 October (6–7 November) 1917 was in fact a meticulously planned paramilitary operation carried out by a political party, the Bolsheviks, who, though strong in the Petrograd Soviet, commanded little popular support in the country at large. What Lenin's party did have, if not popularity, was a clear agenda: ending the war immediately by any means necessary. By announcing a 'decree on peace' which amounted to a unilateral ceasefire in the war, the Bolsheviks in effect surrendered the world war to Russia's enemies. When General Nikolai Dukhonin, Commander-in-Chief of what remained of the Russian armies, refused to obey the Bolshevik ceasefire order (which was accompanied by the mischievous instruction that soldiers begin 'fraternizing' with the enemy), Lenin broadcast a wireless message to the troops denouncing him as a 'counter-revolutionary' (taking the cue perfectly, a mutinous mob lynched Dukhonin in early December).[9] The final nail in the coffin of the Tsarist army was the Bolshevik 'decree on land', which all but invited peasant-soldiers to desert and rush home to claim their fair share of 'socialized' landed estates. The proud *muzhiks* of the Caucasian army may not have been happy about forfeiting their victories over the Turks – in fact the soldiers' committee roundly condemned the Bolshevik coup as 'illegitimate' in a resolution passed on 8 November 1917 – but few wanted to be the last soldier standing in far-off Anatolia when the great peasant land-grab began.[10]

It is only when we understand the intimate connection between Bolshevism and German foreign policy that we can begin to make sense of the astonishing 'self-demobilization' of the still undefeated Army of the Caucasus.[11] It was precisely in order to sabotage the Russian war effort that the Wilhelmstrasse had sent Lenin from Switzerland to Petrograd in April 1917. Whereas before Lenin's arrival in Russia the Bolsheviks had no newspapers at all, within days of his arrival they had more than 100,000 copies of three pacifist-revolutionary dailies, including *Soldatskaia Pravda* (targeting rearguard soldiers and enlistees), *Golos Pravdy* (aimed at sailors), and *Okopnaia Pravda* (pitched at front-line troops). There is no longer any question that funding for these newspapers – which urged Russian troops to realize that their true enemies were not Germans, but their own 'capitalist' oppressors – came from the German Foreign Office, which was now disgorging Communist literature no less meretricious than the jihad propaganda cooked up by Oppenheim in 1914.[12]

The Bolshevik seizure of power in November provided an immediate pay-off for the Germans. To accompany his 'decree on peace', Lenin personally contacted the German General Staff on 25 November 1917 with a telegram sent *en clair*, requesting an immediate ceasefire – without the slightest precondition (followed by Trotsky's public announcement of a Russian ceasefire the following day).[13] What little morale was left at the front following the 'decree on land' desertion free-for-all was sundered by the Bolsheviks' amazing decision actively to disband the existing Russian army in order to allow a new, revolutionary ('Red') army to be raised from scratch, as if Lenin wished in the meantime to invite in the Germans to take over the country.[14] As if this was not enough, Trotsky's notorious publication of the 'secret treaties' of the Entente powers exposed Russia's own expansionist war aims to international opprobrium, which cut the legs out from under any effort to hold on to conquests in Turkish Anatolia. (A popular Bolshevik anti-war slogan was 'We don't want the Dardanelles!')[15] So sweeping was the collapse of the once-mighty army that some of the Germans who had organized Lenin's trip to Russia became embarrassed by how aggressively their man was sabotaging the Russian war effort. Kurt Riezler, State Secretary Kühlmann's liaison to the Bolshevik Foreign Mission in Stockholm, pointedly warned his Foreign Office colleagues to conceal in public their glee (*Freude*) at how well the whole operation was going.[16]

Even the Germans were amazed by the stunningly rapid disintegration of the Russian army following the Bolshevik takeover of the Russian government. But it was no accident. Sabotaging the Tsar's army with revolutionary propaganda, as we saw in chapter 4, had been a cardinal goal of the German Foreign Office since the start of the war. In the 16 August 1914 'Overview of Revolutionary Activity We Will Undertake in the Islamic-Israelite World', prepared by Otto von Wesendonck for Under-Secretary Zimmermann's Foreign Office sabotage bureau, Wesendonck had woven together the idea of spreading sedition through Jewish-dominated exile groups hostile to the Tsar with the jihad stratagem aimed at toppling the British Empire.[17] If the latter gambit had proven a costly failure, the former had now come to world-famous fruition. Following the catastrophe which had befallen the Ottomans in 1916, the October Revolution offered a new lease of life for the Turco-German holy war. As Wesendonck himself declared (from Tiflis, where he had recently been posted by the Wilhelmstrasse as special envoy) in the initial wave of euphoria following Lenin's coup, 'even the idea of a German land-route to China can no longer be dismissed as a fantasy'.[18]

There was, however, a serious problem. By 1917, as we saw in chapter 18, there was little trust left between Berlin and the Porte. The Ottoman Empire stood poised to reap the greatest benefit from the collapse of her northern nemesis. But in truth the Turks had had little to do with it. Neither the Second nor the Third Ottoman Armies had so much as staged a single serious offensive in 1917. The Russians had been broken not in eastern Anatolia, but by the relentless advance of the Germans in eastern Europe, which produced panic in Petrograd and paved the way for German-sponsored Bolshevik sedition. As the Turks themselves must have known, the fortuitous melting away of the Caucasian army was mere spillover from the general destruction of the Tsarist armies. And the Germans were damned if they were going to let Turkey share in the spoils of their great victory. As soon as news of the October Revolution reached the Porte in mid-November 1917, Turkish newspapers like *Sabah* and *Tasvir-i Efkar* were loudly advocating 'the immediate recovery of lands in eastern Anatolia and Transcaucasia'.[19] Even the normally unexcitable Talaat thought that the Russian Revolution had 'opened the doors to the realization of Turkey's eastern empire'. It was no longer enough that the Ottomans win back Bitlis, Erzincan, Erzurum, Muş and Trabzon to restore the status quo ante of 1914: nationalistic Turks now wanted *Elviye-i Selâse*, the three lost provinces of Batumi, Ardahan and Kars, to reverse Russian gains during the war of 1877. By December, Count Johann Heinrich von Bernstorff, the new German Ambassador to the

Porte, had heard enough. On 17 December 1917, just three days before peace negotiations began at Brest-Litovsk, Bernstorff launched a pre-emptive strike, warning Berlin not to countenance the Turks' 'Oriental haggling'.[20]

It was not only growing impatience with Turkish extortions which lay behind Berlin's reluctance to grant Ottoman demands in the Caucasus. With tanks, lorries and aeroplanes playing an increasingly important role on the western front, the Germans were desperate for oil. Whereas France and Britain could draw on the Abadan refinery in the Persian Gulf and colossal American reserves as well (the US had joined the Entente as an 'associated' power in April 1917), the Central Powers' Galician oilfields had been destroyed by the retreating Russian army and they now only had Romania's Ploesti oilfields, which had been severely damaged by a British sabotage team in November 1916. True, there were tremendous oil deposits in northern Mesopotamia, but after the fall of Baghdad in March 1917 these were bound to fall under British control. With the great Baku oilfields now in play due to Russia's collapse, the Germans were not about to let the Turks beat them to the Caspian.[*21] Nor was Berlin eager to restore Batumi, wrested away by Russia in the 1877 war, to the Porte: for whoever ruled this Black Sea port would control the crucial terminus of the Transcaucasian oil pipeline (completed in 1903), from which Caspian oil was exported to European markets. In between Baku and Batumi, the pipeline and the railway parallel to it ran through Tiflis, where the Georgian population was known to be enthusiastically pro-German. With Mesopotamia in British hands, marking the end of the Kaiser's Berlin-to-Baghdad dreams, the Transcaucasian railway and oil pipeline were at the heart of the new German Great Game strategy, the axis of which would now run, in Pomiankowski's formulation, 'across the Black Sea, then over Batumi, Tiflis and Baku' to 'Persia and Afghanistan'.[22]

As the representatives of Germany, Austria-Hungary and the Ottoman Empire descended on Brest-Litovsk on 20 December 1917 to impose a punitive peace on Bolshevik Russia, the Transcaucasus was the elephant in the room which threatened to undermine what little comity

---

* Following the Bolshevik coup the German Foreign Office ordered up a thorough study of Baku's oil reserves.

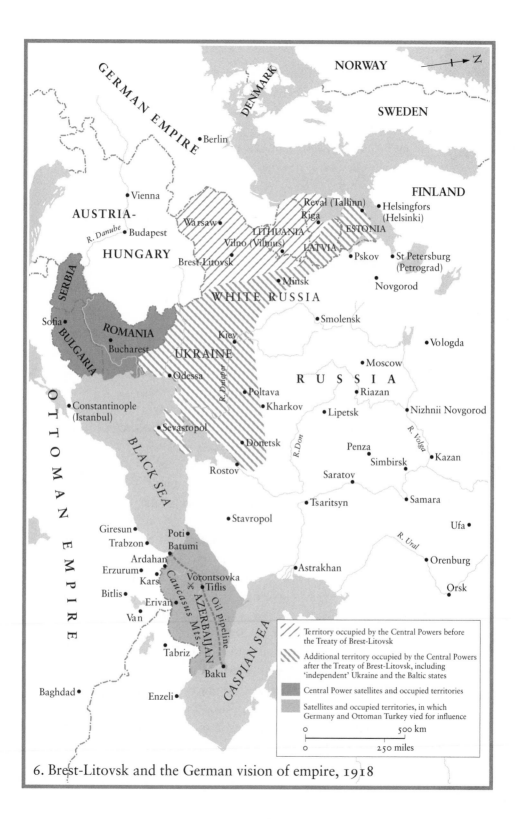

6. Brest-Litovsk and the German vision of empire, 1918

remained between the Central Powers. It was not so hard to agree on detaching Ukraine, White Russia and the Baltic provinces from the Russian Empire. So long as Ukrainian grain reached Constantinople and Vienna – both of which were feeling the pinch of food shortages – the Turks and Austrians were happy to let the Germans to take up the bulk of occupation duty and run the new satellite states.

The Caucasus, however, was another matter. For centuries the Porte had been in a life-and-death struggle with the Russians for control of Turkish Armenia and Transcaucasia. In the give and take of a hundred battles, the borders had moved, now east, now west, although since the seventeenth century things had mostly gone Russia's way. Now, following two centuries of humiliation, it was Turkey's turn for revenge – if only the Germans would let her have it. Baku, with its large concentration of Azeri Turks and port access to the Caspian and the Turkic peoples of Central Asia beyond, was just as glittering a prize for the Porte as for Berlin. Nor was the CUP leadership ignorant of the strategic importance of oil in modern warfare, particularly as Turkey remained too poor to import more than a bare minimum of her potential petroleum needs on the open market. Far from being the blindly romantic pan-Turanian of legend, who dreamed only of conquering the Central Asiatic steppe on horseback, Enver had coolly calculated the importance of Caspian oil for the Ottoman future, and – again contrary to his reputation as Germany's gullible tool – he was not willing in the least to trust the Germans to supply it to Turkey. With the stakes this high, neither side would give up easily.[23]

Of course, the future of Baku was not the only contentious issue at Brest-Litovsk. Before ironing out the political future of the Caucasus, the Central Powers had first to get the Russians to surrender it. While the Bolsheviks had wasted little time in destroying the fighting strength of the Russian army, they were in no rush to ratify a Carthaginian peace sure to humiliate whichever government signed it. As 'internationalists' expecting copycat mutiny-revolutions to sweep across Europe as soon as their stop-the-war message got out, the Bolsheviks believed time was on their side. As Trotsky explained, 'We began peace negotiations in the hope of arousing the workmen's parties of Germany and Austria-Hungary as well as those of the Entente countries. For this reason we were obliged to delay the negotiations as long as possible to give the European workmen time to understand ... the Soviet revolution ... and particularly its peace policy.'[24]

Trotsky's hope that the belligerent powers would fall one after another to Russian-style revolutions may have been misplaced. Still, the delaying tactics he urged on the Bolshevik negotiating team seemed sensible in light of the onerous peace terms the Central Powers were insisting on. The Germans wanted to detach from Russia her most prosperous European provinces: Finland, the Baltic states (then known as Estonia, Livonia and Courland), Poland and the Ukraine. The Turks were demanding an immediate Russian troop withdrawal from the Caucasus, which was obviously meant to be a prelude to a Turkish invasion. Not surprisingly, the Russian delegation, led by Adolf Joffe, hemmed and hawed its way through the first week at Brest-Litovsk, departing for Petograd on 28 December without signing any such agreement.

Having themselves sponsored the revolution which brought Lenin to power, the Germans were willing to indulge Bolshevik prevarication, but only up to a point. Reaching a settlement during the first December session at Brest-Litovsk was not imperative for Berlin, as the Wilhelmstrasse had given the Entente Powers (which had refused to recognize Lenin's regime, viewing it as a German puppet government) until 4 January 1918 to join in the negotiations. After this deadline came and went, talks resumed at Brest-Litovsk in January with a much greater sense of urgency on the German side. The Bolsheviks, of course, were just as intent on stalling as before; but to avoid angering the Germans they needed to appear to take the negotiations seriously. As Joffe told the Bolshevik Foreign Minister, Lev Trotsky, in order to recuse himself, 'to delay negotiations there must be someone to do the delaying'. Trotsky took the hint, travelling to Brest-Litovsk himself to take charge of the Bolshevik team on 8 January 1918.[25]

Trotsky's theatrical performance at Brest-Litovsk has become an integral part of his political legend. Subjecting his diplomatic opponents to endless harangues in which he accused them of 'nauseating him' with their imperialistic greed and hypocrisy – the Russian's stubborn insistence that the Germans simply admit they were 'annexing' Russian territory, rather than allowing satellites to hold plebiscites on whether or not to declare 'independence', was a particular gem – Trotsky progressively drove his interlocutors mad. Count Czernin, the Austrian Foreign Minister, was so fed up with the 'endless spiritual wrestling matches' with this 'wild beast' that, in his diary, he fantasized that a 'Charlotte Corday' would appear on the scene to assassinate Trotsky.*[26]

Richard von Kühlmann, the German State Secretary who had overseen German support for Lenin in 1917, was somewhat friendlier than Czernin to Trotsky.†[27] Unlike Ludendorff and the German military brass, Kühlmann was genuinely interested in ending the war, as he did not believe the Kaiser's government could survive the popular strain of another year's fighting – and he was particularly anxious about the ambitious offensive he knew Ludendorff was planning on the western front. But Kühlmann could not control General Max Hoffman, Ludendorff's liaison officer at Brest-Litovsk. As commander of the German armies on the eastern front, Hoffman had no intention of evacuating his troops from Russian territories already captured – as he betrayed to everyone at Brest-Litovsk (and to those who read newspaper reports of the proceedings) in a notoriously blunt diatribe on 12 January 1918. Following Hoffman's tirade, even Kühlmann, against his better wishes, was forced to concede to Trotsky that Germany would not 'recall its army from the occupied territories, even a year after the conclusion of [peace]'.[28]

Six days later, Trotsky returned to Petrograd in apparent triumph. Not only had he won yet more time without signing a humiliating treaty, Trotsky had greatly embarrassed the Central Powers, whose leaders would now have to explain to increasingly impatient domestic critics why they were still at war with a country (Russia) which no longer had an army. Annoying he certainly was, but Trotsky was also something of a genius. Who else would have come up with the impractical, yet catchy, theoretical doctrine of 'no war, no peace' (Trotsky's position as the Brest-Litovsk negotiations resumed in February), by which was meant that Russia would declare the war over and order a 'general demobilization on all fronts' without actually surrendering?

---

* Charlotte Corday was the notorious assassin of Jean-Paul Marat, the rabid and bloodthirsty French Revolutionary radical who had cheered on Robespierre's terror.

† Kühlmann was also friendlier to Turkish aspirations. As against Bernstorff's blanket denial of the Turkish demand for restoration of the 1877 borders, he told Hakkı Pasha that 'we will be very pleased if you can get [them], but it will be difficult'.

So bewildered was Hoffman upon hearing Trotsky's bizarre proposal on 9 February that he could muster only a single word in reply: *Unerhört!* ('Unheard of'). It was likely with this performance at Brest-Litovsk in mind that Colonel Raymond Robins, the US liaison to Lenin's as yet unrecognized Russian government, called Trotsky 'a four-kind son of a bitch, but the greatest Jew since Jesus'. If it was true that the 'German General Staff had bought Trotsky', Robins helpfully added, 'they bought a lemon'.[29]

Or had they? Just as Hoffman's impolitic diatribe had injected fuel into the engine of Bolshevik 'peace' propaganda back in January, so now did Trotsky's self-infatuated 'no war, no peace' gambit in February bring the Central Powers together in mutual disgust. If it was a bluff, it was a bluff very easily called. If the Bolsheviks were really going to demobilize what remained of the Russian army on all fronts, then why not simply move across the armistice lines? The beleaguered Austrians, to be sure, were in no position to strike, but this was all the better for the Germans, who could now take the Baltic provinces and Ukraine for themselves: and promptly did so in one of the most peculiar routs in military history.* Trotsky may have got a rise out of Hoffman, but the general had the last laugh. As he later recalled the February campaign, 'This is the most comic war that I have ever experienced ... One puts on the train a few infantry with machine guns and one artillery piece, and proceeds to the next railroad station, seizes it, arrests the Bolsheviks, entrains another detachment, and moves on. The procedure has in any event the charm of novelty.'[30] As if to defeat Trotsky on the intellectual plane as well, Hoffman gloated publicly that 'Trotsky's theories could not resist facts'.[31]

Following Hoffman's lead, Enver ordered the Ottoman Third Army on the offensive without delay. The Turks proceeded with only slightly less efficiency than the Germans, recapturing Erzincan on 14 February, Trabzon ten days later, and Erzurum on 12 March. By the first week of April, the Third Army had retaken Ardahan and Sarıkamış, scene

---

* Delegates from the Ukrainian Rada signed a 'peace' treaty with imperial Germany at Brest-Litovsk on 8 February, independent of Moscow. Since the Bolsheviks had captured Kiev the previous day, there was little doubt that the Ukrainians, despite proclaiming independence, had agreed, in effect, to a German protectorate in which Hoffman was expected to move in and expel any remaining Russian troops.

of Enver's catastrophe in January 1915. With no Russian Caucasian army left to oppose them, the Turks had reversed three years of Russian gains in less than two months, restoring the 1914 borders (and going slightly past them) while hardly breaking a sweat.[32] So infuriated were the Germans by Trotsky's delaying tactics that they forgot all about their earlier opposition to Turkish expansion as Enver's army advanced. Far from protesting at the latest Ottoman offensives, in the ultimatum dispatched to the Bolsheviks on 23 February 1918 the Germans even demanded that 'Russia shall do everything in her power to guarantee a speedy and orderly return of the East Anatolian provinces to Turkey'. For good measure, the Germans also insisted that Lenin's regime accept the abolition of the Capitulations. In the final Brest-Litovsk treaty, signed by the Bolsheviks on 3 March 1918, the Germans implicitly accepted Enver's demand for the old 1877 borders by stipulating that 'the districts of Ardahan, Kars and Batumi will likewise and without delay be cleared of Russian troops'.[33] Taking this as permission for Turkish penetration of the Caucasus, Enver recalled his brother Nuri from Libya, to put a trusted relative in charge of the Third Army's relentless push to the Caspian.[34] In this way, the 'greatest Jew since Jesus' helped unleash Islamic holy war in the Caucasus.

Of course, Enver had not really needed German permission to win back Turkey's old borders. As early as 23 January, long before Trotsky had exhausted Berlin's patience with his 'no war, no peace' grandstanding, Enver had ordered preparations for a Third Army offensive to begin, dispatching two infantry divisions and 120 motor-driven trucks across the Black Sea to Giresun.[35] There were sound strategic reasons for the resumption of the Turkish offensive, not least a decree 'On Armenia' co-signed by Lenin and Stalin on 11 January 1918, which proposed self-determination, rather than Ottoman rule, in eastern Anatolia. While Trotsky was prevaricating with theatrical flair at Brest-Litovsk, the Bolsheviks had begun quietly repatriating – and arming – some 100,000 Armenian veterans of the Tsarist army to the Caucasus, with an eye to resisting Turkish penetration. It was this pro-Armenian move which convinced policy-makers at the Porte, notably Talaat, that, despite all the pacifist rhetoric emanating from Moscow, 'the Russian leopard had not changed its spots'.[36] With Armenian militia units bent on revenge mobilizing against them,

Ottoman infantrymen were not lacking in motivation, particularly after witnessing horrendous scenes in many of the cities they recaptured from the departing Tsarist Army of the Caucasus. In Erzincan, the Turks reported that 'all the wells were stuffed with corpses', nearly all of them Muslims.[37] Many of these atrocities could well have been committed by Russian soldiers, but the same was not true in Baku, where on 31 March–1 April 1918 several thousand Azeri Turkish Muslims were massacred, reputedly by Armenian bandits. The bloodbath in Baku may or may not have been conceived in retaliation for the 'Shamkhor massacre' in January, which had seen an Azerbaijani band slaughter several hundred disarmed Tsarist army soldiers, mostly Russians.[38] Whoever bore the blame for the latest round of Muslim–Christian violence, the Turks were hardly going to abandon their Azerbaijani 'brothers' in a time of need. As Vehip Pasha, commander of the Ottoman Caucasian Army Group, justified the Turkish advance beyond the 1914 borders in a telegram dispatched to Russian military headquarters, 'the Armenians are resolved to destroy and annihilate Ottoman Muslims'.[39] The fall of Kars on 25 April 1918, reversing Russia's last conquest from the Berlin Treaty of 1878, was a historic occasion in Constantinople. Even if she had lost Arabia, Mesopotamia and Palestine, Ottoman Turkey had now fully restored the 1877 borders against her hereditary Russian enemy, just as Enver had dreamed.

Had the Turks stopped in Kars to consolidate their gains and reinforced defences in Anatolia and Thrace, Enver might have gone down in history as the greatest living Turk.* But to call a halt at this favourable juncture would have contradicted everything in his nature. At Sarıkamış, Enver had risked everything when the odds were stacked against him. Facing little but Armenian and Georgian militiamen, where before had stood the entire Tsarist Caucasian Army, Enver was not about to back down now. In Batumi, Turkish diplomats were now imposing their own peace terms on the 'Transcaucasian Federated Republic' (which had declared independence on 22 April), and they were even more onerous than those of Brest-Litovsk, notably including

---

* One might easily say the same of Ludendorff as the 'greatest living German', had he taken Kühlmann's advice to sue the Allies for peace following the German victory on the eastern front, instead of staking everything on one last great offensive in the west.

'the free use by the Turks of all Transcaucasian railways' and the ominous hint that 'the Ottoman Government will provide military support to the Azerbaijani Government if this is seen as necessary by the latter for domestic stability and national security'.[40] The threat was clear. Whether by invitation or invasion, the Turks would take the Transcaucasus – and Baku.

Enver's aggressive manoeuvres could not fail to arouse the jealous interest of other powers, not least his own Teutonic ally. Having reawakened from the spell of Turcophilia which had overcome them as they endured Trotsky's February harangues, the Germans were again on full alert – and they were not much further from the Caspian than the Turks were. After pausing to allow the Bolsheviks to digest the draconian Brest-Litovsk treaty in March, Hoffman had resumed his eastward advance, reaching Kharkov on 20 April and Sevastopol and Rostov a week later. General von Lossow was dispatched to Batumi to keep an eye on the Turks, while a detachment of armed German railway engineers were sent ahead to inspect the Baku–Tiflis line. As if to confirm that the Baku oilfields and the Caspian had replaced Cairo and the Suez Canal as the strategic objectives of the *Drang nach Osten*, none other than Colonel Kress was now accredited to Tiflis as military plenipotentiary to mastermind German operations in the Caucasus.[41]

Having barely survived the strain of defeat in Mesopotamia and Palestine, the Turco-German partnership now threatened to go off the rails just as victory beckoned in the Caucasus. Kress wasted no time in gumming up the works of the Turkish advance, mobilizing every German he could find – some from nearby prisoner-of-war camps, others German-speaking civilian settlers who had never even lived in Germany – in a new Germano-Georgian regiment tasked with securing the Transcaucasian railway. To Georgians, recalled one veteran, 'the word German was … a symbol of salvation'.[42] Seizing the moment with great dramatic flair, on 27 May 1918 Kress proclaimed Georgia an independent republic – under German protection – from the town hall in Tiflis, as if daring the Turks to invade the country. German and Georgian flags now flew together above all the important train stations in the area. Viewing Georgia not only as the vital Transcaucasian gateway to Baku and its oil, but as an important source of manganese deposits (German rights to which Kress had already secured in writing), Ludendorff was suddenly seized with enthusiasm: he recalled all German soldiers manning the Ottoman defences in Syria and sent them to the Caucasus and detailed the entire 217th Infantry Division from occupied Crimea to Kress in Tiflis. Two German battalions and a small air force detachment, dispatched across the Black Sea, promptly landed at Sukhum and Poti, just north of Batumi – from which General Lossow now left for Berlin, in protest against Turkish encroachment beyond the Brest-Litovsk lines. The race for Baku was on.[43]

It was not a race the Germans could win. The Ottoman Third Army, commanded by Vehip Pasha (Enver's brother Nuri was still en route for the front), disposed of 'nine well-equipped infantry divisions', although only two divisions, numbering about 10,000 men, ultimately pushed on to Baku. Kress had only two proper German companies and, at most, several thousand irregulars, to cover all of Georgia. This was the force which, on 10 June 1918, came into contact with advance units of the Ottoman 9th Caucasian Infantry Division at Vorontsovka on the Tiflis road, in the first exchange of hostile fire between Turks and Germans in the world war. In a heated, though brief, skirmish, the Turks won in a rout, taking 'a considerable number of prisoners'. Not surprisingly, the Germans were livid (not to say embarrassed). If Vehip Pasha did not return his prisoners to Kress, Ludendorff warned from General Staff headquarters, Germany would recall all troops and civilian personnel from Turkey.[44]

It was the most serious crisis to date in Turco-German relations, of which the 'scandalous incident' at Vorontsovka was merely a symptom. General Lossow, complaining to the Austrian military attaché in Constantinople after deserting the peace talks at Batumi, said that 'the Turks wanted to control the entire Transcaucasus, especially the oilfields of Baku'. Interestingly, Lossow told Pomiankowski that he had no political objection as such to the Porte ruling Azerbaijan. The problem, rather, was that the Turks were 'incapable of administering the country and regulating petroleum production'.[45] Never was the polite fiction which lay behind German pan-Islam more baldly revealed than in the race for Baku. For Berlin, the Turks were no more than a tool to exploit the resources of the Orient – a tool which was now long past its expiration date.

At the centre of the storm stood the enigmatic figure of Enver Pasha. It was Enver's promise to fan the flames of pan-Islam for the Kaiser which had convinced the Germans to sign a far-reaching alliance treaty in August 1914. It was Enver's opportunistic manoeuvring that autumn which had brought Turkey into the war in October over the objections of the Grand Vizier, to the Germans' delight. It was only because of their confidence in Enver's reputed Germanophilia that Berlin had continued subvening the Ottoman war effort through all the disasters of 1916 and 1917, and that Kühlmann and Hoffman had reluctantly indulged his imperial pretensions at Brest-Litovsk. So it was natural that Ludendorff called on Enver to right the ship now, by forcing the return of Kress's prisoners, sacking Vehip Pasha, and travelling to the region to work out a solution to the Turco-German impasse. To keep Enver in line, the Germans sent none other than Hans von Seeckt – the brilliant 'Sphinx with the Monocle' who would run the General Staff in the early years of the Weimar Republic – to accompany him to Batumi.[46]

Enver's solution to the problem was clever. Conceding Georgia to Kress and the Germans, Enver simply reoriented the Ottoman offensive further south, dividing his forces into two separate armies, one to strike at Baku through Armenia, the other to face the British in northern Persia. Although the new strategy did mean bypassing the main stretch of the Transcaucasian railway and pipeline which wound through Tiflis, it also fitted in well with the increasingly popular Young Turk idea of 'pan-Turanianism', a movement to unify the Turkic peoples of Central Asia, Afghanistan, Persia and the Caucasus with Turkey. Enver himself encouraged the Ottoman media to promote pan-Turanianism in 1918, even if his own strategic objective may simply have been to create a series of pro-Ottoman buffer states between Anatolia, Russian Central Asia and British-controlled Persia (although Enver still held out hope for expelling the British from Mesopotamia). Once the Armenian Dashnaks and the Russo-Armenian Bolsheviks now dominating the Baku Soviet were expelled from Azerbaijan, the new strategic pan-Turanian arc would form a 'solid Muslim bloc'.[47] Such was the thinking behind the ominously named 'Caucasus Army of Islam' Enver's brother Nuri was now tasked with raising from the Muslim native population of the Transcaucasus to spearhead the attack on Baku.

With the Germans no longer involved, Enver's drive to the Caspian appeared to be a true Islamic jihad – and truly terrifying to the Armenian population of Baku which stood to be its principal victims.* Following the bloody riots of 31 March–1 April 1918, the Azeri Muslim population of Baku had mostly fled to the hills, as if in anticipation of the arrival of the Turks to help them avenge the spring massacre. Although the city had been majority Muslim, by summer most remaining residents were Christians, whether Armenians (many of them refugees, from as far away as eastern Anatolia), Georgians or Russians. Uniting against the Ottoman threat, local Bolsheviks had teamed up with the Dashnaks in the Baku Soviet, conscripting 'all non-Muslim males older than eighteen' into a sort of Armenian-dominated Red Army. By June, this makeshift revolutionary militia was strong enough to advance westwards along the railway to take up defensive positions against the advancing Turks, burning down 'over fifty Muslim villages' along the way. With the Army of Islam camped out on the heights overlooking the city, the Armenian-dominated Baku Soviet convened on 31 July 1918 to vote on whether or not to invite in British troops led by General Dunsterville, then encamped at Enzeli, a Caspian port in northern Persia, to save them. By 259 votes to 236, the answer was yes.[48]

Never in the First World War was the order of battle more confusing than in the struggle for Baku in August 1918. Inside the city, British 'imperialists' cooperated with revolutionaries to stave off the Ottoman army, out of the entirely mistaken fear that if Baku fell to the Turks it would portend a German advance on India. In Berlin, Adolf Joffe, the Soviet Ambassador to Germany, was begging the Wilhelmstrasse to stop its erstwhile ally, the Turks, from attacking Baku. The Germans agreed, so long as Moscow would guarantee German access to Caspian

---

* The purely Islamic nature of what was formally titled the 'Caucasus Army of Islam' was dubious, particularly as Nuri had great difficulty recruiting Muslim volunteers. Nuri may himself have viewed his 'Islamic' brief somewhat cynically: one of his recruiters reportedly told an unimpressive-looking Muslim *hoca* volunteer that 'the Army of Islam had no place for men of religion'. Nevertheless, Enver's own directive creating the army stated as its primary mission 'to establish in the Caucasus the interests of Islam and political and military ties to the Caliph of the Sacred Law and the Ottoman State'.

oil – which Lenin immediately granted. So desperate were the Bolsheviks to keep the Turks out of Baku that they even agreed, in a supplement to Brest-Litovsk negotiated in August, to Georgian independence – under German protection. The Germans were further enjoined to 'prevent the military forces of any third Power', i.e. Turkey, 'in the Caucasus [from] overstepping the following lines', which included most of Azerbaijan. In exchange for promising to keep the Turks out of the Transcaucasus, Germany was to receive from Moscow a permanent quota of 25 per cent of all the 'crude oil products produced in the Baku district'.[49] In fact, the Bolsheviks were already delivering oil to the German army in the Ukraine by way of the Caspian and Volga, as Nuri informed Enver on 13 August 1918. Far from – as the British feared – goading on their allies in their push to the Caspian, the Germans were actively sabotaging the Turkish war effort in Georgia, 'going so far as to burn down a bridge to prevent the Ottomans from making use of the railroad from Batumi through Tiflis for the shipment of men and ammunition'. So fed up was the supposedly Germanophile Enver with the grasping Germans by this point that he authorized his brother to engage German units in battle if any stood in his way. Playing tit for tat, the Turks blew up a bridge on the Georgian border to stave off German infiltration.[50]

For the Germans, the battle of Baku was predetermined for disappointment. Having lost the vote in the city Soviet to a coalition dominated by Social Revolutionaries and Armenian nationalists and Dashnaks, most of Baku's Bolsheviks had left for Astrakhan, only to be captured several miles offshore and imprisoned. With the de-Bolshevized city now defended by Russian SRs, Armenians and (after they finally landed on 17 August) Dunsterville's 1,000-odd British troops against the entirely German-free Caucasus Army of Islam, Berlin had no dog in the fight. When Nuri's army finally crashed into Baku on 15 September 1918 (after he had allowed Azeri Muslim militiamen free rein to kill some 9,000 Armenians in retaliation for the Muslim massacres of March–April), the news was received in Berlin with indifference.* With the German army crumbling on the western

---

* Many Armenians escaped on refugee boats across the Caspian.

front, it was a matter of little import to the Wilhelmstrasse whether Baku fell to the British, the Bolsheviks, the Armenians or the Turks.

The capture of Baku, of course, proved to be just as hollow a victory for the Porte. In a reversal which must have been stunning to the masses of Constantinople, fed all summer on pan-Turanian propaganda, the armistice the British forced on Turkey at Mudros, on the Aegean island of Lemnos (30 October 1918) obliged the Ottoman army to evacuate Transcaucasia. So enraptured had Enver and Nuri been as the Caucasus Army of Islam set off for the Caspian that they seem to have scarcely noticed the British advancing into Syria, or the collapse of Bulgaria on 28 September which opened the invasion route to the Ottoman capital for the Allied army based at Salonica, across Thrace. The bill for Enver's Caspian gambit was high indeed: the Turks were forced to abandon all recent gains, from Baku and Batumi to Ardahan and Sarıkamış, going all the way back to the 1914 borders. Worst of all, the British fleet now sailed unopposed through the Straits, achieving in one afternoon what the combined Allied forces at Gallipoli had failed to do all through 1915.

London, of course, proved unable to hold on to the trophies of Mudros. By March 1919, the overstretched British had withdrawn all troops from the Transcaucasus except for a small garrison at Batumi. That summer the Turks, regrouping under Mustafa Kemal, made common cause with the Bolsheviks on the basis of shared enmity to London. The future of the Transcaucasus would, in the end, not be decided in the far-away imperial capitals of Berlin and London, but between anti-imperialist Bolsheviks and Turks on the ground, both keen on denying Caspian oil to the British and the Germans. The treaty which fixed the eastern borders of Turkey – a compromise, with Kemal giving up claims on Baku and Batumi in exchange for Soviet recognition of Turkish rule in Kars and Ardahan – was signed in Kars in October 1921, with none of the Western powers present. Although it took them another two long years of gruelling fighting, by 1922 the Turks had at last freed themselves from the shackles of the European powers, winning their war of independence with Greece (some 100 years after the Greeks had won a similar war against the Turks) and abolishing the Capitulations for ever. It was certainly not how Enver had drawn up the plan, but in the end Turkey arguably gained as much as any other belligerent out of the wreckage of the First World War.

The Germans were not so fortunate. With what we now know of Berlin's fundamental culpability for the July crisis and the outbreak of war in 1914, the crushing reversal of 1918 was richly deserved. And yet there is much to learn from the *Götterdämmerung*. While many Germans justifiably wanted their poor-performing allies to share the blame for the defeat of the Central Powers, the ultimate responsibility must rest on the shoulders of the power which dragged the others into the war. Had the coalition been victorious, the Germans would have taken most of the spoils, including much of Baku's oil, by the terms of the August 1918 Supplementary Agreement with the Bolsheviks. Considering that the Turks held Baku for barely a month before allowing in the British (who themselves held it for only several months more), it is hard to imagine the Porte holding onto the city if the Red Army had made a push for it in 1918–19 (the Bolsheviks indeed took Baku in April 1920). For better or worse, the Soviet government was Germany's tool – so long as the German army was in the field. The Bolsheviks were thus the first, and greatest, beneficiaries from Germany's collapse, which allowed them to gain true independence four years before the Turks did.

It is one of the strangest ironies of the First World War that the two powers fated to fill the vacuum left by the failure of the *Drang nach Osten* were Kemalist Turkey and Bolshevik Russia. That London stood to gain from Berlin's loss was obvious enough; although inheriting the poisoned chalice of Mesopotamia and Palestine proved to be more headache than blessing for the British Empire. But who could have imagined that the Kaiser's pan-Islamic gambit would bring Muslim Central Asia and the Caucasus under the thumb of the world's first explicitly atheist regime in Moscow, which would prove to be a bitter enemy of Muslims? Or that Enver's own pan-Islamic scheming would destroy the Ottoman Caliphate and ease into power an aggressively laicist government in Ankara? Mustafa Kemal, as victorious *ghazi* warrior of the Turkish war of independence, could have simply named himself Caliph. Instead he chose to kill off this troublesome Islamic institution which had brought his country nothing but devastation in the modern era.

The great Turco-German holy war had in the end been a great dis-appointment – at least to the Germans. Rather than inspiring Muslims to fight arm-in-arm with Germany against Britain and Russia, the Ottoman jihad had instead exposed the immense divisions in the Muslim world, which London, Moscow and Paris would now learn better to exploit. Worst of all from the German perspective, Zionism, originally conceived and cultivated by Germans, had now been hijacked by the hated British, not least because Berlin – erstwhile home of the international Zionist executive – had been cynically turned into the world capital of Islamic jihadism and its inevitable corollary, anti-Semitism. Reversing the logic of Marx's famous dictum, Germany's pan-Islamic *Drang nach Osten* would repeat itself twenty years later, the first time as farce, the second as tragedy.

Epilogue: The Strange Death of German Zionism and the Nazi-Muslim Connection

In this war the interests of Russian Jews and those of the German Reich are identical.

> Max Bodenheimer, past President of the German Zionist Federation and founder of the 'German Committee for the Liberation of Russian Jewry', to fellow German Zionist Otto Warburg, November 1914[1]

The interests of the German government are identical with those of the Russian revolutionaries.

> Alexander Israel 'Parvus' Helphand to Ambassador Wangenheim, January 1915[2]

I thank God that the interests of Islam are entirely identical with those of Germany.

> Feisal, son of Hussein, Sherif of Mecca, and future Hashemite king of Syria and Iraq, to Baron Max Oppenheim, April 1915[3]

As we survey the political and humanitarian wreckage of the modern Middle East, it is hard to resist the temptation to imagine scenarios in which history would have turned out for the better. If only Turkey had stayed out of the war, the Caliphate might have survived and a fragile Sunni equilibrium endured in Syria, Palestine, Iraq and Arabia, thus avoiding a century of bitter warfare in the Islamic world.

340

If the British and French had not cynically carved up Asiatic Turkey between them in the Sykes–Picot Agreement, say the anti-imperialists, then Arabs might have learned to govern themselves, just as the Turks did after achieving their own independence. If only Arthur Balfour had not issued his declaration wedding Zionism to British interests, we often hear from supporters of the Palestinian cause, then Israel would never have come into existence, sparing the world its most intractable contemporary conflict. In the years since 9/11, yet another lament has been added to the chorus, in which Nazi propaganda in the Middle East is said to have tragically seeded the fevered anti-Semitism of the region, with Israel serving only as a convenient scapegoat for a new and generalized prejudice.[4]

There is something to be said for all of these arguments. Nevertheless, a curious amnesia is common to each of them about the actual events of the First World War which produced the post-Ottoman predicament. Whether in Edward Said's famous critique of Western *Orientalism* or in books celebrating Zionism, we hear again and again about the Entente powers, particularly Britain, as the prime mover, whether for good or ill (or for both, in the case of Israel). From Sykes–Picot and Lawrence's Arab revolt to the Balfour Declaration, the key events in the story have entered the political lexicon.

What is missing from the story is the colossal and almost totally forgotten role of imperial Germany in the drama. To begin with, there is the extraordinary physical legacy of the German-built Baghdad and Hejaz lines, which still form the backbone of the railway systems of modern Turkey, Syria, Jordan, northern Arabia and even a good deal of Israel and Palestine.[5] As we have seen, the Kaiser's promotion of pan-Islam, while a strategic failure in the world war, threw up flames of revolutionary jihadism as far afield as Libya, Sudan, Mesopotamia, the Caucasus, Iran and Afghanistan, which never entirely died down after the war, not least because of ever-more brutal British (and Bolshevik) measures to douse them. In the end, the pan-Islamic cause proved to be only as strong as the Turco-German war effort. Had the Baghdad railway – including the last Taurus and Amanus mountain tunnels – been finished by 1915 or 1916 instead of, as in reality, August 1918, a decisive blow might well have been struck at the Suez Canal, severing the lifeline of the British Empire and forcing London to sue for a compromise peace – which would surely have seen Germany emerge as the leading power in the Near East.

In searching for reasons for the ultimate failure of the *Drang nach Osten*, we should not overlook the strategic fall-out of the Young Turk revolution of July 1908. The resulting political turmoil and weakening of Sultan Abdul Hamid's authority cost the Germans two years on the Baghdad railway – and arguably five if we see the Italian and Balkan wars as the fruit of perceived Ottoman weakness born of the revolution. More damaging still was the chasm in the Islamic world opened up by the Young Turks' forceful deposition of Abdul Hamid in April 1909, so fatefully exposed by Sherif Hussein in the Arab revolt – itself inconceivable had the Hejaz railway been extended to Mecca, as it certainly would have been if not for the deposition of the Sultan. For good or for ill, the fall of Abdul Hamid weakened Turkey, the Baghdad railway and Sunni Muslim solidarity just enough to cut the legs out from under the Kaiser–Oppenheim holy war.

Germany's historic role in the Middle East, however, is hardly confined to the legacy of the botched jihad stratagem. Easy as it is to forget today, living as we do in the long moral shadow of Nazi Germany and the Holocaust, Wilhelmine Germany was also the spiritual and political home of Zionism. As the London *Times* famously complained in 1911 – the same year poor Djavid Bey was ritually abused as a crypto-Jew at the CUP congress for British edification – the leaders of the Zionist movement were 'Yiddish-speaking Jews all of whom understand German'. Indeed, the prevailing view in the British government both before and during the First World War was that 'Zionism was merely a tool of the German Foreign Ministry'.[6] As Sir Ronald Graham wrote to Arthur Balfour shortly before the latter issued his famous declaration, 'We might at any moment be confronted by a German move on the Zionist question and it must be remembered that Zionism was originally if not a German Jewish at any rate an Austrian Jewish idea.'[7]

It is easy to dismiss British wartime fears about the potency of German Zionism, which were of a piece with the general exaggeration of Jewish influence worldwide common in Whitehall. Certainly English notions about crypto-Jewish *Dönme* Freemasons pulling strings in the CUP government were completely overblown. Even more wrong-headed was the British expectation, expressed by Sir Mark Sykes after the February Revolution, that a public embrace of Zionism would help keep Russia in the war by enlisting her millions of Jews behind the Allied cause.[8] The notion that Jews were secretly running Constantinople or Petrograd was a lurid fantasy.

In the German case, however, the British idea of pervasive Zionist influence was on more solid ground. When war came to Europe in 1914, the international Zionist Executive was based in Berlin at 8 Sächsische Strasse, and two of its six members were Germans. While Kaiser Wilhelm had cooled considerably in his support for Zionism since his ill-fated dalliance in 1898, most German Zionists remained strong supporters of the Hohenzollern throne, especially after Germany joined battle with Tsarist Russia, universally regarded as the greatest enemy of world Jewry. The German Foreign Office, as we saw in the August 1914 'Overview of the Revolutionary Activity We Will Undertake in the Islamic-Israelite World', viewed Zionism as a political weapon just as dangerous to Russia as Oppenheim's jihad was to Britain. No less than the British who feared the German-Jewish connection, Wesendonck saw international Zionism as 'similar to the Jesuit order in the tightness of its discipline', with members observing 'strictest obedience towards their leaders'. It was therefore feasible, he proposed, for Berlin to 'win over the entire organization of the Zionists for our cause', which would prove 'a tool of incalculable value' in destroying Russia's war effort.[9]

Of course, that the Wilhelmstrasse believed Zionists to be loyal does not mean that they really were all in the German camp – or that, if they were, this would truly have been 'of incalculable value' to the war effort. And yet it would be wrong to see German Zionists as hapless tools called into service for cynical German geopolitical ends. When we look more closely at the origins of Wesendonck's revolutionary memorandum of August 1914, an astonishing fact emerges: it was the Zionists' idea. Specifically, it was the suggestion of Max Bodenheimer, long-time President of the German Zionist Federation, who had been promoting the idea of a strategic alliance between the German imperial government and Zionism for over a decade. In 1902, Bodenheimer had first broached this idea in a long memorandum to the Wilhelmstrasse. To be sure, little came of his suggestion then: but the German Zionist leader never gave up. Just as Baron Oppenheim's jihad prophecy met its moment in August 1914, so too did Bodenheimer seize the moment at the outbreak of the war to reprise his theme, submitting an 'Exposé on the Synchronization of German and Jewish Interests in the World War' to German military headquarters in Cologne on 4 August 1914. Because of Bodenheimer's great stature in the Zionist movement, his memorandum was forwarded post-haste to Berlin – along with Bodenheimer himself, who was invited to pitch his idea to Count Hutten-Czapski of the General Staff, in charge of sabotage operations on the eastern front. Hutten-Czapski, in turn, invited his friend Baron Diego von Bergen, who handled Polish affairs for the Foreign Office. With support from both the General Staff and the Wilhelmstrasse, Bodenheimer, along with half a dozen German Zionist colleagues, established the 'German Committee for the Liberation of Russian Jewry' on 17 August 1914 – the day after Wesendonck wrote his fateful sabotage memorandum.[10]

It should be emphasized that Bodenheimer was not acting in the name of the international Zionist Executive in establishing his new committee. Officially, the Executive maintained a posture of neutrality in the world war, and began holding meetings in neutral Copenhagen instead of Berlin to distance Zionism from the German war effort.[11] After throwing in his lot with the Germans, Bodenheimer even resigned his chairmanship of the Jewish National Fund (which supported land purchases and investments in Palestine) to avoid the appearance of a conflict of interest. And yet he consulted continuously with the Zionist Executive in Berlin while he was setting up his initiative with the General Staff and Wilhelmstrasse. One of the German members of the Executive, Arthur Hantke, formally joined Bodenheimer's German Committee for the Liberation of Russian Jewry. The other German, Otto Warburg, who was chairman of the international Zionist Executive, wrote to Bodenheimer on 17 August 1914 to express his full support. That Warburg was in the loop of Bodenheimer's Russian revolutionary stratagem is further confirmed in Wesendonck's 16 August 'Overview', which mentions Warburg prominently. In addition, the leading members of the German Zionist Federation were on board, including Adolf Friedemann, the chairman of that body; Adolf Klee; Leo Motzkin; Hermann Struck; and Franz Oppenheimer, who took over the chairmanship of Bodenheimer's new organization. If not all Zionists threw their support behind the German war effort, it is nevertheless true that 'the members [of Bodenheimer's committee] were almost exclusively Zionists'. For better or for worse, these German Zionists now pledged, in the mission statement of the Committee for the Liberation of Russian Jewry, 'to support those powers lined up against Russia on the field of battle in both word and deed'.[12]

It was a fateful decision. While Bodenheimer later came to regret compromising the cause by so closely aligning German Zionists with the war effort, in the early days he was caught up in the general patriotic frenzy. As he wrote to Zionist Executive chairman Otto Warburg in November 1914, 'in this war the interests of Russian Jews and those of the German Reich are identical'. Like Parvus-Helphand, who made an almost identical declaration to Ambassador Wangenheim in Constantinople two months later (substituting only 'Russian revolutionaries' for 'Russian Jews'), Bodenheimer wanted desperately for the German army to destroy the power of the Tsarist empire, at least in the Baltic states, Poland, White Russia and the Ukraine, where he envisioned an 'East European Federation' in which 'all ethnic groups were to enjoy national autonomy' – including, of course, the Jews in the Pale of Settlement. Translated (by the General Staff) into the form of a war propaganda leaflet dated 14 August 1914, Bodenheimer's vision sounded like this:

> Jews of Russia! Rouse yourselves! Take up arms! Leave all the quarrels aside, whether you are Nationalists, Zionists, or Socialists! Help to chase out the Muscovite from the Western territories, from Poland, Lithuania, White Russia, Volhynia, and Podolia! Freedom is coming to Europe ... Organize yourselves! And send men you trust [across front lines] to the German and Austro-Hungarian commanders!

After approval was granted by the Wilhelmstrasse and the Austrian Foreign Ministry, no fewer than 150,000 German- and Yiddish-language copies of this pamphlet were printed up and dropped by German aeroplanes behind Russian front lines in Galicia.[13]

Bodenheimer had not approved this text, and was deeply unhappy when he read it. Before the German and Austro-Hungarian armies had expelled the Tsarist armies from Jewish-inhabited territories, he warned Count Bergen on 16 August 1914, insurrectionary propaganda would only give the Russians a pretext for another brutal pogrom.[14] In order to distance himself and his fellow Zionists from German-Austrian propaganda, Bodenheimer changed the name of his 'German Committee for the Liberation of Russian Jewry' in October to the more innocuous-sounding 'Committee for the East'. On 27 October 1914, the Zionist Executive in Berlin further requested (but did not require) its members to withdraw even from Bodenheimer's watered-down committee, not only to avoid provoking Russian suspicions of Jews and Zionists, but also because several non-German members had expressed doubts, in the wake of the Allied victory at the Marne, that the Germans would win the war.[15]

By then, however, the damage had been done. Propaganda leaflets dropped behind the front lines in Russian Poland and Galicia had already 'triggered off unwarranted suspicions of espionage' and provoked the Russian Stavka into ordering 'mass expulsions of Jews from the war-zone'.[16] In all, at least 500,000 Russian Jews, and possibly as many as one million, were deported from their homes during the war.[17] Bodenheimer could rail all he liked about being misused by the German generals, but his own mission statement had vowed that German Zionists would support the war effort 'by word and deed': one can hardly blame Bergen and Hutten-Czapski for taking him literally. Whether or not Bodenheimer and his Zionist supporters intended to harness themselves quite so unequivocally to the German war machine, this is certainly how Bodenheimer's memorandums had been interpreted at General Staff headquarters and in the Wilhelmstrasse. It is true that, following the failure of a Jewish insurrection to ignite behind Russian lines in the autumn of 1914, the German generals dropped Bodenheimer's idea.[18] But the Russians, of course, did not know this. Try though Bodenheimer might to turn back the clock, the genie of Judeo-cum-Zionist sedition against the Tsar had been prised loose from the bottle, and there was no putting it back.

Thus, in a mixture of happenstance and miscommunication, was born the dangerous conflation of Jews and revolution in the fevered atmosphere of wartime Russia. Cool heads may well have reminded both German and Russian policy-makers that many Russian Jews had actually volunteered to serve the Tsar in the war.

Counting reservists, there were at least 400,000 Jews serving in the Russian army in 1914. True, by the end of 1915 five million of the 6.5 million Russian Jews had become subjects of imperial Germany, but this was because of the incompetence of the Tsarist armies; it was not the fault of Russia's Jews that her army was beaten in the field.[19] Nor did these former Tsarist subjects display any particular loyalty towards the German occupation authorities, despite being ostentatiously granted civil equality, which had been denied them under Russian rule – a key theme in German war propaganda, particularly in America. 'Jews in the [newly] occupied territories,' writes Egmont Zechlin, 'took a wait-and-see attitude towards the Germans, behaving with the utmost reserve.'[20]

As the war cut its vast swathe of destruction through the European social fabric, however, cool heads were increasingly hard to find in belligerent capitals. This was true not only in conquest-mad Berlin or in beleaguered Petrograd, scene of the world-historic revolutions of 1917 which so crippled Russia's war effort, but in London, where policymakers already obsessed with the idea of a Judeo-German revolutionary combine observed these revolutions with foreboding. Considering that the British Foreign Office (mis)interpreted the Young Turk convulsions of 1908–1909 as the work of crypto-Jewish Freemasonry, it is hardly surprising that many Britons ascribed the Russian Revolution to an 'apparent conjunction of Bolsheviks, Germans, and Jews'.[21]

Like all conspiracy theories, this one overreached considerably. While many Bolsheviks, along with Parvus-Helphand and other conspirators behind the Lenin operation, Karl Radek and Olof Aschberg for example, were indeed Jewish, Lenin himself was not. Moreover, neither Bodenheimer's committee of German Zionists, nor the Zionist Executive, nor any kind of organized international Jewish network, had much of anything to do with either the February or October Revolution. Just as fantastic was the idea which began percolating around Whitehall in summer 1917, that a British embrace of Zionism (as in the issuance of something along the lines of what would become the Balfour Declaration) would win world Jewry for the Allied cause and doom German efforts to knock Russia out of the war.[22]

Grossly exaggerated though it was, the British fear of German Judeo-Zionism was not entirely crazy. The Wilhelmstrasse had indeed been looking very closely into the possibilities of a public embrace of Zionism. As early as 1915, Bodenheimer's theme of a confluence of interests between Germany and Zionism had begun winning converts in German political circles, including many of the same men who had dreamed up the pan-Islamic *Drang nach Osten*, such as Professor Martin Hartmann, who volunteered his expertise that year to Oppenheim's Berlin propaganda bureau; Paul Rohrbach, author of *Die Bagdadbahn*; and the arch Turcophile Ernst Jäckh. Were not many of the Jewish settlers of Palestine, Rohrbach asked in an address to the Prussian parliament in March 1915, ideally placed 'to propagate German *Kultur* and commerce in the Orient'?[23]

So insistent was the growing chorus that Under-Secretary of State Arthur Zimmermann felt compelled to respond formally to Zionist demands in a 15 June 1915 letter to Rabbi Jacobus of Magdeburg. Although less committal than Balfour would be in his letter to Lord Rothschild two years later, Zimmermann did declare that 'the Imperial Government is eager to use its influence with the Turkish Government to remove obstacles in the way of Jewish immigration to Turkey'. As for Jews already in Palestine, there is abundant evidence that the Germans leaned heavily on the Porte to improve their lot during the war. In February 1915, for example, Ambassador Wangenheim secured the removal of Beha-ed-Din, the Kaimakam of Jaffa, who had forbidden all use of Hebrew and 'declared illegal' Zionist institutions and the Zionist flag, along with the release of Jews imprisoned by Beha-ed-Din. Pressure from Berlin was strong enough that Djemal even issued, in March 1915, a proclamation confirming that the Porte viewed Palestinian Jews as a 'good and loyal element' in the Ottoman population.[24]

There were sound strategic reasons for Germany to promote Zionism during the war – and not only because of the potential for disrupting the Russian war effort laid out in the Bodenheimer and Wesendonck memorandums of August 1914. As implied by Wangenheim's pro-Zionist intervention with Beha-ed-Din, Berlin, no less than Paris and London, worried keenly about neutral and particularly US public opinion, at least until America's entry into the war in 1917 rendered this issue moot. Yet another rationale for Zionism was created by the course of the war on the eastern front. By 1916 the

German occupation authorities found themselves ruling some five million formerly Russian Jews, of whom nearly a third had been uprooted from their homes, creating 'a very serious refugee problem'. Some pan-German annexationists warmed up to Zionism in part because the war offered a golden opportunity to get rid of Germany's own Jews, along with those being absorbed into the eastern occupation zone.[25] The same anti-Semitic idea had frequently appeared in the marginalia of Kaiser Wilhelm, who once happily prophesied that Germany's 'Social Democratic elements' (i.e. Jewish socialists) 'will stream into Palestine'.[26] Of course, later it would also occur to the Nazis, who actively encouraged Jewish migration to Palestine in the late 1930s, and did not really abandon the idea until 1941.[27]

Much as the Germans would have loved to have flooded Palestine with the generally pro-German Zionist Jews of eastern Europe, however, the Turks were considerably less keen on the idea. It was the Ottoman Foreign Minister's warning to Wilhelm which had put the damper on official German support for Zionism back in 1898. In similar fashion, it was concern for the Porte's reaction which prevented the German Under-Secretary of State from issuing his own Balfour Declaration in June 1915. As Zimmermann delicately concluded his letter to Rabbi Jacobus, 'the suggestion of the gradual creation of a Jewish province with an autonomous administration would encounter great difficulties'.[28]

The issue of Ottoman Zionist policy during the war remains controversial. Talaat, who as Interior Minister is usually blamed for the worst excesses of the Armenian deportation campaign, was notably more friendly to Jewish minorities in Turkey. During the war, Talaat made every effort to stay on good terms with US Ambassador Morgenthau, who was himself Jewish and, like many Americans, keenly interested in the fate of the Jewish settlers of Palestine.[*29] Djemal, who ran most of Syria and Palestine during the war as a virtual dictator, was not a supporter of further Zionist migration, but this did not mean he was hostile to Jewish settlers already living on Ottoman territory. While Djemal had at first acquiesced in Beha-ed-Din's anti-Zionist crackdown in

---

[*] Talaat reportedly told Ambassador Bernstorff following the Balfour Declaration, 'We have done much harm to the Armenians, but we won't do anything to the Jews'.

Jaffa during the first winter of the war, he later recanted. Djemal worked closely with several Jewish engineers and agronomists who came to work in his administration. Djemal found these Zionist settlers 'so skilful and trustworthy' that he 'rejected an offer from Berlin to provide his army with German technicians and doctors', and even boasted that the achievements of the armaments factory in Damascus were due to 'our man' – a Jewish subject – 'not the result of German initiative'.[30]

Despite his appreciation for the contributions of Jewish settlers to Ottoman economic life, however, Djemal refused to embrace Zionism. It is not hard to see why. While very few Jewish settlers participated in seditious activity of any kind during the war, the increasingly strident Zionist propaganda emanating from Entente capitals in 1916 and 1917, not to mention Vladimir Jabotinsky's open recruitment of a 'Jewish regiment' to join the British push into Palestine, was hard for the Ottoman government to ignore. Ottoman minority populations had long been used, wittingly or not, by outside powers as Trojan horses for intervention and invasion: the Crimean War had been literally fought over disputed 'protection rights' for Levantine Christians. Had not Armenian partisans aided the Russians at Sarıkamış and Van? Were not most of the Arab conspirators Djemal executed in 1915–16 compromised by a connection to France (as exposed in captured documents from the Damascus Consulate)? And what of Hussein's rebellion, openly aided and abetted by British agents? One does not have to defend Ottoman brutality during the war to appreciate that the potential for sedition was very real, whether or not British-backed Zionists ever put armed men into the field of battle.

As the intrigue surrounding the Zionist question came to a head in summer 1917, Djemal was the man of the hour. Both the Turks and Germans knew perfectly well that Zionists in London were closing in on a British endorsement. But could Berlin beat them to the punch? Without the consent of its Turkish ally, the German government was unable to go public; nor could German newspapers (the Wilhelmstrasse even leaned on the *Frankfurter Zeitung* at one point to kill a pro-Zionist editorial 'in view of the Turkish government's suspicions about Zionist aspirations').[31] So when Djemal came to Berlin in late August, German Zionist leaders gave him the hard sell. In a meeting with

Arthur Hantke and Richard Lichtheim on 28 August 1917, Djemal repeated his earlier pledges to protect Ottoman Jews, and even encouraged further Jewish migration to the empire – so long as newcomers would settle anywhere but Palestine. It was not simply the potential for Entente-sponsored sedition in Palestine which concerned Djemal, but the overwhelming hostility of the Arab population there to Jews.[32] Echoing Djemal's point in even stronger language, shortly before the Balfour Declaration was issued Talaat (now Grand Vizier) told German Ambassador Bernstorff that 'I would be happy to establish a national home for the Jews [in Palestine].' But there would be little point to the enterprise, Talaat warned, since in the end 'the Arabs would only kill the Jews'.[33]

Djemal and Talaat both had a point. It was not simply that Arab hostility to the Jewish settlers in Palestine was widespread. But had not the Germans themselves promoted anti-Christian, anti-Semitic prejudice with their own jihad stratagem? It was not incidental to the question of Arab-Jewish relations in wartime Palestine that holy war pamphlets had been printed in November 1914 on orders of Hassan Bey, the military governor of the Jaffa district, 'which included the statement that it was incumbent upon every devout Muslim to kill the infidels: Christians and Jews alike'.[34] Terrified that news of massacres in Palestine might prejudice US public opinion against Germany, Wangenheim had pointedly intervened then with Talaat, as he would again with him over the Armenians in 1915 (although with less effect). The Germans thus found themselves in the awkward position during the war of trying to restrain Levantine Muslims from anti-Semitic and anti-Christian pogroms that their own jihad propaganda was promoting.

Nowhere was this contradiction more apparent than in the fieldwork of intelligence agents like Curt Prüfer. In autumn 1915, the dragoman travelled widely through Syria, Lebanon and Palestine, canvassing public opinion on behalf of Djemal. Upon returning to Damascus in December, Prüfer filed a long report, in which he contrasted the generally seditious inclinations of Christians with those of Jews, who remained loyal. While there were signs of sympathy with the Entente among Zionist-style colonies in Beirut, Jerusalem and Palestine, Prüfer emphasized that 'they form only small circles of no importance. The Jews will never dare attempt subversive activities.'[35] So confident of the loyalty of Palestinian Jews was the dragoman that he actively lobbied Berlin for a pro-Zionist declaration to fend off the British in summer 1917, although to no avail.[36]

Endorsing Zionism was an odd position for a holy war fieldman to take. The dragoman implicitly recognized this in his efforts to recruit Jewish agents for the jihad, since he found Arab Muslims 'neither intelligent, nor courageous, nor reliable'. It was only the Jews, Prüfer decided, who were both intelligent enough and 'possessed the necessary sangfroid' to make good spies.[37] It does not seem to have occurred to the dragoman that Zionist settlers may not have wanted to become Islamic holy war agents, if that cause meant promoting vengeance killings against infidels like themselves.

The British made a very similar mistake in trying to unleash Arab nationalism and Zionism simultaneously in their own efforts to destroy the Ottoman Empire. Some of the more wizened hands in the Foreign Office, like General Allenby's political adviser Gilbert Clayton, foresaw the inherent difficulty in basing London's regional policy on an 'Arab-Jewish-Armenian combination', in view of the fact that 'Mecca [i.e. Islam and Muslims writ large] dislikes Jews and Armenians' alike. To bring such an alliance into being on the battlefield, Clayton warned Mark Sykes, was 'an attempt to change in a few weeks the traditional sentiment of centuries'.[38] And yet the Balfour Declaration, coming on top of the promises to the Arabs already made in the Sykes–Picot Agreement (not to mention the vague oral promises about Arab sovereignty Lawrence had made to Feisal), amounted to just such a wishful-thinking wager on Arab-Jewish collaboration. It was exactly the sort of leap of blind faith which appealed to a fantasist like Colonel Lawrence. 'Lawrence of Arabia' was, improbably, a closet Zionist. Despite his reputation as the patron saint of English Arabists, Lawrence 'actually had a sort of contempt for the Arabs ... He felt that only with a Jewish state would the Arabs make anything of themselves.'[39]

In Lawrence's blend of cynicism and baseless optimism, we can see how shallow was the strategic thinking behind the Balfour Declaration. The idea of a public embrace of Zionism had been percolating around London since the February Revolution, and the US entry into the war had put the 'Jewish' issue front and centre in world politics.* And yet the final push came not from anything occurring in America or Russia (much less in Palestine itself), but from a German newspaper editorial which seems to have frightened Whitehall. In the *Vossische Zeitung* on 18 October 1917, Richard Lichtheim exhorted his fellow Zionists not to give up on Germany and her Ottoman ally, because, 'while the Entente can only make promises, Turkey, being in virtual possession of Palestine', could offer 'more tangible concessions'.[40] Denouncing this statement as 'insidious propaganda', the London *Times* – which, in conditions of wartime censorship, was more or less the official organ of Whitehall – printed a historic leader on 26 October 1917, demanding that the government endorse Zionism, on the grounds that 'Germany has been quick to perceive the danger to her schemes and to her propaganda that would be involved in the association of the Allies with Jewish national hopes, and she has not been idle in attempting to forestall us'. After receiving Cabinet approval on 31 October, two days later Foreign Secretary Arthur Balfour made his famous declaration that 'His Majesty's Government view with favour the establishment in Palestine of a national home for the Jewish people,' while promising to protect 'the civil and religious rights of existing non-Jewish communities in Palestine'.[41]

The most astonishing thing about the Balfour Declaration is not that the British tried so blatantly to win over world Jewish opinion, but that they did so in a fit of pique against the Germans, and entirely oblivious to the political price they would pay with their Arab allies. Gilbert Clayton was a rare voice in advocating caution. Far more typical was the famous reaction of Mark Sykes to the news ('Dr Weizmann, it's a boy!'). Years later, once it had become clear that the locals had not exactly welcomed Zionist settlers with open arms, Lloyd George admitted that they had not been consulted before the issuance of the Balfour Declaration. 'We could not get in touch with the Palestinian Arabs,' he wrote with bitterness, 'as they were fighting against us.'[42]

---

*The idea was that both America and Russia had substantial Jewish populations. If Britain could harness world Jewry to the Entente side, British thinking went, then Russia, following the February Revolution, would return to the fold, while President Woodrow Wilson (himself a supporter of Zionism) would speed up US mobilization.

It is interesting to reflect that Djemal and Talaat, who had real-life experience administering the often mutually hostile minority populations of the Ottoman Empire, were much less sanguine about Arab-Jewish relations than the British. While Djemal was coming under fire repeatedly during the war for his anti-Semitic persecutions, as we have seen, he actually thought rather highly of the Jews who worked for him. Revealingly, the Ottoman Fourth Army commander admitted at one point early in 1915 to Albert Antebi, spokesman of the Jewish Yishuv settlement in Palestine, that his persecutions of Jews were politically motivated, because of his 'need to appease the Arabs'. Talaat, for his part, was convinced that further Zionist settlement would inflame the Arabs against the Jews, regardless of which power controlled Palestine after the war. Presciently, the Grand Vizier predicted in July 1918 (after Jaffa and Jerusalem had fallen to Allenby) that, following the inevitable explosion of inter-ethnic tensions, 'England would emerge as protector of the Arabs'. Bernstorff, the German Ambassador who recorded these remarks, was likewise convinced that Balfour's promise to the Zionists was insincere, because it ran directly against London's desire 'to found an Anglo-Arab empire'.[43]

Bernstorff and Talaat were right to be suspicious of English motives. Inevitably, as Arab-Jewish tensions in Palestine exploded following the war, the British took the Arab side. When an angry Muslim mob raged through Jerusalem in April 1920 looking for Jewish targets, the militia organized by Vladimir Jabotinsky from veterans of the Jewish Legion of Allenby's army succeeded in protecting the Jewish community of New Jerusalem. In the Old City, however, 'British army units prevented Jabotinsky's force from entering'. Some of the rioters were even heard to shout that 'The Government [i.e. the British Mandate authority] is with us!' It was hard to argue with this conclusion, particularly after a military tribunal acquitted most of the rioters, while sentencing Jabotinsky to 'fifteen years' hard labour' for the crime of trying to defend his people from a murderous mob. Amazingly, a 'court of inquiry' convened by the British army to examine the conduct of the Jerusalem authorities, headed by Richard Meinertzhagen of Cairo military intelligence, agreed with Jewish complaints of egregious bias – and this despite Meinertzhagen admitting that he was himself 'imbued with anti-Semitic feelings'. While the evidently anti-Semitic military government of Palestine was now recalled (and replaced with a civilian authority), it was clear that British policy-makers had no real stomach for sticking up for Jewish settlers against the hostile Arab majority.[44]

Whether the Germans were any more sincere in their own on-again, off-again wartime dalliance with Zionism is another question. The Wilhelmstrasse was more cautious than Whitehall, at least in part because the Germans took the question more seriously. If the promotion of Jewish emigration to Palestine was for London in 1917 a kind of geopolitical parlour game involving 'world Jewish opinion', for Berlin, which even before the collapse of the Tsarist armies that year had absorbed five million Russian Jews into the Reich, the 'Jewish question' was more concrete. Had a Brest-Litovsk style settlement reigned following a German victory (if, say, Ludendorff had taken Kühlmann's advice and called off the spring offensive), Germany would have most likely promoted Jewish migration to Palestine, if only to defray the financial and social costs of absorbing millions of Russian Jews into the Reich. For this reason, it would be wrong to conclude that Zionism came to prominence only because the Entente won the war.[45]

Of course, the Germans did not win the war. Since it is the victors of great conflicts who write the history, Germany has therefore largely been written out of the story of Zionism, remembered by most Jews not for the great flowering of German Zionist thought, literature and organization in the Wilhelmine era but for the destruction of European Jewry by the Nazis in the Second World War. As Kaiser Wilhelm himself lamented following the Balfour Declaration, perfidious Albion, in its typically backhanded way, had unfairly won 'the sympathy of the Jews' while 'we as usual trail behind'.[46]

For this, Hajji Wilhelm had only himself to blame. In 1898, he had knowingly thrown Germany's lot in with Abdul Hamid and Ottoman pan-Islam, dropping his promising flirtation with Herzl and the Zionists as soon as the Sultan's Foreign Minister had told him he must. In 1914, the Kaiser had intervened with Wangenheim – and again with Liman – to make sure Turkey would enter the war, so that he could unleash Oppenheim's great global jihad to destroy the British Empire. During the entire war, the Porte retained a veto on Berlin's Zionist policy, which tied German hands and allowed the British to seize control over what had been primarily a German-inspired movement. As the Germans discovered in the Baghdad railway bottleneck caused by the Armenian massacres of 1915, and as the British would later learn trying to govern Palestine, one could not have it both ways in the Near East: you could base a regional policy on the Muslim majority or on the Jewish and Christian minorities, but not on both at the same time. To their credit and their shame, both Talaat and Djemal realized this unwritten law, and acted accordingly (if sometimes ruthlessly). Policy-makers in Berlin and London alike could have saved themselves much grief had they listened more closely to Turkish officials with real governing experience in the region.

Curiously, the British and the Germans focused their frustration on the same scapegoat as their respective Near Eastern policies burst into flames. Despite mounting evidence that Feisal and his Hashemite clan had little popular following in the Arab world – not that they would have fared much better on their new thrones if they had – the Colonial Office continued to put far more stock in Arab nationalism than in Zionism, which was treated in Whitehall as a nuisance at best. The Jerusalem riots of 1920 taught the Mandate authorities not that Palestinian Jews needed more protection, but that Arab Muslims must be appeased by every means possible. And so in 1921 the British created a 'Supreme Muslim Council' to direct religious affairs in Jerusalem, and appointed as senior judge Muhammad Amin al-Husseini, in 'one of the most fatal appointments in modern history'.

Al-Husseini, a veteran of the Ottoman army who had evidently taken Oppenheim's murderous jihadi propaganda to heart, had been one of the few Muslims punished for the riots of April 1920, sentenced – then – to ten years' hard labour for having 'provoked bloody anti-Jewish riots'. This 'dedicated killer' was now pardoned by the British and anointed 'Grand Mufti for life' of the interfaith city of Jerusalem. Al-Husseini would later come to fame as a key adviser on Jewish issues to Adolf Hitler and Heinrich Himmler (on which more below). It was not that the British shared the Mufti's virulent strand of murderous anti-Semitism. Rather, the idea seems to be that his views were shared by the Arab majority, and so must be indulged. The Zionists, by contrast, were smaller in numbers, and ideally they would stay that way so as to avoid further provocation. By the time of the 1939 'White Paper' which recommended a halt to further Zionist settlement in Palestine, Britain had repudiated the Balfour Declaration in both the spirit and the letter, calling its original good faith into question.[47]

Just as the earnest Germans had taken pan-Islam and Zionism more seriously than had the cynical British, so now did the Germans take anti-Semitism to heights previously unimaginable in England. The story of the *Dolchstosslegende*, the 'stab in the back' legend by which German *völkisch* nationalists like Hitler came to blame Germany's defeat in 1918 on a cabal of Jewish-cum-socialist politicians, is far too well known to require repetition here. Whether the particular virulence of the German strain in the wave of anti-Semitism which swept across Europe in the 1920s owed more to the fact that most Germans had believed (not entirely unreasonably) that they were winning the war before the shocking collapse of the western front in August–September 1918, or to some innate German propensity to take all ideas to their most extreme logical conclusions, is an interesting but ultimately academic question.* For whatever reason, anti-Semitism gained a broad spectrum of support in post-war Germany, with fateful consequences.

It was not that German Zionism disappeared. To some extent it thrived: during the early Weimar years the 'Pro-Palestine Committee' created in April 1918 to counter British Zionist influence experienced 'unprecedented growth'.[48] Still more unprecedented, of course, was the growth of German anti-Semitism, which dwarfed that of Zionism. That Berlin had lost the political influence the Kaiser had once enjoyed in the Ottoman Middle East further rendered German Zionism impotent. The German-built Baghdad and Syrian-Hejaz railways were taken over by Kemalist Turkey and the French and British Mandate authorities, respectively, just as the minority populations of the Levant were now under Entente, not German, protection. This result is not surprising when we remember that the Kaiser had chosen not to base his regional policy on these prospering, generally pro-European Christians and Jews, but rather on the often resentful Muslim majority, which

---

* As John Buchan wrote in *Greenmantle*, Germany 'produced good and bad, cads and gentlemen, but she could put a bit of the fanatic in them all'.

357

had proved hard to control and had even, in the case of the Mecca Sherifiate, sabotaged the Turco-German holy war in a way far more damaging than anything Zionists or Christians had done in Palestine or Syria.

One might expect that the Kaiser and the architects of his Near Eastern policy would have concluded that pan-Islam was, at best, unreliable and, at worst, actively inimical to German interests. Zionists, by contrast, had arguably helped the Germans turn the tide in Russia, and could not have done more than token damage to the Ottoman position in Palestine. Despite often brutal treatment by Djemal's lieutenants – no less than 9,000 Jews were deported from Jaffa in April 1917, even as Muslim inhabitants 'were treated with conspicuous indulgence' – Judeo-Zionist sedition in Palestine never did rear its head. Jabotinsky's vaunted Jewish Legion, meanwhile, did not reach the battlefield until February 1918, by which time Jaffa and Jerusalem had already fallen.[49]

Of course, these men concluded nothing of the kind. While reminiscent of the British view of the Young Turk revolution of 1908 propagated by Fitzmaurice, the Kaiser's burgeoning anti-Semitism after the war was actually closer in spirit to Nazism. In one letter dated 2 December 1919, Wilhelm blamed Jews for 'the lowest, most abject outrage ever to be perpetrated by any nation in history'. The Germans, he claimed, had been

> egged on and misled by the tribe of Juda whom they hate, who were guests among them! That was the thanks they got! Let no German ever forget this, nor rest until these parasites have been wiped out from German soil and been exterminated! This poisonous mushroom on the German oak-tree![50]

Hitler himself could not have said it better.

Wilhelm had good company in his post-war plunge into the fever swamps of anti-Semitism. Curt Prüfer's stock had risen higher and higher during the war, from trusted dragoman of Djemal and Kress to head of the intelligence bureau of the German Embassy in Constantinople. It was in this capacity that he had proposed a German endorsement of Zionism in 1917, albeit in vain. Prüfer's next pet project, a restoration of the deposed Egyptian Khedive Abbas Hilmi's ruptured relations with Berlin in case the Germans rode the momentum of Brest-Litovsk to a compromise peace which would have split the Middle East between Britain and Germany, had met with more success: the two men were invited to an audience with the Kaiser at German military headquarters in Spa on 31 July 1918. Prüfer had finally arrived at the heights of his social ambition. In his 'parting reply', Prüfer reported proudly to his superiors in the Wilhelmstrasse, Wilhelm had touchingly promised him that he and the Khedive would 'see me next time in a free Egypt'.[51]

Like his beloved Emperor, Curt Prüfer could never reconcile himself to the idea that Germany had lost the war. Ominously, following the Kaiser's abdication, the dragoman angrily blamed the defeat on 'the Jewish slogan, "shed no blood"'. By 1920, the dragoman had seen enough of democracy. 'It is repulsive,' he wrote in his diary, 'to see how the stupid Germans allow themselves to be ensnared by international Jewry.' With views like these, it is not hard to see why Prüfer offered his services to the Nazis. After the passage of the Nuremberg laws in September 1935, Prüfer was put in charge of personnel at the Wilhelmstrasse, in which capacity he helped Nazify the Foreign Office and cleanse it of Jewish influence. Invited to the famous Nuremberg Rally that year, Prüfer sent a postcard to his wife which began, 'Dearest, there is great joy everywhere'.[52]

If anyone could have been expected to avoid the plague of self-pitying anti-Semitism which spread through Germany's disgraced governing classes after 1918, it would be Prüfer's erstwhile mentor, Max von Oppenheim. The Baron, after all, was himself of Jewish ancestry, a scion of one of Europe's greatest Jewish banking dynasties who had lived off the Oppenheim family fortune his entire life. The Oppenheim bank itself was, not incidentally, molested by the Nazis in the usual fashion, although a semi-voluntary 'Aryanization' of the bank in 1936 in accordance with the Nuremberg Laws did allow many, though not all, of the Jewish Oppenheims to survive the war unscathed.[53] Surely the Baron, despite his lifelong Arabophilia, Anglophobia and pan-German enthusiasm, must have realized just how dangerous the Nazi racial programme was to the Jews of Europe and (if German Great Power influence were restored in the Middle East) those living in Palestine as well.

It is astonishing to report that Baron Oppenheim realized nothing of the kind. Having spent his entire adult life trying to erase his Judaic heritage, Oppenheim eagerly accepted 'honorary Aryan' status when it was offered to him following passage of the Nuremberg Laws. The Baron was put on the Nazi government payroll as early as 1 April 1933, through the offices of Franz von Papen, the former Chancellor who had fatefully convinced Hindenburg to turn the Chancellery over to Hitler that January: Papen was an old friend of Oppenheim's from wartime Turkey. In recognition of his service to the German cause in the First World War by promoting the global anti-Entente jihad, Oppenheim was even given an 'Honour Cross for front-line soldiers' (*Ehrenkreuz für Frontkämpfer*) 'in the name of the Führer and Reichskanzler' on 29 January 1937.[54]

Never one to resist flattery from social superiors, Oppenheim happily volunteered his services to the Nazis when war broke out again in 1939. Showing that he had neither forgotten nor learned anything in the preceding twenty-five years, Oppenheim reprised his early tune in a style verging on self-parody, composing yet another monster 'Memorandum on the Revolutionizing of the Middle East' on 25 July 1940, in which he advised his Führer that 'the struggle against the Jews and English in Palestine must be resumed afresh'.[*][55] As ruler of soon-to-be *Judenrein* Palestine, Oppenheim proposed his good friend al-Husseini, the Grand Mufti of Jerusalem, who had shown himself 'an energetic, clever, and crafty ... militant' in his campaign 'against Jewish infiltration'.[56]

Hitler was happy to take Oppenheim's advice. The Mufti was a pioneer in race-murder, having incited Arab mobs to lynch hundreds of Palestinian Jews in Jerusalem riots in 1920, 1921, 1929 and 1936. Al-Husseini had excelled himself in organizing the anti-Semitic pogrom in Baghdad in June 1941, following the failure of a pro-Nazi coup, in which some 110 Jews were murdered, hundreds more were wounded, and thousands deprived of their property. Although most

---

* To be fair to Oppenheim, he did not propose here to Hitler that *all* Jews in Palestine be expelled. Rather, he specified that 'only those who were [living] there before the world war' be allowed to remain. With a Jewish population of some 400,000 in 1940, this meant Oppenheim wanted in the neighbourhood of 300,000 Palestinian Jews cleansed, to restore the pre-1914 population of under 100,000.

Iraqi Jews had already been expelled during Feisal's short-lived reign, the 1941 pogrom was one of the ugliest episodes in the process which saw Baghdad's once thriving Jewish population reduced to almost zero in the twentieth century.*[57] Little wonder Hitler, impressed with the vigour of Oppenheim's anti-Semitic man of action, agreed to meet with the Mufti on 28 November 1941, just as the serious logistical planning for the Holocaust began.

Predictably, Hitler and the Mufti got along famously during their historic encounter, which was lubricated by 'Arabic' coffee. It may have helped al-Husseini that, unlike many Levantine Arabs, he had blond hair and blue eyes: he was the spitting image of an 'honorary Aryan'.[58] Hitler assured his new friend that Germany would carry out 'an uncompromising struggle against the Jews', which would include measures to make impossible 'the formation of a Jewish state in Palestine'. The Mufti, for his part, offered his 'full trust in the Führer, who was fighting against the same three enemies which were shared by the Arabs: namely the English, the Jews and the Bolsheviks'. Giving the first semi-public hint of the destruction of European Jewry he was planning, Hitler told al-Husseini that he would 'solve the Jewish problem in one European country after another'. Even more explicitly, Hitler declared that one of Germany's main strategic goals was 'the annihilation of the Jews living under British protection in Arab lands' (*die Vernichtung des im arabischen Raum unter der Protektion der britischen Macht lebenden Judentums*). Hearing this promise with 'an air of gratification', the Mufti assured Hitler of his trust and promised to do everything he could to help.[59]

These were not idle words. Hitler, true to his word, put the Mufti on the payroll, to the tune of 75,000 Marks per month. The Nazis also gave al-Husseini 'a luxurious home on Berlin's fashionable Klopstock Street, a full staff of servants, a chauffeured Mercedes limousine ... as well as four other residences and suites in two of Berlin's most luxurious hotels'. These he used to entertain Arab exiles from British Palestine, who were assured that German military might would soon allow them revenge against their English and Jewish oppressors.[60]

---

* Among the Mufti's fellow plotters in 1941 was General Khairallah Talfah, Saddam Hussein's uncle and later his 'guardian, mentor and father-in-law'.

This was the subject of the Mufti's radio addresses from Berlin, in which he exhorted the Arab world to join another global jihad targeting Bolsheviks, Englishmen and Jews. In one such broadcast, the Mufti told his Arab listeners 'in the name of the Koran and for the honour of Islam, to sabotage the oil pipe lines ... [and] kill British troops'. Another stock theme was that Arab Muslims 'could achieve eternal salvation by rising up and killing the Jewish infidels living in their countries'. The Mufti's tone grew more urgent in summer 1942, as the Wehrmacht pushed into the Caucasus, while Rommel's desert offensive threatened British Egypt. In view of the genocidal plans the Mufti cooked up with Adolf Eichmann that year involving a 'mobile SS squad' called 'Einsatzgruppe Ägypten' which was 'on standby in Athens' in case Rommel took Cairo – not to mention a plan the Mufti himself organized in late 1944, which saw five German parachutists sent carrying 'ten containers of a toxin to poison Tel Aviv's water system'* – we may infer that the Nazi defeats at Stalingrad and El-Alamein saved the entire Jewish population of Palestine, now nearing 500,000, from annihilation.[61]

Europe's Jews, of course, were not so fortunate. Perhaps in order to compensate for his inability to murder Jews in Palestine, in 1943 the Mufti travelled to Sarajevo to help Heinrich Himmler form volunteer Muslim SS battalions in the Balkans. As Himmler himself explained, Muslims were seen as 'among the most honourable and true followers of the Führer Adolf Hitler due to their hatred of the common Jewish-English-Bolshevik enemy'.[62] Inspired by Himmler's words, the Mufti formed three mostly Muslim Waffen-SS divisions, which by 1944 numbered some 100,000 recruits in all.† The most notorious of the Mufti's death squads, the *Handschar* SS division, 'slaughtered 90 percent – 12,600 – of Bosnia's 14,000 Jews'. Himmler was so pleased that he 'established a special mullah military school in Dresden to train the Bosnian Muslim recruits.'**[63] The Mufti formed his own 'Imam

---

* The parachutists were captured by the British somewhere near Jericho.
† In one of the Mufti's Muslim Waffen-SS divisions, some 15 per cent of the volunteers were Catholic Croats.
** Himmler was less pleased, however, when the Mufti sabotaged a propaganda stunt which would have seen 5,000 token Balkan Jewish children allowed to emigrate via Turkey, in exchange for the release of 20,000 German POWs. The Mufti insisted the children be sent to the gas chambers in Poland instead. His wish was granted.

School' in Berlin, which trained German SS officers in the convergence of Nazi and Muslim ideas, which they could then instil in their Muslim volunteers. So enthusiastically did these recruits respond to Nazi anti-Semitic propaganda, boasted Division Commander Sauberzweig, 'that the Muslims in our SS division ... are beginning to see in our Führer the appearance of a Second Prophet'. Little wonder German tourists were still being greeted decades later with enthusiastic 'Heil Hitler!' salutes by Muslims in Casablanca, Cairo, Damascus and Baghdad.[64]

In the years since 9/11, the Nazi-Muslim connection in the Second World War has inspired a growing literature as journalists seek to understand the roots of 'radical Islam'. Even more shocking than the extent of cooperation has been the revelation that many Arab Muslims have expressed public regret that Hitler did not finish the job. The Saudi news agency's description of Adolf Eichmann (another friend of the Mufti's) as the man who 'had the honour of killing six million Jews' has become justly notorious, but it is hardly the only example of its kind. On 29 April 2002, to take a random sample from the Cairo media, Fatma Abdallah Mahmoud wrote in *Al-Akhbar*, 'But I, personally, complain to Hitler, even saying to him from the bottom of my heart, "If only you had done it, brother, if only it had really happened, so that the world could sigh in relief".'[65]

Germany's own jihadis were similarly unrepentant. While some of those involved in Oppenheim's holy war, like Frobenius, Hentig, Kress and Niedermayer, kept their distance from the Nazis (which is not to say that any of them actively opposed Hitler),* both Oppenheim and Prüfer distinguished themselves in their moral blindness to the plight of

---

* Although Oskar von Niedermayer expressed reservations about the brutal German invasion of the Soviet Union, this was due less to concern for the Nazis' genocidal policy of racial extermination than to his dismay over the strategic foolishness of the enterprise, not least because it destroyed the fruitful Soviet-German partnership he had done much to create: Niedermayer had personally drafted many of the financial terms of the Rapallo Treaty of 1922. Despite his reservations, Niedermayer actively assisted the Wehrmacht in Ukraine, putting his regional and linguistic expertise to use training units of Caucasian and Central Asian 'Osttruppen' defectors from the Red Army.

Niedermayer was, it is true, later interned in a prison camp in Torgau in October 1944 for 'defeatist' anti-Hitler remarks. But Nazi friends, including Heinrich Himmler, intervened on his behalf to secure favourable treatment. There is a popular theory that

Europe's Jews. Prüfer did resign from the Foreign Office in September 1943, but this was in the manner of leaving a sinking ship and in no way a protest at Nazi war crimes. The defeat of Hitler's war machine in 1945, Prüfer's biographer Donald McKale writes, actually 'heightened his hatred of the Jews'.[66]

Oppenheim's reaction to Germany's downfall, while less openly anti-Semitic, was more revealing. In the section of his memoirs touching on the war, composed in 1946, the Baron blamed Hitler for having unleashed a war in which 'millions of Germans had fallen on the battlefield, and nearly all of Germany's cities, along with her immense and irreplaceable cultural possessions, have been destroyed by enemy bombs'.[67] There is not a single word in Oppenheim's voluminous memoirs about the mass murder of the Jews during the war in Germany, Europe or the Near East. While the Baron had been estranged from the Jewish banking side of his family for most of his life – his father Albert's conversion to Catholicism in 1858 had provided him with useful insurance following the passage of the Nuremberg Laws – Max von Oppenheim was still the grandson of Salomon Oppenheim Jr, the bank's founder. Although it was understandable that he would keep his distance from his Jewish kinsmen in the interest of self-preservation during the Nazi period, one might think the Baron would have spared a thought for Jewish suffering once the world had learned about the Holocaust. One would be wrong.

Oppenheim was not the only exemplar of Jewish self-abnegation in the Nazi era. In *The Orientalist* (2005), Tom Reiss tells the improbable story of Lev Nussinbaum, scion of a rich Jewish oil dynasty from *fin de siècle* Baku, who later reinvented himself as 'Essad Bey', a pro-Nazi Muslim writer in Weimar Berlin.[68] In both of these men, we can see a powerful longing for a mythical realm where Jews could blend into the

Niedermayer, as a result of a childhood acquaintance with Colonel Klaus von Stauffenberg, was peripherally involved in the 20 July 1944 plot to kill Hitler, but as Hans-Ulrich Seidt writes in his fine recent biography, *Berlin, Kabul, Moskau* (p. 372), 'there is no evidence at all that [Niedermayer] knew of, endorsed, or in any way supported the conspiracy [to kill Hitler]'. Certainly the Soviets did not see Niedermayer as a hero of the anti-Hitler resistance: he was interned by the Red Army in 1945 and deported to the USSR. Niedermayer died in a Russian prison in Vladimir, near Moscow, in 1948.

ethnic mosaic of the Orient, escaping not only the demands of Judaic tradition and stereotyping by Gentiles but the cold light of Western reason altogether. Nussinbaum/Essad Bey, like many other great Jewish Orientalists of the time, found this realm in his imagination.

Oppenheim, by contrast, had tried to make his fantasy world flesh. So sweeping was his rejection of his Jewish heritage that he openly endorsed race murder in the First World War, and again in the Second, when in 1940 he advised Hitler to support his friend al-Husseini's efforts to cleanse British Palestine of Jews. The Grand Mufti of Jerusalem clearly learned a great deal from Oppenheim, whose 1914 jihad *fetvas* targeting Entente subjects probably inspired al-Husseini's own jihad *fetvas* of 1921, 1929, 1937 and 1941, which targeted British nationals and Jews – as well as his far more significant jihad *fetva* of 1948 which declared the murder of Israeli Jews a Muslim duty for ever after. The Mufti had fought in the Ottoman army, after all, which had been bombarded in 1914 and 1915 with Oppenheim's holy war propaganda.[69] The Baron even created a precedent for Shia jihad *fetvas* with the Grand Mufti of Karbala's anti-Entente holy war proclamation in 1915. One does not have to saddle Oppenheim with personal responsibility for the actions of murderous Muftis and Mullahs to see that his idea of a worldwide holy war targeting innocent civilians set an extremely dangerous precedent.

It was not only in his invention of global jihad that Oppenheim was a pioneer. In the Baron's self-pitying rejection of his Judaic heritage, we can see at work that virulent syndrome of bourgeois self-loathing so common in the modern West. To secure acceptance in the Wilhelmstrasse (and later, with the Nazis), Oppenheim was willing to expunge his racial and religious heritage. To avenge the British persecutors in Cairo who had deprived him of his hard-won status in the German Foreign Office before the war, he sought to unleash the murderous rage of Muslims against Albion, even if it meant also ensnaring Christians and Jews – despite being a converted Christian of Jewish heritage himself. While it is easy to dismiss the Baron as a common buffoon (as German Orientalists like Ernst Jäckh did), Oppenheim's complexes were dangerous precisely because they *were* common: common enough to appeal both to intellectual mediocrities like the Kaiser and to brilliant (if immature) scholars like Curt Prüfer. The anti-Semitism which gripped so many Germans after 1918 was born of the same poisonous brew of self-pity in a people which, by all rights, had done pretty well for themselves in the world and were substantially responsible for the catastrophe which had befallen them in the First World War.

Since Hitler was defeated in 1945, there has been a tendency to say 'goodbye to all that', as if the exposure of the Nazi death camps truly taught the world 'a lesson it will never forget'.[70] And yet the toxic self-pitying disease which gave rise to Nazism is still abroad in the world, if no longer so prevalent in Germany itself. At its most glaringly obvious, the syndrome manifests itself in common Arab anti-Semitism, with Israel blamed for every evil which has occurred in the Middle East in modern times. But there is a subtler version of the virus coursing through the veins of the West, such as in the fashionable Third Worldist autocritique which decries every sin of European imperialism while absolving the world's most wicked post-colonial regimes of responsibility for their crimes. Tellingly, the self-loathing 'my people are not my own' syndrome tends to strike not the poor, but instead 'limousine liberals' like Baron Oppenheim, a man who literally spent a Jewish banking fortune fomenting anti-Semitic jihad. Zionism, whatever its merits or demerits as a political programme, had emerged from the heart of German Judaeo-Christian culture at the time of its greatest flowering. Ungrateful recipients of all the best their flourishing empire had to offer, Max von Oppenheim and his foolish Emperor spent their civilizational inheritance promoting an atavistic version of pan-Islam devoted to the destruction of that civilization and to the murder of the Christians and Jews who had forged it. It was a breathtaking error in judgement, and we are all living with the consequences today.

Notes

Prologue

1. Canon J. T. Parfit, *Twenty Years in Baghdad and Syria*, p. 32.

1 The Kaiser, the Baron and the Dragoman

1. 'To banish the demons [i.e. born of modern democracy], we need a prophet': Louis-Philippe to Guizot, cited by Michael Balfour in *The Kaiser and His Times*, p. 27.

2. 'The German Emperor's Visit to Constantinople' in *The Levant Herald and Eastern Express* (Special Edition), Constantinople, Saturday, 9 November 1889.

3. See Margaret Lavinia Anderson, '"Down in Turkey, far away": Human Rights, the Armenian Massacres, and Orientalism in Wilhelmine Germany' in *Journal of Modern History*, 79 (March 2007), p. 111.

4. For a critique of the 'Pomeranian-grenadier-bones thesis' about Bismarck's supposed aversion to 'any political, economic and military ties with the Ottoman Empire', see Jehuda Wallach, 'Bismarck and the "Eastern Question" – A Re-Assessment' in Wallach (ed.), *Germany and the Middle East 1835– 1939*, pp. 23–9.

5. 'Aufzeichnungen Seiner Majestät Kaiser Wilhelms II', unpublished memoir, in GPA, BPH/53/165, section 'Beziehungen S.M. zu Europäischen Fürsten-höfen. Stambul', pp. 3–5.

6. Ibid., p. 8; 'The German Emperor's Visit to Constantinople'; and Balfour, *The Kaiser and His Times*, p. 142.

7. John C. Röhl, *The Kaiser and his Court*, pp. 13, 25–6; Balfour, *The Kaiser and His Times*, p. 125; and Oberst Walter Nicolai, *Kaiser Wilhelm II*, unpublished persönliche Erinnerungen, in GPA, BPH/53/342, pp. 21–2.

8. 'Aufzeichnungen Seiner Majestät Kaiser Wilhelms II', pp. 9–10.

9. Balfour, *The Kaiser and His Times*, p. 190.

10. 'Aufzeichnungen Seiner Majestät Kaiser Wilhelms II', pp. 6–7; and Peter Hopkirk, *On Secret Service East of Constantinople*, p. 21.

11. Ibid., p. 23.

12. Prince (Bernhard) von Bülow, *Memoirs*, vol. 1, p. 251.

13. Bülow, *Memoirs*, vol. 1, pp. 249–50. See also Isaiah Friedman, *Germany, Turkey, and Zionism*, pp. 75–9; Balfour, *The Kaiser and His Times*, p. 216; and Hans Rall, *Wilhelm II. Eine Biographie*, p. 185.

14. Bülow, *Memoirs*, vol. 1, p. 253.

15. Wilhelm II, 'Tischrede in Damaskus (8 November 1898)' in Ernst Johann (ed.), *Reden des Kaisers*, p. 81; Hopkirk, *On Secret Service East of Constantinople*, p. 23.

16. Bülow, *Memoirs*, vol. 1, p. 254.

17. Wilhelm II, *The Kaiser's Letters to the Tsar*, Isaac Don Levine (ed.), p. 58.

18. Ibid., pp. 66–7.

19. Thomas L. Hughes, 'The German Mission to Afghanistan 1915–1916' in Wolfgang Schwanitz (ed.), *Germany and the Middle East 1871–1945*, p. 29.

20. Maurice Larcher, *La guerre turque dans la guerre mondiale*, pp. 8–9.

21. Max von Oppenheim, 'Meine Beziehungen zu seiner Majestät dem Kaiser Wilhelm II', MvO, 1/7, p. 160.

22. Oppenheim, 'Jugendzeit in Köln, Straßburg und Berlin 1860–83', in MvO, 1/1, pp. 45–6, 57–65; and 'Referandar und Assessor 1883–92', in MvO, 1/2, p. 11 and *passim*.

23. Oppenheim, 'Erste Reisen im Vorderen Orient u. in Afrika 1883–93', in MvO, 1/3, pp. 1–10.

24. Citation in Teichmann and Völger, *Faszination Orient*, p. 22.

25. Max von Oppenheim, *Vom Mittelmeer zum Persischen Golf* (2 vols, 1899–1900). The Lawrence quote is cited in Teichmann and Völger, *Faszination Orient*, p. 27.

26. Ibid., p. 112.

27. 'Bericht über eine im Jahr 1899 ausgeführte Forschungsreise in der asiatischen Türkei, von Dr. Max Frhr. V. Oppenheim' in PAAA, R 14558, p. 70.

28. Oppenheim, 'Meine Beziehungen zu seiner Majestät dem Kaiser Wilhelm II' in MvO, 1/7, pp. 160–62.

29. This is confirmed by most of the Kaiser's tabletalk companions, such as his intelligence chief, Colonel Walter Nicolai. See Nicolai, *Kaiser Wilhelm II*, in GPA, BPH/53/342, pp. 22–4.

30. Oppenheim, 'Meine Beziehungen zu seiner Majestät dem Kaiser Wilhelm II' in MvO, 1/7, p. 162.

31. Oppenheim report from Cairo, 25 June 1903, in PAAA, R 14559.

32. On the Armenians in Cairo, see Oppenheim's 29 April 1904 dispatch to Berlin, in PAAA, R 14560. Oppenheim filed voluminous reports on the Mahdi before his (apparent) death in 1902, in PAAA, R 14559. On Mahdism and the Sanussis, see chapter 15.

33. See, for example, Oppenheim reports from Cairo dated 1 and 7/15 April 1905, in PAAA, R 14560.

34. See, for example, 'Kaiser Wilhelm II. Und der Islam', *Berliner Tageblatt*, 23 October 1905, in which Mustafa Kemal Pasha endorsed the German position on the Moroccan dispute. Clipped in PAAA, R 14560. See also Donald McKale, *Curt Prüfer*, p. 16.

35. Oppenheim, 'Dienst in Kairo. Eingeborene Welt, 1896–1909', in MvO, 1/6, pp. 1–12.

36. See 'Intrigues Allemandes au Caire. Comment on joue du Panislamisme' in *Les Pyramides*, 15 February 1906; 'Lettre d'Egypte' in *Journal des Débats*, 4 February 1906; 'Baron Max Oppenheim', *New York Daily Tribune*, 9 April 1906; and articles on Aqaba in *Mokattam*, the Cairo version of the *Daily Mail*, all clipped in PAAA, R 14561. For the British perspective on the Kaba crisis, see Roger Owen, *Lord Cromer*, pp. 333–41.

37. Sir Charles Hardinge to His Majesty's Foreign Secretary Lord Grey, 2 June 1906, in PRO, FO 371/65.

38. Oppenheim to Berlin from Cairo, 9 May 1906, in PAAA, R 14561.

39. Oppenheim to Berlin from Cairo, 8 August 1906, in PAAA, R 14561.

40. 'L'Agent Allemand Oppenheim' in *La Libre Parole*, 25 December 1910, clipped in PAAA, R 14565.

41. Letter from Habib Anhoury, Cairo businessman, to the President of the Reichstag, passed on by Reichstag deputy Freiherr von Hertling to the Foreign Office, 9 December 1909, in PAAA, R 14565.

42. Teichmann and Völger, *Faszination Orient*, p. 124.

43. McKale, *Curt Prüfer*, pp. 2–8.

44. See Shawish dossier prepared by Schabinger von Schowingen, 21 May 1915, in PAAA, R 21133.

45. Lord Kitchener MS, signed letter from Cairo to His Majesty's Foreign Secretary Lord Edward Grey, 30 September 1911, in PRO, FO 371/1114.

46. McKale, *Curt Prüfer*, p. 20.

47. Kitchener to Grey, 29 September 1911, in PRO, FO 371/1114.

48. Kitchener to Grey, 26 October 1911, in PRO, FO 371/1114.

49. McKale, *Curt Prüfer*, p. 22.

50. Kitchener to Hatzfeldt, 4 November 1911, and Kitchener reply, 6 November 1911, in PRO, FO 371/1114.

2 Berlin to Baghdad

1. Cited in Erich Lindow, *Freiherr Marschall von Bieberstein*, p. 48.

2. Cited in Edward Mead Earle, *Turkey, the Great Powers, and the Bagdad Railway*, pp. 16–17.

3. Quoted by Elie Kedourie, *England and the Middle East. The Destruction of the Ottoman Empire 1914–1921*, p. 90.

4. See Maybelle Kennedy Chapman, *Great Britain and the Baghdad Railway*, pp. 12–18.

5. Kuropatkin to French Ambassador at St Petersburg, M. le Marquis de Montebello, 30 January 1900, in QO, Corr. Pol. Nouvelle Série. Turquie, vol. 334. See also clippings in the same folder from the French-language Petersburg press, such as the cover stories in *Nouveau Temps*, 18/30 November and also 24 November/6 December 1899. For an overview of the objections to the Baghdad railway (and rail projects abutting the Black Sea) voiced by Russian diplomats over many years of frustrating negotiations, see, for example, the letter from Marschall von Bieberstein, German Ambassador at the Porte, to Reich Chancellor Bernhard von Bülow, 17 March 1907, in PAAA, R 13554.

6. Quoted by Jonathan S. McMurray, in *Distant Ties*, p. 20.

7. See Herbert Feis, *Europe, the World's Banker 1870–1914*, pp. 343–4.

8. Cited in Erich Lindow, *Freiherr Marschall von Bieberstein*, p. 48.

9. Chapman, *Great Britain and the Baghdad Railway*, p. 24; McMurray, *Distant Ties*, p. 28.

10. This agreement, dated 6 May 1899, is reproduced in Earle, *Turkey, the Great Powers, and the Bagdad Railway*, pp. 59–60. There is some dispute as to whether the Germans had agreed to take only an equal share (40 per cent) to the French, but, according to Siemens himself, the Germans reserved the right to keep a controlling majority. See Chapman, *Great Britain and the Baghdad Railway*, p. 33, especially footnote 46.

11. Somewhat confusingly, there was a provision for revenue guarantees of 15,000 francs per kilometre, but they were to come only out of 'excess' revenues raised by ordinary taxes in the Ottoman vilayets through which the railway passed, the idea being that commerce stimulated by the railway would ensure such easy revenue surpluses. The Ottoman government in Constantinople would not be responsible for plugging any gaps. See Earle (who interviewed Rechnitzer), *Turkey, the Great Powers, and the Bagdad Railway*, pp. 60–61, and p. 85 (footnote 7).

12. Widely cited, as in Balfour, *The Kaiser and His Times*, pp. 226–7.

13. The text of this agreement is widely available, as for example in 'The Baghdad Railway', *The Times* (London), 3 January 1900, clipped in QO, Corr. Pol. Nouvelle Série. Turquie, vol. 334.

14. Ibid.

15. See Ambassador Marschall von Bieberstein's complaint sent from Pera to Reich Chancellor Hohenlohe, 1 March 1900, in PAAA, R 14148.

16. Quoted by McMurray, in *Distant Ties*, p. 32.

17. Tevfik Pasha to German State Secretary Bernhard von Bülow, 23 June 1899, in PAAA, R 14155.

18. Oppenheim to Bülow, 12 May 1903, in PAAA, R 14559.

19. A copy of this secret decree is preserved in PAAA, R 13757.

20. See Deutsche Bank director Arthur Gwinner's letter to the German Foreign Office, 9 July 1906, in PAAA, R 14562.

21. On the Stemrich expedition and its findings, see McMurray, *Distant Ties*, pp. 44–8.

22. Earle, *Turkey, the Great Powers, and the Bagdad Railway*, pp. 83–4; and McMurray, *Distant Ties*, pp. 50–51.

23. Headline clipped and translated from *Novoe Vremya*, 9 March 1903; 'Le Chemin de fer de Bagdad', commissioned by the 2ème Bureau of the French army, March 1903; and Cambon to Quai d'Orsay, 13 March 1903: all in QO, Corr. Pol. Nouvelle Série. Turquie, vol. 334. On the British government reaction after a heated debate in the Commons on 23 April 1903, see Feis, *Europe, the World's Banker 1870–1914*, p. 351.

24. See McMurray, *Distant Ties*, p. 52; and Feis, *Europe, the World's Banker 1870–1914*, p. 353. A French group put up 540,000 francs, or 18 per cent of the total; another 25 per cent was put up by the ARC and BRC (both dominated by Deutsche Bank), with the remainder coming almost entirely from other German banking institutions.

25. Paul Rohrbach, *Die Bagdadbahn*, p. 16.

26. See McKale, *War by Revolution*, pp. 19, 239 (note 5).

27. Quoted by McMurray, in *Distant Ties*, p. 61.

28. See 'Note' labelled 'Bagdadbahn', sent as attachment to Marschall's report to Berlin from Therapia, 20 October 1905, in PAAA, R 13553.

29. Earle, *Turkey, the Great Powers, and the Bagdad Railway*, pp. 95–6.

30. See the tentative Isvolsky–Schoen agreement, 20 February 1907, and updated draft dated 3 July 1907, in PAAA, R 13554.

31. Marschall to Chancellor Bülow from Pera, 17 March 1907, in PAAA, R 13554.

32. Erich Lindow, *Freiherr Marschall von Bieberstein*, p. 75.

33. Earle, *Turkey, the Great Powers, and the Bagdad Railway*, p. 96.

34. See McMurray, *Distant Ties*, pp. 70–71.

3   Young Turks and Old Caliphs

1. Letter clipped from the 13 August 1906 London *Times* and reproduced, with annotations, in PAAA, R 14158.

2. Marschall to Berlin from Therapia, 7 October 1909, in PAAA, R 14159.

3. Sir Edward Pears, *Life of Abdul Hamid*, pp. 108–109.

4. See M. Naim Turfan, *Rise of the Young Turks*, p. 62.

5. On the impact of these events on Abdul Hamid and his view of the European powers, see Orhan Koloğlu, *Avrupa'nın Kıskacında Abdülhamit*.

6. M. Şükrü Hanioğlu, *The Young Turks in Opposition*, pp. 84–6. See also Bernard Lewis, *The Emergence of Modern Turkey*, pp. 162–3, 176, 198–9; and Erik Zürcher, *The Unionist Factor*, pp. 9–16.

7. Hanioğlu, *The Young Turks in Opposition*, pp. 142–3.

8. Letter from 'Mahmoud Pacha. Beau-frère de S. M. I. Le Sultan' to Kaiser Wilhelm II, 4 February 1900, and follow-up attempt from Sabahaddin and Lütfullah, 11 April 1900, in PAAA, R 14156. The Kaiser did not reply to any of these queries.

9. See Hanioğlu, *The Young Turks in Opposition*, p. 143.

10. 'Deutschland und die Affaire Mahmud Pascha', *Die Post*, 27 December 1899; 'Aus der Türkei', *Neue Preussische Zeitung*, 9 February 1900; cover story in *Frankfurter Allgemeine Zeitung*, 31 December 1899; 'Ausland' in *Der Bund*, 14 August 1900; 'Mahmoud Pacha and the Sultan' in *The Standard*, 22 January 1900; *Le Matin*, 16 January 1900, etc. All clipped in PAAA, R 14155 and 14156.

11. This promise was passed on to State Secretary Bülow by the Swiss Ambassador in Berlin, 30 March 1899, in PAAA, R 14156.

12. Several of Richthofen's letters to Munir Bey were seized and photographed by the Swiss police on the grounds that he was acting as a 'spy or *agent provocateur*'. They were reproduced in a number of Swiss newspapers in 1901–1902, including *Gazette de Lausanne* and *La Suisse*. Clipped and reproduced in PAAA, R 14158.

13. Ahmed Rıza, letter addressed to 'Sa Majesté Impériale Guillaume II Empereur d'Allemagne', 15 November 1898, in PAAA, R 14155.

14. See Marschall dispatch from Therapia, 1 June 1902, 'Geheim' in PAAA, R 14158.

15. Bodman from Therapia, 9 August 1905, and follow-up reports from the Munich Staatsrat to Prussian representative in Bavaria (Geschaftsträger) Freiherr von Werthern, 4 September 1905, and from Werthern to Bülow, all in PAAA, R 14158.

16. Rotenhan to Bülow from Rome, 8 March 1906, in PAAA, R 14158.

17. M. 2ükrü Hanioğlu, *Preparation for a Revolution. The Young Turks, 1902–1908*, pp. 124–5, and pp. 398–9 (notes 484–9).

18. Ibid., pp. 125 and 399, note 488; and Rotenhan to Bülow from Rome, 8 March 1906, in PAAA, R 14158.

19. See, for example, 'Mémoire des Libéraux Turcs Relatif à la Question d'Orient. Le Prince Sabehedine Aux Chancelleries' (Paris, December 1906); 'Aux Arméniens Ottomans' (Paris, September 1905); and Sabahaddin's letter to His Majesty's Foreign Secretary Edward Grey, published in *The Times*, 13 August 1906, in PAAA, R 14158.

20. Sabahaddin's letter, written in French, was published (in English translation) in *The Times* (London), 13 August 1906. It is excerpted, at length, in Hanioğlu, *Preparation for a Revolution. The Young Turks, 1902–1908*, pp. 126–7. Because it better captures the spirit of the original French than *The Times* translation (which blandly renders 'between East and West' ('zwischen Abend- und Morgenland' in the German translation) as 'between two worlds', and also uses the misleading 'Islamism' in place of 'Islam'), I have used the German translation in PAAA, R 14158.

21. On Abdul Hamid's attempt to revive the Caliphate for political purposes, see Turfan, *Rise of the Young Turks*, pp. 62–3.

22. So observed Baron Oppenheim, who was intimate with most of the Egyptian nationalists worked up about the Aqaba business, and who interviewed a number of hajj pilgrims on the subject (no doubt suggestively). See, for example, his report from Cairo, 16 May 1907, in PAAA, R 14563.

23. 'The Caliphate. The Sultan and England', *Egyptian Gazette*, 24 May 1906, clipped in PAAA, R 14562.

24. As Oppenheim complained in a report filed from Cairo, 16 May 1907, in PAAA, R 14563, with several examples from the *Egyptian Gazette* attached.

25. See David Fromkin, *A Peace to End All Peace*, pp. 104–105.

26. On this question, see especially Elie Kedourie, 'Egypt and the Caliphate, 1915–52', in *Chatham House Version*, pp. 177–81.

27. I have drawn here primarily on the fine analysis of the Sherifiate by Dr C. Snouck Hurgronje, in *Revolt in Arabia*, pp. 3–18.

28. As noted by Baron Oppenheim, among others, who socialized with many would-be Sherifs in Cairo, and met Hussein himself in Constantinople (on this meeting, see chapter 11 below). Oppenheim to Bülow, 1 April 1905, in PAAA, R 14560.

29. Ibid.

30. Oppenheim to Bülow, 26 May 1908, in PAAA, R 14563. In a similar vein, see also Oppenheim to Bülow, 31 July 1906, in PAAA, R 14562; and McKale, *War by Revolution*, p. 22.

31. As Hurgronje explains, in *Revolt in Arabia*, p. 32.

32. Figures given in Justin McCarthy, *Death and Exile*, p. 135; and Kemal Karpat, *Ottoman Population*, pp. 254, 274.

33. Cited by Turfan, in *Rise of the Young Turks*, pp. 65–6. Turfan's translation.

34. Exception should be made here for Hanioğlu's *Preparation for the Revolution*, Turfan's *Rise of the Young Turks*, and Feroz Ahmad, *The Young Turks*. Still, the so-called 'classic accounts' by Western historians, including Bernard Lewis's *Emergence of Modern Turkey* and Erik Zürcher's *Unionist Factor*, glide rather quickly over the events of 1908, as if conceding their inability to explain them. The present author makes no claim to have done any better.

35. Kiderlen-Wächter to Bülow, 10 July 1908, in PAAA, R 14159.

36. Heathcote to Foreign Office, 13 July 1908, in PRO, FO 371/544.

37. Cited by McMurray, in *Distant Ties*, p. 73. McMurray's translation.

38. Consul-General Harry H. Lamb from Salonika to Foreign Office, 2 August 1914 in PRO, FO 371/545.

39. McMurray, *Distant Ties*, p. 75.

40. Cited in ibid., p. 77. Marschall's moniker as the 'Giant of the Bosphorus' is cited in Weber, *Eagles on the Crescent*, p. 6. On the importance of the Austrian annexation of Bosnia, see also Turfan, *Rise of the Young Turks*, pp. 148–9.

41. Gerard Lowther to Grey, 19 August 1908; and Grey's reply, 20 August 1908, in PRO, FO 371/545.

42. Rıza's mother had been born in Munich, although by 1908 she had been living in the suburbs of Constantinople for many years. Lancken from Wilhelmshöhe (on behalf of Kaiser Wilhelm) to Foreign Office, 25 August 1908, in PAAA, R 14159.

43. Ibid.; and Bernard Lewis, *The Emergence of Modern Turkey*, pp. 197–8.

44. In this vein, see ibid., pp. 202–204, and Zürcher, *The Unionist Factor*, pp. 16–18.

45. Cited by Hanioğlu, in *The Young Turks in Opposition*, pp. 200–201.

46. Citations in Turfan, *Rise of the Young Turks*, pp. 134, 144, 148. See also Feroz Ahmad, 'The Young Turk Revolution' in *Journal of Contemporary History*, 3(3) (July 1968), p. 29; and Baron Marschall's dispatch from Pera, 13 April 1909, in PAAA, R 14160, which includes the second two demands ('die Wiederherstellung der Sultansherrschaft' and the demand for Rıza to be turned over, 'um ihn zu hängen').

47. Ibid.

48. Guenter Lewy, *The Armenian Massacres in Ottoman Turkey*, p. 33.

49. McMurray, *Distant Ties*, p. 79; and Lewis, *Emergence of Modern Turkey*, pp. 214–17.

50. Literally translated, 'Hareket ordusu' is 'Action Army', although the political flavour of the thing is lost. The usual rendering into English is 'Army of Deliverance'. See Bernard Lewis, *Emergence of Modern Turkey*, p. 216.

51. Turfan, *Rise of the Young Turks*, pp. 160–61; McMurray, *Distant Ties*, p. 79.

52. Cited by Lewis, in *Emergence of Modern Turkey*, p. 217.

53. Marschall to Berlin from Therapia, 7 October 1909, in PAAA, R 14160.

54. On all this see especially Fromkin, *A Peace to End All Peace*, pp. 41–2. Fromkin is relying here largely on the analysis of Elie Kedourie, in *Arabic Political Memoirs and Other Studies*. For a slightly more sympathetic account of Fitzmaurice, see G. R. Berridge, *Gerald Fitzmaurice (1865–1939), Chief Dragoman of the British Embassy in Istanbul* (2007).

55. Lamb to Foreign Office from Salonica, 2 August 1908, in PRO, FO 371/545.

56. See McMurray, *Distant Ties*, pp. 77–8.

57. Fromkin, *A Peace to End All Peace*, pp. 42, 49.

58. Marschall to Berlin from Pera, 22 and 23 April 1911, in PAAA, R 14160. For the details on Djavid and the British footnoted here, see Marschall from Pera, 1 and 5 May 1911, in PAAA, R 14560.

59. Ibid.

60. Jäckh, *Der aufsteigende Halbmond* (1911). On Jäckh's Ottoman-German PR tour, see Margaret Anderson, '"Down in Turkey, far away": Human Rights, the Armenian Massacres, and Orientalism in Wilhelmine Germany' in *Journal of Modern History*, 79 (March 2007), p. 108.

61. McMurray, *Distant Ties*, pp. 80–83.

62. See Aide-Mémoire from the German Chancellor's office, passed on to the Porte via the German Embassy in Pera, 11 January 1914, in BOA, HR-H 329.

63. The German Embassy in Constantinople was still protesting at the Porte's default on the captured Üsküp base renovations four years later. See Notes verbales dated 7 May 1915, 9 June 1916, etc., in BOA, HR-H 336.

64. See Oppenheim, 'Meine Etablierung in Berlin Ende 1913' in MvO, I/12.

65. Luxburg to Berlin from Calcutta, 16 January 1913, in PAAA, R 14549.

66. Luxburg from Calcutta, 12 March 1913, in PAAA, R 14549.

67. Luxburg from Calcutta, 29 July 1913, in PAAA, R 14549

68. Luxburg from Simla, 7 August 1913, in PAAA, R 14549.

69. Ibid.

70. Lichnowsky from London, 15 July 1913, in PAAA, R 14549.

4 A Gift from Mars: German Holy War Fever

1. The Kaiser wrote this in the margins of a telegram received from Pourtàles, the German Ambassador to St Petersburg, 30 July 1914. Cited in Ulrich Gehrke, *Persien in der Deutschen Orientpolitik während des ersten Weltkrieges*, vol. 1, p. 1; and in Fritz Fischer, *Germany's Aims in the First World War*, p. 121.

2. Norman Stone, *Europe Transformed 1878–1919*, p. 247.

3. For analysis of the evidence surrounding German war guilt, see David Fromkin, *Europe's Last Summer*. The most incriminating evidence that Bethmann himself had war in mind was that he contacted his Hamburg bankers repeatedly in July to rearrange his family's finances. See Norman Stone, *World War One. A Short History*, pp. 20–21.

4. Hopkirk, *On Secret Service East of Constantinople*, p. 53.

5. Cited in Fischer, *Germany's Aims in the First World War*, p. 126. On Moltke's embrace of revolutionary jihad in August 1914, see also Carl Mühlmann, *Das Deutsche-Türkische Waffenbündnis im Weltkriege*, pp. 24–5.

6. Ulrich Trumpener, *Germany and the Ottoman Empire*, p. 22.

7. See Fromkin, *A Peace to End All Peace*, p. 109.

8. Trumpener points out, for example, that Wangenheim was 'overruled' by the Kaiser on 24 July 1914 in his spurning of Enver's overtures towards a military alliance. Trumpener also notes that, on the eve of the Ottoman jihad declaration in November 1914, Wangenheim warned the Wilhelmstrasse that 'the unleashing of religious passions among the Turks was liable to do more harm than good' (this is Trumpener's phrasing, but the gist of this remark is confirmed by Austrian Ambassador Pallavicini, in his 2 November 1914 report to Vienna, in HHSA, Liasse Krieg 21a. Türkei, box 942). Wangenheim was particularly concerned that massacres of Armenians would be blamed on the Germans. See Trumpener, *Germany and the Ottoman Empire*, pp. 15, 22–3, 118–19. While Wangenheim's concerns about possible damage to Germany's reputation ring true (and were shared by many other Germans as news of the Armenian massacres filtered out of Turkey in 1915), this obviously did not preclude support for the jihad, the plans for which Wangenheim personally negotiated over many months with Enver.

9. Wangenheim to Bethmann, 14 August 1914, in PAAA, R 21028, and 18 August 1914, in PAAA, R 20936.

10. Ibid.

11. Donald McKale, *War by Revolution*, pp. 50–51.

12. Moritz reporting to the Wilhelmstrasse from Berlin, after returning home, 26 August 1914, in PAAA, R 21123.

13. John Buchan, *Greenmantle*, p. 21.

14. Hopkirk, *On Secret Service East of Constantinople*, p. 2.

15. Friedrich Kress von Kressenstein, *Mit den Türken zum Suezkanal*, p. 25.

16. Jagow to Stockholm, 7 August 1914, in PAAA, R 21028.

17. Reichenau to Zimmermann from Stockholm, 25 August 1914, in PAAA, R 21028.

18. Otto von Wesendonck, writing for Foreign Office Legation Secretary Friedrich von Prittwitz, 'Überblick über die in der islamitisch-israelischen

Welt eingeleitete Agitationstätigkeit', 16 August 1914, in PAAA, R 21028. For more on the origins of this extraordinary document, see Egmont Zechlin, *Die deutsche Politik und die Juden im Ersten Weltkrieg*, pp. 119–20, and the Epilogue below.

19. Oppenheim to Bethmann, 18 August 1914, in PAAA, R 20936.

20. Tschirschky to Bethmann from Vienna, 22 August 1914, in PAAA, R 21123.

21. Quadt to Bethmann from Athens, 5 September 1914, in PAAA, R 21123.

22. Ibid.

23. Prüfer to Berlin, via Wangenheim, 7 September 1914, in PAAA, R 21124; Wangenheim to Berlin, 4 September 1914, in PAAA, R 21123; and McKale, *Curt Prüfer*, pp. 27–8. On the plans relating to sabotaging the Suez Canal, see also the British interrogation of Mors after he was captured in early November 1914. The transcript is reproduced in the official 'Correspondence Respecting Events Leading to the Rupture of Relations with Turkey . . .' (henceforth 'Turkey Correspondence'), printed by Harrison & Sons for His Majesty's Stationery Office, November 1914.

24. Wangenheim to Berlin, 30 August and 4 September 1914, in PAAA, R 21123.

25. On the role the dispatch of this invitation played in America's decision to enter the war in 1917, see Barbara Tuchman, *The Zimmermann Telegram*.

26. According to Donald McKale, Curt Prüfer's biographer, Wangenheim and Prüfer did not, in fact, get on well. This may well be true, but any mutual mistrust the two men felt seems to have been overridden by their reliance on each other. Prüfer was exceptionally loyal, sending all correspondence via Wangenheim and trusting him implicitly. Likewise, Wangenheim never spoke an ill word about Prüfer in his own correspondence with Berlin. It is clear that the two men respected each other greatly. In a telegram from Therapia on 7 September 1914, Wangenheim did request that he could send Prüfer to Jaffa (i.e. out of town) – but he emphasized that the reason was his dire need for 'a trustworthy man in the field'. In PAAA, R 21124.

27. Bethmann to Wangenheim, 7 September 1914, in PAAA, R 21124.

28. Wangenheim from Therapia, 8 September 1914 (twice); Jagow from military headquarters in Luxemburg, 9 and 13 September 1914, and Bethmann from same (and copied to the Reichsschatzamt), all in PAAA, R 21124.

29. Cited by McKale, in *Curt Prüfer*, p. 28.

30. McKale, *War by Revolution*, pp. 57–8.

31. Hopkirk, *On Secret Service East of Constantinople*, p. 86.

32. See Roloff, 'Meine Pilgerfahrt nach Mekka', *circa* December 1914, and accompanying post-mortems, in PAAA, R 21126. Oppenheim concluded from the meagre results of Roloff's mission that he was a con man who had

never set sail from Rotterdam. McKale, in *War by Revolution* (p. 62), agrees, as does Herbert Müller, in *Islam, gihad ('Heiliger Krieg') und Deutsches Reich*, p. 369. Tilman Lüdke, in *Jihad Made in Germany* (pp. 149–52), takes Roloff's account as truthful. Considering the extreme difficulty of entering Mecca as an infidel in Muslim disguise, Oppenheim's dismissal of Roloff's claim is certainly plausible. But Oppenheim may also have been angered by Roloff's discouraging conclusions about the prospects for German jihad.

33. Niedermayer to Foreign Office from Pera, 2 October 1914, in PAAA, R 21031.

34. Wangenheim to Oppenheim, 15 October 1914, in PAAA, R 21124.

35. Max Freiherr von Oppenheim, 'Denkschrift betreffend die Revolutionierung der islamischen Gebiete unserer Feinde', dated 'Berlin, Ende Oktober 1914', in PAAA, R 20937.

36. Ibid.

5 The War for the Porte

1. I. K. Grigorevich memorandum, on behalf of the Russian Naval Staff, 7 November 1913. Reproduced in *Krasnyi Arkhiv*, vol. 6, pp. 67–9.

2. Frank G. Weber, *Eagles on the Crescent*, pp. 11, 49.

3. Grigorevich telegram no. 320, to Tsar Nicholas II, dispatched at 1.30 a.m. on the night of 25–26 October 1912, and the Tsar's reply ('Soglasen. Nikolai.'), reproduced in *Krasnyi Arkhiv*, vol. 6, pp. 51–2.

4. Reynolds, 'The Ottoman-Russian Struggle for Eastern Anatolia and the Caucasus, 1908–1918', pp. 60–64.

5. The key planning meeting was held in St Petersburg on 21 February 1914, with not only all ranking naval staff personnel, but also Foreign Minister Sazonov, and Girs, the Constantinople Ambassador, present. Sazonov, remarkably, chaired the meeting, indicating how fully the Foreign Ministry was on board with plans to seize Constantinople. The original transcript and the six-point plan to ready the navy for a 'final settlement' of the Eastern Question – i.e. seizure of the Straits and Constantinople – along with the final version approved by Tsar Nicholas II on 5 April 1914, are preserved in AVPRI, fond. 138, opis' 467, del. 462, 9–25 (and backs) and 67–93 (the Tsar's dated signature is on list' 93).

6. Reynolds, 'The Ottoman-Russian Stuggle for Eastern Anatolia and the Caucasus, 1908–1918', pp. 71–4.

7. Ibid., pp. 77–8.

8. Weber, *Eagles on the Crescent*, pp. 38–9.

9. Ibid., pp. 47, 54–5.

10. Henry Morgenthau, *Secrets of the Bosphorus*, p. 2.

11. Weber, *Eagles on the Crescent*, p. 25.

12. Reynolds, 'The Ottoman-Russian Struggle for Eastern Anatolia and the Caucasus, 1908–1918', p. 70.

13. Weber, *Eagles on the Crescent*, pp. 20, 34–9, 43, 49–52.

14. Reynolds, 'The Ottoman-Russian Struggle for Eastern Anatolia and the Caucasus, 1908–1918', p. 186.

15. Fromkin, *A Peace to End All Peace*, pp. 49–50.

16. Trumpener, *Germany and the Ottoman Empire*, pp. 15–16.

17. Fromkin, *A Peace to End All Peace*, pp. 54–61. Trumpener, incidentally, seems to have missed Enver's trick, concluding that Britain was justified in seizing the battleships on 3 August in retaliation for Enver's 1 August offer of the *Sultan Osman* to Germany, without realizing that 1) Britain had already completely impounded and boarded the warships on 29 July; and that 2) Enver knew of this by 1 August. Trumpener, *Germany and the Ottoman Empire*, p. 24.

18. From article 2: 'Dans le cas où la Russie interviendrait par des mesures militaires actives ete créerait par là pour l'Allemagne le casus foederis vis-à-vis de l'Autriche-Hongrie, ce casus foederis entrerait également en vigueur pour la Turquie'. The 2 August 1914 treaty is reproduced in both its French original version and German translation in Carl Mühlmann, *Deutschland und die Türkei 1913–1914*, pp. 94–6.

19. 'Turkey Annual Report, 1913. Mr. Beaumont to Sir Edward Grey', 4 December 1914, in PRO, FO 371/2137.

20. Alan Moorehead, *Gallipoli*, p. 17.

21. Cited by Weber, in *Eagles on the Crescent*, p. 26.

22. Barbara Tuchman, *The Guns of August*, p. 183.

23. Wangenheim to Grand Vizier Said Halim, 6 August 1914, as reproduced in Mühlmann, *Deutschland und die Türkei*, pp. 96–97.

24. Tuchman, *Guns of August*, pp. 177, 182–3.

25. See memorandum from the National Bank of Turkey to the British Foreign Office, 5 August 1914, in PRO, FO 371/2137.

26. Beaumont to Grey from Therapia, 10 August 1914, in PRO, FO 371/2137.

27. Trumpener, *Germany and the Ottoman Empire*, pp. 31–2.

28. See Beaumont to Grey from Therapia, 11 August 1914, from the 'Turkey Correspondence'.

29. Mallet to Grey, 20 August 1914, from the 'Turkey Correspondence'.

30. Reynolds, 'The Ottoman-Russian Struggle for Eastern Anatolia and the Caucasus, 1908–1918', pp. 192–3.

31. Girs to Sazonov, 19 August 1914, reproduced in Pokrovskii, *Tsarskaia Rossiia v mirovoi voine*, vol. 1, p. 28.

32. Sazonov to Girs, 3 (16) August 1914, in ibid., p. 25.

33. Izvolsky to Sazonov, 11 August 1914, reproduced in *Tsarskaia Rossiia*, vol. 1, p. 17.

34. Buchanan to Grey from Petrograd, passed on to Mallet in Constantinople, 21/22 August 1914, in PRO, FO 371/2137.

35. Trumpener, *Germany and the Ottoman Empire*, p. 33.

36. Joseph Pomiankowski, *Zusammenbruch des Ottomanischen Reiches*, p. 78.

37. Trumpener, *Germany and the Ottoman Empire*, pp. 38–9.

38. Mallet to Grey, 26 and 27 August, 10, 21, 24 and 25 September 1914; Sir H. Bax-Ironside from Sofia to Grey, 28 August 1914, all in the 'Turkey Correspondence'. Mallet's 29 August 1914 dispatch to Grey is in PRO, FO 371/2137. The British were not certain about the size of the German naval detachment, guessing 500 or 600, or their ultimate destination; it was only after their arrival in Constantinople that the purpose of the 700-man mission to man the Straits defences became clear. The experts on coastal batteries came from a German unit referred to as the Sonderkommando Usedom. Trumpener, *Germany and the Ottoman Empire*, p. 36.

39. Ibid., pp. 39–40.

40. Girs to Sazonov, 27 July 1914, in *Tsarskaia Rossiia*, vol. 1, pp. 4–5.

41. Citations in Ronald Bobroff, *Roads to Glory. Late Imperial Russia and the Turkish Straits*, pp. 107, 112.

42. Girs to Trubetskoi, 28 September (11 October) 1914, in AVPRI, fond 151, opis' 482, del. 4068, 224.

43. Cited by Fromkin, in *A Peace to End All Peace*, p. 66.

44. On this point see Reynolds, 'The Ottoman-Russian Struggle for Eastern Anatolia and the Caucasus, 1908–1918', p. 195.

45. Trumpener, *Germany and the Ottoman Empire*, pp. 42–4.

46. In this vein, see Pomiankowski (the Austro-Hungarian military attaché at the Porte), *Zusammenbruch des Ottomanischen Reiches*, pp. 80–83.

47. As paraphrased by Trumpener, in Germany and the Ottoman Empire, p. 47.

48. Mallet to Grey, 17 and 23 October 1914, from the 'Turkey Correspondence'.

49. On Russian intelligence on the 11 October 1914 meeting, see Girs to Sazonov, 13 October 1914, reproduced in *Tsarskaia Rossiia*, p. 50.

50. On the financial terms (and the insistence that the gold be physically present before an attack was authorized), see Humann report dated 11 October 1914, in EJP, 1/13. Enver's insistence on a 500,000 (Turkish) pound monthly subsidy was communicated via Humann, on 24 October 1914, in EJP, 1/15. For analysis, see Mustafa Aksakal, *Ottoman Road to War*, pp. 167, 172–3.

51. According to the Austro-Hungarian military attaché. Pomiankowski, *Zusammenbruch des Ottomanischen Reiches*, p. 85.

52. Enver's action programme, sent from Prinz Hohenlohe from Berlin to Vienna, 24 October 1914, and modified agreement sent from Pallavicini to Vienna, 25 October 1914, both in HHSA, Liasse Krieg 21a. Türkei, box 942.

53. Cited in the frontispiece of Tuchman, *Guns of August*, p. 9.

54. Cited by Trumpener, in *Germany and the Ottoman Empire*, p. 54. The Djemal quote is cited by Mustafa Aksakal, in *Ottoman Road to War*, p. 19. On Russian foreknowledge of Djemal's conversion to the war camp, see Girs to Sazonov, 21 September (4 October) 1914, in AVPRI, fond 151, opis' 482, del. 4068, 187.

55. Cited by Aksakal, in *Ottoman Road to War*, p. 177.

56. Pallavicini's secret report labelled 'Actives Eingreifen der Türkei', 22 October 1914, in HHSA, Liasse Krieg 21a. Türkei, box 942. A copy of Enver's final orders to Souchon, dated 24 October 1914, can also be found in EJP, 1/15.

57. Aksakal, *Ottoman Road to War*, p. 179.

58. Pallavicini from Pera, 30 and 31 October 1914, in HHSA, Liasse Krieg 21a. Türkei, box 942.

59. For the Russian intelligence on Souchon's authorization for attack and its relation to the German gold shipments, see Sazonov to Sevastopol, 20 October 1914, in AVPRI, fond 151, opis' 482, del. 4068, 234.

60. Trumpener, *Germany and the Ottoman Empire*, pp. 58–9. See also Aksakal, *Ottoman Road to War*, pp. 180–81.

61. Fromkin, *A Peace to End All Peace*, pp. 72–3. In this vein see also Pomiankowski, *Zusammenbruch des Ottomanischen Reiches*, p. 87.

62. Mallet to Grey, 20, 28 and 29 October 1914, from the 'Turkey Correspondence'.

63. Pomiankowski, *Zusammenbruch des Ottomanischen Reiches*, pp. 84–5.

6   The First Global Jihad

1. Jihad pamphlet submitted to Morgenthau by J. B. Jackson from Aleppo, 8 April 1915, in NA, M 353, roll 6.

2. The sources here are numerous. A good place to begin is Philip H. Stoddard, 'The Ottoman Government and the Arabs, 1911 to 1918: A Study of the Teşkilat-ı Mahsusa', p. 24 and *passim*. A fine summary of the literature can be found in Gottfried Hagen, *Die Türkei im Ersten Weltkrieg*, pp. 3–5. French-language copies of the Sultan's manifesto, and several of the accompanying *fetvas*, including one signed by Enver Pasha, the War Minister, can be found in HHSA, Liasse Krieg 21a. Türkei, box 942.

3. For a fine recent analysis of Ottoman jihad precedents prior to 1914, see Mustafa Aksakal, 'The Trained Triumphant Soldiers of the Prophet Muhammad. Holy War and Holy Peace in Modern Ottoman History', forthcoming.

4. Ibid.; and Stoddard, 'The Ottoman Government and the Arabs', p. 27. See also Ahmed Emin, *Turkey in the World War*, p. 175; and Wolfgang Schwanitz, 'The Bellicose Birth of Euro-Islam in Berlin' in Nathalie Clayer and Eric Germain (eds), *Islam in Interwar Europe* (2008).

5. Snouck Hurgronje, *The Holy War 'Made in Germany'*, pp. 6–7, 33.

6. See, for example, the Tunisian Sheikh Salih's *Haqiqat al-jihad*, or 'The Truth of Jihad', published in Berlin in 1915 under the guidance of Schabinger and Martin Hartmann. For analysis, see Schwanitz, 'The Bellicose Birth of Euro-Islam in Berlin', pp. 193–4; and Stoddard, 'The Ottoman Government and the Arabs', pp. 35–6.

7. See Aksakal, 'The Trained Triumphant Soldiers of the Prophet Muhammad. Holy War and Holy Peace in Modern Ottoman History', p. 28.

8. Enver's holy war promise was point six in the promised Ottoman mobilization programme. As reproduced in Pallavicini to Vienna, 25 October 1914, in HHSA, Liasse Krieg 21a. Türkei, box 942. On the tensions between Enver and the Germans over theological terms, see Aksakal, 'The Trained Triumphant Soldiers of the Prophet Muhammad. Holy War and Holy Peace in Modern Ottoman History', p. 28.

9. See the 'Cihad fetvâsi' telegram to Baghdad, 2 December 1914, in BOA, DH-ŞFR box 47, file 290, which lists nationals of Belgium, Britain, France and Russia as enemy infidels. Serbians were few and far between in Asiatic Turkey, but still they, too, were on the target list. See also Morgenthau, *Ambassador Morgenthau's Story*, p. 130.

10. Ottoman Government Telegram to the Commander of the Ottoman Fourth Army in Damascus, 13 December 1914, in BOA, DH-ŞFR box 47, file 444.

11. Pallavicini to Vienna, 2 and 5 November 1914, in HHSA, Liasse Krieg 21a. Türkei, box 942. For Enver's warning that an open-ended jihad would end up targeting all infidels without discrimination ('der Heilige Krieg logischerweise gegen alle "Ungläubigen" richten müsse'), see Humann to the German Embassy in Therapia, 22 October 1914, in EJP, 1/14.

12. Cited by Tilman Lüdke, in *Jihad Made in Germany*, p. 53.

13. Schabinger von Schowingen, *Weltgeschichtliche Mosaiksplitter*, p. 107; and Gottfried Hagen, *Die Türkei im Ersten Weltkrieg*, p. 5.

14. Schabinger, *Weltgeschichtliche Mosaiksplitter*, pp. 102–106.

15. Ibid., pp. 106–108. For details of the holy war street procession of 14 November, see also Gottfried Hagen, 'German Heralds of Holy War: Orientalists and Applied Oriental Studies', in *Comparative Studies of South Asia, Africa and the Middle East* 24 (2) (2004), p. 145. On the 'burlesque' incident

at the Hotel Tokatlian, see also Humann's secret report of 17 November 1914, in EJP, 1/18.

16. Morgenthau, *Ambassador Morgenthau's Story*, pp. 133, 135.

17. Morgenthau, 'Turks Attempt to Treat Alien Enemies Decently but the Germans Insist on Persecuting Them' in ibid., pp. 130, 134–7, 142.

18. Stoddard, 'The Ottoman Government and the Arabs', p. 31.

19. From the diary of M. Ledoulx, French Embassy dragoman, 18 November 1914, in QO, file 896.

20. Morgenthau, *Ambassador Morgenthau's Story*, p. 138.

21. Official Communiqué from 'Commandant Djemal' passed on to the Entente powers by the US Consul-General of Beirut, 8 November 1914, in NA, M 353, roll 6.

22. Dadini, the Hapsburg Consul in Damascus, to Berchtold, 19 November 1914, in HHSA, Liasse Krieg 21a. Türkei, box 942.

23. 'Rapport de M. Ottavi. Depart des consuls francais et anglais de Damas et d'Alep. Menaces turco-allemandes ... et propagande panislamique' (henceforth 'Ottavi report'), submitted to the Quai d'Orsay from Marseille, 24 November 1914, in QO Guerre 1914–18, file 1650, p. 6. The nature of Kressenstein's threat is confirmed in an Abschrift dated 8 November 1914 and received by the Austrian Embassy in Constantinople, 12 November 1914, in HHSA, Liasse Krieg 21a. Türkei, box 942.

24. Dadini to Berchtold from Damascus, 14 November 1914, in HHSA, Liasse Krieg 21a. Türkei, box 942.

25. See Russell McGuirk, *Sanusi's Little War*, p. 52.

26. Or 'idolators', as sometimes translated, from Koran Sura 9:5. The same exhortation to 'kill them wherever you find them' can also be found in Sura 4:89, in a slightly different context.

27. Telegram from Frank Larken, captain of HMS *Doris*, addressed 'A Son Excellence le Caïmacan d'Iskanderuneh', 20 December 1914, in PRO, FO 371/2483.

28. Morgenthau, passing on Djemal (via US Consul in Damascus), to Larken, 21 December 1914, in PRO, FO 371/2483.

29. Reply to Larken from 'Le Caïmacan d'Alexandrette', 21 December 1914, in PRO, FO 371/2483.

30. Letter written 'on behalf of the British subjects held at Damascus', signed 'DANIEL OLIVER; BARIEZ CLARK, and WILLIAM HOLLOWAY, Chief of Staff of Sir John Jackson (Limited)', 20 December 1914, in PRO, FO 371/2483.

31. Dispatch from J. B. Jackson, US Consul at Alexandretta, 12 January 1915, forwarded to the British Foreign Office, in PRO, FO 371/2483.

32. Ibid.

33. Report by George Horton, US Consul in Smyrna, on 'Political Conditions in the Smyrna District', 4 February 1915, in NA, M 353, roll 6.

34. Buchan, *Greenmantle*, p. 62.

35. See Stoddard, 'The Ottoman Government and the Arabs', p. 31.

36. Report by W. Stanley Hollis, US Consul in Beirut, on 'Political Conditions in Aleppo', 27 November 1914, in NA, M 353, roll 6.

37. Horton to Morgenthau from Smyrna, 14 November 1914, in NA, M 353, roll 6.

38. Ibid.

39. Morgenthau to the Secretary of State in Washington, 12 December 1914, in NA, M 353, roll 6.

40. Jackson to Morgenthau from Aleppo, 8 April 1915, in NA, M 353, roll 6.

41. Oppenheim to Foreign Office, 26 November 1914, in PAAA, R 21125.

42. Morgenthau, *Secrets of the Bosphorus*, p. 110.

43. Jihad pamphlet submitted to Morgenthau by J. B. Jackson from Aleppo, 8 April 1915, pp. 4, 5, 23.

44. Ibid., p. 9.

45. Ibid., pp. 25–7.

46. Ibid., p. 29.

7   Parting the Red Sea

1. Frobenius report no. 6, dispatched from Massaua in Italian Eritrea, 19 February 1915, in PAAA, R 21145.

2. Frobenius from Constantinople, 1 December 1914, in PAAA, R 21145.

3. On Frobenius' early life and works, see Ute Luig (ed.), *Leo Frobenius. Vom Schreibtisch zum Äquator*, and Eike Haberland (ed.), *Leo Frobenius 1873–1973. Eine Anthologie*.

4. Wangenheim (passing on Frobenius) to Oppenheim in Berlin, 27 November 1914; Stempel (for Oppenheim) to Wangenheim, 29 November 1914; Zimmermann to Frobenius (via Wangenheim), 2 December 1914; and Wangenheim to Oppenheim, 29 November and 7 December 1914; all in PAAA, R 21144.

5. Wangenheim (for Frobenius) to Oppenheim, 1, 12, and 18 December 1914, all in PAAA, R 21144; and Abschrift from Captain Tutt of the Hamburg-Amerika line (after rescuing Frobenius' party), datelined Massaua, 26 February 1915, in PAAA, R 21146.

6. Frobenius telegram from Massaua, passed on to Constantinople and Berlin via Damascus, 10 January 1915; and Wangenheim to Berlin, 20 January

1915, both in PAAA, R 21144. On Frobenius' conversion to Islam, see Humann's 'secret report' of 25 November 1914, in EJP, 1/18.

7. Wangenheim to Berlin, 20 October 1914, in PAAA, R 21144.

8. See Wangenheim to Berlin, 18 November 1914, in PAAA, R 21144; and from same, 30 November 1914; Loytved from Haifa, 26 November 1914, in PAAA, R 21126.

9. Frobenius report number 5, dispatched while aboard a German merchant vessel in the Red Sea, 6 February 1915, in PAAA, R 21145.

10. Ibid.

11. Frobenius report number 6, dispatched from Massaua, 19 February 1915, in PAAA, R 21145.

12. Ibid.; and report sent from Massaua by Captain J. Tutt of the *Christian X*, 26 February 1915, in PAAA, R 21146.

13. Frobenius report number 6, dispatched from Massaua, 19 February 1915, in PAAA, R 21145.

14. See, for example, 'La Missione militaire tedesca nell' Eritrea. Una interrogazione alle Camera', 5 March 1915, *La Sera*; 'Il divieto alla missione tedesca di recarsi in Abissinia dell'Eritrea', 7 March 1915, *Corriera della Sera*; 'Le manovre dei tedeschi in Abissinia. La storia di una missione ... che non giunge a Addis Abeba', 7 March 1915, *Il Popolo*, all clipped in PAAA, R 21145.

15. Report of Mohammed Said, Sohn des Emir Ali und Neffe des Emir Abdelkadir, filed in Damascus 6 March 1915, and Wangenheim to Bethmann Hollweg, passing on Emir Said, via Damascus Consul, 3 April 1915, both in PAAA, R 21146.

16. Prüfer to Wangenheim from Jerusalem, 5 April 1915, in PAAA, R 21146.

17. Rochus Schmidt, secret report from Constantinople to the Colonial Office in Berlin, 12 March 1915, in PAAA, R 21146; and Wangenheim to Bethmann Hollweg, 2 May 1915, in PAAA, R 21147.

18. Abdul Djelil, from the Ottoman Regiment no. 128 (Hejaz), 3rd Company, to 'Abdul Kerim Pascha, Excellenz!', 28 April 1332 (i.e. 1915), in PAAA, R 21147.

19. Bülow to Berlin from Rome, 10 April 1915, in PAAA, R 21146.

8   An Austrian in Arabia

1. Cited by John Kirtland Wright, in 'Northern Arabia. The Explorations of Alois Musil', *Geographical Review*, 17 (2) (April 1927), p. 179.

2. On Burton and Doughty, see Robert Kaplan, 'Sand-Mad Englishmen' in *The Arabists*. On Shakespear's travels, see Douglas Carruthers, 'Captain Shakespear's Last Journey' in *Geographical Journal*, 49 (6) (June 1922).

3. Wright, 'Northern Arabia', p. 180. See also the final Alois Musil post-mortem report on his wartime mission, sent from Vienna, 21 April 1916 (henceforth 'Musil report'), in PAAA, R 21148, p. 11.

4. Ibid.; and Karl Johannes Bauer, *Alois Musil. Wahrheitssucher in der Wüste*, pp. 185–94.

5. On this gift, see Musil to Consul Lloytved, from Damascus, 1 December 1914, in PAAA, R 21145; and 'Musil report', p. 8.

6. See Bauer, *Alois Musil*, pp. 202–203.

7. Cited by Wright, in 'Northern Arabia', p. 179.

8. Bauer, *Alois Musil*, pp. 148–9, 200–201.

9. As ably summarized in ibid., pp. 202–203.

10. Tschirschky to Berlin from Vienna, 14 October 1914, in PAAA, R 21144.

11. Musil to Tschirschky, 14 October 1914, in PAAA, R 21144.

12. Tschirschky to Berlin, 14 October 1914, in PAAA, R 21144.

13. Ibid.; Bauer, *Alois Musil*, pp. 206–207; 'Musil report', p. 1; and Austrian Foreign Ministry 'Tagesbericht', 6 October 1914, in HHSA, Liasse Krieg 21a. Türkei, Karton 948. For the Austrian reservations and how this may have flavoured reluctance to pay Musil's expenses, see Wangenheim to Berlin, 28 November 1914, in PAAA, R 21144.

14. Conversation as reported by Musil to Pomiankowski, the Habsburg military attaché to the Porte, as reproduced in Pomiankowski, *Zusammenbruch des Ottomanischen Reiches*, pp. 171–2.

15. 'Musil report', p. 2.

16. Musil to Consul Lloytved, from Damascus, 1 December 1914, in PAAA, R 21145.

17. Pallavicini from Pera, passing on Musil, 28 November 1914, in HHSA, Liasse Krieg 21a. Türkei, Karton 948. On Kress's views of Musil, see his telegram to Berlin from Pera, 19 July 1916, in PAAA, R 21148.

18. Musil to Consul Lloytved, from Damascus, 1 December 1914, in PAAA, R 21145.

19. 'Musil report', p. 3.

20. Musil to Damascus from 'somewhere between al-Hegm and al-Bark', 29 December 1914, in PAAA, R 21145.

21. Kress telegram from Pera, 19 July 1916, in PAAA, R 21148.

22. See Bauer, *Alois Musil*, p. 211.

23. Musil to Damascus from somewhere 'between al-Hegm and al-Bark', 29 December 1914, in PAAA, R 21145.

24. For Musil's various financial requests and responses see, for example, Wangenheim to Berlin, 24, 28 November and 2 December and 18 December 1914, and Tschirschky from Vienna, 1 December 1914, all in PAAA, R 21144.

25. Musil to Damascus from somewhere 'between al-Hegm and al-Bark', 29 December 1914, in PAAA, R 21145.

26. Musil to Consul Lloytved, from Damascus, 1 December 1914, in PAAA, R 21145.

27. Musil to Djemal from Damascus, 12 June 1915, passed on to Berlin by Lloytved, 28 June 1915, in PAAA, R 21147.

28. Ibid.

29. Citations in Bauer, *Alois Musil*, pp. 212–15. For Kress on Bedouin sexual morality, see his *Mit den Türken zum Suezkanal*, p. 52.

9   Showdown at the Suez Canal

1. Kress von Kressenstein, *Mit den Türken zum Suezkanal*, pp. 78–9.

2. As ably summarized, for example, in Prüfer's field report from Jerusalem, filed 31 December 1914, in PAAA, R 21128.

3. Kress von Kressenstein, *Mit den Türken zum Suezkanal*, p. 30. Construction problems on the Baghdad railway, and the way these were exacerbated by the Armenian massacres of 1915, form a principal leitmotif of Kress's memoirs. See also chapter 14 below.

4. Ibid., p. 27.

5. Cited by Weber, in *Eagles on the Crescent*, p. 88.

6. Wangenheim from Pera, 29 August 1914, in PAAA, R 21123.

7. Weber, *Eagles on the Crescent*, p. 90.

8. Ibid., p. 92.

9. Cited by Hopkirk, in *On Secret Service East of Constantinople*, p. 78.

10. Oppenheim memorandum reporting on his visit to the Khedive in Vienna, 22 January 1915, in PAAA, R 21127. See also McKale, *War by Revolution*, pp. 116–17.

11. According to Humann, the German naval attaché. Cited by McKale, in *War by Revolution*, p. 89.

12. Oppenheim memorandum, 22 January 1915, in PAAA, R 21127; and Wangenheim to Berlin, 2 February 1915, in PAAA, R 21128.

13. Prüfer from Jerusalem, 31 December 1914, in PAAA, R 21128

14. Kress von Kressenstein, *Mit den Türken zum Suezkanal*, p. 41.

15. Prüfer from Jerusalem, 31 December 1914, in PAAA, R 21128. See also McKale, *Curt Prüfer*, p. 31.

16. Prüfer from Jerusalem, 31 December 1914, in PAAA, R 21128.

17. Kress von Kressenstein, *Mit den Türken zum Suezkanal*, pp. 78–9.

18. Ibid., p. 79.

19. Ibid., p. 80.

20. Prüfer from Jerusalem, 31 December 1914, in PAAA, R 21128. Also cited in McKale, *Curt Prüfer*, p. 34. The translation here is McKale's.

21. From Prüfer's diary entry for 20 January 1915. Cited in McKale, *Curt Prüfer*, p. 35.

22. Prüfer to Wangenheim, from Hafir el Andscha, 9 February 1915, in PAAA, R 21129.

23. Ibid., and Kress von Kressenstein, *Mit den Türken zum Suezkanal*, p. 90.

24. Weber, *Eagles on the Crescent*, p. 99.

25. Stoddard, 'The Ottoman Government and the Arabs', pp. 70, 104.

26. Kress von Kressenstein, *Mit den Türken zum Suezkanal*, p. 88. Kress uses the word 'Geistlichen', which literally translates to English as 'chaplains', although the term does not properly apply to Islam. The detail about the whirling dervishes was reported by Wangenheim to Berlin, as cited in Weber, *Eagles on the Crescent*, p. 99.

27. Prüfer from Jerusalem, 31 December 1914, in PAAA, R 21128.

28. Maxwell to Kitchener, 2 February 1915, in PRO, WO 33/731. See also McGuirk, *Sanusi's Little War*, p. 83.

29. Cited in McKale, *Curt Prüfer*, p. 36. McKale's translation.

30. See, for example, Fromkin, *A Peace to End All Peace*, pp. 121–2; Weber, *Eagles on the Crescent*; McKale, *Curt Prüfer*, pp. 36–7 and *War by Revolution*, p. 100; and Hopkirk, *On Secret Service East of Constantinople*, pp. 78–80.

31. There are many accounts of the Suez battle, most of which differ slightly on the details, though not on the essentials. The most detailed timeline, which I have used here, is the one sent by Prüfer to Wangenheim from Hafir el Andscha, 9 February 1915, in PAAA, R 21129. Kress goes into more detail about operations, in *Mit den Türken zum Suezkanal*, pp. 91–2. Field reports dated 2–7 February 1915 from Lieutenant General Maxwell, on the British side (in PRO, WO 33/731) corroborate much of what Kress and Prüfer remembered, although making it painfully obvious that no surprise was achieved in the Turco-German attack.

32. Commander-in-Chief, East Indies, to Admiralty, 2 February 1915; and Maxwell to Kitchener, 3 February 1915, in PRO, WO 33/731. It was Staff Officer George Lloyd who compared the operation to a 'grouse drive'. Cited by McGuirk, in *Sanusi's Little War*, p. 84.

33. Prüfer to Wangenheim from Hafir el Andscha, 9 February 1915, in PAAA, R 21129.

34. As the British later claimed. See McGuirk, *Sanusi's Little War*, p. 83.

35. Prüfer to Oppenheim from Hafir el Andscha, 9 February 1915, in PAAA, R 21129.

36. Prüfer to Wangenheim from Hafir el Andscha, 9 February 1915, in PAAA, R 21129.

37. Ibid.

38. Prüfer to Oppenheim from Hafir el Andscha, 9 February 1915, in PAAA, R 21129.

39. The usual figure cited is roughly 90,000 casualties at Sarıkamış, which seems to have originated in Maurice Larcher's 1926 history of *La Guerre turque dans la guerre mondiale*. But, as Edward Erickson has recently noted, Larcher offered no documentation, and his figure was probably 'grossly inflated'. Erickson, who has done the only serious Western study of the Ottoman military records from the war, estimates 33,000 dead, 7,000 prisoners and 10,000 wounded. Erickson, 'The Armenians and Ottoman Military Policy, 1915' in *War in History*, 15 (2) 2008, p. 148. For further exposition, see also Erickson, *Ordered to Die*, pp. 59–60. The best narrative history of the Sarıkamış battle, with accompanying maps, can be found in W. E. D. Allen and Paul Muratoff, *Caucasian Battlefields*, pp. 249–85.

10 Gallipoli: From Disaster to Triumph

1. Alan Moorehead, *Gallipoli*, p. 76.

2. Weber, *Eagles on the Crescent*, p. 127.

3. Liman von Sanders, *Cinq ans de Turquie*, pp. 59–61; and Pomiankowski, *Zusammenbruch des Ottomanischen Reiches*, p. 116.

4. Weber, *Eagles on the Crescent*, p. 108 and *passim*. In this vein, see also Trumpener, *Germany and the Ottoman Empire*, pp. 75–81.

5. See the 'Abschrift eines Briefes des Hofrats Musil an Seine Excellenz den Herrn Minister ddo. Damaskus, 1.Dezember 1914' in PAAA, R 21145.

6. Pomiankowski, *Zusammenbruch des Ottomanischen Reiches*, p. 57.

7. Liman, *Cinq ans de Turquie*, pp. 47–9, 57.

8. Citations in Weber, *Eagles on the Crescent*, p. 132.

9. Cited in Trumpener, *Germany and the Ottoman Empire*, p. 83.

10. Cited in Weber, *Eagles on the Crescent*, p. 133.

11. Morgenthau, *Ambassador Morgenthau's Story*, pp. 185, 187, 193.

12. Alan Moorehead, *Gallipoli*, p. 56.

13. Pomiankowski, *Zusammenbruch des Ottomanischen Reiches*, p. 117; Morgenthau, *Ambassador Morgenthau's Story*, p. 193. That the Ottoman government shipped away its valuables, gold reserves and Islamic artefacts is confirmed in Rochus Schmidt's report from Pera, 12 March 1915, in PAAA, R 21146. On preparations for the evacuation, see also Pallavicini from Pera, 4 January 1915, in HHSA, Liasse Krieg 21a. Türkei, box 943.

14. That Humann refused to panic is strongly confirmed in his report forwarded to Berlin on 2 March 1915, in EJP, 1/22.

15. The sources here are virtually without limit. I have followed mostly Moorehead, *Gallipoli*, pp. 54–93.

16. Stoddard, 'The Ottoman Government and the Arabs', pp. 72–3.

17. Moorehead, *Gallipoli*, p. 76.

18. The sources here, too, are numerous. I have mostly followed Mango, *Atatürk*, pp. 144–7, which includes all of these citations.

19. Moorehead, *Gallipoli*, pp. 51, 138–9.

20. Cited by Mango, in *Atatürk*, p. 145.

21. Liman von Sanders, *Cinq ans de Turquie*, p. 104.

11   The Blood of the Prophet

1. Buchan, *Greenmantle*, p. 27.

2. See Oppenheim's memorandums to Foreign Office from Berlin, 2 and 12 March 1915, in PAAA, R 21129.

3. Oppenheim to Foreign Office, 14 September 1914, in PAAA, R 21124.

4. Cited by Kedourie, in *England and the Middle East*, p. 52.

5. T. E. Lawrence, 'Personal Notes on the Sherifian Family' in the 26 November 1916 *Arab Bulletin*.

6. As recounted by Feisal in his 24 April 1915 meeting with Oppenheim in the Pera Palace Hotel, document labelled 'Compte rendu d'une séance politique' in MvO 1/19, folder labelled 'Algerien, Afrika und Vorderer Orient. 1886–1941' (henceforth 'Oppenheim–Feisal compte rendu').

7. Oppenheim, 'Reisen, Leben 1893–6' in MvO, 1/4, p. 4.

8. 'Oppenheim–Feisal compte rendu', pp. 2–3.

9. Ibid., pp. 3–4.

10. See, among many accounts, Fromkin, *A Peace to End All Peace*, pp. 173–5; and George Antonius, *Arab Awakening*, pp. 149–50.

11. 'Oppenheim–Feisal compte rendu', pp. 6–7.

12. Ibid., pp. 9–10.

13. Ibid., pp. 11–13.

14. 'Texte des instructions au Grand Chérif de Mecque remis à son fils Chérif Faïsal Bey par son Excellence Enver Pacha le 9 mai 1915', and Oppenheim, summary of a 'Besuch bei dem Scherifen Fessal in Bujukdere am 30. April 1915', and both in MvO 1/19, folder labelled 'Algerien, Afrika und Vorderer Orient. 1886–1941'.

15. Oppenheim, 'Besuch bei dem Scherifen Fessal in Bujukdere am 30. April 1915'.

16. Unsigned Oppenheim memorandum, 14 May 1915, in MvO 1/19, folder labelled 'Algerien, Afrika und Vorderer Orient. 1886–1941'.

12   The Shia Stratagem

1. Hans Lührs, *Gegenspieler des Obersten Lawrence*, pp. 11–12.

2. On Kitchener and the Caliphate, see especially Fromkin, *A Peace to End All Peace*, pp. 104–105.

3. Hans Lührs, *Gegenspieler des Obersten Lawrence*, pp. 11–12.

4. McKale, *War by Revolution*, pp. 83–5; and Oppenheim, 'Denkschrift betreffend die Revolutionierung der islamischen Gebiete unserer Feinde', dated 'Berlin, Ende Oktober 1914', in PAAA, R 20937.

5. Lührs, *Gegenspieler des Obersten Lawrence*, pp. 10–11.

6. Ibid., pp. 11–13.

7. Ibid., pp. 13–15.

8. Ibid., p. 20.

13   To the Gates of India

1. Buchan, *Greenmantle*, p. 13.

2. Wangenheim to Berlin, 14 August 1914, in PAAA, R 21028.

3. Wangenheim to Berlin, 30 August 1914, in PAAA, R 21028.

4. Unsigned 'Abschrift', probably authored by Wesendonck or Oppenheim, dated Berlin 26 August 1914, in PAAA, R 21028.

5. Wangenheim to Berlin, passing on Wassmuss's recommendations, 14 September 1914, in PAAA, R 21029.

6. Reichenau to Zimmermann from Stockholm, 25 August 1914, in PAAA, R 21028.

7. On Oppenheim's Berlin Indian revolutionary committee, see McKale, *War by Revolution*, pp. 120–27; and Hopkirk, *On Secret Service East of Constantinople*, pp. 96–7.

8. Hans-Ulrich Seidt, *Berlin, Kabul, Moskau*, pp. 30–31.

9. Ibid., pp. 32–5.

10. Antony Wynn, *Persia in the Great Game*, pp. 232–3.

11. Seidt, *Berlin, Kabul, Moskau*, pp. 36–8.

12. Cited in ibid., pp. 39, 51.

13. Ibid., pp. 51–2.

14. Niedermayer to Oppenheim, 2 October 1914, in PAAA, R 21031.

15. Robert Wonckhaus to Oppenheim, 20 August 1914, in PAAA, R 21028; and Hermann Consten to Reinhard Mannesmann at Foreign Office, Berlin, 2 October 1914, in PAAA, R 21031. On the burgeoning feud between Consten and Wassmuss, see also Wangenheim from Therapia, 15 October 1914, in PAAA, R 21031.

16. Niedermayer to Oppenheim, 2 October 1914, in PAAA, R 21031.

17. Wassmuss to Bethmann Hollweg, via Wangenheim, from Tarsus, *circa* 2 or 3 October 1914, in PAAA, R 21031.

18. Seidt, *Berlin, Kabul, Moskau*, pp. 59–61.

19. Wangenheim from Pera, 8 and 11 December 1914, in PAAA, R 21032.

20. Hopkirk, *On Secret Service East of Constantinople*, p. 159.

21. Citations in Mango, *Atatürk*, pp. 140–41.

22. Wangenheim from Pera, 18 January 1915, passing on Niedermayer from Baghdad, in PAAA, R 21034; and Seidt, *Berlin, Kabul, Moskau*, pp. 60–61. For Rauf's own account of his dealings with the Germans in Baghdad, see Vahdet Keleşyılmaz, *Teşkilat-ı Mahsûsa'nın Hindistan Misyonu (1914–1918)*, pp. 91–4.

23. Von der Goltz to Zimmermann from Constantinople, 30 January 1915, and Wangenheim from Pera, 1 and 6 February 1915, in PAAA, R 21035.

24. 'Besprechung über die türkische Aktion nach Persien und dit Tätikeit [*sic*] der deutschen Expedition', 11 February 1915, in PAAA, R 21036. See also Seidt, *Berlin, Kabul, Moskau*, p. 63.

25. Ibid., pp. 61–5. For Enver's critique of Niedermayer, see also Wangenheim from Pera, 16 April 1915, in PAAA, R 21041.

26. Seidt, *Berlin, Kabul, Moskau*, pp. 66–7; McKale, *War by Revolution*, pp. 80, 130.

27. Hopkirk, *On Secret Service East of Constantinople*, p. 92.

28. Seidt, *Berlin, Kabul, Moskau*, pp. 66–9. On the details of Rauf Bey's offensive, see also Fritz Klein from Baghdad, 13 March 1915, in PAAA, R 21038; and Kardorff from Tehran, 22 April 1915, in PAAA, R 21042.

29. Wangenheim from Pera, 24 March 1915 (two separate dispatches, both passing on Wassmuss via Tehran), in PAAA, R 21038. The Hopkirk quote footnoted is from *On Secret Service East of Constantinople*, p. 242. See also David Kahn, *The Codebreakers* (1967).

30. Seidt, *Berlin, Kabul, Moskau*, p. 70.

31. Wangenheim from Pera, 10 May 1915, in PAAA, R 21042.

32. Seidt, *Berlin, Kabul, Moskau*, pp. 68, 70, 74.

33. Ibid., 72–3.

34. Wangenheim from Pera to Prince Reuss in Tehran, 8 May 1915, in PAAA, R 21042.

35. Seidt, Berlin, Kabul, Moskau, pp. 75–7; McKale, *War by Revolution*, pp. 128–9. For more on Pratap and Barakatullah, see also Hughes, 'The German Mission to Afghanistan 1915–1916' in Wolfgang Schwanitz (ed.), *Germany and the Middle East 1871–1945*, pp. 39–41.

36. Hopkirk, *On Secret Service East of Constantinople*, pp. 99–100.

37. I have mostly followed Hopkirk, *On Secret Service East of Constantinople*, chapters 8 ('The Race for Kabul'), and 9 ('Niedermayer's Bluff'). For his account of the desert journey, Hopkirk relies primarily on Niedermayer's memoir *Unter der Glutsonne Irans*.

38. Citations in Seidt, *Berlin, Kabul, Moskau*, p. 81.

39. Cited by Hopkirk, in *On Secret Service East of Constantinople*, p. 152.

40. Niedermayer, *Krieg in Irans Wüsten*, p. 111.

41. This despite Pratap's generally obliging nature towards Islamic authority figures. Before arriving in Istanbul in May 1915, Pratap had written an effusive letter gushing with praise for 'my dear hero Enver Pasha'. See Keleşyılmaz, *Teşkilat-ı Mahsûsa'nın Hindistan Misyonu (1914–1918)*, pp. 94–6.

42. Ibid.

43. On the treaty terms, see Seidt, *Berlin, Kabul, Moskau*, p. 84.

14 Trouble on the Baghdad Railway

1. Berlin Foreign Office memorandum to the German Embassy in Pera, 15 October 1915, labelled 'Misellania Militaria ex Turcia asiatica' in PAAA, R 13753.

2. Trumpener, *Germany in the Ottoman Empire*, p. 271.

3. Koran, Sura 9:29.

4. Niall Ferguson, *The Pity of War*, p. 337.

5. In this vein, see Wangenheim's dispatch from Pera, passing on Niedermayer from Tehran, 29 May 1915, in PAAA, R 21043.

6. On Balkan diplomacy, see Weber, *Eagles on the Crescent*, pp. 115–27.

7. As paraphrased by Jonathan McMurray, in *Distant Ties*, p. 99.

8. Ibid., p. 98.

9. Ibid., p. 87 and *passim*.

10. Ibid.

11. 'Die Bagdadbahn', report forwarded by Wangenheim to Berlin, 31 December 1914, in PAAA, R 13527.

12. On the bewildering array of exemptions from Ottoman army service, and their evolution over time, see Zürcher, 'The Ottoman Conscription System, 1844–1914' in *the International Review of Social History*, 43 (1998), pp. 437–49.

13. See Wangenheim to Berlin, 12 February 1915, in PAAA, R 13527; and Prüfer to Wangenheim, passing on Kress, 9 February 1915, in PAAA, R 21129.

14. Cited by Trumpener, in *Germany and the Ottoman Empire*, p. 291.

15. See, for example, the transcript of the meeting held with these principals, along with Moltke the Younger, 13 February 1915, in PAAA, R 13527.

16. Wangenheim to Falkenhayn, passing on Böttrich, 16 March 1915, in PAAA, R 13528.

17. McMurray, *Distant Ties*, p. 115.

18. German military headquarters memorandum to Foreign Office, 15 April 1915, PAAA, R 13528; and Jagow-signed memorandum endorsing the earlier credit of 40 million Marks, 19 June 1915, in PAAA, R 13529.

19. Weber, *Eagles on the Crescent*, p. 143.

20. McMurray, *Distant Ties*, p. 118.

21. The subject of the Armenian massacres in 1915 has, of course, inspired a vast and ever-growing literature. By far the best overview is Guenter Lewy's fine recent survey, *The Armenian Massacres in Ottoman Turkey. A Disputed Genocide*.

For strong statements of the Armenian position, one may consult the voluminous works of Vanakh N. Dadrian (e.g. *The History of the Armenian Genocide*) and Richard Hovannisian ((ed.), *The Armenian Genocide in Perspective*, among many other works). A somewhat more moderate line is staked out by Ronald Suny in, for example, 'Empire and Nation: Armenians, Turks and the End of the Ottoman Empire' in *Armenian Forum*, 1 (2) (1998), pp. 17–51, and more recently by Donald Bloxham in *The Great Game of Genocide*. Bloxham accepts the 'genocide' allegation in terms of intent and scale of the killings but rejects the notion that it was premeditated or systematically planned in advance. A notable recent restatement of the essentials of the Armenian position, notable because of the Turkish nationality of the author, is Taner Akçam, *A Shameful Act*.

The Turkish case, i.e. that Armenian uprisings occasioned the deportations, has been most effectively presented in documentary form, as in *Documents on Ottoman Armenians*, published in Ankara (1982–3, two vols) by the Turkish Directorate General of Press and Information. Another important work available in English is Sinasi Orel and Süreyya Yuca, *The Talât Pasha 'Telegrams': Historical Fact or Armenian Fiction?* An important recent work from a pro-Turkish perspective is Justin McCarthy et al., *The Armenian Rebellion at Van*. The most serious analysis to date of the Ottoman military's approach to the perceived Armenian security threat is that of Edward Erickson, 'The Armenians and Ottoman Military Policy'. Erickson argues that the anti-Armenian campaign evolved 'from localized anti-terrorism measures to a generalized campaign of counter-insurgency', of which the deportations were only a part.

22. Olferiev to Girs from Van, 25 March (7 April) 1913, in AVPRI, fond 180, opis' 517-2, del. 3573, 85.

23. Shirkov to Girs from Bitlis, 7/20 March 1914, in AVPRI, fond 180, opis' 517-2, del. 3573, 338–42.

24. Olferiev to Girs from Van, 25 March (7 April) 1913, in AVPRI, fond 180, opis' 517-2, del. 3573, 85; and Chirkov to Girs, from between Van and Bash-Kaloyu, 30 May (12 June) 1913, in AVPRI, fond 180, opis' 517-2, del. 3573, 191.

25. Letter of Zavène Der-Yéghiayan, the Armenian Metropolitan of Bitlis, to Russian Consul Shirkov, 3 (16) March 1914, in AVPRI, fond 180, opis' 517-2, del. 3573, 326–7 (and backs).

26. Shirkov to Girs from Bitlis, 23 March (5 April) 1914, in AVPRI, fond 180, opis' 517-2, del. 3573, 369. On this entire episode, see also Reynolds, 'The Ottoman-Russian Struggle for Eastern Anatolia and the Caucasus, 1908–1918', pp. 127–30.

27. Letter from Dr G. C. Reynolds, Secretary of the American Mission Board, to S. Olferieff (Olferiev), 25 March 1913, in AVPRI, fond 180, opis' 517-2, del. 3573, 72.

28. Olferiev to Girs, 18 (31) March 1913, in AVPRI, fond 180, opis' 517-2, del. 3573, 53–5.

29. Sazonov to Tiflis command (with a copy to War Minister Sukhomlinov), 13/26 August 1914; Yudenich to Stavka from Tiflis, 22 August (4 September) 1914; and enclosed report 'O snabzhenii oruzhiem" turetskikh' armyan", dated 16/29 August 1914, in RGVIA, fond 2000, opis' 1, del. 3851, 7 and 9, 10 and back, 11, 24.

30. 'O snabzhenii oruzhiem' 'turetskikh armyan', and Sazonov to Tiflis command, ibid.

31. Vorontstov-Dashkov to Sukhomlinov, again in response to Sazonov's request, 7/20 September 1914, in RGVIA, fond 2000, opis' 1, del. 3851, 68 and back. According to Vorontsov-Dashkov, the Armenian bands were being concentrated in the border hamlets of Ol'ty, Sar, Kamyishek, Gizman and Igdir.

32. Reynolds, 'The Ottoman-Russian Struggle for Eastern Anatolia and the Caucasus, 1908–1918', pp. 261–4, 268; and Erickson, 'The Armenians and Ottoman Military Policy', pp. 150–52.

33. Stolitsa to Stavka from Tiflis, 23 April (6 May) 1915, in AVPRI, fond 151, opis' 482, del. 3505, 2.

34. Stolitsa to Stavka from Tiflis, 29 April (12 May) 1915, in AVPRI, fond 151, opis' 482, del. 3505, 4.

35. Reynolds, 'The Ottoman-Russian Struggle for Eastern Anatolia and the Caucasus, 1908–1918', pp. 261–4. On the role of Armenian deserters in Van, see the report by the Austrian ski instructor sent to train the Ottoman Third Army in mountain warfare, in packet labelled 'Copia pro actis zu Einsichtstück der k.u.k. Marine-Sektion vom 2. VIII. 1915', passed on from the Pera Embassy, 16 July 1915, in HHSA, Liasse Krieg 21a. Türkei, box 944. Although the Austrian was sympathetic to the Armenians – he described the Turkish retaking of Van as a 'St Bartholomew's massacre' – he conceded that

the Armenians had erected there a 'proper Armenian national government', and that the Russian army had been 'reinforced by some 10,000 deserters' which had furnished enough manpower for the Russians to create 'an entire Armenian regiment'.

36. See, for example, the epic account of the Van uprising written by a special correspondent for *Russkoe Slovo*, 20 June 1915, clipped in AVPRI, fond 151, opis' 482, del. 3505, 7–8. While entirely – and passionately – pro-Armenian, the author makes absolutely no effort to hide the fact that Armenians were resisting the draft and deserting en masse. The idea, rather, is that they were right to do so, and to rise in Van, because the government intended them harm.

37. See, for example, *Mshak*, 30 September 1915, as translated (into Russian) and clipped by Tiflis command and forwarded to Sazonov and Grand Duke Nicholas, in AVPRI, fond 151, opis' 482, del. 3480, 20.

38. Reynolds, 'The Ottoman-Russian Struggle for Eastern Anatolia and the Caucasus, 1908–1918', pp. 261–4, 268. See also Erickson, 'The Armenians and Ottoman Military Policy', pp. 150–52.

39. Erickson, 'The Armenians and Ottoman Military Policy', p. 166.

40. Dadrian, 'The Armenian Question and the Wartime Fate of the Armenians as Documented by Officials of the Ottoman Empire's World War I Allies: Germany and Austria-Hungary', *International Journal of Middle East Studies*, 34 (2002), p. 69.

41. Citations in Lewy, *Armenian Massacres in Ottoman Turkey*, pp. 98, 103.

42. Erickson, 'The Armenians and Ottoman Military Policy', p. 163.

43. Vorontsov-Dashkov to Stavka and the Foreign Office from Tiflis, 7 (20) February 1915, in RGVIA, fond 2000, opis' 1, del. 3851, 82.

44. Citations in Lewy, *Armenian Massacres in Ottoman Turkey*, pp. 104–105.

45. Neratov (Petersburg) to Benckendorff (London), 28 March (10 April) 1915, in RGVIA, fond 2000, opis' 1, del. 3851, 93.

46. See Sazonov to Vorontsov-Dashkov, 27 February (12 March) 1915, in RGVIA, fond 2000, opis' 1, del. 3851, 89.

47. The landing at Dörtyol was confirmed by several German Consuls in the area in reports to Wangenheim. The discovery of the dynamite near Ceyhan, and the reports of attacks in the rear of the Fourth Army, were reported by Ali Fuad, a staff officer in the Fourth Army. Citations in Erickson, 'The Armenians and Ottoman Military Policy', p. 156, text and fns79 and 80.

For a more sceptical view of the security threat posed by British landings and Armenian rebels in Dörtyol, see Bloxham, *Great Game of Genocide*, pp. 81–3.

48. Stolitsa, secret telegram to Stavka, 3 (16) April 1915, in RGVIA, fond 2000, opis' 1, del. 3851, 94.

49. The most cogent analysis of the issue of threat perception is Erickson's, in 'The Armenians and Ottoman Military Policy', pp. 165–6. Although Erickson concedes that the various Armenian uprisings caused 'only minor disruptions to the war effort', he concludes that the communications lines of the Ottoman Third and Fourth Armies were indeed 'highly vulnerable', and that 'the Armenians had the capacity to destroy those lines'. Because 'stockpiles of munitions and supplies for the forward 3rd, 4th, and 6th armies were insufficient for prolonged operations without continual replenishment', even maintenance and hold operations were impossible if supply lines were not secure.

50. Reynolds, 'The Ottoman-Russian Struggle for Eastern Anatolia and the Caucasus, 1908–1918', p. 270.

51. Cited in Lewy, *Armenian Massacres in Ottoman Turkey*, pp. 154–5.

52. Erickson, 'The Armenians and Ottoman Military Policy', p. 165.

53. On the various 'exemptions' declared both by Talaat and by certain regional governors, and their scattershot application, see Bloxham, Great Game of Genocide, p. 89, and Lewy, *Armenian Massacres in Ottoman Turkey*, pp. 180, 184, 205–206.

54. Bloxham, *Great Game of Genocide*, pp. 124–5.

55. Pomiankowski, *Zusammenbruch des Ottomanisches Reiches*, p. 161.

56. Cited in Lewy, *Armenian Massacres in Ottoman Turkey*, pp. 188–9.

57. 'Information from Two Arab Officers Recently Arrived in England from the Caucasus and Examined by Sir M. Sykes', submitted to the British War Office, 25 September 1916, in PRO, FO 371/2781.

58. So anointed by Wilhelm Litten, a German diplomat who travelled the route in January and February 1916. Cited by Lewy, *Armenian Massacres in Ottoman Turkey*, p. 212.

59. According to Dr Winkler, a BRC engineer, reporting from Adana, 16 September 1915, in PAAA, R 13531.

60. Günther reporting to BRC headquarters in Berlin via the German Consulate in Damascus, 1 September 1915, in PAAA, R 13531.

61. Winkler from Kushchular, outside Adana, 16 September 1915, in PAAA, R 13531.

62. Citations in Lewy, *Armenian Massacres in Ottoman Turkey*, p. 184.

63. From two separate Winkler reports, both filed from Kushchular, outside Adana, 16 September 1915, in PAAA, R 13531.

64. Ibid., and Wangenheim, passing on Günther to Gwinner, 30 October 1915, in PAAA, R 13531.

65. Falkenhayn to Enver, 3 November 1915, passed on via the Constantinople Embassy 4 November 1915, in PAAA, R 13531.

66. See Falkenhayn to Treutler, 19 November 1915, in PAAA, R 13531. On the Böttrich document controversy, see Dadrian, *History of the Armenian*

Genocide, p. 261; Böttrich communiqué 'Au Commissariat de la ligne d'Anatolie', 3 October 1915, in PAAA, R 13531; and Günther to Berlin, 3 December 1915, in PAAA, R 13532.

67. *Ambassador Morgenthau's Story*, pp. 370, 374.

68. Ibid., pp. 381–2.

69. Pallavicini to Burian, 24 June 1915, in HHSA, Liasse Krieg 21a. Türkei, box 947.

70. Pallavicini to Burian, 12 November 1915, in HHSA, Liasse Krieg 21a. Türkei, box 944.

15   The Reluctant Mahdi

1. Oppenheim to Bülow, 8 April 1902, in PAAA, R 14559.

2. John Buchan, *Greenmantle*, p. 27.

3. For the German troop figures footnoted, see Keith Neilson and Roy Arnold Prete (eds), *Coalition Warfare: An Uneasy Accord*, p. 35. On the German-Turkish military relationship generally, see Mühlmann, *Das Deutsche-Türkische Waffenbündnis im Weltkriege*.

4. From the *Egyptian Gazette*, 16 August 1902, following al-Mahdi's death. Cited in Russell McGuirk, *The Sanusi's Little War*, p. 24.

5. Oppenheim to Bülow, 19 April 1903, in PAAA, R 14559.

6. Oppenheim to Bülow, 20 April 1903, in PAAA, R 14559.

7. Oppenheim to Bülow, 23 April 1903, in PAAA, R 14559.

8. Oppenheim to Bülow, 21 June 1903, in PAAA, R 14559.

9. As reported by Wilfred Jennings Bramley, a British intelligence officer. Cited in McGuirk, *Sanusi's Little War*, p. 64.

10. Cited in McGuirk, *Sanusi's Little War*, p. 77.

11. According to an Egyptian officer debriefed by Leo Royle, cited in McGuirk, *Sanusi's Little War*, p. 35.

12. The Germans insisted repeatedly to the Italian government that Libya 'aus dem Spiel bleibt'. In this vein, see Wangenheim from Therapia, 8 September 1914, reporting on his conversations with Italian Ambassador Marquis Garroni, in PAAA, R 21124

13. Interview cited in McGuirk, *Sanusi's Little War*, p. 61.

14. Cited in ibid., p. 63.

15. The *Teşkilat-ı Mahsûsa* has become notorious in recent years since being implicated in the Armenian massacres of 1915 by Dadrian, among others. See his 'The Role of the Special Organization in the Armenian Genocide during the First World War' in *Minorities in Wartime: National and Racial Groupings in Europe, North America and Australia in Two World Wars*, edited by Panikos

Panayi, pp. 58–63. Lewy, in *Armenian Massacres in Ottoman Turkey* (pp. 82–8), disputes this claim. The most thorough examination of the subject is in Erickson, 'Armenian Massacres: New Records Undercut Old Blame' in *Middle East Quarterly*, 11 (3) Summer 2006, pp. 67–75.

On the role of the Special Organization in general, see Stoddard, 'The Ottoman Government and the Arabs'; Zürcher, *Unionist Factor*, pp. 58, 85–6; Emin Demirel, *Teşkilat-ı Mahsûsa'dan Günümüze Gizli Servisler*, pp. 150–62 and *passim*; and Keleşyılmaz, *Teşkilat-ı Mahsûsa'nın Hindistan Misyonu (1914–1918)*; and Atilla Çeliktepe, *Teşkilat-i Mahsûsa'nın Siyasi Misyonu*. On the Special Organization in Libya during the war, see Rachel Simon, *Libya between Ottomanism and Nationalism. The Ottoman Involvement in Libya during the War with Italy (1911–1918)*, pp. 125–8.

16. McGuirk, *Sanusi's Little War*, pp. 85–6, 92–3. On the German decision to allow Enver's 'Muslim emissaries' to try to win over the Sanussi, see Wangenheim from Pera, 23 January 1915, in PAAA, R 21127.

17. McGuirk, *Sanusi's Little War*, p. 108.

18. As reported by Wangenheim from Pera following a conversation with Enver, 13 April 1915, in PAAA, R 21131.

19. McGuirk, *Sanusi's Little War*, p. 111.

20. Ibid., p. 113.

21. Wangenheim from Pera, 4 July 1915, in PAAA, R 21134.

22. Hohenlohe from Pera, 26 July 1915, in PAAA, R 21135.

23. Humann's report of a conversation with Enver, 4 July 1915, in EJP, 1/25. See also McKale, *War by Revolution*, p. 148.

24. McGuirk, *Sanusi's Little War*, p. 106.

25. Nadolny, passing on Mannesmann's requests from military headquarters to the German Foreign Office, 5 July 1915, in PAAA, R 21134.

26. Krüger from Canea, passing on Mannesmann's requests to the German Foreign Office, 17 July 1915, in PAAA, R 21135.

27. 'Islam and the War' in *The Standard*, 31 August 1915. Clipped and filed in PAAA, R 21135.

28. Citations in McGuirk, *Sanusi's Little War*, pp. 143, 145–6.

29. As Mannesmann reported on 5 November 1915, cited in ibid., p. 131.

30. See Krüger from Canea, 17 July 1915, in PAAA, R 21134.

31. Mirbach for Consul Kanea, passing on Mannesmann, 12 November 1915, R 21136.

32. Cited in McGuirk, *Sanusi's Little War*, p. 115.

33. For details of the outbreak of the conflict, see ibid., pp. 145–8; and McKale, *War by Revolution*, pp. 150–51.

34. From the Sir John Maxwell Papers, cited in McGuirk, *Sanusi's Little War*, p. 151.

35. See Pinhas Walter Pick, 'German Railway Constructions in the Middle East', in Wallach (ed.), *Germany and the Middle East 1835–1939*, pp. 76–7, 81–2.

36. Oppenheim to Foreign Office, Berlin, passed on by Hohenlohe from Pera, 9 August 1915, in PAAA, R 21135.

37. Zimmermann to Pera Embassy, 26 November 1915, in PAAA, R 21137.

38. Cited by McGuirk, in *Sanusi's Little War*, pp. 144–5.

39. Cited in ibid., p. 217.

40. Ibid., pp. 159–60, 216.

41. Ibid., p. 151; and Falkenhayn telegram to Enver, 11 November 1915, in EJP, 1/28.

16   Iranian Implosion

1. Wassmuss to Sarre, sent via Shiraz, 8 January 1916, in PAAA, Nachlass Wassmuss, 790–91.

2. According to a damage report assessment prepared by the Anglo-Persian Oil Company for fiscal year 1915, reproduced in Lührs, *Gegenspieler*, p. 94.

3. On Rauf's strategic justification for his incursions into western Persia, see Kanitz from Baghdad, 20 August 1915, in PAAA, R 21047.

4. Sarre to Nadolny, 20 April 1915, in PAAA, R 21042.

5. Wangenheim from Pera, 10 May 1915, in PAAA, R 21042.

6. Lührs, *Gegenspieler*, pp. 167, 188.

7. McKale, *War by Revolution*, p. 129; and Seidt, *Berlin, Kabul, Moskau*, pp. 71–5.

8. Lührs, *Gegenspieler*, p. 166.

9. Hohenlohe from Pera, passing on Sarre from Baghdad, 23 September 1915, in PAAA, R 21049.

10. McKale, *War by Revolution*, pp. 138–9.

11. Lührs, *Gegenspieler*, pp. 166–86 and *passim*.

12. Lossow passing on Baghdad (Sarre?), 15 September 1915, and passed on by Nadolny to Bethmann Hollweg, 24 October 1915, in PAAA, R 21052.

13. Hohenlohe from Constantinople, 23 September 1915, in PAAA, R 21049; and Lossow/Wangenheim to Nadolny, 21 October 1915, in PAAA, R 21051.

14. McKale, *War by Revolution*, pp. 139–40.

15. Niedermayer from Herat or Kabul, passed on by Sarre/Lossow/Wangenheim, 16 October 1915, in PAAA, R 21051.

16. Lührs, *Gegenspieler*, p. 192.

17. See Hopkirk, *On Secret Service East of Constantinople*, p. 174.

18. Ibid., p. 176. See also Ulrich Gehrke, 'Germany and Persia up to 1919' in Wallach (ed.), *Germany and the Middle East 1835–1939*, pp. 114–15.

19. Lührs, *Gegenspieler*, p. 188.

20. McKale, *War by Revolution*, p. 141.

21. Cited by Hopkirk, *On Secret Service East of Constantinople*, p. 175.

22. Ibid., pp. 167–71, 176–7, 221–4.

23. Lührs, *Gegenspieler*, pp. 187–200.

24. McKale, *War by Revolution*, pp. 142–3; Hopkirk, *On Secret Service East of Constantinople*, pp. 204–10.

25. Kanitz from Baghdad, 17 July 1915, in PAAA, R 21046.

26. 'German Plot in Persia. Turkish Invasion Encouraged' in *The Times* (London), 19 March 1915.

27. Lührs, *Gegenspieler*, p. 192.

28. Hopkirk, *On Secret Service East of Constantinople*, p. 176.

29. Lührs, *Gegenspieler*, pp. 201–20.

30. In this vein, see Hopkirk, *On Secret Service East of Constantinople*, pp. 105–106 and *passim*.

31. Wassmuss 13 September 1915, passed on via Kermanshah, Baghdad etc. to Neurath in Berlin 6 November 1915, in PAAA, R 21052.

32. Wassmuss to Sarre, sent via Shiraz, 8 January 1916, in PAAA, Nachlass Wassmuss, 790–91.

17   Betrayal in Mecca

1. Cited by Hurgronje, in *Revolt in Arabia*, p. 43 and *passim*.

2. Quai d'Orsay position paper on 'les affaires musulmanes', 8 December 1915, in QO, Guerre 1914–1918, file 1655.

3. McKale, *War by Revolution*, p. 191.

4. Projet de loi, 9 December 1915, reproduced with annotations, commentaries etc., in QO, Guerre 1914–1918, file 1658.

5. Huguet report on the 'Sending of sacred carpet to Mecca', 10 October 1915, in PRO, FO 371/2491.

6. On the fall of Erzurum, see Allen and Muratoff, *Caucasian Battlefields*, pp. 355–72; and Erickson, *Ordered to Die*, pp. 120–28.

7. Fromkin, *A Peace to End All Peace*, p. 219. See also Cemal (Djemal) Pasha, *Memories of a Turkish Statesman*, p. 214.

8. Pomiankowski, *Zusammenbruch des Ottomanischen Reiches*, pp. 196–205.

9. See, for example, Loytved-Hardegg to Wolff-Metternich, 26 February 1916, in PAAA, R 21139; and Djemal, *Memories of a Turkish Statesman*, p. 217.

10. Ibid., p. 215. Oppenheim also reproduces a copy of this telegram, in his memoirs, section labelled 'Personalien … Stammbaum der Sherifen v. Mekka. Fesal. Aufstand im Hedjaz' in MvO, I/19.

11. On the various Arab conspiracies and Djemal's crackdowns in Beirut and Damascus, see Fromkin, *A Peace to End all Peace*, pp. 218–19; Antonius, *Arab Awakening*, pp. 184–7; Kedourie, *England and the Middle East*, pp. 62–4. On the Stotzingen mission, see McKale, *War by Revolution*, pp. 172–5; Lüdke, *Jihad Made in Germany*, pp. 177–85; and chapter 18 below.

12. Antonius, *Arab Awakening*, p. 189.

13. Prüfer to Djemal, 5 December 1915, in PAAA, R 14131.

14. Citations in Lewy, *Armenian Massacres in Ottoman Turkey*, pp. 112, 196–8.

15. Ibid.; Kress, *Mit den Türken zum Suezkanal*, p. 30; Pomiankowski, *Zusammenbruch des Ottomanisches Reiches*, p. 199.

16. The correspondence surrounding Djemal's (probably mythical) peace offer, in a file dated 29 and 30 December 1915, can be found in PRO, FO 371/2492.

17. David Fromkin and Franz Weber both credit the possibility Djemal's offer was genuine. Weber, *Eagles on the Crescent*, pp. 153–6; and Fromkin, *A Peace to End All Peace*, pp. 214–15. Ulrich Trumpener, for his part, said that he 'had found no evidence to substantiate this story'. Trumpener, *Germany and the Ottoman Empire*, p. 151, n. 29. Turkish historians, in general, treat the idea as too incredible to be indulged seriously. They are almost certainly correct to do so: an examination of Russian Foreign Office files reveals that Zavriev had been intriguing with the Russians for years to set up an independent Armenia, making elaborate promises which rarely, if ever, panned out. His famous December 1915 'Djemal' initiative was almost certainly fraudulent.

18. Djemal, *Memories of a Turkish Statesman*, p. 197.

19. For a summary of the inter-Allied negotiations, see Fromkin, *A Peace to End All Peace*, pp. 214–15. Copies of most of the essential correspondence can be found in PRO, FO 371/2492.

20. Kress, *Mit den Türken zum Suezkanal*, p. 73.

21. See Djemal, *Memories of a Turkish Statesman*, pp. 214, 222.

22. McKale, *War by Revolution*, p. 175.

23. Djemal, *Memories of a Turkish Statesman*, pp. 220–23. For Enver telling Humann Feisal was used as a hostage, see Humann report, 12 July 1916, in EJP, 1/35.

24. Humann report, 12 July 1916, in EJP, 1/35.

25. Hopkirk, *On Secret Service East of Constantinople*, pp. 225–6.

26. Kedourie, 'The Capture of Damascus, 1 October 1918', and appendix, in *Chatham House Version*, pp. 33–51.

27. Kedourie, 'Cairo and Khartoum on the Arab Question' in *Chatham House Version*, p. 18.

28. See Kedourie, 'Egypt and the Caliphate, 1915–52', in ibid., p. 182.

29. Cited by McKale, *War by Revolution*, p. 49. Oppenheim himself, incidentally, was less heartbroken by the Arab revolt than Prüfer thought, or at least

he was when recalling it a quarter-century later in his memoirs. Oppenheim blamed the affair on Djemal's brutality in suppressing Arab treachery in Damascus, arguing that had the Turks instead curried Hussein's favour by offering him a hereditary claim to the Hejaz, they could have avoided the rebellion. See Oppenheim, 'Zur Angelegenheit des Aufstandes des Hedjaz während des Weltkrieges', MS dated 23 January 1943, in MvO, 1/19.

30. French-language translation of English pamphlet intercepted by Ottoman intelligence in Arabia, *circa* summer 1916, in BOA, HR.SYS 2318-6.

31. Pick, 'German Railway Constructions in the Middle East' in Wallach (ed.), *Germany and the Middle East 1835–1939*, p. 84.

32. For details, see Pomiankowski, *Zusammenbruch des Ottomanischen Reiches*, pp. 227–9; McKale, *War by Revolution*, pp. 178, 182–3.

33. Fromkin, *A Peace to End All Peace*, pp. 220, 223, 226.

34. 'Twenty-Seven Articles by T. E. Lawrence', article 11, first published in the *Arab Bulletin*, 20 August 1917.

35. See Wingate from Cairo, 29 January 1917, in PRO, FO 371/3048.

36. Cited, among many places, in Fromkin, *A Peace to End All Peace*, p. 497.

18   The Holy War Devours its Children

1. Lossow from Pera, 11 March 1916, in PAAA, R 21139.

2. British spy report of agent in Constantinople from 3 to 27 June 1916, forwarded from Alexandria on 11 July 1916, in RGVIA, fond 2000, opis' 1, del. 3888, 168.

3. Pomiankowski from Pera, 18 December 1915, in HHSA, Liasse Krieg 21a. Türkei, box 944. For exposition of the theme, see also Pomiankowski, *Zusammenbruch des Ottomanisches Reiches*, pp. 240–43.

4. On this point see especially Neilson and Prete (eds), *Coalition Warfare*, p. 36.

5. Kress von Kressenstein, *Mit den Türken zum Suezkanal*, pp. 35–8.

6. As reported by Sarre, in Baghdad, to Nadolny in Berlin, 20 April 1915, in PAAA, R 21042.

7. Wangenheim reporting on his conversation with Enver, 16 April 1915, in PAAA, R 21041.

8. Russian military intelligence intercept of the dispatch of Kh. Khogopian, correspondent for the *New York World*, in AVPRI, fond 151, opis' 482, del. 4073, 103.

9. Lührs, *Gegenspieler des Obersten Lawrence*, pp. 81–2.

10. Ibid., pp. 133–147.

11. Dandini to Burian (from Aleppo), 9 March 1915, in HHSA, Liasse Krieg 21a. Türkei, box 943.

12. 'Musil report', pp. 19–21.

13. Weber, *Eagles on the Crescent*, pp. 173–4.

14. Hopkirk, *On Secret Service East of Constantinople*, p. 219.

15. McGuirk, *Sanusi's Little War*, p. 277.

16. Khogopian dispatch intercepted by Russian army intelligence, in AVPRI, fond 151, opis' 482, del. 4073, 99–100.

17. British agent report, circulated 24 August 1916, in RGVIA, fond 2000, opis' 1, del. 3888, 297.

18. Bakherakht to Sazonov from Bern, passing on Russian spy Mandel'shtam's report, 15/28 June 1916, in AVPRI, fond 151, opis' 482, del. 4073, 114. See also British spy's report passed on to the Russians in Petrograd, 19 April 1916, in RGVIA, fond 2000, opis' 1, del. 3888, 126.

19. Lossow from Pera, 11 March 1916, in PAAA, R 21139.

20. McKale, *War by Revolution*, p. 178. On Neufeld's marriage ceremony, see Stotzingen from El-Ula, 5 May 1916, in PAAA, R 21142.

21. Stotzingen post-mortem from Damascus, 16 July 1918, in PAAA, R 21142.

22. Buchan, *Greenmantle*, p. 144.

23. Stresemann from Constantinople, via Zimmermann, 14 March 1916, in PAAA, R 13750.

24. Wolff-Metternich from Pera, passing on Mecklenburg from Baghdad, June 1916, in PAAA, R 13751.

25. Harry Stuermer, *Zwei Kriegsjahre in Konstantinopel*, pp. 134–42. On the German advisers appointed in 1916, see Weber, *Eagles on the Crescent*, pp. 175–7.

26. On the wartime diplomacy between the Porte and the (other) Central Powers surrounding the Capitulations issue, see Trumpener, *Germany and the Ottoman Empire*, pp. 122–30.

27. See the complaint lodged (in French) on 26 November 1912 by the German Embassy in Pera with the Porte, in BOA, HR-H 336.

28. Wolff-Metternich from Pera, 17 January 1916, in PAAA, R 13750. Some Germans, like Humann, did think Wolff-Metternich exaggerated the extent of anti-German sentiment. See Humann to Jäckh, 28 January 1916, in EJP, 1/7.

29. Trumpener, *Germany and the Ottoman Empire*, p. 271.

30. Pallavicini from Pera, 12 November 1915, in HHSA, Liasse Krieg 21a. Türkei, box 944. The Djemal quote footnoted is cited in Sina Akşin, *Jön Türkler ve İttihat ve Terakki*, p. 415.

31. Pomiankowski, *Zusammenbruch des Ottomanisches Reiches*, p. 263.

32. Matthias Erzberger from Pera, via the German Embassy, 13 February 1916, in PAAA, R 13750.

33. As paraphrased by Weber from Tschirschky's 15 January 1916 report to Bethmann Hollweg, in *Eagles on the Crescent*, pp. 166–7.

34. Wolff-Metternich from Therapia, 21 September 1916, in PAAA, R 13753.

35. McMurray, *Distant Ties*, pp. 125–6, 131.

36. Erickson, *Ordered to Die*, p. 127.

37. Schulenberg to Nadolny, passed on via the military attaché in Pera, 28 February 1916, in PAAA, R 21018.

38. Lewy, *Armenian Massacres in Ottoman Turkey*, pp. 204–205.

39. Bloxham, *Great Game of Genocide*, pp. 98–9.

40. Reynolds, 'The Ottoman-Russian Struggle for Eastern Anatolia and the Caucasus', pp. 293–6 and *passim*. Reynolds is one of the few scholars to have examined in depth Russia's pre-war and wartime cultivation of the ethnic minorities of the Near East, including Armenians, Assyrians, Kurds and Circassians.

41. British agent report passed on via Alexandria on 18 July 1916, in RGVIA, fond 2000, opis' 1, del. 3888, 222.

42. Bakherakht to Sazonov from Bern, passing on Russian spy Mandel'shtam's report, 4/17 June 1916, in AVPRI, fond 151, opis' 482, del. 4073, 105.

43. Weber, *Eagles on the Crescent*, p. 195.

44. Wolff-Metternich from Therapia, passing on Werth from Sivas, 13 August 1916, in PAAA, R 13753.

45. Werth from Sivas, 14 August 1916, in PAAA, R 13753.

46. Wolff-Metternich from Pera, passing on Schmidt from Jerusalem, 9 January 1916, in PAAA, R 13750.

47. Stuermer, *Zwei Kriegsjahre in Konstantinopel*, pp. 118–24.

48. See Wolff-Metternich from Therapia, 15 September 1916, in PAAA, R 13753.

49. See Enver's complaint to Hindenburg, lodged via Lossow and Radowitz, 2 November 1916, in PAAA, R 13753.

50. Humann to Jäckh, 15 November 1916, in PAAA, R 13753. This letter is also preserved in EJP, 1/8.

51. Ibid.; Weber, *Eagles on the Crescent*, p. 196; and Pomiankowski, *Zusammenbruch des Ottomanisches Reiches*, p. 244.

52. Trumpener, *Germany and the Ottoman Empire*, p. 130.

53. Zimmermann, from Berlin, to Kühlmann (the new German Ambassador at the Porte), 6 March 1917, in PAAA, R 13754.

54. Kühlmann from Pera, 2 April 1917, in PAAA, R 13754.

55. Stumm from Foreign Office, Berlin to the Pera Embassy, 1 April 1917, in PAAA, R 13754.

56. See Kurt Grunwald, 'Pénétration pacifique – the Financial Vehicles of Germany's "Drang nach dem Osten"' in Wallach (ed.), *Germany and the Middle East 1835–1939*, p. 95.

57. See Bibikov to Sazonov from Bern, 5/18 April 1917, passing on Mandel'shtam, in AVPRI, fond 151, opis' 482, del, 4073, 169.

58. Trauttmansdorff to Czernin, 3 March 1917, in HHSA, Liasse Krieg 21a. Türkei, box 945.

59. Pallavicini to Czernin, 17 March 1917, in HHSA, Liasse Krieg 21a. Türkei, box 945.

60. Ludendorff to the Embassy in Pera, 16 August 1917, in PAAA, R 13755.

61. Nadolny from Berlin to the Embassy in Pera, 29 August 1917, in PAAA, R 13755.

62. See transcript of a 28 October 1918 radio broadcast, clipped by the German Foreign Office, in PAAA, R 13758.

63. Trautsmandorff from Yeniköy, 11 September 1917, in HHSA, Liasse Krieg 21a. Türkei, box 945. See also the Russian intelligence report on the Haydarpasha explosion cited in Reynolds, 'The Ottoman-Russian Struggle for Eastern Anatolia and the Caucasus, 1908–1918', p. 306, n. 32.

19   Consolation Prize? The Race for Baku

1. Bernstorff to Kühlmann, 17 December 1917, in PAAA, R 13755.

2. Norman Stone, *The Eastern Front 1914–1917*.

3. Erickson, *Ordered to Die*, pp. 160–61. Likewise, the classic study by W. E. B. Allen and Paul Muratoff of *Caucasian Battlefields* devotes only ten pages to the long stretch between the Russians' summer advance of 1916 and the Turkish offensive of spring 1918. Confirming the general pattern, the eastern Anatolian sector merits only passing mention in Allan Wildman's two-volume study of *The End of the Russian Imperial Army*, in which the Army of the Caucasus is not mentioned until vol. 1, p. 325, in a brief discussion of the Tiflis soldiers' congress of April–May 1917. While Bolshevik agitation and related morale problems in individual regiments of the Army of the Caucasus are discussed, Wildman does not really discuss the eastern Anatolian front as such in his narrative of the breakdown of the Tsarist armies – doubtless because, in his words, 'in most [Russian] armies only one or two major operations resulted in disbanding [i.e. the literal disintegration of one or more military units], and on the Rumanian and Caucasian fronts, none at all'. Allan K. Wildman, *The End of the Russian Imperial Army*, vol. 2, p. 141.

4. An exception should be made here for Michael Reynolds' fine recent dissertation, 'The Ottoman-Russian Struggle for Eastern Anatolia and the Caucasus, 1908–1918', Princeton University, 2003.

5. Reynolds, 'Buffers, not Brethren: Young Turk Military Policy in World War One and the Myth of Panturanism', forthcoming in *Past and Present*. See also Pomiankowski, *Zusammenbruch des Ottomanisches Reiches*, p. 272; and

Reynolds, 'The Ottoman-Russian Struggle for Eastern Anatolia and the Caucasus, 1908–1918', p. 296.

6. Cited in Kazemzadeh, *Struggle for Transcaucasia*, p. 61.

7. Ibid., pp. 43–4.

8. Particularly the 78th, 717th, and 732nd Regiments. See Wildman, *The End of the Russian Imperial Army*, vol. 2, p. 135.

9. John Wheeler-Bennett, *Brest-Litovsk: The Forgotten Peace*, pp. 70–73.

10. Cited in Reynolds, 'The Ottoman-Russian Struggle for Eastern Anatolia and the Caucasus, 1908–1918', p. 362.

11. The phrase is that of Allen and Muratoff, in *Caucasian Battlefields*, p. 457.

12. Richard Pipes, *Russian Revolution*, p. 410. For analysis of the current state of knowledge on German financing of the Bolsheviks, see McMeekin, *History's Greatest Heist*, chapter 5.

13. Telegram from Kurt von Lersner at Gr. Hauptquartier to the Foreign Office in Berlin, 25 November 1917, in PAAA, R 10085.

14. Pipes, *Russian Revolution*, pp. 609–10.

15. Cited in Allen and Muratoff, *Caucasian Battlefields*, p. 457.

16. Riezler telegram from Stockholm to the Foreign Office in Berlin, 26 November 1917, in PAAA, R 2000.

17. Otto von Wesendonck, 'Uberblick über die in der islamitisch-israelischen Welt eingeleitete Agitationstätigkeit', 16 August 1914, in PAAA, R 21028. See chapter 4 above, and the Epilogue below.

18. Cited in Norman Stone, *World War One*, p. 130. On Wesendonck, see also Fischer, *Germany's Aims in the First World War*, p. 125.

19. Citations in Bülent Gökay, *Clash of Empires*, pp. 17–18.

20. Bernstorff to Kühlmann, 17 December 1917, in PAAA, R 13755.

21. The report on Baku's oil reserves referenced in the footnote is preserved in PAAA, R 21025.

22. Pomiankowski, *Zusammenbruch des Ottomanisches Reiches*, p. 336. On the logistics of oil pipelines and transport by ship and rail in the *fin de siècle* era and beyond, see John P. McKay, 'Baku Oil and Transcaucasian Pipelines, 1883–1891: A Study of Tsarist Economic Policy' in *Slavic Review*, 43 (4) (Winter 1984), pp. 604–23. On Germany's strategic aims in the Caucasus more generally, see Fischer, *Germany's Aims in the First World War*, esp. pp. 550–62.

23. On the importance of Baku and its oil to the Caucasian plans of the CUP leadership (as opposed to the influence of pan-Turanian ideas, which has been greatly exaggerated in most of the literature), see Reynolds, 'Buffers, not Brethren: Young Turk Military Policy in World War One and the Myth of Panturanism'. For the Turkish side on Brest-Litovsk generally, see Dr Akdes Nimet Kurat, 'Brest-Litovsk Barışı' in *Türkiye ve Rusya*, pp. 339–52 and *passim*.

24. Cited in Wheeler-Bennett, *Brest-Litovsk: The Forgotten Peace*, p. 115.

25. Ibid., p. 139.

26. Cited in ibid., pp. 165–6.

27. The Kühlmann quote footnoted is cited by Reynolds in 'The Ottoman-Russian Struggle for Eastern Anatolia and the Caucasus, 1908–1918', p. 314.

28. Wheeler-Bennett, *Brest-Litovsk: The Forgotten Peace*, p. 115.

29. Citations in ibid., pp. 152, 226–8.

30. Cited in Richard Pipes, *Russian Revolution*, pp. 586–7.

31. Cited in Reynolds, 'The Ottoman-Russian Struggle for Eastern Anatolia and the Caucasus, 1908–1918', pp. 345–6.

32. Pomiankowski, *Zusammenbruch des Ottomanischen Reiches*, p. 335.

33. The ultimatum is reproduced in Wheeler-Bennett, *Brest-Litovsk: The Forgotten Peace*, pp. 255–6, and the Brest-Litovsk Treaty on pp. 403–408.

34. Allen and Muratoff, *Caucasian Battlefields*, p. 468.

35. Erickson, *Ordered to Die*, p. 182.

36. Reynolds, 'The Ottoman-Russian Struggle for Eastern Anatolia and the Caucasus, 1908–1918', p. 333.

37. Ibid., p. 377.

38. The number initially reported by Azeri Turks was 12,000 killed in Baku, which was almost certainly exaggerated; local Armenian leaders, like Stepan Shaumian, estimate 3,000 were killed, not exclusively Muslims. Likewise, some have estimated as many as 1,500 Russians and Armenians killed at Shamkhor, while the real number is probably only several hundred. Nevertheless, there is no denying that massacres of some kind took place in both locations. See Kazemzadeh, *Struggle for Transcaucasia*, pp. 70–73, 83–4; Pipes, *Formation of the Soviet Union*, p. 103; Gökay, *Clash of Empires*, p. 23.

39. Reynolds, 'The Ottoman-Russian Struggle for Eastern Anatolia and the Caucasus, 1908–1918', p. 372.

40. On these terms, see ibid., p. 467; and Gökay, *Clash of Empires*, p. 26.

41. Jehuda Wallach, *Anatomie einer Militärhilfe*, p. 241. See also Pomiankowski, *Zusammenbruch des Ottomanischen Reiches*, pp. 336–7.

42. Cited in Kazemzadeh, *Struggle for Transcaucasia*, p. 147.

43. For details, see Reynolds, 'The Ottoman-Russian Struggle for Eastern Anatolia and the Caucasus, 1908–1918', pp. 416–19.

44. Citations in Allen and Muratoff, *Caucasian Battlefields*, pp. 476–8. For further details, see also Pomiankowski, *Zusammenbruch des Ottomanischen Reiches*, pp. 361–3; and Erickson, *Ordered to Die*, pp. 186–7.

45. Pomiankowski, *Zusammenbruch des Ottomanischen Reiches*, p. 362.

46. Ibid., p. 363.

47. Ibid., p. 368.

48. Hopkirk, *On Secret Service East of Constantinople*, p. 329. See also Kazemzadeh, *Struggle for Transcaucasia*, pp. 138–9, and Reynolds, 'The Ottoman-Russian Struggle for Eastern Anatolia and the Caucasus, 1908–1918', pp. 453–4. Citations on the 'Islamic character' of Nuri's Army of Islam are in Reynolds, 'Buffers, not Brethren', pp. 34–5.

49. The Treaty Supplement, dated 27 August 1918, is reproduced in Wheeler-Bennett, *Brest-Litovsk: The Forgotten Peace*, pp. 427–34. See also Kazemzadeh, *Struggle for Transcaucasia*, pp. 135, 150.

50. Reynolds, 'The Ottoman-Russian Struggle for Eastern Anatolia and the Caucasus, 1908–1918', pp. 468–9.

EPILOGUE

1. Cited in Isaiah Friedman, *Germany, Turkey, and Zionism*, p. 230.

2. Cited in Zeman (ed.), *Germany and the Revolution in Russia*, pp. 1–2.

3. See chapter 11 above.

4. In this last vein, see particularly Matthias Küntzel, *Jihad and Jew-Hatred: Islamism, Nazism and the Roots of 9/11*, or the various articles and books of Paul Berman, Christopher Hitchens and Norman Podhoretz, who have all promoted the term 'Islamofascism' – i.e. the idea that contemporary Islamic terrorism is an outgrowth of European-style fascism/Nazism. For a more academic treatment of the subject, see Martin Cüppers and Klaus-Michael Mallmann, *Halbmond und Hakenkreuz. Das dritte Reich, die Araber und Palästina*.

5. For a fine summary of the traces of the German-built Baghdad and Hejaz railways in the region, see Pinhas Walter Pick, 'German Railway Constructions in the Middle East' in Wallach (ed.), *Germany and the Middle East 1835–1939*, pp. 72–85.

6. Walter Laqueur, *A History of Zionism*, p. 143.

7. Cited by David Fromkin, in *A Peace to End All Peace*, p. 296.

8. Ibid., p. 287.

9. Wesendonck, 'Uberblick über die in der islamitisch-israelischen Welt eingeleitete Agitationstätigkeit', 16 August 1914, in PAAA, R 21028.

10. Egmont Zechlin, *Die deutsche Politik und die Juden im Ersten Weltkrieg*, pp. 117–18. See also Friedman, *Germany, Turkey, and Zionism*, pp. 230–31.

11. Fischer, *Germany's Aims in the First World War*, p. 142.

12. Zechlin, *Deutsche Politik und die Juden im Ersten Weltkrieg*, pp. 118–19.

13. Cited in ibid., p. 121, and for the number of pamphlets printed, p. 124, n. 46.

14. Cited in ibid., p. 122.

15. Friedman, *Germany, Turkey, and Zionism*, pp. 232–5.

16. The phrases are Friedman's, in *Germany, Turkey, and Zionism*, pp. 232–3.

17. Eric Lohr, 'The Russian Army and the Jews: Mass Deportation, Hostages, and Violence During World War I' in *Russian Review*, 60 (July 2001): 404.
18. Zechlin, *Deutsche Politik und die Juden im Ersten Weltkrieg*, pp. 124–5.
19. Friedman, *Germany, Turkey, and Zionism*, pp. 253 and 239, n. 33.
20. Zechlin, *Deutsche Politik und die Juden im Ersten Weltkrieg*, pp. 136, 142–3.
21. As nicely explained by Fromkin, in *A Peace to End All Peace*, pp. 247–8.
22. See ibid., especially chapters 32–4, 'Lloyd George's Zionism', 'Toward the Balfour Declaration' and 'The Promised Land'. On the Parvus–Radek–Aschberg nexus surrounding the financing of Lenin's return to Russia and Bolshevik propaganda, particularly the Stockholm connection, see McMeekin, 'Brest-Litovsk and the Diplomatic Bag', chapter 5 in *History's Greatest Heist*.
23. As paraphrased in Friedman, *Germany, Turkey, and Zionism*, p. 253.
24. Citations in ibid., pp. 198–9, 255. On Beha-ed-Din's recall, and Djemal's intervention, see Zechlin, *Deutsche Politik und die Juden im Ersten Weltkrieg*, pp. 322–3.
25. Friedman, *Germany, Turkey, and Zionism*, pp. 252–3.
26. Cited by David Yisraeli, in 'Germany and Zionism' in Wallach (ed.), *Germany and the Middle East 1835–1939*, p. 142.
27. For a thorough timeline of the evolution of Nazi policy as regards forced emigration/expulsion of Jews, whether to Palestine or other possible locations like Madagascar, see Philippe Burrin, *Hitler and the Jews*. For a more recent take on the subject, see Christopher Browning, *Fateful Months: Essays on the Emergence of the Final Solution*.
28. Cited in Friedman, *Germany, Turkey, and Zionism*, p. 255.
29. See Zechlin, *Deutsche Politik und die Juden im Ersten Weltkrieg*, p. 353. Talaat's remark to Bernstorff is cited in ibid., p. 371, n. 114.
30. Friedman, *Germany, Turkey, and Zionism*, pp. 274–5.
31. Cited in Yisraeli, 'Germany and Zionism' in Wallach (ed.), *Germany and the Middle East 1838–1939*, p. 148.
32. Friedman, *Germany, Turkey, and Zionism*, pp. 329–30; and Zechlin, *Deutsche Politik und die Juden im Ersten Weltkrieg*, pp. 369–70. See also Walter Laqueur, *A History of Zionism*, p. 177.
33. From Bernstorff's memoirs, as cited by Zechlin, in *Deutsche Politik und die Juden im Ersten Weltkrieg*, p. 371, n. 116.
34. Friedman, p. 199. See also Emin, *Turkey in the World War*, pp. 174–7.
35. Prüfer report from Damascus for Djemal, 10 December 1915, passed on to Berlin by Wolff-Metternich to Bethmann Hollweg, 30 December 1915, in PAAA, R 14131.
36. See Friedman, *Germany, Turkey, and Zionism*, pp. 328–9.

37. Prüfer from Jerusalem, 1 March 1915, in PAAA, R 21131.

38. Cited in Fromkin, *A Peace to End All Peace*, p. 321.

39. Donald Macintyre, 'Lawrence of Arabia was really a Zionist, historian claims' in the *Independent*, 24 February 2007.

40. Cited in Friedman, *Germany, Turkey, and Zionism*, p. 335.

41. Cited in Fromkin, *A Peace to End All Peace*, p. 297.

42. Citations in ibid.

43. Citations in Friedman, *Germany, Turkey, and Zionism*, pp. 224, 408, 409.

44. Fromkin, *A Peace to End all Peace*, pp. 447–8.

45. See Friedman, *Germany, Turkey, and Zionism*, p. 417.

46. Cited in ibid., p. 402.

47. Paul Johnson, *A History of the Modern World*, pp. 481–2. See also J. H. Patterson, *Behind the Palestine Betrayal*, pp. 3–9.

48. Friedman, *Germany, Turkey, and Zionism*, p. 416.

49. Ibid., pp. 350–51.

50. Röhl, *The Kaiser and his Court*, p. 14.

51. Cited in McKale, *Curt Prüfer*, pp. 540–55.

52. Citations in ibid., pp. 57, 61, 101, 130.

53. The bank took on a gentile, Robert Pferdmenges, as managing director and namesake, which corporate name it retained until 1947 (except during 1944–1945 when, following the arrests of Waldemar and Carl Friedrich von Oppenheim, it essentially ceased operations). See Michael Stürmer, Gabriele Teichmann and Wilhelm Treue, *Sal. Oppenheim jr. & Cie. Geschichte einer Bank und einer Familie*, pp. 365–411.

54. Oppenheim, 'Leben im NS-Staat. 1933–1945' in MvO 1/14, pp. 7, 12; and copy of Oppenheim's 'Ehrenkreuz' bestowal by Hitler, 29 January 1937, also in MvO 1/14.

55. Citation in Cüppers and Mallmann, *Halbmond und Hakenkreuz*, p. 101.

56. Oppenheim, 'Der Mufti und Giliani', attachment to 'Leben im NS-Staat. 1933–1945', dated 28 June 1946, in MvO 1/14, pp. 8–9.

57. David G. Dalin and John F. Rothmann, *Icon of Evil*, p. 44.

58. Ibid., p. 49.

59. Cited in Cüppers and Mallmann, *Halbmond und Hakenkreuz*, pp. 106–108. The source is the notes of the Hitler–Mufti meeting taken by Dr Fritz Grobba, a former Minister to Mesopotamia who was now 'Commissioner for Arab Affairs' in the German Foreign Office, and reinforced by a second transcription of the meeting, which agrees with the Grobba text on all main points. That the meeting took place is exceedingly well documented; a photograph of the two men engaged in friendly conversation graces the cover of *Halbmond und Hakenkreuz*.

60. Cüppers and Mallmann, *Halbmond und Hakenkreuz*, p. 107.

61. Dalin and Rothmann, *Icon of Evil*, pp. 52–3, 59–60. See also Matthias Küntzel, *Jihad and Jew-Hatred*, p. 36.

62. Cited in Cüppers and Mallmann, *Halbmond und Hakenkreuz*, p. 227.

63. Dalin and Rothmann, *Icon of Evil*, p. 57; and Cüppers and Mallmann, *Halbmond und Hakenkreuz*, p. 227. The story about the Balkan children footnoted is in Klaus Gensicke, *Der Mufti von Jerusalem el-Husseini und die Nationalsozialisten*, p. 156.

64. Ibid., pp. 231, 253.

65. Cited from MEMRI report no. 375, 3 May 2002, available online at http://memri.net/bin/articles.cgi?Page=subjects&Area=antisemitism&ID=SP 37502. Also cited in Küntzel, *Jihad and Jew-Hatred*, p. 61.

66. McKale, *Curt Prüfer*, p. 175.

67. Oppenheim, 'Leben im NS-Staat. 1933–1945', dated 28 June 1946, in MvO 1/14, pp. 14–15.

68. Tom Reiss, *The Orientalist. In Search of a Man Caught between East and West.*

69. See Dalin and Rothmann, *Icon of Evil*, pp. 131–4.

70. This phrase appears, for example, on the back jacket cover of Joachim Fest's *Hitler*.

Bibliography

Archives and Principal Collections

Arkhiv vneshnei politiki Rossiiskoi Imperii (AVPRI). Moscow, Russia.
  Fond 135. Osobyi politicheskii otdel.
  Fond 138. Sekretnyi arkhiv ministra.
  Fond 180. Posol'stvo v Konstantinopole.
  Fond 151. Politicheskii arkhiv.
  Fond 129. Turetskii stol.

Başbakanlik Osmanlı Arşivleri (BOA). Istanbul, Turkey.
  Hariciye Nezareti Hukuk Kısmı (HR-H). Sublime Porte Legal Corres-
    pondence. Boxes 328–9, 336. 'Almanya. Muhtelif Yazışmalar.' 1914–1918.
  Hariciye Nezareti Siyasi (HR.SYS). Ottoman Foreign Ministry.
    Box 2318. Wartime correspondence, esp. relating to jihad. 1914–16.
  Dahiliye Nezareti. Şifre Kalemi (DH-ŞFR). Ottoman government telegrams.
    Boxes 47–8. Wartime communiqués, esp. relating to jihad. 1914–16.

Deutsches Bundesarchiv Berlin (DBB), Lichterfelde, Berlin, Germany.
  R 901. Auswärtiges Amt.

Ernst Jäckh Papers (EJP), Yale University, New Haven, Connecticut.
  Enver Pasha, Correspondence (1911–18). Autobiography. Clippings.
  Humann, Hans, Correspondence and Reports (1911–16).
  Oppenheim, Max A. S., Freiherr von. Correspondence and Reports (1914).
  Mehmed Talât Pasha: Correspondence (1914, 1919). Autobiography.
    Clippings.

Geheimes Preussisches Staatsarchiv (GPA). Berlin, Germany.
  BPH. Rep. 53. 165/1–8. 'Aufzeichnungen Seiner Majestät Kaiser Wilhelm II'.
  BPH Rep. 53 Nr. 342. *Kaiser Wilhelm II.* persönliche Erinnerungen von
    Oberst Nicolai.

BPH Rep. 53 F III d. Nr. 2a. News clippings, particularly relating to the Kaiser's visits to Constantinople in 1889 and 1898.

Haus-, Hof- und Staatsarchiv (HHSA), Vienna, Austria.
Politisches Archiv I, Liasse Krieg 21a. Türkei und Krieg 22–4.
Kartons 942–8. Turkey wartime correspondence, 1914–18.
Karton 841. Deutschland 1918.
Karton 467. Türkei (misc.).

Kriegsarchiv Wien (KW). Vienna, Austria.
Generalstab. Militärattachees Konstantinopel.
Evidenzbüro. Türkei.

Max von Oppenheim Stiftung (MvO), Sal. Oppenheim jr. & Cie KGaA, Cologne, Germany.
Nachlass Max von Oppenheim. Lebenserinnerungen (memoirs).
1/1. 'Jugendzeit in Köln, Straßburg und Berlin 1860–83'.
1/2. 'Referandar und Assessor 1883–92.'
1/3. 'Erste Reisen im Vorderen Orient u. in Afrika 1883–93.'
1/4. 'Reisen, Leben 1893–6.'
1/5. 'Dienst in Kairo. Europäisches Leben 1896–1909.'
1/6. 'Dienst in Kairo. Eingeborene Welt. 1896–1909.'
1/7. 'Dienst in Kairo. Politisches etc. 1896–1909.'
1/12. 'Der Erste Weltkrieg. 1914–18.'
1/13. 'Bekanntschaft aus dem Auswärtigen Amt, 1914–45.'
1/14. 'Leben im NS-Staat. 1933–45.'
1/19. 'Erster Weltkrieg. 1914–18. Politisches.'
  – 'Compte rendu d'une séance politique. A Pera Palace Hotel. Constantinople Samedi 24 Avril 1915.'
  – 'Mitteilungen des Botschafter Dr. Prüfer über seine Begegnung mit Fe[i]sal im Jahre 1916.'
  – 'Personalien. Nachrichtenstelle in Konstantinopel. Kaiserlampe im Grabmal Sala Errins 10.8.1916. Stammbaum der Sherifen v. Mekka. Fesal. Aufstand im Hedjaz 1943.'
  – 'Zur Angelegenheit des Aufstandes des Hedjaz während des Weltkrieges.'

National Archives of the United Kingdom (PRO). Kew Gardens, London, UK.
FO 371. Foreign Office Correspondence.
Boxes 65, 245, 1174, 1261. Cairo corr., Prüfer and Oppenheim, etc., 1906–11.
Boxes 544–5. Turkey Files, 1908–09 (on the Young Turks, etc.)
Boxes 2135–41. Turkey Files, 1914 (up to Turkey's entry into war).

Boxes 2147, 2482–92, 2769–72, 2781, 3046–60, 3391–9.
    Turkey (War) Files, 1914–18.
FO 882/25. Arab Bulletin Nos. 1–36. 1916–18.
WO 33/731. War Office Correspondence, esp. 1914–18.

National Archives of the United States (NA). US Embassy, Ankara, Turkey.
M 353. Turkey correspondence, 1914–1915 (roll 6).

Politisches Archiv des Auswärtigen Amtes (PAAA), Berlin, Germany.
    Berichte des Freiherrn von Oppenheim über orientalische Verhältnisse.
        – R 14555–65. 1896–1909.
    Deutsche wirtschaftliche und industrielle Unternehmungen in der Türkei.
        – R 14148. 1899–1901.
    Deutschland 131. Geheime Akten.
        – R 2000–1. German financing for Lenin etc.
    Eisenbahnen in der asiatischen Tuerkei. (Tuerkei 152).
        – R 13456–13557. 1898–1917.
    Die Juden in der Turkei.
        – R 14131. 1 August to 31 December 1915.
    Die Jungtürken. Vorgänge i.a. Orient.gen.
        – R 14155–62. 1898–1920.
    Krieg 1914. Unternehmungen und Aufwiegelungen gegen unserer Feinde.
        – R 20936–39 (Allgemeine).
        – R 21008–25. (Kaukasus).
        – R 21123–48. (Egypten, Syrien, Arabien).
        – R 21028–62. (Afghanistan und Persien).
        – R 21283. ('Die Senussi').
    Muhamedanismus.
        – R 14549. 1 October 1912 to 30 August 1916.
    Nachlaß Curt Prüfer.
    Nachlaß Schabinger von Schowingen.
    Nachlaß Wilhelm Waßmuß (1880–1931).
    Rußland 61. Geheime Akten.
        – R 10073–85. German financing for Lenin etc.
    Das Verhaeltnis der Tuerkei zu Deutschland. (Tuerkei 152).
        – R 13742–60. 1898–1918.

Quai d'Orsay Archives (QO), Paris, France.
    Guerre 1914–18. Affaires Musulmanes. I. Panislamisme. Guerre Sainte. La
        Turquie dans la Guerre Européenne. Files 1650, 1654, 1655, 1658, 1662.
    Guerre 1914–18. Turquie. Files 845–8.
    Guerre 1914–18. Turquie. Notes Journalières. Files 896–9.

Corr. Pol. Nouvelle Série. Turquie. Vol. 334. Chemins de fer. Réseau asiatique. Chemin de fer de Bagdad.

Rossiiskii Gosudarstvennyi Voenno-Istoricheskii Arkhiv (RGVIA). Moscow, Russia.
Fond 2000. Opis' 1. Glavnoe upravlenie General'nago Shtaba.
Fond 165. Opis' 1. Kuropatkin.
Fond 450. Opis' 1. Turtsiia.

Printed and Online Works, including Memoirs

'L'Agent Allemand Oppenheim' in *La Libre Parole*, 25 December 1910.

Ahmad, Feroz, *The Young Turks. The Committee of Union and Progress in Turkish Politics*, Oxford: Clarendon Press, 1969.
——, 'The Young Turk Revolution' in the *Journal of Contemporary History*, vol. 3, no. 3 (July 1968), pp. 19–36.

Akçam, Taner, *A Shameful Act. The Armenian Genocide and the Question of Turkish Responsibility*, trans. Paul Bessemer, New York: Metropolitan Books, 2006.

Aksakal, Mustafa, *The Ottoman Road to War in 1914: The Ottoman Empire and the First World War*, Cambridge: Cambridge University Press, 2008.
——, 'The Trained Triumphant Soldiers of the Prophet Muhammad. Holy War and Holy Peace in Modern Ottoman History', forthcoming.

Akşin, Sina, *Jön Türkler ve İttihat ve Terakki*, Istanbul: Remzi Kitabevi, 1987, p. 415.

Allen, W. E. D. and Paul Muratoff, *Caucasian Battlefields. A History of the Wars on the Turco-Caucasian Border, 1828–1921*, Cambridge: Cambridge University Press, 1953.

Anderson, Margaret Lavinia, '"Down in Turkey, far away": Human Rights, the Armenian Massacres, and Orientalism in Wilhelmine Germany' in the *Journal of Modern History*, 79 (March 2007), pp. 80–111.

Antonius, George, *The Arab Awakening. The Story of the Arab National Movement*, New York: Capricorn Books, 1946.

'Aus der Türkei' in *Neue Preussische Zeitung*, 9 February 1900.

'Ausland' in *Der Bund*, 14 August 1900.

'The Baghdad Railway' in *The Times* (London), 3 January 1900.

Balfour, Michael, *The Kaiser and His Times*, London: Cresset Press, 1964.

'Baron Max Oppenheim' in the *New York Daily Tribune*, 9 April 1906.

Bauer, Karl Johannes, *Alois Musil. Wahrheitssucher in der Wüste*, Vienna: Böhlau, 1989.

Berridge, G. R., *Gerald Fitzmaurice (1865–1939). Chief Dragoman of the British Embassy in Istanbul*, Leiden: Martinus Nijhoff Publishers, 2007.

Bloxham, Donald, *The Great Game of Genocide: Imperialism, Nationalism, and the Destruction of the Ottoman Armenians*, Oxford: Oxford University Press, 2005.

Bobroff, Ronald Park, *Roads to Glory. Late Imperial Russia and the Turkish Straits*, London: I. B. Tauris, 2006.

Browning, Christopher, *Fateful Months: Essays on the Emergence of the Final Solution*, New York: Holmes & Meier, 1991.

Buchan, John, *Greenmantle* (1916), London: Penguin, 2001.

Burrin, Philippe, *Hitler and the Jews: The Genesis of the Holocaust*, trans. Patsy Southgate, New York: Edward Arnold/Routledge, 1994.

Bülow, Bernhard, Fürst von, *Memoirs of Prince von Bülow*, 2 vols, trans. F. A. Voigt, Boston: Little, Brown and Company, 1931–32.

'The Caliphate. The Sultan and England' in the *Egyptian Gazette*, 24 May 1906.

Carruthers, Douglas, 'Captain Shakespear's Last Journey' in the *Geographical Journal*, vol. 49, no. 6 (June 1922), pp. 321–34.

Çeliktepe, Atilla, *Teşkilat-ı Mahsûsa'nın Siyasi Misyonu*, Istanbul: IQ Kültür Sanat, 2002.

Chapman, Maybelle Kennedy, *Great Britain and the Baghdad Railway, 1888–1914*, Northampton, Massachusetts, 1948.

'Correspondence Respecting Events Leading to the Rupture of Relations with Turkey', printed by Harrison & Sons for His Majesty's Stationery Office, November 1914.

Cüppers, Martin, and Klaus-Michael Mallmann, *Halbmond und Hakenkreuz. Das dritte Reich, die Araber und Palästina*, Darmstadt: Wissenschaftliche Buchgesellschaft, 2006.

Dadrian, Vanakh N., 'The Armenian Question and the Wartime Fate of the Armenians as Documented by Officials of the Ottoman Empire's World War I Allies: Germany and Austria–Hungary' in the *International Journal of Middle East Studies*, vol. 34 (2002), pp. 59–85.

——, *The History of the Armenian Genocide: Ethnic Conflict from the Balkans to Anatolia to the Caucasus*, New York: Berghahn Books, 2003.

——, 'The Role of the Special Organization in the Armenian Genocide during the First World War' in *Minorities in Wartime: National and Racial Groupings in Europe, North America and Australia in Two World Wars*, edited by Panikos Panayi, New York: St Martin's Press, 1993.

Dalin, David G. and John F. Rothmann, *Icon of Evil: Hitler's Mufti and the Rise of Radical Islam*, New York: Random House, 2008.

Demirel, Emin, *Teşkilat-ı Mahsûsa'dan Günümüze Gizli Servisler,* Istanbul: IQ Kültür Sanat, 2002.

'Deutschland und die Affaire Mahmud Pascha' in *Die Post*, 27 December 1899.

'Il divieto alla missione tedesca di recarsi in Abissinia dell'Eritrea' in *Corriera della Sera*, 7 March 1915.

Djemal Pasha, Ahmed, *Memories of a Turkish Statesman, 1913–1919*, New York: George H. Doran, 1922.

Documents on Ottoman Armenians, 2 vols, Ankara: Turkish Directorate General of Press and Information, 1982–3.

Earle, Edward Mead, *Turkey, the Great Powers, and the Bagdad Railway. A Study in Imperialism*, New York: Russell & Russell, 1966.

Emin, Ahmed, *Turkey in the World War*, New Haven: Yale University Press, 1930.

Erickson, Edward, 'Armenian Massacres: New Records Undercut Old Blame' in *Middle East Quarterly*, vol. 11, no. 3 (Summer 2006), pp. 67–75.

——, 'The Armenians and Ottoman Military Policy, 1915' in *War in History*, vol. 15, no. 2 (2008), pp. 141–67.

——, *Ordered to Die: A History of the Ottoman Army in the First World War*, Westport, Connecticut: Greenwood Press, 2001.

Feis, Herbert, *Europe, the World's Banker 1870–1914. An Account of European Foreign Investment and the Connection of World Finance with Diplomacy before World War I*, New York: Norton, 1965.

Fest, Joachim, *Hitler*, London: Penguin, 2002.

Ferguson, Niall, *Empire: How Britain Made the Modern World*, New York: Penguin, 2004.

——, *The Pity of War*, New York: Basic Books, 1999.

Fischer, Fritz, *Germany's Aims in the First World War*, New York: Norton, 1967.

Friedman, Isaiah, *Germany, Turkey, and Zionism, 1897–1918*, New Brunswick: Transaction Publishers, 1998.

Fromkin, David, *A Peace to End All Peace: Creating the Modern Middle East, 1914–1922*, New York: H. Holt, 1989.

——, 'The Importance of T. E. Lawrence' in the *New Criterion*, vol. 10, no. 1 (September 1991).

——, *Europe's Last Summer: Who Started the Great War in 1914?*, New York: Alfred A. Knopf, 2004.

Gehrke, Ulrich, 'Germany and Persia up to 1919' in Jehuda Wallach (ed.), *Germany and the Middle East 1835–1939*, Tel Aviv: Institute of German History, 1975.

——, *Persien in der Deutschen Orientpolitik während des ersten Weltkrieges*, 2 vols, Stuttgart: W. Kohlhammer, 1960.

Gensicke, Klaus, *Der Mufti von Jerusalem und die Nationalsozialisten*, Darmstadt: Wissenschaftliche Buchgesellschaft, 2007.

'The German Emperor's Visit to Constantinople' in *The Levant Herald and Eastern Express* (Special Edition), 9 November 1889.

'German Plot in Persia. Turkish Invasion Encouraged' in *The Times* (London), 19 March 1915.

Gökay, Bülent, *A Clash of Empires: Turkey Between Russian Bolshevism and British Imperialism*, London: I. B. Tauris & Co. Ltd, 1997.

Die Grosse Politik der Europäischen Kabinette 1871–1914. Sammlung der Diplomatischen Akten des Auswärtigen Amtes, Berlin: Deutsche Verlagsgesellschaft für Politik und Geschichte, 1927.

Grunwald, Kurt, 'Penetration pacifique – the Financial Vehicles of Germany's "Drang nach Osten"' in Wallach (ed.), *Germany and the Middle East 1835–1939*, Tel Aviv: Tel Aviv University, Institute of German History, 1975.

Guse, Felix, *Die Kaukasusfront im Weltkrieg*, Leipzig: Koehler & Amelang, 1940.

Haberland, Eike (ed.), *Leo Frobenius 1873–1973. Eine Anthologie*, Wiesbaden: F. Steiner, 1973.

Hagen, Gottfried, 'German Heralds of Holy War: Orientalists and Applied Oriental Studies' in *Comparative Studies of South Asia, Africa and the Middle East*, vol. 24, no. 2 (2004), pp. 145–62.

——, *Die Türkei im Ersten Weltkrieg: Flugblätter und Flugschriften in arabischer, persischer und osmanisch–türkischer Sprache aus einer Sammlung der Universitätsbibliothek Heidelberg*, Frankfurt am Main:P. Lang, 1990.

Hanioğlu, M. Şükrü, *A Brief History of the Late Ottoman Empire*, Princeton: Princeton University Press, 2008.

——, *Preparation for a Revolution. The Young Turks, 1902–1908*, New York: Oxford University Press, 2001.

——, *The Young Turks in Opposition*, New York: Oxford University Press, 1995.

Hopkirk, Peter, *On Secret Service East of Constantinople: The Plot to Bring Down the British Empire*, London: John Murray, 1994.

Hovannisian, Richard (ed.), *The Armenian Genocide in Perspective*, New Brunswick, New Jersey: Transaction Books, 1986.

Hughes, Thomas L., 'The German Mission to Afghanistan 1915–1916' in Schwanitz (ed.), *Germany and the Middle East 1871–1945*, Princeton: Markus Wiener Publishers, 2004, pp. 25–62.

Hurgronje, C. Snouck, Dr, *The Holy War 'Made in Germany'*, New York: G. P. Putnam's Sons, 1915.

——, *Revolt in Arabia*, New York: G. P. Putnam's Sons, 1917.

'Intrigues Allemandes au Caire. Comment on joue du Panislamisme' in *Les Pyramides*, 15 February 1906.

'Islam and the War' in *The Standard*, 30 August 1915.

Jäckh, Ernst, *Der aufsteigende Halbmond. Auf dem Weg zum deutschtürkischen Bündnis*, Berlin: Deutsche Verlagsanstalt, 1915.

Johnson, Paul, *A History of the Modern World: From 1917 to the 1980s*, London: Weidenfeld & Nicolson, 1983.

Kahn, David, *The Codebreakers: The Story of Secret Writing*, London: Weidenfeld & Nicolson, 1967.

'Kaiser Wilhelm II. Und der Islam' in *Berliner Tageblatt*, 23 October 1905.

Kaplan, Robert, *The Arabists: The Romance of an American Elite*, New York: Free Press, 1995.

Karpat, Kemal, *Ottoman Population 1830–1914: Demographic and Social Characteristics*, Madison: University of Wisconsin Press, 1985.

Kazemzadeh, Firuz, *The Struggle for Transcaucasia, 1917–1921*, New York: Philosophical Library, 1951.

Kedourie, Elie, *Arabic Political Memoirs and Other Studies*, London: Cass, 1974.

——, *The Chatham House Version and Other Middle-Eastern Studies*, Chicago: Ivan R. Dee, 2004.

——, *England and the Middle East. The Destruction of the Ottoman Empire 1914–1921*, London: Mansell, 1987.

Keleşyılmaz, Vahdet, *Teşkilat-ı Mahsûsa'nın Hindistan Misyonu (1914–1918)*, Ankara: AKDTYK Atatürk Araştırma Merkezi, 1999.

Koloğlu, Orhan, *Avrupa'nın Kıskacında Abdülhamit*, Istanbul: İletişim, 1998.

Krasnyi Arkhiv. Istoricheskii zhurnal, volume 6, Moscow, 1924. 'Konstantinopol I prolivyi', pp. 48–76.

Kress von Kressenstein, Friedrich, *Mit den Türken zum Suezkanal*, Berlin: Vorhut-Verlag, 1938.

Küntzel, Matthias, *Jihad and Jew-Hatred: Islamism, Nazism, and the Roots of 9/11*, trans. Colin Meade, New York: Telos Press, 2007.

Kurat, Akdes Nimet, Dr, *Türkiye ve Rusya*, Ankara: Kültür Bakanlığı, 1990.

Laqueur, Walter, *A History of Zionism*, New York: Schocken Books, 1972.

Larcher, Maurice, *La guerre turque dans la guerre mondiale.*, Paris: E. Chiron, 1926.

Lawrence, Thomas Edward, 'Personal Notes on the Sherifian Family' in the *Arab Bulletin*, 26 November 1916.

——, 'Twenty–Seven Articles by T. E. Lawrence' in the *Arab Bulletin*, 20 August 1917.

'Lettre d' Egypte' in *Journal des Débats*, 4 February 1906.

Lewis, Bernard, *The Emergence of Modern Turkey*, 3rd edn, New York: Oxford University Press, 2002.

Lewy, Guenter, *The Armenian Massacres in Ottoman Turkey: A Disputed Genocide*, Salt Lake City: University of Utah Press, 2005.

Lindow, Erich, *Freiherr Marschall von Bieberstein als Botschafter in Konstantinopel,1897–1912*, Danzig: A. W. Kafemann G.m.b.H., 1934.

Lohr, Eric, 'The Russian Army and the Jews: Mass Deportation, Hostages, and Violence During World War I' in *Russian Review*, 60 (July 2001), pp. 404–19.

Lüdke, Tilman, *Jihad Made in Germany: Ottoman and German Propaganda and Intelligence Operations in the First World War*, Lit Verlag, 2006.

Lührs, Hans, *Gegenspieler des Obersten Lawrence*, Berlin: Otto Schlegel, 1936.

Luig, Ute (ed.), *Leo Frobenius. Vom Schreibtisch zum Äquator: afrikanische Reisen*, Frankfurt-am-Main: Societäts-Verlag, 1982.

McCarthy, Justin, *Death and Exile: The Ethnic Cleansing of Ottoman Muslims, 1821–1922*, Princeton: Darwin Press, 1995.

McCarthy, Justin et al., *The Armenian Rebellion at Van*, Salt Lake City: The University of Utah Press, 2006.

McGuirk, Russell, *The Sanusi's Little War. The Amazing Story of a Forgotten Conflict in the Western Desert, 1915–1917*, Arabian Publishing (UK), 2007.

Macintyre, Donald, 'Lawrence of Arabia was really a Zionist, historian claims' in the *Independent*, 24 February 2007.

McKale, Donald, *Curt Prüfer. German Diplomat from the Kaiser to Hitler*. Kent: Kent State University Press, 1987.

——, *War by Revolution: Germany and Great Britain in the Middle East in the Era of World War I*, Kent: Kent State University Press, 1998.

McKay, John P., 'Baku Oil and Transcaucasian Pipelines, 1883–1891: A Study of Tsarist Economic Policy' in the *Slavic Review*, vol. 43, no. 4 (Winter 1984), pp. 604–23.

McMeekin, Sean, *History's Greatest Heist. The Bolshevik Looting of Russia*, New Haven: Yale University Press, 2008.

McMurray, Jonathan S., *Distant Ties. Germany, the Ottoman Empire, and the Construction of the Baghdad Railway*, Westport, Connecticut: Praeger, 2001.

'Mahmoud Pacha and the Sultan' in *The Standard*, 22 January 1900

Mango, Andrew, *Atatürk*, London: John Murray, 1999.

'Le manovre dei tedeschi in Abissinia. La storia di una missione ... che non giunge a Addis Abeba' in *Il Popolo*, 7 March 1915.

'La Missione militare tedesca nell' Eritrea. Una interrogazione alle Camera' in *La Sera*, 5 March 1915.

Moorehead, Alan, *Gallipoli*, London: H. Hamilton, 1956.

Morgenthau, Henry, *Ambassador Morgenthau's Story*, New York: Doubleday, 1918.

——, *Secrets of the Bosphorus*, London: Hutchinson & Co., 1918.

Mühlmann, Carl, *Deutschland und die Türkei, 1913–1914*, Berlin: Dr Walther Rothschild, 1929.

——, *Das Deutsche-Türkische Waffenbündnis im Weltkriege*, Leipzig: Koehler & Amelang, 1940.

Müller, Herbert, *Islam, gihad ('Heiliger Krieg') und Deutsches Reich: Ein Nachspiel zur wilhelminischen Weltpolitik im Maghreb, 1914–1918*, Frankfurt-am-Main: P. Lang, 1991.

Neilson, Keith and Roy Arnold Prete (eds), *Coalition Warfare: An Uneasy Accord*, Ontario: Wilfrid Laurier University Press, 1983.

Niedermayer, Oskar von, *Krieg in Irans Wüsten. Erlebnisse der deutschen Expedition nach Persien und Afghanistan*, Hamburg: Hanseatische Verlaganstalt, 1940.

——, *Unter der Glutsonne Irans. Erlebnisse der deutschen Expedition nach Persien und Afghanistan*, Dachau: Einhornverlag, 1925.

Oppenheim, Max von, *Vom Mittelmeer zum Persischen Golf* (2 vols, 1899–1900), Berlin: Dietrich Reimer, 1900.

Orel, Sinasi and Süreyya Yuca, *The Talât Pasha 'Telegrams': Historical Fact or Armenian Fiction?*, Nicosia: K. Rustem & Brother, 1986.

Owen, Roger, *Lord Clomer: Victorian Imperialist, Edwardia Proconsul*, Oxford: Oxford University Press, 2004.

Parfit, Canon J. T., *Twenty Years in Baghdad and Syria: Showing Germany's Bid for Mastery of the East*, London: Simpton, Marshall, Hamilton, Kent, 1916.

Patterson, J. H., *Behind the Palestine Betrayal*, New York: American Friends of a Jewish Palestine, 1940.

Pears, Edward, Sir, *Life of Abdul Hamid*, New York: Henry Holt, 1917.

Pick, Pinhas Walter, 'German Railway Constructions in the Middle East' in Jehuda Wallach (ed.), *Germany and the Middle East 1835–1939*, Tel Aviv: Institute of German History, 1975.

Pipes, Richard, *The Formation of the Soviet Union: Communism and Nationalism, 1917–1923*, Cambridge, MA: Harvard University Press, 1954.

——, *The Russian Revolution*, New York: Alfred Knopf, 1990.

Pokrovskii, M. N. (ed.), *Tsarskaia Rossiia v mirovoi voine*, vol. 1, Leningrad, 1926.

Pomiankowski, Joseph, *Der Zusammenbruch des Ottomanischen Reiches. Erinnerungen an die Türkei aus der Zeit des Weltkrieges*, Zurich: Amalthea, 1928.

Rall, Hans, *Wilhelm II. Eine Biographie*, Graz: Styria, 1995.

Reiss, Tom, *The Orientalist: In Search of a Man Caught between East and West*, New York: Random House, 2005.

Reynolds, Michael A., 'Buffers, not Brethren: Young Turk Military Policy in World War One and the Myth of Panturanism', *Past and Present*, vol. 203, issue (May 2009), pp. 137–79.

——, 'The Ottoman-Russian Struggle for Eastern Anatolia and the Caucasus, 1908–1918', unpublished Princeton University dissertation, 2003.

Röhl, John C., *The Kaiser and his Court: Wilhelm II and the Government of Germany*, New York: Cambridge University Press, 1994.

Rohrbach, Paul, *Die Bagdadbahn*, Berlin: Wiegandt, 1911.

Sabahaddin, Prince Mehmed, 'Aux Arméniens Ottomans', Paris, September 1905.

——, 'Mémoire des Libéraux Turcs Relatif à la Question d' Orient. Le Prince Sabehedine Aux Chancelleries', Paris, December 1906.

Sanders, Liman von, *Cinq ans de Turquie*, trans. Commandant Mabille, Paris: Payot, 1923.

Schabinger von Schowingen, Karl Friedrich Maximilian, *Weltgeschichtliche Mosaiksplitter*, Baden-Baden: K. F. Schabinger Frhr von Schowingen, 1967.

Schwanitz, Wolfgang, 'The Bellicose Birth of Euro-Islam in Berlin' in Nathalie Clayer and Eric Germain (eds), *Islam in Interwar Europe*, C. Hurst & Co. Ltd, 2008.

—— (ed.), *Germany and the Middle East 1871–1945*, Princeton: Markus Wiener Publishers, 2004.

Seidt, Hans-Ulrich, *Berlin, Kabul, Moskau: Oskar Ritter von Niedermayer und Deutschlands Ostpolitik*, Munich: Universitas, 2002.

Shaw, Stanford, *The Ottoman Empire in World War I*, Ankara: Turkish Historical Society, 2006.

Simon, Rachel, *Libya between Ottomanism and Nationalism. The Ottoman Involvement in Libya during the War with Italy (1911–1918)*, Berlin: K. Schwarz, 1987.

Stoddard, Philip H., 'The Ottoman Government and the Arabs, 1911 to 1918: A Study of the Teskilat-ı Mahsusa', Ph.D. dissertation, Princeton University, 1963.

Stone, Norman, *The Eastern Front 1914–1917*, New York: Charles Scribner's Sons, 1975.

——, *Europe Transformed 1878–1919*, Cambridge, MA: Harvard University Press, 1984.

——, *World War One. A Short History*, London: Allen Lane, 2007.

Stuermer, Harry, *Zwei Kriegsjahre in Konstantinopel. Skizzen deutsch-jungtürkischen Moral und Politik*, Lausanne: Payot, 1917.

Stürmer, Michael, Gabriele Teichmann, and Wilhelm Treue, *Sal. Oppenheim jr. & Cie. Geschichte einer Bank und einer Familie*, Munich: Piper, 1989.

Suny, Ronald, 'Empire and Nation: Armenians, Turks and the End of the Ottoman Empire' in *Armenian Forum*, vol. 1, no. 2 (1998), pp. 17–51.

Teichmann, Gabriele and Gisela Völger, *Faszination Orient: Max von Oppenheim – Forscher, Sammler, Diplomat*, Cologne: Dumont, 2003.

Trumpener, Ulrich, *Germany and the Ottoman Empire, 1914–1918*, Princeton: Princeton University Press, 1968.

Tuchman, Barbara, *The Guns of August*, New York: Macmillan, 1962.

——, *The Zimmermann Telegram*, New York: Viking, 1958.

Turfan, M. Naim, *Rise of the Young Turks: Politics, the Military, and the Ottoman Collapse*, New York: I. B. Tauris, 2000.

Wallach, Jehuda, 'Bismarck and the "Eastern Question" – A Re-Assessment' in Wallach (ed.), *Germany and the Middle East 1835–1939*, Tel Aviv: Tel Aviv University, Institute of German History, 1975, pp. 23–9.

——, *Anatomie einer Militärhilfe. Das preußisch-deutschen Militärmission in der Türkei 1835–1919*, Düsseldorf: Droste, 1976.

Weber, Frank G., *Eagles on the Crescent. Germany, Austria, and the Diplomacy of the Turkish Alliance, 1914–1918*, Ithaca: Cornell University Press, 1970.

Wheeler-Bennett, John, *Brest-Litovsk: The Forgotten Peace. March 1918*, London: Macmillan, 1938.

Wildman, Allan K., *The End of the Russian Imperial Army*, 2 vols, Princeton: Princeton University Press, 1980/1987.

Wilhelm II (Emperor of Germany), *The Kaiser's Letters to the Tsar*, edited by Isaac Don Levine, London: Hodder & Stoughton, 1920.

————, *Reden des Kaisers. Ansprachen, Predigten, und Trinksprüche*, edited by Ernst Johann, Munich: Deutscher Taschenbuch-Verlag, 1966.

Wright, John Kirtland, 'Northern Arabia. The Explorations of Alois Musil' in the *Geographical Review*, vol. 17, no. 2 (April 1927), pp. 177–206.

Wynn, Antony, *Persia in the Great Game*, London: John Murray, 2004.

Yalman, Ahmet Emin (Ahmed Emin), *Turkey in the World War*, New Haven: Yale University Press, 1930.

Yisraeli, David, 'Germany and Zionism' in Jehuda Wallach (ed.), *Germany and the Middle East 1835–1939*, Tel Aviv: Tel Aviv. University, Institute of German History, 1975

Zechlin, Egmont, *Die deutsche Politik und die Juden im Ersten Weltkrieg*, Göttingen: Vandenhoeck und Ruprecht, 1969.

Zeman, Z. A. B. (ed.), *Germany and the Revolution in Russia, 1915–1918. Documents from the Archives of the German Foreign Ministry*, London: Oxford University Press, 1958.

Zürcher, Erik, 'The Ottoman Conscription System, 1844–1914' in the *International Review of Social History*, vol. 43 (1998), pp. 437–49.

——, *The Unionist Factor. The Role of the Committee of Union and Progress in the Turkish National Movement, 1905–1926*, Leiden: E. J. Brill, 1984.

Acknowledgements

Two writers above all deserve recognition for having inspired this book: John Buchan, author of the great First World War yarn *Greenmantle*, and Peter Hopkirk, who did the first serious exploration of the Turco-German jihad in English, in *On Secret Service East of Constantinople*. If I have sometimes picked nits with Hopkirk's reasoning or sourcing, it is only by way of honouring his achievement in bringing the 'story behind *Greenmantle*' to life. I have enjoyed all of Hopkirk's books on Great Game intrigue in Asia. Let this book serve as homage to a wonderful writer whose gift for storytelling has been an inspiration to me, however far I fall short of his fine example.

I should also confess a scholarly debt to Jonathan McMurray, on whose fine recent study of the Baghdad railway, *Distant Ties*, I have drawn heavily; and to Mustafa Aksakal, who was kind enough to let me read his groundbreaking and as yet unpublished article on Ottoman jihad declarations, 'The Trained Triumphant Soldiers of the Prophet Muhammad. Holy War and Holy Peace in Modern Ottoman History'. Likewise, Michael Reynolds of Princeton University has generously shared with me his forthcoming article 'Buffers, not Brethren: Young Turk Military Policy in World War One and the Myth of Panturanism', along with his still unpublished dissertation on 'The Ottoman-Russian Struggle for Eastern Anatolia and the Caucasus, 1908–1918'. Mike Reynolds is a fantastic scholar, whose work in this little-known field deserves much wider circulation than it has thus far received.

The project out of which this book grew could not have been undertaken without generous financial support from the Alexander von Humboldt Foundation. I would like to thank Georg Schütte at Humboldt headquarters for his continued support, along with Heinz Kramer, my gracious host at the Stiftung Wissenschaft und Politik. My stay in Germany was made much more pleasurable by the hospitality of Anna Kossatz and Heiko Kosel (in Cottbus), Tom Grant (in Heidelberg), Jan Dirk Kemming (in Cologne), and Gereon Mänzel (in Berlin). Since 2008, I have also been able to exploit the wonderful Sterling library at Yale, thanks to the generosity of International

Security Studies and the Brady-Johnson Program in Grand Strategy. For this, heartfelt thanks to Professors John Gaddis, Paul Kennedy and Charlie Hill for inviting me and providing such excellent facilities in which to work, along with stimulating company.

Among the many fine archivists who facilitated my work, I must single out for special praise Mareike Fossenberger of the Politisches Archiv des Auswärtigen Amtes in Berlin. Yes, dear Mareike, I confess proudly to being an 'Aktenfresser'; and I could not have devoured so many files without your help. Likewise Dr Leopold Auer, Director of the Haus-, Hof- und Staatsarchiv in Vienna, whose informative invitation allowed me to begin plugging away as soon as I arrived, and Joachim Tepperberg, who helped me photocopy huge reams of files with a very quick turnaround time. Betil Gurun of the US Embassy archives in Ankara was a delightful host each time I took the Bilkent bus downtown.

At the Oppenheim Bank archive in Cologne, Thorsten Maentel was tireless in retrieving old files and processing my photo requests. Gabriele Teichmann was gracious enough to share her tremendous expertise on all things Max von Oppenheim, and to allow me to lunch in the bank caféteria. If I come to somewhat different conclusions about the Baron than Teichmann, I should emphasize that I find Oppenheim equally interesting and by no means unsympathetic as a character. In any case, I would not have been able to write my book without Teichmann's help – and her own study of the Baron.

At Bilkent, I am grateful to Ali Doğramaci, Abdullah Atalar and Ali Karaosmanoğlu for their continued support. Muge Keller and Nilüfer Genç often went well beyond the call of duty with logistical support for my research trips. James Alexander and Sandy Berkovski helped tighten and discipline my ideas. Hasan Ali Karasar introduced me to Turkish government archives: reading the document registers I would have been literally lost without him. I would have been even more lost without the Ottoman Turkish expertise of Abdürrahim Özer, who generously transliterated more than a dozen documents for me from the Başbakanlık Osmanlı Arşivleri, and helped me poke my own way through a dozen more. Onur Önol unearthed the wonderful Djemal quote footnoted in chapter 18. Ian Sherwood was a fantastic host, as always, in Istanbul. Bilge Criss shared her encyclopaedic knowledge of Ottoman Turkish history, including her cavernous personal library. Norman Stone has been a part of this project from the beginning. Norman helped in the deciphering of several handwritten letters, and read through the entire manuscript. Of course he bears no responsibility for the final result. The same goes double for Peggy Anderson of Berkeley, who continues to be a close and careful reader of my work, even if she does not always agree with me on the fine points. Back home in the States, my sister Michele has been a constant source of good cheer and encouragement. And I am grateful to Simon Winder of Penguin for believing in the book and ushering it through, and also to Richard Duguid for all his help. Similarly, my thanks to Jane Robertson and Stephen Ryan, who have performed wonders in cleaning up my prose.

Finally, there is Nesrin Ersoy, the love of my life, without whom I could not have written this book. She has been a keen and critical reader of the manuscript, saving me from numerous errors of both translation and interpretation, while all along patiently enduring my erratic travel and writing schedule. Thank you again, Nesrin, for your love and support.

Index

Abadan oil refinery, 204, 209, 277–8, 324

Abbas Hilmi II, Khedive of Egypt, 25, 91, 169–71, 169fn, 173, 194, 201, 205, 358

Abdul Hamid II, Ottoman Sultan, 4, 7, 24, 35, 54–6, 61, 61fn, 72, 72fn, 81, 192, 233, 263; and Armenian subjects, 49, 57; assassination plots against, 59–60; and Baghdad railway convention(s), 37, 39–43, 46, 48–9, 51–3, 239, 249; as 'Bloody Sultan,' 10–11, 57, 78; as Caliph of Sunni Islam, 62–4, 66, 373n21; deposition by Young Turks and downfall of, 74–5, 77–8, 193, 291, 297, 342; and dissolution of Ottoman parliament, 56; German courtship of, 4, 37, 56; and Kaiser Wilhelm II, 4, 7–9, 11–12, 24, 37, 58, 69, 101; and pan-Islam, 48, 62, 66, 193; paranoia of, 55, 60; and suspicions of Great Britain and other European powers, 35, 372n4; under house arrest, 102, 102fn; and Young Turk revolution of 1908, 68–9, 72–3; and Zionism, 10, 24, 355

Abdullah bin al-Hussein of Mecca, later Abdullah I, King of Jordan, 192–3, 299

Abdullah Effendi, Sheikh of Damascus, 14

Abdul Aziz, Sultan of Ottoman Empire, 54–5

Abyssinia, 143, 143fn, 149

Adana, 32, 35–6, 52–3, 74, 238, 248, 250, 254

Adana rail station, 32, 53, 254. *See also* Baghdad railway

Afghanistan, 3, 89, 91, 96, 98, 184, 202, 204–5, 208; its role in German designs on India, 209, 212, 216–17, 219, 223–9, 223fn, 276–7

Ahmad, Feroz, 374n34

Ahmad Shah (of Persia), 276, 281–2. *See also* Germany, tries to bring Persia into World War I against Britain and Russia

Akçam, Taner, 394n21

Aksakal, Mustafa, 382, 427

Al-Akhbar, 363

Albania, 104

Al-Baruni, Suleyman, 266

Aleppo, 96fn, 116, 133–4, 191, 217, 240, 250

Alexander the Great, 3, 35, 44

Alexandretta (Iskenderun), 41, 116, 130–31, 218, 238, 248f, 250

Alexandria, 92, 95, 142, 266, 273

Al-Hassan ibn Ali, 192